D1519826

The Early Modern Englishwoman: A Facsimile Library of Essential Works

Part 1: Printed Writings, 1500–1640

Volume 8
Margaret Tyler

The Early Modern Englishwoman:
A Facsimile Library of Essential Works

Part 1: Printed Writings, 1500–1640

Volume 8
Margaret Tyler

Selected and Introduced by
Kathryn Coad

General Editors
Betty S. Travitsky and Patrick Cullen

SCOLAR
PRESS

The Introductory Note copyright © Kathryn Coad, 1996

Published by
SCOLAR PRESS
Gower House
Croft Road
Aldershot
Hants GU11 3HR
England

Ashgate Publishing Company
Old Post Road
Brookfield
Vermont 05036-9704
USA

British Library Cataloguing-in-Publication data.

Early Modern Englishwoman: Facsimile Library of Essential Works. – Part 1: Printed Writings, 1500–1640. – Vol. 8: "Mirrour of Princely Deedes and Knighthood" by D. Ortúñez De Calahorra. – facsim. of 1579(?) ed
    I. Tyler, Margaret
    863.3

Library of Congress Cataloging-in-Publication data.

The early modern Englishwoman: a facsimile library of essential works. Part 1. Printed writings, 1500–1640 / general editors, Betty S. Travitsky and Patrick Cullen.

See page vi for complete CIP Block 95-20837

The woodcut reproduced on the title page and on the case is from the title page of Margaret Roper's translation of Erasmus's *A Devout Treatise upon the Pater Noster* (circa 1524).

ISBN 1 85928 099 4

Printed in Great Britain by Antony Rowe Ltd, Chippenham

CONTENTS

Preface by the General Editors

Introductory Note

The Mirrour of Princely Deedes and Knighthood

Library of Congress Cataloging-in-Publication Data

The early modern Englishwoman : a facsimile library of essential works.
  Part 1. Printed writings, 1500–1640 / general editors, Betty S. Travitsky
  & Patrick Cullen.
    Contents: v. 1. Anne Askew / intro. J.N. King – v. 2. Works by and
  attributed to Elizabeth Cary / intro. M.W. Ferguson – v. 3. Katherine
  Parr / intro. J. Mueller – v. 4. Defences of Women, Jane Anger, Rachel
  Sowernam, and Constantia Munda / intro. S.G. O'Malley – v. 5.
  Admirable events / S. DuVerger / intro. J. Collins – v. 6. M. Sidney
  Herbert, A discourse of life and death / intro. G. Waller – v. 7. Alice
  Sutcliffe / intro. P. Cullen – v. 8. Margaret Tyler / intro. K. Coad –
  v. 9. Anne Wheathill / intro. P. Cullen – v. 10. Mary Wroth / intro.
  J.A. Roberts.
  ISBN 1-85928-226-1 (set) – ISBN 1-85928-092-7 (v. 1) –
  ISBN 1-85928-093-5 (v. 2) – ISBN 1-85928-094-3 (v. 3) –
  ISBN 1-85928-095-1 (v. 4) – ISBN 1-85928-096-X (v. 5) –
  ISBN 1-85928-097-8 (v. 6) – ISBN 1-85928-098-6 (v. 7) –
  ISBN 1-85928-099-4 (v. 8) – ISBN 1-85928-100-1 (v. 9) –
  ISBN 1-85928-101-X (v. 10)
    1. English literature—Early modern, 1500–1700. 2. Women—
  England—History—Renaissance, 1450–1600—Sources. 3. Women—
  England—History—17th century—Sources. 4. English literature—
  Women authors. 5. Women—Literary collections. 6. Women—
  England—Biography.
  I. Travitsky, Betty S. II. Cullen, Patrick.
  PR1121.E19 1995
  820.8' 09287' 09031—dc20
                                                          95-20837
                                                            CIP

PREFACE
BY THE GENERAL EDITORS

Until very recently, scholars of the early modern period have assumed that there were no Judith Shakespeares in early modern England. Much of the energy of the current generation of scholars has been devoted to constructing a history of early modern England that takes into account what women actually wrote, what women actually read, and what women actually did. In so doing the masculinist representation of early modern women, both in their own time and ours, is deconstructed. The study of early modern women has thus become one of the most important – indeed perhaps the most important – means for the rewriting of early modern history.

The Early Modern Englishwoman: A Facsimile Library of Essential Works is one of the developments of this energetic reappraisal of the period. As the names on our advisory board and our list of editors testify, it has been the beneficiary of scholarship in the field and we hope it will also be an essential part of that scholarship's continuing momentum.

The Early Modern Englishwoman is designed to make available a comprehensive and focused collection of writings in English from 1500 to 1700, both by women and for and about them. The first series in the facsimile library provides a comprehensive if not entirely complete collection of the separately published writings by women. In reprinting these writings we intend to remedy one of the major obstacles to the advancement of feminist criticism of the early modern period, namely the unavailability of the very texts upon which the field is based. The volumes in the facsimile library reproduce carefully chosen copies of these texts, incorporating significant variants (usually in appendices). Each text is preceded by a short introduction providing an overview of the life and work of the writer along with a survey of important scholarship. These works, we strongly believe, deserve a large readership – of historians, literary critics, feminist critics, and non-specialist readers.

The Early Modern Englishwoman: A Facsimile Library of Essential Works is published in two parts: *Printed Writings, 1500–1640* and *Printed Writings, 1641–1700*. We project that it will be complemented by separate facsimile series of *Essential Works for the Study of Early Modern Women* and of *Manuscript Writings*, and by a series of original monographs on early modern gender studies, also under our general editorship.

New York City
1996

vii

INTRODUCTORY NOTE

The biography of Margaret Tyler remains speculative, and the identification of even her class and religion is difficult and controversial. The information which Tyler gives about herself in the prefatory material provides the only certainties about her life: she wrote the prefatory material for Thomas East's edition of *The First Part of the Mirrour of Princely Deedes and Knighthood* at an age at which she considered the reading of romance somewhat inappropriate (she refers to her 'years' three times in 'M.T. to the Reader'), and she served the Howard family (Thomas Howard, Duke of Norfolk) in some capacity. Tyler's social standing and economic position are uncertain and in no way defined by her level of education, which Tina Krontiris describes as 'amazing' for a woman outside the aristocracy ('Breaking' 19); however, Louise Schleiner thinks Tyler's education feasible although not frequent for a middle-class servant (4). Tyler's claim that she has published *The Mirrour* for financial gain does not clarify the situation. Tyler's religion is similarly unknown. Moira Ferguson notes that Tyler may have been Catholic, a suggestion which Schleiner further discusses, providing credible evidence for both sides of the question. Ferguson further conjectures that Tyler may have been a pseudonym for Margaret Tyrrell, who was related by marriage to the Howard family (51).

Tyler's translation of Diego Ortúñez de Calahorra's romance, *Espejo de principes y cavalleros (El Caballero del Febo)* Part I, from the original Spanish marks not only a notable moment in book history but also the beginning of the popularity and availability of continental romance in England. The translation registers two firsts in book history: Tyler is both the first woman to publish a romance in England and the first English translator to work from an original Spanish romance rather than from a French translation of the Spanish. After *The Mirrour*'s publication, the popularity of continental chivalric romance increased in England, as the surge in printing romances and the negative reactions to their wide readership indicate. Francis Meres in his *Palladis Tamia: Wits Miscellany* (1598) condemns *The Mirrour* by name as inappropriate reading for youth.

The First Part of the Mirrour of Princely Deedes and Knighthood includes the three books of the original first part which were written by Ortúñez de Calahorra. According to Daniel Eisenberg, the first part was published in 1555, not 1562 as is usually listed (*Romances* 103). The *Espejo de principes y cavalleros* remained popular in Spain into the seventeenth century, with a total of six editions (49). Ortúñez de Calahorra's biography is sparse: the *Espejo* is his only known work; from the preface we know he was in his twenties at its composition (94), which Eisenberg calculates as shortly before its 1555 publication, during the last years of the reign of Carlos V (48).

We can only theorize about why Tyler judged the meager financial benefits of selling her translation to East worth the risk of reproof for trespassing in the masculine domain of romance, a genre denigrated as youthful, secular, and frivolous. The *Espejo* was a particularly wise choice for Tyler's translation because of the narrator's tendency to moralize his story. Eisenberg suggests that in constructing a uniquely didactic tone, Ortúñez himself may have been responding to the increasingly pejorative criticism of romance (*Espejo* 1:lxvi). The narrator offers moral instructions on a variety of topics although his favourite is the inconstancy of fortune.

Because of the negative association of women with romance and the general cultural restrictions on female authorship, Tyler's bold defence of her translation in the dedication and preface is remarkable, and as it is the earliest Englishwoman's defence of women's literary work, it has sometimes earned her the title of the first English feminist (Todd 681).

After Tyler's first edition (STC 18859), licensed in 1578 but probably published in 1579 or 1580 (see Joseph de Perott for dating of the first edition), two later editions appeared in 1580 [?] (STC 18860) and in 1599 (STC 18861). The other three parts of the Spanish continuation were written by two authors: the second part (two books) by Pedro de la Sierra; the third and fourth parts (two books each) by Marcos Martínez. The printer, Thomas East, further sponsored translation of the entire romance, making all nine books available in English by 1601.

Reprinted here is the first edition (1578) of the first part, a quarto volume (13 × 17.3 cm.; sig. C 9 × 17.2 cm.) in the possession of The Huntington Library, chosen because of minor changes to the prefatory material of later editions, changes which almost certainly would not have been Tyler's corrections (especially since she does no further translation work for East, possibly because of her age). Some lexical differences occur in the prefatory material throughout the three editions. In the dedication to Lord Howard, the second edition differs from the first and third in the following two phrases: 'the consideration of my insufficiency' reads 'the consideration of my sufficiency', sufficiency having financial implications absent from insufficiency; 'reserving for my selfe the order for the dedication' (1578) reads 'referring for my selfe' (1580) and then 'reserving for my selfe' (1599). In the letter 'M.T. to the Reader', the first edition differs from the second and third in the following two changes: 'the inheritance of all warlike commendation' later reads 'the inheritaunce of all worldly commendation'; 'And thus much as concerning this present story' reads 'And thus much concerning this present storie', eliminating 'as' from the later two versions. Later editions also have changes in the translation and orthography, notably in the names of some of the characters. In the 1580 and 1599 editions, for instance, Clavergudo is changed to Claverindo, and Trebatio's enchantment develops differently. A careful comparison of Ortúñez's *Espejo* and Tyler's

Mirrour, as well as of the textual variations in the three editions of Tyler's translation, are areas for further research.

References

STC 18859

Blain, Virginia, Patricia Clements & Isobel Grundy, (ed.), *The Feminist Companion to Literature in English: Women Writers from the Middle Ages to the Present*, New Haven, CT: Yale UP, 1990

Eisenberg, Daniel, *An Edition of a Sixteenth-Century Romance of Chivalry: Diego Ortúñez de Calahorra's 'Espejo de principes y cavalleros [El Caballero del Febo]'*. Baltimore, MD: Johns Hopkins, 1971

———— *Romances of Chivalry in the Spanish Golden Age*. Newark, Del.: Juan de la Cuesta, 1982

Ferguson, Moira (ed.), *First Feminists: British Women Writers 1578–1799*, Bloomington: Indiana UP; Old Westbury, NY: Feminist Press, 1985

Koeppel, E., *Ben Jonson's Wirkung auf zeitgenössische Dramatiker und andere Studien zur inneren Geschichte des englischen Dramas* (Anglistische Forschungen, 20), Heidelberg, Winter 1906, 210–222

Krontiris, Tina, *Oppositional Voices: Women as Writers and Translators of Literature in the English Renaissance*, London, New York: Routledge, 1992

———— 'Breaking Barriers of Genre and Gender: Margaret Tyler's Translation of *The Mirrour of Knighthood*' (1988), *English Literary Renaissance*, 18, 19–39

Mackerness, E.D. 'Margaret Tyler: An Elizabethan Feminist', *Notes and Queries*, 190, 23 March, 1946, 112–113

Perott, Joseph de, 'The Mirrour of Knighthood', *The Romantic Review*, 4, October–December 1913, 397–402

Schleiner, Louise, 'Margaret Tyler, Translator and Waiting Woman', *English Language Notes*, 29, March 1992, 1–8

Santoyo, Julio César, 'En el IV centenario de Margaret Tyler, primera traductora español–inglés', *ES: Publicaciones del Departamento de Inglés, Universidad de Valladolid*, 9, 1979, 133–48

Todd, Janet (ed.), *British Women Writers: A Critical Reference Guide*, New York: Continuum, 1989

KATHRYN COAD

The Mirrour of Princely deeds and Knighthood (STC 18859) is reproduced, by permission, from the copy of The Huntington Library. Its text block measures 9 × 17.2 cm.

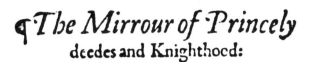

¶ *The Mirrour of Princely*
deedes and Knighthood:

Wherein is shewed the worthinesse of the
Knight of the Sunne, and his brother
Rosicleer, sonnes to the great Emperour Trebetio : with the strange
loue of the beautifull and excellent Princesse Briana,
and the valiant actes of
other noble Prin-
ces
and Knightes.

Now newly tranſlated out of Spaniſh
into our vulgar Engliſh
tongue, by M. T.

¶ Imprinted at London
by Thomas Eaſt.

To the right honourable the Lord Thomas Haward.

NOT being greatly forwarde of myne own inclination, (right honourable) but forced by the importunity of my friends to make some triall of my selfe in this exercise of trāslation. I haue aduentured vpon a peece of worke not in deede the most profitablest, as entreting of arms, nor yet altogether fruitlesse, if example may serue, as being historicall, but the while, either to be born withal for the delight, or not to be refused for the strāgenes: farther I mean not to make boaste of my trauaile, for the matter was offred not made choice off, as ther appeared lykewise little lybertie in my first yelding. The earnestnesse of my friends perswaded me that it was conuenient to lay forth my talent for encrease, or to sette my candle on a candlesticke, and the consideration of my insufficiency droue me to thinke it better for my ease, eyther quite to bury my talent, therby to auoyde the breaking of thriftlesse debtes, or rather to put my candle cleane out, then that it should bewray euery vnswept corner in my house, but the opinion of my friendes iudgement preuailed aboue mine owne reason. So vpon hope to pleafe them I first vndertooke this labour, & I haue gone thorow withall, the rather to acquaint my selfe with mine olde reading: wherto since the dispatch theroff, I haue made my friends priuie, & vpon their good liking with requeft thereto, I haue passed my graunt vnto thē for the publicatiō, reseruing to my selfe the order for the dedication, so as I should thinke best either for the defence of my worke, or for some perticuler merite towards me. And heerein I tooke no long leysure to finde out a sufficient personage. For the manifolde benefits receyued from your honourable parents my good

A.ii.   Lord

The Epistle Dedicatorie.

Lord and Lady, quickly eafed me of that doubt, and prefented your honour vnto my viewe: whome by good right I ought to loue and honour in efpeciall, as being of them begotten, at whofe handes I haue reaped efpeciall benefit. The which benefit if I fhould not fo gladly profeffe openly, as I willingly receiued being offred, I might well be challenged of vnkindeneffe: but were I as able to make good my part, as I am not ignoraunt what may be required at my hands, I would hope not to be founde vngrateful. In the meane time this my trauaile I cōmend vnto your Lordfhippe, befeeching the fame, fo to accept thereoff, as a fimple teftimony of that good will which I bere to your parēts while they liued thē being their feruāt, & now do owe vnto their ofspring after their deceafe, for their demerits. Vnder your honours protectiō I fhal leffe fere the affalt of the enuious, & of your honours good acceptaciō I haue fome hope in the mildenes of your Lordfhips nature, not doubting but that as your Lordfhippe hath giuen no fmal fignification in this your noble youth of wifedome and courage to fo many as knowe you, it being the only fupport of your aunceftours lyne: fo the fame lykewife will maynteine your aunceftours glorye & the hope of your owne vertues with affabilitie & gentleneffe, which was the proper commēdation of your parents. The almightie encreefe this hope with the other vertues before named, to the good hope of your countries peace, your Princeffe fafetie, and your owne honour, with the ioy of your kinred & friēds, whom not a few your parents good deferuing hath affured vnto you, and of whofe erneft prayers you fhal not faile, to further your wel doing. Amongft them though laft in worthineffe, yet with the formoft in well wifhing and defire of wel deferuing, your honour fhall finde me.

Your honours humbly moft affured,
Margaret Tyler.

M T. to the Reader.

Thou hast heere, gentle Reader, the historie of Trebatio an Emperour in Greece: whether a true storie of him in deede, or a fained fable, I wot not, neither dyd I greatly seeke after it in y translation, but by me it is done into English for thy profit & delight. The chiefe matter therin conteined is of exploits of wars, & the parties therin named, are especially renowmed for their magnanimitie & courage. The authors purpose appeareth to be this, to animate thereby, and to set on fire the lustie courages of youg gentlemen, to the aduauncement of their line, by ensuing such like steps. The first tongue wherein it was penned was the Spanish, in which nation by common report, the inheritance of all warlike commendation hath to this day rested. The whole discourse in respect of the ende not vnnecessary, for the varietie & continuall shift of fresh matter very delightfull, in y speaches short & sweet, wise in sentence, and wary in the prouision of contrary accidents. For I take the grace thereof to be rather in the reporters deuice then in the truth of this report, as I would that I could so well impart with thee y delight which my selfe findeth in reading the Spanish: but seldome is the tale carried cleane from an others mouth. Such deliuery as I haue made I hope thou wilt friendly accept, y rather for that it is a womans woork, though in a story prophane, and a matter more manlike then becometh my sexe. But as for y manlinesse of the matter, thou knowest y it is not necessary for euery trumpettour or drumslare in the warre to be a good fighter. They take wage onely to incite others though themselues haue priuy maimes, and are thereby recurelesse. So Gentle Reader if my trauaile in Englishing this Authour, may bring thee to a liking of the vertues herein commended, and by example therof in thy princes & countries quarrel to hazard thy person & purchase good name, as for hope of well deseruing my selfe that way, I neither bend my selfe therto nor yet feare the speach of people if I be found backward. I trust euery man holds not the plow, which would y greud

A.iij.   were

were filled:& it is no sinne to talke of Robinhood though
you neuer shot in his bow: Or be it that ẏ attempt were
bolde to intermeddle in armes,so as the auncient Ama-
zons did,and in this story Claridiana doth, & in other stories not a fewe,yet to report of armes is not so odious
but ẏ it may be borne withal,not onely in you men which
your selues are fighters,but in vs women,to whom the
benefit in equal part apperteineth of your victories,either
for that the matter is so commendable that it carrieth no
discredit from the homelinesse of the speaker, or for that
it is so generally knowen that it fitteth euery man to
speake thereoff,or for that it iumpeth with this common
feare on all partes of warre. and inuasion. The inuenti-
tion,dispositiõ,trimming,& what els in this story,is wholy an other mans,my part none therein but the translation,as it were onely in giuing entertainment to a stran-
ger,before this time vnacquainted with our ceũtry guise.
Mary the worst perhappes is this,that amonge so many
straungers as dayly come ouer,some more auncient,and
some but new set foorth,some penning matters of great
weight and sadnesse in diuinitie or other studies,the pro-
fession whereof more nærely besæmeth my yeares.other
some discoursing of matters more easy & ordinary in common talke,wherein a gentlewoman may honestly employ
hir trauaile.I haue notwithstanding made countenance
onely to this gentleman,whõ neither his personage might
sufficiently commend it selfe vnto my sexe, nor his beha-
uiour(bæing light & souldierlike)might in good order ac-
quaint it selfe with my years. So ẏ the question now a-
riseth of my choice,not of my labour,wherfore I preferred
this story before matter of more importance. For answere
whereto gentle Reader,ẏ truth is, that as ẏ first motion
to this kinde of labour came not frõ my selfe,so was this
pæce of worke put vpon me by others,& they which first
counsailed me to fall to worke,toke vpon them also to be
my taskemasters and ouersærs least I should be idle,and
yet bicause the refusall was in my power, I must stand to
answere for my easy yelding, & may not be vnprouided of

That a vvo man of your yeares maye vvrite in this argu-ment.

XI

excuse, wherin if I should alledge for my selfe ý matters
of lesse worthynesse by as aged years haue bene taken in
hand, & that dayly new deuises are published, in songs, sonets, enterludes, & other discourses, and yet are borne out
without reproch, only to please the humour of some men:
I thinck I should make no good plea therein, for besides ý
I should finde therby so many known enimies as known
men haue ben authors of such idle conceits, yet would my
other aduersaries be neuer the rather quieted : For they
would say ý aswel the one as the other were al naught, &
though peraduenture I might passe vnknown amongst a
multitude, & not be ý onely gaze or ý od party in my il doing, yet bicause there is lesse merit of pardon if the fault
be excused as common, I wil not make ý my defence which
cannot help mee, & doth hinder other men. But my defece
is by example of the best, amongst which many haue dedicated their labours, some stories, some of warre, some phi-
sick, some lawes, some as concerning gouernment, some diuine matters, vnto diuers ladies & gentlewomen. And if
men may & do bestow such of their trauailes vpon gentlewomen, then may we woṁe read such of their works as
they dedicate vnto vs, and if we may read them, why not
farther wade in thē to ý serch of a truth. And then much
more why not deale by translatiō in such argumēts, especially this kinde of exercise being a matter of more heede
then of deep inuention or exquisite learning, & they must
needs leaue this as confessed, ý in their dedications they
minde not only to borrow names of worthy personages,
but ý testimonies also for their further credit, which neither the one may demaund without ambition, nor ý other
graunt without ouerlightnes: if women be excluded from
the biew of such workes as appeare in their name, or if
glory onely be sought in our common inscriptious, it mat-
tereth not whether ý parties be men or women, whether
aliue or dead. But to retourn whatsoeuer the truth is,
whether that women may not at al discourse in learning,
for men lay in their claim to be sole possessioners of knowledge, or whether they may in some maner ý is by limita-

or appointment in some kinde of learning, my perswasion hath bene thus, that it is all one for a woman to pen a story, as for a man to addresse his story to a woman. But amongst al my il willers, some I hope are not so straight ỹ they would enforce me necessarily either not to write or to write of diuinitie. Whereas neither durst I trust mine own iudgement sufficiently, if matter of controuersy were handled, nor yet could I finde any booke in the tongue which would not breed offence to some, but I perceiue some may be rather angry to see their Spanish delight tourned to an English pastime, they could wel alow the story in Spanish, but they may not afford it so chepe, or they would haue it proper to themselues. What Natures such men be off, I list not greatly dispute, but my meaning hath ben to make other parteners of my liking, as I doubt not gentle reader, but if it shal plese thee after serious matters to sport they self with this Spaniard, ỹ thou shalt finde in him the iust reward of mallice & cowardise, with the good speed of honesty & courage, beeing able to furnish thee with sufficient store of forren example to both purposes. And as in such matters which haue bene rather deuised to beguile time, then to breede matter of sad learning, he hath euer borne away the price which could season such delights with some profitable reading, so shalt thou haue this straunger an honest man when nede serueth, & at other times, either a good companiõ to driue out a wery night, or a merry iest at thy boord. And thus much as concerning this present story, that it is neither vnseemly for a woman to deale in, neither greatly requiring a lesse staied age then mine is. But of these two points gentle reader I thought to giue thee warning, least perhaps vnderstanding of my name & yeares, thou mightest be carried into a wrong suspect of my boldnesse and rashnesse, frõ which I would gladly free my selfe by this plaine excuse, & if I may deserue thy good fauour by lyke labour, when the choice is mine owne I will haue a speciall regard of thy liking.   So I wish thee well.
                    Thine to vse, M.T.

Margin notes:
That you made not write of diuinitie.
That you meant to make a common benefit of your paines.
The vse & profit of this Spanish translation.
The conclusion.

¶CAP. I.

After that the greate Emperour Constantine had peopled the Citie of Constantinople, with the race of the noble Citizens of Rome, & had rectified ý auncient buildings founded by Pansanias king of the Parthes. Among all the Emperours which succeeded in that Empire of Greece, none seemed to haue raysed his owne name, or to haue made it so famous, as the great and mightie Emperour Trebatio. Whose worthy deedes with the valiant actes of the Knights of his time, I will report here, according as Artimidoro the Grecian hath left them written in the great volumes of his Cronicle.

The story sayth thus: That if at any time Fortune, being alwaies vncerteine and variable, shewed hir selfe more freindly to the Greekes, then to all men besides: and if euer the Grecians were feared in all the worlde, it was in the time of Trebatio the sonne of Alicante, which man by right line discended from the noble and auncient blood of Molosso, the second sonne of strong Pyrrhus, and in the third discent from the great Achilles, which was slayne in the warres at Troye.

This Trebatio, in the xx. yeare of his age, reigned in Epirus, wher the sayd Pyrrhus & his auncestours had bene kings. He was strong and valiant in armes, and endowed with so many graces, that his fame in ý time was spred ouer all the world, and that there was neither king nor Emperour but he was glad to hold him for his friend.

Now it happened in his time by the death of the Emperour Theodoro, the state of the Empire to be voyde, for that Theodoro had no sonne, and the Empire was to be giuen by election: So that the Electors not fynding any whom with so good reason they might chuse for Emperour as the great Trebatio, as well for his great valure, as for his discent from so noble a race. They with the willing & ioint assent of all the Emperials named him vnto the Empire, and brought him with great honour to Constantinople. Where, (if before, for his great fame they had praised and honored him) now much more they held him deere, hauing in some part seene & knowen him. Bicause he was of conditions very noble, pleasant, louing to all, liberall, courteous, sufferable, pitifull, and aboue all very desirous to entertein in his court, valiant and worthy knights, whom he honoured aboue all the Princes of the earth. So that his court florished with princes & knights, as wel subiects as straungers, which much magnified his great estate, & him selfe held continuall exercise in armes with them, as being like enclined to nothing. His vertue by the report of such as knew him, was so rare that it was generally thought none of his predecessors to haue had aduauntage ouer him, but rather he was of greater force then any one of them all. For many men were witnesses of his mightie strokes.

He was called the great Trebatio, bicause he was viii. foote in height, & very strong timbred, so that without proofe of his manhood, they might therby make coniecture of his force.

In his life, customes & conditions he was alway so affable, and courteous, that neuer might be noted in him one little fault. Wherfore his historians say, that he was the crown of the Greeks, and the cleere mirrour of all the Princes & knights of the world. Whence also this his chronicle boroweth this title, especially hauing therein to remember the meruailous deedes of the knight of the Sunne with Rosicleer both sons vnto Trebatio. Since whose time, all the aduentures of the auncient & famous knights were cleane forgotte, & since whose time, neither Vlisses, of whom Homere speaketh, neither any other songs or sonets, ballads or enterludes, wer heard in Greece, onely with these two knightes they were familiarly acquainted. Of these they made great volumes, and with a thousand deuises in verse they

they sang of their loue. Thei made no building nor pasture without some storie of them and their memorie therin declared. In such sort that you might passe by no part of all Greece where was not recited, song or painted ẙ histories and noble deeds of these knights. As if no other thing but armes or loue were fitting for them.

And bicause that in the time to come so noble things should not be put in obliuion, some of ẙ Grecians compiled this noble Historie, to the encouraging of all Nations, that shall either heare or reade this Historie.

¶The king of Hungary pretending a title to the Empire, setteth him selfe against the Emperour Trebatio. Cap. 2.

IT appeareth by an auncient Greeke Chronicle, ẙ the Emperour Helio, ẙ third predecessor in the Empire of Trebatio had two sons, ẙ eldest of the which two, ẙ father being deceased, was chose Emperour, the other was married with a Princesse inheritrix of the kingdome of Hungary, whereby he became Lord & ruler of that kingdome. The first son which was elected for Emperour departed without issue. For which cause ẙ Grecians chose an other which was ẙ predecessor of Theodoro. This seeing ẙ second son of Helio which then reigned in Hungary, and iudging ẙ with most reason ẙ Empire was his, as greeued with ẙ election he assembled his power against ẙ Grecians, thinking to be Lord ouer them by force. In the end as he was not so mightie as they, so he was vanquished and slaine before he might atteine his purpose. Yet frō that time forth al the kings which succeded in Hungary, pretended alway ẙ the right of the Empire rested in them by way of inheritaunce, and there neuer failed warres & dissentions betweene the Hungarians & the Greeks vpon this occasion.

In like manner when the great Trebatio was chosen for Emperour (then reigning in Hungary ẙ king Tiberio, a very strong man & of great courage, besids of more might

B.ij. th.u

then all his auncestours. For he held in his subiection beside the kingdome of Hungary many other prouinces, as
Holland, Zeland, Flaunders, Zweueland, Bauare, Austrich,
Almaine, Alba, Denmarke, Marcomandia, Persia, and o-
ther regions, with the which he deemed himselfe one of
the mightiest kings in the world. This Tiberio knowing the election of the Emperour Trebatio, and beinge
more attached with the desire of the Empire then any
of his predecessors were, (as it was to bee gotten by war)
so he assembled by summons ÿ greatest of estate throughout his lande, and declaring vnto them his will, hee com-
manded to gather all the people they might for to inuade Greece. Besides this, to the ende his power might
yet bee greater, he determined to marry his daughter vnto such a one, as would and could mainteine his quarrel.
This maiden was called Briana, the most beautifull Princesse that was to be found in all those partes, beinge by
the onely reporte of hir excellencie, sued vnto by many
worthy Princes, especially by Prince Edward, sonne of
Olyuerio king of the great Britaine. This yonng knight
strong and valiant, and greatly enamored on the Princesse Briana, through the great fame of hir beautie, had before dispatched his ambassadors towards the king hir father, to request hir for wife. To the which hir father bicause hee had already vndertooke the battaile against the
Emperour Trebatio, easely condescended, vpon condition
that the Prince should come into Hungary with 20000
chosen men of warre for to aide him in the pursuite of his
claime, against the Emperour.

  This, when Prince Edward vnderstoode, hee had
so great desire to haue the Princesse Briana, that by and
by he graunted his request, and so as speedely as he might,
he gathered the people that the king Tiberio required of
him, and with the consent of his father hee departed
from great Britaine towarde Hungary, giuing intelligence before vnto the king Tiberio, of his comming. The
king

king knowing the succours which came vnto him, appointed a day when all his hoast should meet together, and
finding him selfe of so great power, in the meane while
vntill the Prince came, hæ resolued to make a rode into
Greece, sacking all the little townes he might, before that
the Emperour Trebatio should perceiue it. Afterwardes
if ý Emperour Trebatio should come to succour his subiectes, then to ioyne battaile with him, at such time as the
Prince should apporch, which thing he put in practise diligently. For with that power which he had, he entered into Greece forraging the countrey, taking little townes of
no great force, burning and wasting so much as he might,
to the intent that the people of other fenced cities stroken
with feare, might abandon themselues to flight, and en-
feable their forces. Howbeit king Tiberio had not passed in
Greece xxx. myles, when the Emperour Trebatio hauing
knowledge of it, came against him vv an hoast of knights
so valiant, that at the first alarme, the Hungarian reculed,
and by the chase of his enimies was forced to retire home
into the citie of Belgrado, which is in Hungary. Ther he
fortified himselfe, and manned the twone, vnwilling as
yet to gœ vnto the fælde, vntill the Prince of greate
Britaine should arriue: by whose comming their powers bæing ioyned, he thought he might giue the battaile
vnto ý Emperour Trebatio. Albeit he caryed about him
a mayme incurable in his body, not by any stroke lent him
by his enimie, but by the onely conceit of the Emperours
vertue. For he had sæne the Emperour demeane him selfe
more worthely, then any of those which came with him, &
namely in a kinsman of his, a very strong knight, whom
the Emperour at one blow, as it were, deuided in two pæces. This, as it might be, made, him kœpe his chamber, bicause he himselfe confessed ý valour of the Emperour to
be aboue the report of men, notwithstanding he had heard
sufficiently of the Emperours prowesse. But bicause these
things are not mentioned, but to giue beginning to this

history,we run them briefly ouer, not rehearsing ý great
deds of armes that the Emperour and his people did in
besieging ý citie,bicause we haue other matters more noble in hand,in comparison whereoff,these thinges were
needlesse. The story hereoff,begins in ý chapter following.

¶ The Emperour Trebatio by the hearesay of hir beautie,
was surprised with the loue of the princesse Briana. ca.3

CErteine daies the Emperour Trebatio lay at ý siege
of Belgrado,hoping that the king Tiberio would come
out to giue them battaile , for that he had greate desire
to be auenged of the great harmes which he had receiued
in Greece,but the king would in no wise leaue the towne,
still abiding the comming of Prince Edward and his army out of England. The Emperour meruailing much at
it,comaunded a prisoner to be brought before him, whom
he had taken in the former battaile,of him he demaunded
the cause why the king Tiberio helt himself so clese with
so many good knights mewed vp in the citie,and why hee
came not out to giue the battaile, with promise of life ¢
liberty if he told trouth,otherwise ý certeintie of most cru-
death. The prisoner thus placed before ý Emperour,what
with feare of death,and hope of libertie,durst not declare
other then ý truth,¢ therfore thus made answere vnto him.

„ Know you mightie Emperour, that when the king of
„ Hungary my master,first tooke vpon him the entry into
„ Greece,he would not haue done it, (although he hath so
„ mightie an hoast as is sene)but in hope ý before he should
„ be espied and met withall,there should come to his helpe
„ Prince Edward,sonne to the king of great Britaine with
„ 20000.knights. This number was promised vpon condi-
„ tion that the prince should haue the kings daughter , the
„ princesse Briana to wife,which princesse I beleue is the
„ fayrest maide in all the world,and by such fame ý prince
„ is become enamored of hir,so as we here that he is al-
„ ready departed from greate Britaine with the number
appointed

appointed, & shal take landing very soone in this countrey, „
the king Tiberio abideth his comming,& is determined to „
giue the onset,as soone as their forces shalbe vnited.   „

This sayd the prisoner,but the Emperour minding to „
knowe more of the matter,demaunded of him where the „
Princesse Briana remayned,and of what age shee myght „
be.The prisoner aunswered him.My Lord,she is with the „
Queene Augusta hir Mother in the monastary of the ry- „
uer which is nere to Buda,a pleasant and delectable house, „
wherin none are lodged but Nonnes,& the Queenes gen- „
tlewomen.The princesse is of y age of xiiij.yeares,& be you „
assured that so many as shal see hir, wil iudge hir rather a „
goddesse then a woman,so much hir beautie doth excell all „
the gentlewomen of the world.Now so soone as y prince „
shall land,he will straight waies take his iourney towards „
the monastery of y riuer,bicause it is so appointed by the „
king hir father.The king him selfe will not be there, bi- „
cause he will not be absent in such a busy time from the
citie.When the prisoner had thus sayde, the Emperour
Trebatio commaunded him to be set free without speaking
other thing to his people,but with a sorowfull & troubled
countenaunce,he withdrew himselfe into a secret chamber
of his Imperiall tent.Where tossing in his conceit diuers
& sundry fancies,he endured a wilful imprisonment,with-
out any baile or maynprise. Thus that force,which nei- „
ther by tilt, turney,nor barriers , neither by speare nor „
sword, neither by mallice of the enimy,nor pride of the „
mightie,mught at any times be subdued,was nowe van- „
quished by y onely hearesay of a gentlewomans commen- „
dation. Nay y valiant heart which he held forcible inough „
against all the world, failed in his own defence against a „
delicate damzel whom he had neuer seene.What force is „
it y may repulse this euil,sith y with such flattering closes, „
it ouerthroweth so many noble hearts and strong bodies. „

But to retourne,the Emperour Trebatio so much bur-
ned in loue with the Princesse Briana,that already he hath
B.iiij.   forgotten

forgotte the damage receiued in his countrey, his trauaile out of his countrey with a huge army, the consuming of his treasure for to wreake his anger on the king Tiberio, onely he deuised vpon this, howe to giue remedie vnto his amorous passion. For as ẙ fire was great which enflamed him, so was the remedy by all semblaunce farre from him. Because that on ẙ one part he was hindred by the enmitie betwéene him and hir father, so that he durst not require hir for wife, and on the other side she was already promised to the Prince of greate Britaine, who had put himselfe on his iourney for ẙ atteining of hir person, so that likewise ẙ king could not take hir from him to giue vnto his enmy. These things bred such griefe vnto ẙ Emperour as ẙ he hoped for nothing, but to dye. And so tourning & ouertourning in his thought a thousand sort of remedies, without finding any which might satisfie him, he conuaied him selfe into his most secret tent, & ther remained iii daies, not suffering any of his people to haue accesse vnto him or speach wt him, except some squiers seruitors, from who likewise he would willingly haue exempted himself, but that he would not die so desperately. Those of the camp which sawe the sodeine chaunge & alteration in the Emperour, as they knew not the cause of it, so were they much abashed and carefull to know what it might bée. Some immagined that the delay of the warre, and the comming of prince Edward were the occasions of his trouble, and so hoping that he should well ouercome that griefe shortly, they left him to his rest, vntill he had resolued vpon the pursuite of this which followeth in the next Chapter.

¶Prince Edward entereth into Belgrado: The Emperour bethincketh himselfe of his remedie.   Cap. 4.

FOure daies after ẙ the Emperour Trebatio was thus wounded with the loue of the Princesse Briana, Prince Edward wt rr.M. entered into the citie of Belgrado, where he was welcomed by the king who had great desire to

see

fee him,foz he thought not only to depart with ȳ citie, but
also to adde therbnto a great part of ȳ empire of Greece.
So foone as these newes wer spzed in the enimies campe,
the emperour was cast into greater melancholy,as by the
shoztnes of time not being able to finde an issue foz his late
deuise,only this he thought,ȳ foz to assure his bncerteine
hope(if ther might be any)he had none other way then to
cut of pzince Edwards enterpzise, and so by shoztning his
life,better ¢ moze easely to compasse ȳ obteining of ȳ pzin⸗
ces.Upon this resolution he made to call into his tent.xii.
knights.ȳ most baliant ¢ wozthiest of all his hoast,among
whom one was Alceo,father of Rodomarte,pzince of Sar⸗
dinia,of whom ther is made great account in this histozy:
the second was Alpinco L.of ȳ Iland Lemnos: the third
was called Alfonte L.of ȳ Iland Sicile:the iiii. was cal⸗
led Alcino king of Thrace:ȳ fifte,Liberio L.of Nicropon⸗
te: ȳ sixt Boristhines whose son was Rodopheo pzince of
Rhodes:ȳ seuenth Dardante pzince of Dalmatia: ȳ eight
Melides L.of Ithaca wher Vlysses reigned king:ȳ ix.Ar⸗
gante L.of Pathmos:ȳ x. Arimont L.of ȳ Ilands Cycla⸗
des:ȳ xi.Artedoro pzince of Candia:ȳ xii.¢ last Nicoleon⸗
te L.warde of ȳ streights wher Corinth stod.All knights
of great account,young ¢ bery strong foz to bndertake a⸗
ny enterpzise, all subiects bnto the emperour,¢ all welbe⸗
loued of him,bscause he was pziuie bnto their great ber⸗
tues.Now when ȳ emperour saw all these knights in pze⸗
sence,with some shamefastnes which ȳ weight of ȳ mat⸗
ter caused , he reueled to them wholy his grǽfe, giuing
thē to bnderstād withall,ȳ bnles he had some help his life
wer spilt.Among all ȳ best which he had found,he reckned
specially bpon one,which was,ȳ secretly they shold auoyd
the campe ¢ follow him.The knights hauing great desire
to serue him,¢ esteeming themselues happy that he would
communicate with them part of his minde , they frǽly
offered bnto him their persons foz ȳ accomplishing of that
which he should commmaund them,¢ they all agrǽd to
depart

depart with him in such order as he had deuised. Then ye emperour made to cal before him ye king of Boheme, which was his vnckle, a very wise and expert man in armes, to

,, whom he declared,ye he had vrgent occasion to be absent a

,, while from his army:ye circumstances wherof saith he,you

,, shall further know at our returne,in ye meane time, I com=

,, mend vnto you ye charge of ye warre,& for your greater cre=

,, dite with ye people I deliuer vnto your hands the Imperi=

,, all scepter.The king meruailing at this ye the Emperour did; without more demaunding of him whether or wher about he would go,accepted ye charge & promised therein to employ his trauaile.Well,ye night approching with the houre agreed vpon,ye emperour & the xii.knights, armed at all points with rich & costly armour and with Hungarian bases, secretly left ye campe without being heard or know en of their enimies,wherin they trauayled all night vntill the day appeared , then they alighted to rest their horses, and fed vpon such victuals,as thei had brought with them: after taking again their horses,they posted on their iour ney till they wer in the myd way,betwæen Buda and Bel grado,which way prince Edward of force must haue passed when he should go to ye monasterie of ye riuer.Ther in a thicke wood somewhat aside out of ye way,they put them selues hauing prouision & furniture of all things necessa ry,wher they remained very close:vntill ye Fortune friend ly to ye emperour & enimie to ye prince,gaue ye prince into ye emperours hads,which shalbe shewed in ye chap.folowing.

Prince *Edward* ryding towards the Monasterie of the riuer, was by the Emperour *Trebatio* encountred & slayne. Cap. 5.

VVen prince Edward had once set footing in Belgrado, he had great desire to sæ the princes, so ye the third day after his comming,he would næds depart tewards ye monasterie of ye riuer.The king Tiberio vnderstäding his desire(albeit he him selfe might not accópany him,yet) he set him on his way thetherward,(only to haue his aide & assistäce in ye battaile)wt foure aged knights in his com pany,being best knowu by ye Q. & the princes.These fielo

be

be in ý prince retinue, & other xii. knights mo which he had brought out of his coūtry, & by these ý king sent letters to ý Q. & the princes Briana, ý contents wherof wer, ý the prince might spedaly bebetrothed vnto hir, but more company would he not send therby to haue the mach kept secret till the war which he held with the emperour wer finisht. For this matter was husht no man almost being priuie vnto it, yet ý prisoner which bewrayed it vnto the emperour, had vnderstanding of it by meanes of the kings seruice. In this time the Q. & hir daughter hauing intelligence of the princes comming, attended his comming in the monasterie with preparation for his enterteinment. Prince Edward departing frō ý king one night ý most couertly ý he might, went out of ý citie with his owne xii. knights, & foure of ý kings: with these he tooke his way a whole night & a day withall ý hast he might, to ende the great desire he had to sée ý beautifull princes. This way albeit short, yet it semed long vnto him, as being ignorāt of ý sower sauce & wofull wedding which was in prouiding. O mariage, ý slender & weake foundation of world- „
ly things, how is it not onely regarded by men but high- „
ly reuerenced: how seldome was it euer stedfast, and how „
many thousands hath it beguyled. (I meane not the base „
and common people, but euen Kinges and Emperours. „

O how many impediments be therin left to hinder vs „
from enioying it: O what a common thing is it do die : & „
how many euer saw happie ende in it: How ioyfull & plea- „
sāt was to Paris ý desired match of Helena, & how sorrow- „
full & lamentable was the end, not onely to him but to his „
parents & brethren & the greatest part of all Asia: For not „
only in Greece, but in all ý out Ilands therabouts was be- „
wept his bitter bridall. With how great care & diligence „
do men hasten on ý causes of their care, occasions of their „
heauines, means of their paines, & matter for their griefe, „
and do not content themselues with the continuall afflic- „
tion wherin fortune scholeth them: but by new meanes „
they inuente newe matters of daunger whiche cros- „
seth

" seth the at euery step, they frame new causes, & as it wer,
" forge vnto themselues sharp spurs to prick foreward this
" woful life, wher they thinke to finde pleasure & rest, there
" they finde for their losse trauaile, & trouble for the death
" which they would fly frō. To escape either nipping coldes,
" or scalding heat, this only one remedy they haue to climbe
" vp vnto ẏ mountains, wher yet ẏ winde hath most force, &
" ẏ sun doth soonest parch: aboue all this hath not ẏ vnsatia-
" ble couetousnes of man broken through ẏ sturdy waues of
" the sea, & cut out new passages on ẏ moūtaines? But why
" do we cōplaine on Fortune, do not we bend hir armies to
" fight with vs, do not we maintain hir weapōs which per-
" aduenture lighteth on our own necks. As for example if
" Paris had not made a way through ẏ dæpe waues of ẏ sea
" A egean (which the gods had placed as a peaceable bound
" betwene Europe & Asia) & if he had not sought Greece, sith
" Asia was large enough to haue found a fair wife in, & (so it
" may be) much more honest then Helene was, then the A-
" chians had not transported thēselues into Asia, to destroy
" Troy. And tourning againe to our matter, prince Edward
" might haue sought him a wife in his own coūtrey or more
" nære home, of whose beautie his own eies might haue ben
" witnesses, and not haue sought hir in a straunge land by
" ẏ onely brute of a running tale, especially vpon so hard &
" sore conditions as to bring his owne person & people to
" the war. Whosoeuer cōns to seeke pleasure and delight
" for his youth, let him take that he findes, and think it not
" straunge, because that bawnde Fortune hath vsed the like
" vnto others. The prince then being on his way, two of ẏ
kings knights were dispatched before by some secreate
by wayes very well knowne vnto them to aduertise ẏ
Quene & princesse of ẏ approching of ẏ prince. These ii.
held on their way, not afrayed by the ambush, but so soone
as ẏ prince w̄ his knights had entred in the thicket, they
wer presētly discouered by ẏ Emperour, who was alredy
armed w̄ his rich armor & moūted vpō a strōg & light horse

The

The Emperour taking a great speare in his hande very sharpe, and well steeled for the purpose, went alone aside out of the woode with a softe pace, to encounter with the Prince and his knightes, and beeing come right before them, sayd vnto them. Knowe you knights that this passage is forbidden you, except you leaue your shieldes and your names in them. For that a Ladie whom I honour and serue hath commaunded me to doe it, whose loue I could not otherwise obteine. The Prince Edward was by nature very stoute, and by inclination giuen to somewhat lesse modestie in his talke then behoued suche a Prince, howbeit for this and other faultes he was a very valiaunt and streng knight, such a one as neither in great Britaine, neither in the kingdome of Hungary, was thought to haue his peere. But as he vnderstoode the demaunde of the knight, very wroth he aunswered him. By God knight, if the king Liberio were as certeine of the victorie against the Emperour Trebatio, as I hope to chastise thy follie, then the Prince of England shoulde not neede to come from so farre a countrey to giue him helpe. Take then quickly that part of the fielde as shall seeme good vnto thee, and with one onely chofe thou shalt see howe deere and bitter thy loue hath bene vnto thee.

As the Prince had sayd this, and had pronounced with his owne mouth, that cruell doome, not well foreseeinge his owne fall, he tooke a great speare fró one of his knights and brocht his horse with the spurres to meete the Emperour. (This he did, not for that his knights woulde not haue put themselues in the aduenture before him, euery man claiming to be first, but for that no reason suffised him. For his stoutnesse & his vnmeasurable pride, made him to forget the force of his enemie, and put his enimie stode before him so great and so bigge made, that he seemed to be a gyant.) But this Princes aduerse fortune and vnhappie destinies woulde him to be the formost, so that the mightie Trebatio knewe it, as well by the riches of

his

his armour as by the talke which had passed betwéen him
& his knightes, and beeing very glad to sée him the firste
which he met, he sayd vnto himselfe, O that my speare
were nowe greater and stronger and the head forged by
Vulcan, that it might not stay in ỹ armour of this knight,
for that according as I sée him great & stronge, so I feare
hée will escape my handes, and then my trauaile shall be
all in vaine. Thus as he sayde, they by and by did put
both their speares in their restes, and giuing either horse
hys bridle, they ranne together with such fury, that they
made the earth to tremble, and yet the lightnesse of their
horses was such, that it seemed the grasse yelded not vnder
their féete. The Prince hit the Emperour in the middest of the shéelde, and pearcing farther left the head remaining in the fine and well stéeled armour, whereby
the staffe broken in many shiuers made a great whistle-
ling in the ayre. But the Emperours stroke was muche
more fell, for he leuelled it with such force that it entred
not onely into the shéeld and strong armour of the Prince,
but passed through vnto his amerous heart all bedewed
with bloud a whole armes length.

Then the Prince fel dead executing the sentence which
he had giuen in these wordes, that that loue shoulde bée
very deere & bitter. When his people sawe him stretched
vpon the grounde, there might no sorowe be compared
vnto theirs, and as raging madde they ranne altogether
vppon the Emperour thinckinge to put in practise their
deadly anger vpon his carcase. Some with speares and
other with swordes strake hym on all partes with great
rage and hast, so that if his armour had not bene verie
good, in short space they had hewed it in peeces. But that
most valiant Greke, no lesse strong, then any of his aunce-
tors, bearing his fine and sharp sword, tourned himselfe a-
mong them in such manner, that he shethed it in their bodies. The first whom he met he cleaued vnto the eyes, the
seconds arme he cut of by the elbow, & being sore woun-

ded

ded he ouerthzewe the third at an other blowe, neither
ftaied he here, but in his rage, he dealt blows and wounded many, whiche foz feare accounting him rather a
diuell of hell then a knight put themfelues to flight. Albeit, they might haue recouered fome courage in ȳ they wer
many ⁊ chofen knights, alwaies againft one knight onely.
But the reafon was foz that at this time the Emperours
knightes fhewed themfelues out of the woode. So that indeede by the great manhood of their Lozd they found none
left on liue faue two knights of ȳ king which wer know-
en by their Hungarian bafes. Thofe the Emperour commaunded to be kept carefully foz ȳ thing befoze touched.

This being done, the knights and other footmen which
the Emperour had bzought with him to guid his cariage
tooke all ȳ dead bodies vpon their hozfes, wout leauing a-
ny thing which was theirs, ⁊ altogether they caried thē into ȳ thick of ȳ wood, frō whence they befoze came out, ther
in ȳ thickeft therecf, they made a great pit, into ȳ which
they thzew ȳ prince ⁊ the knights faue ȳ Englifh bafes, ⁊
ȳ kings letters which were needful foz his purpofe. They
couered thē with earth in fuch fozt, that ther was neuer
memozy of them. At the time that the Pzince was entered, the Emperour being of conditions pitiful, felt fo great
doloz in his heart ȳ the teares iffued abundantly from his
eyes, ruing the loffe of fo great a Pzince flaine out of his
own country in the bewtie of his age, when alfo yelding a
great figh which fæmed to haue come frcm ȳ bottome of
his heart, he fad with a troubled ⁊ low voice in this wife.

O vnhappie and vnfoztunate Pzince, God knoweth „
how fozowful and grieuous thy death is to mæ, and how „
faine I would haue giuen remedy in fome other manner „
to that I moft defired, and although thou waft mine ene- „
mie and come in fauour of ȳ kinge Tiberio to take from „
me my land ⁊ high eftate, yet woulde I not haue bene fo „
cruel an enimie vnto thæ, but ȳ entire loue of the pzinceffe „
Briana dzaue me moze therto, then mine owne enmitie, „

Nowe

,, Nowe I wish that by some other meanes I might haue
,, bene relieued, and not to haue bought my life by thy losse.
,, But as loue is tirannous, so meruaile not though he want
,, pittie towardes thee, which could not otherwise purchase
,, it to himselfe: Pardon me therefore. O mightie and wor-
,, thy prince, I iudge if thou wert aliue what thou wouldest
,, doe if by my death thou mightest finde remedie of thy
,, loue. The Emperours knights which heard these words,
and sawe the teares trickling downe his manly cheekes,
perceiued well howe much the death of the Prince disquieted him And they sayd amongst themselues, that by
god right the Emperour deserued the prayse of the most
noble and worthy Prince of the worlde. But hauing
made an ende, the Emperour caused to be brought before
him the two knightes belonging vnto Tiberio. These two
were very fearfull of the death, seeing the thinges which
were already done, and especially when they knewe him
to be the Emperour Trebatio, whom they helde as their
mortall enimie. Nowe when they came before him, the
Emperour sayd to them. If you will doe that whiche I
,, commaunde you, and keepe secreate that which I tell
,, you, I will not onely pardon you the death which I haue
,, giuen to your felowes, but also I will bring you with me
,, into mine Empire, where you shall be very well conten-
,, ted. The knightes better satisfied then they were, because
he promised them life, before not hoping but the death,
with god will they yelded themselues to doe all that hee
would, withall, swearing into his emperiall handes their
,, faith and obeisaunce. Then sayde the Emperour, that
,, which I would haue you doe is this, I haue great desire
,, to haue the Princesse Briana for wife, and this maye not
,, be done, except I goe in the name of Prince Edward,
,, to ensure my selfe with hir in the monastery of the riuer,
,, for the which it is necessary that you two being kinsmen
,, of the Queene and the Princesse, shoulde goe in my com-
,, panie, and say that I am Prince Edward. Nowe first

diſcouer not my ſecreat to any perſon, vntil ý you be licen⸗ ,,
ſed therevnto by me, and in ſo doing, you ſhall do naught ,,
either againſt your Lord o2 kingdome , ſith in this bar⸗ ,,
gaine the p2inceſſe loſeth not, and the king with all hys ,,
ſubiectes winne perpetually, fo2 that by this meane, the ,,
great wars and contentions begun, ſhall take ende.   ,,

After that the Emperour had ſaid theſe and other things,
whereby the knights vnderſtode his will, it grieued them
not a whit of this talke, but they were rather ioyous. wey⸗
ing the benefit which the king, the kingdome, the p2inceſſe
Briana, and all his ſhould reape thereby, and eſpecially the
P2inceſſe, by obteining to huſband the moſte noble and
wo2thy P2ince of all ch2iſtendome, as well fo2 his perſon
as fo2 his eſtate, and ſo with good will they ſubmitted
themſelues to doe him pleaſure and what els he cōmaun⸗
ded them . With this the Emperour and his knightes
toke the letters which were directed to the Quæne and
the p2inceſſe, and with mo2e hope to achiue their enqueſt,
they put on the Engliſh baſes , which made them ſæme
Engliſh men, then taking their way towarde the mona⸗
ſtery of the ryuer . In the way the kings knightes tolde
the Emperour howe two of their felowes were gone be⸗
fo2e to gyue notice vnto the P2inceſſe of P2ince Edwards
comming, and that therefo2e it were good to goe well ad⸗
uiſed, fo2 they ſhould mæte them by the way. The Em⸗
perour alowed their aduice, and charged his people vntill
they app2oched nære them not to diſcloſe themſelues, leaſt
they retiring, their ſecreats might be layd open. Now fo2⸗
tune iumped ſo euen with the Emperour, as that al things
ſucceded on his ſide, vntill the accompliſhment of his de⸗
ſire, which ſhall be recited in the Chapter following.

¶The Emperour Trebatio was receiued at the monaſta⸗
rie by the Archbiſhop of Belgrado, and there betro-
ched by the name of Prince Edward.   Cap.6

C.   The

The Emperour with his knightes departed from the Wodde, where the vnfortunate Prince was slaine, and toke their way towards the citie of Buda, vntil they came within vj. miles of the monastery, where they saw a farre the two other knightes which had retourned to bringe the Prince on his way, when their fellowes had espyed them, they tolde it to the Emperour, vpon this the Emperour commaunded his knights to kepe together, least they should be knowne, and so they kept on till they met. The other two seing the English bases, thought him to bee ye prince of England with his knights. But ye Emperours knightes as soone as these were within their reach laide holde on their brideles, and with courteous woordes stayed them vntill the other two knightes of the kings had talked with them. These two declared vnto the other that which had happened betwéen prince Edward & the Emperour Trebatio, & in ye end made plaine the meaning of the Emperour, both praying them to kéepe it secreate, and threatening them with death if they did otherwyse. No doubt they wondred at that which chaunced, but what the Emperour would that they promised him, & were nothing repentaunt of their exchaunge.

The Emperour béeing asserteined of their faith, went with them towards the monastery of the riuer, wherevnto béeing come, they founde not in the menasserie but the Quéene, the Princesse and other gentlewomen béeinge seruitors to attend vpon them, and the Archbishoppe of Belgrado which there taryed for to ensure them. This Archbishop receiued the Emperour at the gate, & thincking him assuredly to be the Prince of England, conducted him with his knightes, where the Quéene & the Princesse were in the company of beautifull and discreate Ladies, abiding his comming. When they had saluted each other, and that the Emperour had taken a full biew of the princesse, he was greatly abashed to sée hir beautie, for he could not be perswaded that so great comlinesse had bene in He-

lene,

lene, although dærely bought by his aunceltors, hæ iudged it more heauenly or angelicall, then humaine or earthly, belides she was of a goodly stature excelling the other gentlewomen in height a span. The Princelle when she fawe the Emperour before hir, shæ iudged him to bæ the goodlieſt knight that might be in the world, which his beautiful face and pleaſant countenaunce ſhewed eſpecially. When thus by the eies each of them were indifferently ſatiſæd, the Emperour would haue kiſſed the hand of the Quæne Auguſta, but ſhe with great good will embraced him. By and by, tourning himſelfe againe towardes the Princeſſe, hæ tæke hir by the hand, and ſayde in effect thus much.

The fame of your great beautie, excellent Princeſſe, „ hath in ſuch ſort paſſed through the world, that the onely „ report thereof hath forced the prince of England to leaue „ his naturall kingdome and ſoile, to come and ſerue you „ in this countrey, and to beholde with his owne eies „ that whiche his eares woulde ſcarſely belæue. God „ hath made me ſo fortunate that I haue obteined the good „ will of the king your father, and of the Quæne your mo- „ ther for to haue you to wife. Onely nowe I want the „ conſent of your part, which the king by his letters praieth „ you to giue vnto me, & I for the deſire that I haue to bæ „ yours, beſæch you not denie it me, for with it I maye ac- „ count my ſelfe the happieſt knight of all the world. And „ with theſe wordes, kiſſing the kings letters he deliuered it into hir handes, which the Princeſſe receiuing with a graue & ſober countenaunce, and after taking it to ý Archbiſhop for to read, the meane time made aunſwere ſoftly, on this wiſe.

I would to God moſt worthy Prince, that I were ſuch „ a one as with reaſon might deſerue ſome part of ý paines „ which you haue taken onely to ſæ me, or that I might in „ ſome little reſpect recompence the great pleaſure you haue „ done to me, & to al this kingdome in cōming, to ſuccour vs „

with

,, with your great force and power, but sith desert doth want
,, so much in me, I will accomplish that which the duetie of
,, obedience vnto the king my father forceth me vnto, for y I
,, must subiect my wil vnto his comaundement. yet I so con-
,, sider of this your offer & request, as that from this time
,, I will dare to compare with you in like happinesse.

While these wordes were in speaking, the Archbishoppe began to reade the kinges letters, wherein onely
was conteined his consent with the desire of dispatch, that
presently vpon the princesse comming they should be married. The Archbishop with both their consents taking
their handes, married them with all the ceremonies and
wordes which the Church ordeineth. After this the Emperour embraced the faire Princes, and with vnspeake-
able gladnesse kissed hir on the white and red chakes, and
from thence brought hir into a gorgeous chamber, where
they draue foorth the rest of the day with very amorous
and delectable talke, which so much the more set his loue
on fire, as he proceeded farther in his pleasant dalliaunce.
Albeit ere night the most puissant Emperour was not
altogether quieted in his thought, for feare least some one
which knewe the Prince might haue betrayed them, at
length beeing certeine that none in the monastery had
seene either the one or the other, but onely the kinges. iiif.
knightes, and his owne men which kept that matter close
inough, when the houre of supper approched, hee supped with some pleasure, and so helde on a greate parte of
the night till it was time to take his reste. Then the
Emperour was ledde to one side of the monasterie,
wherein there was a riche and stately lodginge, where
he lengthened the night with many fancies, not hauinge
as yet reached into the very depth of his enterprise, albeit stilled a little with y which already had happened. The
bautiful princesse after leaue taken of y Emperour, accompanied y Queene hir mother. Because vntil y the war was
ended betweene y king hir father & the emperour, she was
desirous

deſirous to kæpe hir ſelfe vnknowen,and ſo the kinge hir father,and the Quæne hir mother had commaunded,leaſt if ought ſhould happen amuſſe to the prince in theſe battailes,the princeſſe ſhould haue remained both a maiden, and a widowe,this deuiſe little auayled, as ſhal be manifeſted in the ſequele.

¶ The Emperour Trebatio driueth in his conceit,the order how to conſummate the marraige,which in the end he bringeth to paſſe accordingly.　　　Cap.7

THE Emperour Trebatio remained. iij.dayes in the monaſtery of the ryuer , not hauing opoztunitie to talke with the Princeſſe alone,bicauſe ſhe was not willing to giue conſent to his deſire,vntil the warre with the emperour ſhould be finiſhed. This inconuenientie troubled his thought & increaſed his melancholy, as nothing moze foz that the terme which the king had ſet foz his retourne was all ready expired,and bæing afraide leaſt the kinge would ſend foz him,whereby his fault ſhould be diſcoue= red,without giuing remedy to that which had bene the o= riginall of his griefe,in ſuch wiſe he was tozmented that he could neither ſlæpe noz eate. And in his imagination he did naught els but gaſe on the princeſſe,expecting time when he might alay the heate of his amozous paſſion.But whether it were Foztune,oz the will of God,it fell ſo out that there was begotten betwæne them the fruite of their deſire. Foz one mozning walking in his chamber,he eſpied out of a windowe the Princeſſe alone in hir night gowne, going towards a freſh and pleaſant gardein butting vpon his lodging,(the gardein befoze he had not ſæne) . In= to this gardeine entered none but the Princeſſe and hir gentlewomen . As hæ ſawe ſo good and pzoſperous a time , the moſt ioyfull man that euer was, hæ went to= wardes the pleaſaunt gardeine , and findinge no entery but by the chamber of the Princeſſe , the doze where=

of was shutte, hee tooke two of those speares which his knightes had brought, and rearing them vp against the wall with the blunt ende vpwards,(as he was very nimble,he lifted himselfe vpon them lightly,and easely slode downe betwixt them into the gardeine , without beeinge seene of any,especially not of the Princesse, who was vnwitting of such a leape.

The Princesse was nigh a fountaine wel set about with Roses and Iessamines,kembing & dressing of hir yeelow haire. Nowe when she sawe hir selfe thus sodeinly taken by the Emperour, with a fearefull starte shee rose from whence she was,and gentely smiling as somewhat ouertaken with shamefastnesse,she bespowed him in this
,, sort. Assuredly my Lord,nædes must the hurt bee greate
,, which you haue susteined by your leape,and great is the
,, iniury which the gardeine hath receiued by your entery,
,, bicause that in it none haue come, but either my selfe , or
,, my gentlewomen : for whose solace it was first plotted
,, out. For this cause God hath shewed mee such fauoure,
,, aunswered the Emperour,bicause I haue lodged my heart
,, in your excellent beautie,and well maye the body lawe-
,, fully enter where the heart is harboured. Let not there-
,, fore my entrie,good madame,seeme straunge vnto you,sith
,, that neither heure nor moment I may departe from you.
,, And if this my rudenesse hath procured you any paine,by
,, the freedome which you haue giuen me my heart shal make
,, excuse vnto your beautie, vnder whose safe conduct with-
,, out demaund of leaue,my body hath entered. The good
Emperour hauinge thus sayd,embraced & kissed hir,& not leauing any leasure of reply,made hir to sit downe by him neere vnto the well.This place was so hedged & compassed about with coodiferous Roses & sweet smelling Iessamines,y they might not be perceyued by any.And y gentle murmure that the running water made vppon the pibble stones,agreeing with the delicate layes which diuerse birdes made vppon the grene boughes, encreased so
much

much the longing desire of the Emperour, that casting
howe to winne the fauour of his lady, already his tounge
failed to speake, and his hearing to receiue that which she
spake. She then all trembled, as knowing his purpose,
& through feare greatly desired to haue shunned that place,
but the Emperour caught hir betwœne his armes, and
with such haste to ende his suite left hir vnfurnished of
hir aunswere.

At that time as the burning beames of the Sunne began
with his golden rayes to looke through the thicke Iessamines, al the fortunate aspectes intermedling their forces,
at that time, by the grace of the Almightie, were begotten
these two noble children, The Knight of the Sunne, and
Rosicleer. The beames of whose knightly deeds so shined
through the world, as that the worthy prowesse of their
predecessors were thereby eclipsed.

This was the Plaudite of his passion, and the beautiful
princesse now became a wife somewhat against hir will,
but when she sawe no remedy to that which was past,
she comforted hir selfe in that he was hir lawfull husband, and therefore she pardoned him his boldnesse in trou-
bling hir. These two louers shortened the time with good
agrœment, vntill the Emperour at his departure tooke his
leaue of hir to mounte vp the way hee came, and to retourne into his lodging. The princesse remained alone
in the gardeine, vntill hir gentlewomen came for hir to
dinner.

After this, yet the Emperour soiourned ther three daies,
at the ende whereoff, fearing the kinges ielousie ouer his
tarrying, and the euent of his sending for, hee tooke hys
leaue of the Quéene and the Princesse, not without the courtesie of many teares on each parte,
and especially of the Princesse whom he left
very dolefull, albeit sadder woulde shœ
haue bene, if she had forefœne the
longe time of his absence.

C.iiii.   The

¶The Emperour Trebatio purſuing thoſe which had
ſtolen his Lady, leſte all his knights and tooke an o-
ther way.　　　　　　　　　　　　　Cap.8

The Emperour Trebatio thus hauing departed from
the monaſtery of the riuer, became very ſorowfull in
his heart, with the leauing of the Princeſſe Briana , for
that ỹ fire which enflamed him after he had knowen hir,
was greater then ỹ affection which he bare to hir before
by the hearing of hir beautie, and that which cauſed his
moſt griefe, was that he knew not how either to retourne
ſpeadely vnto hir, or to ſalue that ſore which he had already chaffed . He thought in himſelfe, that if hee made
peace with the king Tiberio letting him vnderſtand of the
matter, the king would not accept of it, either for the great
enmitie which was betwixt them, or for the bond wherein he was bound to the Prince of great Britaine . And
therefore it would be a thing neither reaſonable, nor agrœ-
ing with his honour, in lieu of the princes paines which
hee had taken to come from his countrey accompanied
with ſo great a number of knightes to ſerue him, and in
regard of the death which he there receiued in his ſeruice,
nowe to become a friend to his foe, and to giue his daughter before eſpouſed to the Prince, vnto the deadlyeſt foe
which the Prince had, debating theſe and other thinges
in his minde about the time that they had got ouer their
heads the thicke woode wherein they had bene before,
nowe to the ende not to tyre their horſes, they lighted
downe, vnbridled their horſes, and tourned them to graſſe.
They themſelues feeding on ſuch victualls as they had
brought with them, although the meat whereon the Emperours ſtomack tyred, was meſt of all ſobs and ſighes,
as receiuing no pleaſure in the abſence of ỹ princeſſe. Now
the night aſſailed them, and hauing not in them to make
reſiſtaunce, they yelded their forces, euery one taking hys
reſt where it liked them beſt. But ỹ Emperour ſomwhat a
　　　　　　　　　　　　　　　　　　　　　　part

parte from the reſſe , caſting himſelfe vppon the greene
graſſe,& ſtaying his back againſt a tree, he there remained
moze then two houres bzoad awake ſtaring at the cleareneſſe
of the ayze,& the brightneſſe of the ſtars,when his thoughts
renued,and the amozous paſſion, if befoze not cleane buried now reuiued a freſh by the ſolitarines of his conceipt:
at length his cares, the wearineſſe of his way,and the ſweet
noiſe of the pleaſaunt leaues through the hiſſing of the winde,
bzought him in a gentle ſlomber : wherin he had ſcarſely
bene an halfe houre but that his fancie pzeſented to him
againe his Lady Briana. He dzeamed that ſhe was taken
by foze of two Giants,the meſt fierce & ſtrong that euer
he had ſeene in all his life , and that ſhe ſeing him, cried
foz helpe.Through the griefe wherof he awaked bery much
afrighted: and in dæde this dzeame pzoued no game vnto
him, foz by and by he heard a great noyſe neere vnto him,
& liſtening what it might be,he beheld a faire charist dza-
wen wt iiij.hozſes , & in the top of it two great burning torches ſet in ſiluer candleſticks,by the light wherof he ſaw
a Lady in the chariot clothed with rich & pzincely robes,
and reſembling ſo much the Pzinceſſe Briana,that he verely beleued it was ſhe. The gentlewoman leaning on hir
elbow,and caſting downe hir countenaunce,paſſed on ſtil
ſighing, as one enduring ſome great foze & tozment.The
Emperour pzying about to ſee who were the guides of the
chariot perceiued that ſhe was caried away by two ſtrong
and huge Gyants,with great battell axes in their hands,
being on foote at the foze ende of the chariot. Theſe two
had ſo fell and cruell loks,that they would haue daunted
the courage of any man which ſhould haue beheld them.
But the Emperour aſſured in his thought,that this was
the Pzinceſſe, with great anger ſtart vp, and not remembzing to call any of his knights,with his ſwozd he paced
towazds the Gyaunts,where without either good euen oz
good mozrow, he lent the firſt whom he appzoched vnto
ſuch a ſtroke, that the Gyaunt would haue mozgaged his

C.v.   part.

part in the Lady, to haue made sufficient paiment of that blowe, for lifting vp his battell are to receiue the blowe, the sword cut it into the myddest of the helme, and from thence gliding downe vpon his armour hewed it into many peeces. Then y other Giant hastening to smite the emperour, layde at his head with mayne force: but the Emperour warded it on his shælde, in which the Gyants battell are stacke so fast, that he might no more drawe it out, vntill the emperour strake him on the right arme, that he made him forgoe his holde. The two Gyants thus being left weaponles, with much lightnesse, more then was likely for their bignesse, leapt vnto the chariot, whereby the Emperour had no time to bestowe an other blowe on them. Then a dwarfe being in the one ende of the chariot, lasht foorth the horses, so that they ranne with such swiftnes as if they had flyne. With this noise the knights awaked, and with their swordes in their handes came to learne what it should be, in the ende much abashed to see their Lord in such a heat, as they demaunded of him what befell, he was so troubled in his heart, the Princesse thus being ledde away, that he made them no annswere, but taking his horse, he commaunded them to folow him. The Emperour spurred his horse with such furie, that he made him to runne as fast, as the swallowe flyeth in the ayre. It could not be that the palfrayes which drew the chariot were horses, bicause his horse was one of the best & most precious in the world, & his Lord hauing desire to ouertake the Princesse made him gallop more then an indifferent pace, but the other were sprightes of the ayre, and infernall furies I thincke, forced by Arte Magicke both to fly and runne. Yet the Emperour folowed the chase, without loosing the sighte of them, although it was all in vayne. The knightes which remayned in the wood, being loth to be farre behind their Lorde, went to catche their horses, but were it that naturally they feared the Gyants, or that the wicked sprites had bewitched them, they all

brake

brake out of that place, and strayed héere and there, so
that the knightes spente moze then two houres ere they
might take them. By this the Emperour was so farre
from his knightes with the haste he made, that they knew
not what waye to take, and in déede it was not possible
for them to get within ý sight of him, albeit they hat helt
on ý beaten way, which they thought that the Emperour
had taken. They rode one waye and the Emperour belyke posted an other way, for they neuer met, but the emperour pursued so lóg vntil, ung ende he came to ý brinke
of the riuer Danubia, there where it deuideth it selfe into
fiue armes, at the shoze wherof there was a godly and
tall shippe, as the Emperour might well sée, being a bow
shotte behind the Gyants. In this they put the chariotte
& withal hoysed their sailes, & through ý middle arme sailed with god spéede. This outraged ý Emperour so that
with spurring he caused his hozse to fall downe dead vnder him. Being thus left on foote, notwithstanding he
dismayed not, but helde on to that place from whence the
chariot was taken, where he carefully lokt about him to
sée if peraduenture on the one side oz on the other, hee
might trace out a way to followe: so loathe he was to
loose the sighte of it. But as all this was deuised by enchauntment, so lykewise it happened him to see a little
shippe sayling in the riuer, with greate swiftnesse: in
the which there sate an olde man with a white bearde, by
his countenaunce seeming to be a very honest man. To
him ý emperour called with a loude voyce, desiring him tó
take towardes the shoze. The olde man which had the
same thinge in charge, incontinently stéered towardes
him, and asked what he woulde haue. That which J
would haue quoth the emperour, is to be conuayed in thy „
ship, to that other ship which rideth before vs. For they „
haue in it stollen from me the thing which J loue best in „
all the worlde. This paines, if thou wilt take for me, J „
wyll so well contente thee, as thou shalt thincke thy „

trauaile

,, trauaile well employed. Affuredly fayd the old man, J am
,, content to doe it, bicaufe your courtefie induceth me to a
,, greater hope of your merit. Saying this he guided his ship
fo nære the fhoze, that the emperour leaped vp into it, and
being on the hatches, tourning him felfe to the olde man
to geue him thancks, the olde man banifhed away: and
the Emperour neuer fawe him after. The fhippe kept the
fame courfe that it began with, and the Emperour was
much aftonifhed at it, ý rather foz that he wift no man els
aboord to rule ý fhip, not knowig what els to fay oz thinck
of this great wonder, he thẽ befœched God fo to direct his
viage ý he might yet obtein his lady: foz he verely dæmed
hir to be Briana which was in ý chariot. In this ozder being ftil win fight of ý fozmer fhyp, & not frayig frõ ý way
which he had kept, the Emperour fayled thzée dayes and
thzée nightes in the ryuer without any lacke of fufficient
fœde. By reafon of this trauell and thought, the meate
which he eate was no moze then would fuffice nature. In
the fourth day by mozning the fhip with the chariot was
dziuen into the great and large Sea, called Pontus Euxinus, thzough the which he yet fayled within the view of
the other, vntill the fozewarder fhippe ariued in a fayze
and delectable Jlande, where the chariot tœke landing.
Halfe an houre after the emperours fhippe rufhed on the
fhoze with fuch fozce that the fhippe rent in pæces, and
with the violence of the rufh thzew the Emperour vppon the bancke flatlings on his backe. where after he had
ftretched himfelfe, he began againe to trauaile on fœte
that way which he gefled ý chariot had gone. In this way
ftraunge things befel him, as fhall appeare in the chapter
folowing.

¶ The aduentures of the Emperour in folowing the enchaunted chariot.   Cap.ix.

                                                    The

He Emperour being as you heard caſt on lande, he behelde well how the Ilande was as it were walled about with a faire & freſh water, the faireſt that euer he had ſeene, then loking farther into ŷ lande, he marked alſo how it was furniſhed with ſo many trees, and of ſo diuers ſortes that it was verie ſtraunge in reſpect of their vnmeaſurable height & greatneſſe, vnderneth theſe the grounde was beautified with ſweet roſes & other fragrant flowers, amongs the beddes wherof there ran by chanells a very cleare and chriſtallin water, able to delight the moſt weryed ſences & trauailed minde that might be. Beſides theſe, to make vp a full meſſe of diſport, there was a ſweete and pleaſaunt ſong of birdes, which ſeemed to reioyce in the brighte and cleare morning, beſides a thouſand other paſtimes which I let paſſe, to long to make a tale off. But yet of al theſe, ŷ noble Emperour toke no care, for the thought of his lady detained from him, but onely he beat all both knowen and vnknowen wayes, to finde out that wherein the chariot had gone. At length he winded one, but an vnvſed way, which by all lykelyhood was the ſame which he would haue, in that the graſſe ſeemed new preſſed downe. This tract the noble Emperour followed on foote, without ŷ either the heauineſſe of his armour or the length of the way, made him to reſt any whit. From the morning a full halfe day the Emperour had continued his iourney, not meeting any perſon, at whome he might alke newes of that, which he moſt deſired. But afterwards leuing the thicke and pleaſaunt woode, he came into a faire greene & medow full of roſes and other ſweet hearbs and flowers of all colours, without any other ſhade in all the medowe then thoſe trees which ſerued for an hedge vnto it. The length of this medow ſeemed three bowe ſhotte vnto the myddeſt, where was ſituated a goodly caſtle, and in good proportion. It was foure ſquare, hauing at eache corner a toure, and on euery ſide one in the middeſt of the ſide, all

of

of them so high as if they should haue edged with the clouds. This great castle was enclosed and shut in with a high and thicke wal, the stones whereof and the toures, dyd shine lyke Chrystal, or the well polyshed steele against the sunne beames. Rounde about the walll there was a déepe moate, the water being so broad, as a man might scarce cast a stone from the one side to the other. Ouer the water there was a bridge, verie large and well toured so strong accordyng to the depth of the water, that it might haue withstoood a thousand men. Thrée toures it had in al, one in the enteraunce, an other in the middle, and the third at the furthest ende: each of them very high and greate, and wrought with the same stone, that the great castle was buylded with. The two outermost toures of the bridge, aswell the entry as that towards the castle, were gated and barred with dores and locks of fine filed steele, being so shéene that it serued for a looking glasse vnto the passengers. The lockes were so shut, that vnlesse they were opened on ẙ inside, it was vnpossible to vndoe them. The good Emperour scanned vpon all this, the like wherof he had not séene in all his life, and concluding fully that no such buylding might be made by mans hand, yet hee meruailed that of an Ilande so faire and delectable, there was no more noyse bruted, especially standing as it séemed to him in a sea so saileable. He beleued that the princesse was within, bicause there appeared to him no other building in all ẙ Iland, & therfore taking wide steps, hee passed on towards the gate of steele, wher finding it closed, he toke a great hámer hanging therby, & bounsed at ẙ gate with such force vpon the sounding steele, that the fury of the rap was heard through all ẙ toures, and a great part of ẙ Iland. For all this none shewed themselues to make him aunswer, although he had stood more then an whole houre calling and knocking, at length with some trouble he departed from thence to coast the water, if perchaunce he might light vpon any other way into the castel. When

be

he had gone a tourne about,at one part of ẙ wall he hap
pened vpon a gentlewoman,which was in a little boate
newly taking land at a little postern doze of yzon,when ẙ
gentlewoman had taken footing on ẙ lande,she opened the
gates,making shew as if she would haue entred,leauing
the vessell in ẙ water.The Emperour strained his voice to
call vnto hir ẙ she should stay, but she feigning as though
she heard him not , made to ẙ wicket,wher as she was to
fasten ẙ doze:ẙ Emperour cryed yet lowder,then she tour
ned toward him,ꝓ as though she had but then espyed him,
she sayd vnto him.What would you haue sir knight?The ,,
Emperour przayed hir to come nærer,foz ẙ he would onely
demaund a certein thing of hir:with this she tooke hir boat
againe ꝓ with a little ower,rowed towards the land,wher
the Emperour was:whē she came somewhat nere ẙ banck
there staying,she sayd vnto him.What is it ẙ you would ,,
haue sir knight,in that you haue called mée so lowd.That ,,
which I would fayze gentlewoman,answered ẙ emperour ,,
is ẙ you would ferry me euer in yonr boat vnto the castle, ,,
foz ẙ I haue to do with one of ẙ Giants which are within. ,,
If you haue to dele with thē said ẙ gétlewomā,they be no ,,
people on whom you way win honour. That is true said ,,
ẙ emperour, I haue no desire to trouble them,if they wil ,,
do ẙ which I require them.Sith it so said ẙ gentlewoman ,,
I will do your commaundement , bicause you looke like a ,,
knight wozthy of this seruice.I giue you great thanks foz ,,
your courtesie answered ẙ emperour,ꝓ with this he entred ,,
the boat,ꝓ shouing with ẙ rudder towards ẙ castle he got
thether.The gétlewoman went in,leading ẙ emperour w̄
hir,ꝓ closed ẙ doze after hir,cōducting him thzough a little
court to an other pziuie doze, which was not ẙ cōmon en
trie. She opened a wicket w̄ a key which she had at hir
girdel,ꝓ bzought him farther into a gardeine the most de
lightsōe ẙ art might deuise.The emperour now tooke him
selfe to be in a terrestrial paradise,ꝓ gasing a while theren,
w̄out remēbzing ẙ occasiō of his thether cōming he was so
estranged from

from him selfe. Out of this garden by an other doze, they came into a large courte of the castle, buylt with brighte Alablaster, the excellencie wherof in ye ymagerie & workemanshippe cannot be declared. For in comparison of this enchaunted Castle, either the sumptuous buylding of Mansolus tombe, oz the famous Pyramides of Aegypt, oz the maze of Dædalus making, founde in Crete, may wel be forgotten. And as the Emperour mused on all this, the gentlewoman knowing him to be distraught, caught him by the hande, and bzought him to a payze of stayzes, the steppes whereof were all of Jasper, by them he mounted with hir into a chamber foure square, of the largenesse of a stones cast. In this yet she opened a nother doze, with thzee steppes of siluer plate, out of the goldsmithes shoppe, through which she bzought ye emperour into a moze stately chamber, foure square as the other was and very rich, whereof the sæling and rœfe were engrauen gold embossed with many pzecious stones, sending fœzth such a light as it was meruaylous. The Emperour tœke no keepe of the riches of the place, but of the beautie of a number of faire gentlewomen whome he saw, sitting richly apparailed in euerie part of ye chamber. Among these one seemed to be the pzincipall, stalled in a seate higher then the other, and passing them all, so well in beautie as in rich apparel. She, as lady and mistres aboue them all, held in hir hand a Lute, whereon she played and sung together with such an harmony, that it was no lesse daungerous vnto the pœze Emperour, then the alluring song of ye Mermaides should haue bene vnto Vlysses company. She sange swetly and she withal reached hir warbling notes so high and so shzill, that it much pleased the Emperour. Hir faire & golden haire hung downe hir backe, and couered both hir shoulders. And you must pardon the Emperour if by this he was wholy possessed with hir loue, & forgot his late wife the Pzincesse Briana. The entertainment was great, and yet this chaunge pzocœded not thzouh the beautie of

the

the enchauntreſſe,foꝛ his owne wife was much fairer,but
rather by the ſecreate vertue of the place, which was
therto deuiſed , accoꝛdinge as ſhall bee recited hereafter.
By this time the Emperour had cleane loſte the re-
membꝛaunce of his wife , his Empire, countrey , and
what els perteined to him , onely reioyſing in the loue
of Lindaraza, (foꝛ ſo thys Lady was called) this hee
eſteemed foꝛ his pꝛincipall happe and good Foꝛtune.
When the Emperour had ſtoode ſtone ſtill a while,
this Lady roſe from hir ſeate, and laying downe hir lute
which ſhe helde in hir hand,with hir gentlewomen way-
ting on hir,and with a good grace ſhe made towardes the
Emperour,to take him by the hand,ſaying vnto him.You
are welcome moſt noble and woꝛthy Emperour Trebatio,
foꝛ whoſe cōming I haue long time wiſhed . The Emperour glad of ſuch a welcome,& making not ſtraunge of his
courteſy,albeit he could not finde wherby ſhe ſhould know
his name,he aunſwered hir.Madame my arriuall cannot ,,
be but good,ſith by it,I may beholde the pꝛicke & pꝛice of ,,
all the beautie in the woꝛld,conſpiring as it were in your ,,
excellencie , and ſith you receiue me with ſuch fauour, I ,,
beſéech you tell me who you are,leaſt by not knowing you ,,
I might foꝛeſlow that duetie which I owe vnto your per- ,,
ſon.This account replied the Lady,ſhall be made in better ,,
time.Now know you that I am all yours,and there ſhal ,,
not be done by me oꝛ my gentlewomen other thing,but to ,,
doe you pleaſure in my pallaice. The Emperour was in- ,,
trapped with hir pleaſant ſpeach, and knew not whether
he were in heauen oꝛ in the earth,and willing to kiſſe hir
hand foꝛ the grace ſhe ſhewed him,ſhe thought no ſcoꝛne
of a kiſſe on hir chéeke when it was pꝛofred . Then ſhe
led hym by the hande vnto the place where hir owne
thꝛone was,there the Emperour felte in himſelfe a great
contentment by the touching of hir white and delicate
handes, imagining with himſelfe that he was tranſferred
into a ſecond heauen.

D.   Some

Some of the ladies helped to vnarme him, & other were not well, either playing on their harpes, or singing and making such musike, as well eased the mindes of the enamored, some brought rich robes to attire the Emperour withall, other conserues and comfettes very comfortable, with delicate wine in great plates and cups of golde to refresh him as he had had, by reason of the trauaile he had taken on foot, although other meat liked him better which was the sight of the faire Lindaraza and hir companie, & she no lesse enamored with him beheld him goodly, & with hir knife in one hand, and a napkin in the other, she hir selfe carued vnto him of those pleasant conserues. I do not thinck that the Emperour refrained vpon strauingenes, but she to qicken his stomake with many a pleasaunt deuise and other amorous perswasions made him eat a good, and very swéte were those morsels vnto him. When this collation was ended, with some solempnitie ye faire Lindaraza lead him a side vnto a great bay window, opening vpon ye fresh & gladsome gardein, through which the Emperour with the gentlewomen had before passed. There they both beguiled the time with pleasaunt speach & melodie which the ladies made in a fresh arbour vpon ye top of two trées the Lawrel & the Cipres, the Tenor béeing mainteined among them onely by Nightingales. I denie not but the sauour also of ye swéet smelling flowers refreshing their sprits did encrease their appetites, and gaue hope of better ioy to come. When it was time to sup, the tables béeing spred, they were serued of exquisit deinties. Supper being done, the two estates fell to their wonted discourses. It was now night, and yet there needed neither torch nor candel. The brightnes of the stones enchaffed in ye walles made the chambers as light as the daye, when it was time to sléepe, the fayre Princesse Lindaraza brought the Emperour to hir owne lodging, richly adorned with silke and golde where was a riche and stately bedde, and there vnclothed by hir gentlewomen both of them wente to
bed

bed,& remaining thus,both of the reioysed of their leues to
their contentations. As ẏ Emperour had thus liued wan-
tonly many dayes,depriued of his vnderſtanding, ſauing
onely in honoꝛing hir which was befoꝛe him. In the end,ẏ
beautiful Lindaraza was great with childe,& bare him a
daughter of rare beautie called Lindaraza,by hir mothers
name:from whō iſſued a great & noble race,which bicauſe
in his place it ſhall be largely declared, I ſhall ouerpaſſe
now,briefly touching ſuch occurrents as I read off,in the
meane time.

¶ The Emperours knightes finde not their Lord,and the
  Hungarians miſſe the Prince of England.   Cap.10

VVHen the Emperour Trebatio was in his queſt of the
     inchaunted chariot,the ſtoꝛy telleth that his knights
might not come nere him,ſome bicauſe they could not take
their hoꝛſes,and ſome bicauſe his hoꝛſe ranne ſo faſt,foꝛ
he ouercame in halfe a daies iourney the trauaile of.viij
dayes(as I thinke)foꝛ that he was caried both by his own
deſire & the diuels dꝛiuing,otherwiſe it had ben impoſſible to haue endured ſo great paines. Foꝛ this cauſe I ſay,
although the knightes rode ſo faſt as they might,yet they
could not come within the ſight of him,noꝛ finde whiche
way he was gone,yet with ſoꝛꝛowe and griefe,eſpecially
thꝛough the feare which they conceiued by his medling
with ẏ Giants,they parted companies,euery man taking
a ſeuerall way to ſæke the Emperour, and they agræd
at the monthes ende to mæte at one place . The moneth
came when as yet none of them had heard any news of
him,although they ſought him in diuers partes. They all
meruayled,but not knowing what to ſay,in the end,they
determined at ſome other time to mæt & to enter into this
queſte againe. Foꝛ this time they altogether tæke towardes the campe which they lefte befoꝛe the Citie
of Belgrado, where they abode not longe , but remembꝛing themſelues of their pꝛomiſe,they met at the place
appointed , and deuided themſelues accoꝛdingly .

The

The iiii. Hungarian knights, fering to be diſcried by thoſe
which went to ſeeke prince Edward the courtlieſt which
they might, they went toward the campe of the Emperour
& ther remained ſometime, after they folowed into Greece,
wher they tarried til ẙ retourne of ẙ Emperour, according
as ſhall be mentioned hereafter. Now by this time with
no leſſe care & diligẽce, prince Edward was ſought by many
knights in all ẙ kingdome, for that the king had giuen him
no longer time to remaine in ẙ monaſtery of the riuer then
three dayes. There was already tolde xx. daies when he
came not. Firſt thẽ he ſent many of his knights to know ẙ
cauſe of his tarrying, theſe retourned vnto ẙ king with anſwere ẙ they neither found him in ẙ minſter, nor could here
tidings of him by the way. Then the king diſpatched other
meſſengers to enquire after him and his knightes in all
the land, but they brought the like aunſwere, yet again he
ſent more then 1000 well prepared for warre, with authoritie of ſerch through al his kingdome, that they might
bring newes of life or death. But al was one, laſt of al, fearing leaſt peraduenture he had ben taken priſoner by ẙ
enimies, he wrote vnto the Emperours camp to know the
truth, to the ende he might ranſome him, if ſo it were, but
not hearing any newes, he then bewailed the loſſe of the
prince, and became very ſorowfull, like as contrary wyſe
ẙ emperials bemoned their Emperour. Theſe things happened ſo in the necke one of an other, that Tiberios iudgment failed to decide ẙ truth, & he pittied him with no leſſe
griefe then if he had bene his owne ſonne, partly for hys
daughters ſake, who muſt needs be partener of hir huſbãds
miſaduenture, & partly for the princeſſe parents who could
not wont ſome ſorow cõceiue of his miſſing, albeit al this
happened more by ẙ miſgiuing of his own minde, then by
any certeintie be found. You haue heard perticulerly the
care of the king Tiberio, now you muſt conſider of the diligence of ẙ king of Boheme by ẙ ſemblable. An other month
had end & ẙ knights votaries ſped thẽ homwards to ẙ camp

of

of the Empereur without any newes of their Lorde, which no doubte much molested the whole hoast, but in especiall it afflicted the kinge of Boheme to see them come without him . As they made declaration of the whole monethes trauaile, it little pleased the king, enely for the loue hee bare to the Emperour and the wante of his presence in a time so daungerous , hee wept as sore for him, as if he had scene his little childe giue vp the ghost . The losse of the Emperour thus published through the armie, there was no one which sorowed not inwardly, for he had the loue of all his subiects.

· Albeit this was bootelesse, yet his loue beguiled him, for ÿ king yet charged more then 2000. knights with ÿ search of ÿ Emperour in al places, as well by sea as by land, but it naught auailed, for ÿ iland of Lindaraza held him so sure that he could not be found, and if he had bene found, yet he was so wel garded, that the whole hoast had not ben able to haue deliuered him from the inchaunted castle. While these things were in dowing, the king of Bohome him selfe set the remainder on woorke to assalt the cite, with ful purpose not to leaue the siege, till either he knew where the Emperour was, or had lien a halfe yeare longer, at the ende whereoff he would raise the siege and so depart into Greece againe. In this time the Hungarians issued out of their citie against the Grecians, and there was betweene them many cruell and bloudy skirmishes. The Greekes did nobly, as you may reade in their seuerall histories, at this time bicause they are not of the substaunce of my matter I will not name them, onely I will recount vnto you the perticuler truth of that which followeth.

¶The Princesse Briana taketh great sorowe at the losse of Prince Edward. Cap.11.

Reat was the diligence which the king of Hungary commaunded his knightes to make, in seeking the

Prince Edward, and as greate was his griefe in not finding him by the consideration of the towardnesse of the noble knight, and the dole of his parentes bæing their dære and onely sonne. But greater must nædes bée and inexpressible, the mortall dolor which the Princesse Briana conceiued when shée once heard of the misse of Prince Edward. And as I reade, at the thrée moneths ende, when nothing was reported, for very anguish of heart, (besides hir often sowninges) after when shée recouered out of that traunce, shée sæmed to them nærer the death, then the Prince hir husbande was, as they thought: for belæuinge that hée was deade, shée would neither eate, drincke, nor slæpe, but became weake and fæble, and wasted hir dayes with sorrowe. She layde a part all hir princely robes, and precious iewels, and tired hir selfe in course mourning wædes of a widow. She kept hir selfe in a secret chamber, onely with the comfort of hir gentlewomen, and cōming not foorth one step, demeaned rather the life of an Anchresse, or religious woman, then of a Princesse. The Quéene mother then abidinge at Buda, came often times to visite hir, and in hir company other great Ladyes, but they could not remoue the dulnesse of hir melancholy.

Ere the Princesse had long led this solitary life, she felt hir selfe quick with childe, whence she tæke some ioy, but yet fearing the disclosing of it vnto hir friends whom she would not haue pertakers of it for all Hungary, before the solemnization of the marriage was openly performed, & being notwithstanding desirous in time to sæke remedy therevnto, she concionated hir secret onely with one of hir gentlewomen named Clandestria, whom she best loued, and with whom she was best acquainted, for the good counsayle she often gaue hir. Shée which was wise and discrete kissed hir ladies handes for the honour she did vnto hir, in reuealing suche a secrete, onely a little withstandinge hir entent of concealement at the first, and

perswa-

perſwading that it was no reaſon why ſhee ſhoulde not
bewray hir childbering vnto the king hir father, and the „
Queene hir mother, for that ſeeing it pleaſed God to giue „
you a childe by a lawfull huſbande , it were not amyſſe „
if it were knowen abroade,be it ſonne or daughter.And „
ſayth ſhe moreouer, if God gyue you a man childe,prince „
Edward thus periſhing, as we knowe no other,this your „
chylde is lawfull inheritour of great Britaine in the right „
of his father,the king nowe liuing hauing no iſſue male. „
Wherefore me thinckes you ſhoulde doe him wronge, „
ſeeing he hath loſt his father, to depriue hym alſo of hys „
lawefull ſucceſſion . The Princeſſe aunſwered,perſwade „
me not to this good Clandeſtria , for though the chylde „
which ſhall bee borne of mee,ſhould be Lorde of the whole „
world,I would not tell this ſecrete to any bodie, but to „
thee.And if it ſhall pleaſe God that the Prince Edwarde „
ſhall ſee vs once agayne,it ſhall ſuffice,let him diſcouer it „
when he ſees time. If it fall out otherwiſe,my ſonne may „
well beare the loſſe of great Britaine, and it bee but to accompany mee in the loſſe of ſo worthy an huſbande.
Clandeſtria woulde haue entred farther in thys per-
ſwaſion with the Princeſſe , but ſeeing it would not bee,
ſhe gladly made offer of hir ſeruice. Then ſayde the
Princeſſe , what doeſt thou thincke is beſt to bee done
in this thing . The beſte which I can aduiſe you ſayd
the gentlewoman,is that you madame gouerne the childe „
ſo that it periſh not in your wombe , and when the time „
of your trauaile ſhall bee at hande, that you faine vnto „
your gentlewomen a ſolempne faſt and prayer xl. dayes „
without to be ſeene or biſited of your gentlewomen or a- „
ny perſon ſauinge mee , whome you will haue to wayte „
on you onely for your neceſſarye repaſt . The glaſe „
which you ſhal ſet on it ſhal be this,that you will praie to „
God for prince Edward your huſband,ỹ ſhew wil be cre- „
ible inough by means of your life hitherto. This would „
I haue you do madame,for this cauſe take your lodging „
D.iiij. in „

in one part of the house ioyning to the wood being very good & solitary for this purpose. If you be deliuered in this time, I will conueigh it to a sister of mine lately married, and dwelling in the citie of Buda. She bare a sonne about a month past, and will nourse your child carefully. This counsell liked wel the Princesse, because it was consonant to hir desire. The Princesse now expecting the time of hir lying down, told hir gentlewomen ý she had vndertaken a deuotion of fast and praier, and before she entred into this obseruaunce she said she would a little take hir rest, eating and sleeping somewhat more then shee was wont, which in deed she did, to preserue that which was in hir belly, albeit it was well coloured by hir continuall sadnesse. In this time the Queene hir mother was brought to bed of a beautifull boy, which much gladded al the kingdome, his name was Liriamandro, a noble prince much aduauncing the honour of ý Hungarians, as shal be shewed you in his historie. But this childing of the Queene was very commodious for the Princesse, for that when the Queene was brought to bed, she could not visite hir daughter at the monastery as she was accustomed.

¶The Princesse Briana was deliuered of two sonnes, Clandestria christeneth them, and causeth them to be noursed.   Cap. 12.

The Princesse as you haue heard, liued somewhat contented after that she felt hir selfe to be with childe, but yet not so, but that hir colour much abated, and impaired hir beautie, & so driuing on hir daies vntill the approch of hir trauaile, she now feined to begin hir voluntary fast of fortie daies, which she before had signified vnto them, and withdrawing hir selfe into a chamber prouided for hir, she forbad the entery to all, except onely Clandestria for hir table, this they thought the Princesse had done vpon meere deuotion.

The

The same night after she was nowe professed a holye vowesse, Clandestria tooke the keyes of the backe gates belonging to her lodginge, and opening a dore into the woode, she passed by the fieldes to Buda, standing but a mile off, and entring into hir sisters house, secretly declared the cause of hir comming, desiring hir to be as secret, bicause the Princesse would in no wise haue it manifested, she willingly promised silence, and withall departed with hir towards the monasterie, ere it was long, they came before the Princes, whom they found sitting alone, not altogether voyde of dreade, as being vnacquainted with those pangs, and hartely wishing for their comming, as without knowledge to be hir owne mydwife. When she felt the fittes of hir trauaile, she was somewhat comforted with their comming, and Clandestria with hir sister, enforced their diligence to doe hir seruice, giuing themselues to prayer vntill it pleased God to manifest his workes in this noble Princesse.

She bare two sonnes so straunge and rare for beauty, that the gentlewomen not a little wondred, and yet they were more moued to see the tokens which either of them brought seuerally from their mothers wombe. For they marked well how that the first borne, had vpon his left side a little face figured, shining as bright as if it had ben a little Sunne, & how that the other had in the middest betwene his brests, a white Rose fashioned of so perfect making, that it seemed to be gathered, from some arbour of Roses.

Before they swadled them, they layd the little boyes betwene the Princesses armes, comforting hir with that that God had giuen hir, two so excellent children. The mother ful of paine with ye trauaile which she had susteined, as well as she coulde laying them to hir brests, kissed & embraced them wyth such loue and pittie, that the teares trickled downe from hir faire eyes, & with a low and softe voyce, she sayd thus.

D.b.

,, O my sonnes, I beseech the Lord, who hath made you
,, so exceedingly faire, to blesse you also with good happe, that
,, you may ease your mother of that sorrowe wherein shee
,, remaineth as nowe plunged, and that you proue such, as
,, by your valours, you may recouer that which your mother
to couer hir falte hath made you lose. These and other
wordes spake the Princesse, weping bitter teares, vntill
the nurse toke the children from hir bed, to swaddle them
in clothbands, & to giue them hir brest. Now least peraduenture they shold be heard to cry, Clandestria sayd to ŷ
Princesse, that it were good hir sister shoulde retourne
to hir owne house, where she would bring vp the younge
Princes as carefully as if she were daily in hir presence.
The Princesse very loath to parte with hir children, bad
hir do notwithstanding what she wold with them, so that
she baptised them ere they went, for feare they should pe-
rish in the way. Let it be so madame sayd Clandestria, for
you haue sayd very well. The nurse then toke water and
pouring it on their heads, she christened thē in ŷ name of
God, with other formal wordes of baptisme, as she coulde
best do. Clādestria with a very good grace, gaue names to
the little boyes, the first she named Caualiero del Febo,
for the figure that she saw in his lefte side nære vpon the
heart, the younger she called Rosicleer for the Rose betwæne his breasts. Of this the Princesse toke some ioy,
saying she had giuen them names as they deserued. The
nurse toke leaue of the Princes, and with hir husband
which came on the way, and which had not stayed farre
off, she gotte redily into Buda before broad light, where she
festred these noble babes as carefully as hir owne. Clandestria after she had shutte fast the dores, went vp againe
to the Princesse, whome she founde discomforted for hir
children. The gentlewoman paincd hir selfe to comforte
hir, and soberly spake vnto hir, in this sort.

,, O madame, how vnthankefull are you to God for the
,, great grace he hath bestowed on you, in giuing you two
sonnes

sonnes of so excellent beautie , and that with so little pe- ,,
rill of your person . I beleue and holde for certeyne,that ,,
God hath not left you such sonnes, neuer to knowe their ,,
father, nor made you such a Princesse, neuer more to see ,,
your husband. The workes of God are wonderfull , and ,,
that which we thincke is sette for our griefe and disease, ,,
he tourneth to our commoditie,what know you madame ,,
if God willing to preserue your husband,hath by some ad- ,,
uenture brought him where he shal escape the great daun- ,,
gers and perils of death in which he was hourly like to ,,
incurre , in the battaile that the kinge your father hath a- ,,
gainst Trebatio. God madame quiet your selfe,God will ,,
bringe him vnto you at such time, when you shalbe leaste ,,
mindefull of him. And if you can so ill brooke the absence ,,
of your sonnes they are not hence but one myle , thether ,,
maye you sende me , when it pleaseth you,to knowe of ,,
their welfare.

Thus Clandestria discoursed with hir Lady the Princesse Briana still beating vpon this one poynt , that she
sholo rest hir selfe vpon Gods prouidence,and in the ende
she so aswaged hir griefe that she after well endured the
fortie dayes penaunce. In the ende being better at ease,
and feeling hir selfe more pleasauntly disposed withall as
fresh as if she had neuer abode any childebedde , toke hir
lodging among hir gentlewomen , who seing hir so well
and somewhat more merie then before, were glad of that
alteracion, for they loued hir so hartely,that they willingly, would haue giuen their liues , to haue redeemed hir
from that discontentment wherein she liued.

¶The king of Boheme raised the siege, and the king of
    Hungarie retourned the Princes knights into Eng-
    lande.   Cap.xiij.

M Any and hotte bickeringes there were betwene the
    Emperours people and the kinge of Hungarie,
while the siege lasted againste the citye of Belgrado:
                                                    but

but bicause the history hath more to intreate of other especiall aduentures,it remēbreth not euerie particuler,which
happened in the skirmish. It sayeth in effect that as those
of the citie were many,so they were well prouided of all
furniture, that the Greeks might not enter into the citie,
albeit many of them had done meruailous deds in armes.
After one yeare was come and gone, the king of Boheme
with all the principall of his hoast , thought it beste to
raise the siege then lying before the citie,and with bag &
baggage to marche homewardes to Constantinople , to
the ende, to giue out a new order , for the finding of the
Emperour. So within two dayes they had all charge to
packe and prepare thē selues for their retourne : the soul-
dyers not yet forgetting the losse of their Lorde, which
they shewed by their chære.The king of Boheme the emperours vnckle well perceiuing it, and knowing how the
good Emperour, was wont to encourage and comforte
them,he tooke some paine in it at that time,and being well
setled in Constantinople , for the better pacifiyng of all
tumults, the army as yet not disperscd,he tooke vpon him
the gouernment of the Empyre in his nephewes name,
at the humble sute of all the Emperialls, after he prouided the best that he might, for a newe search of the Emperour,swearing many good knights vnto this enterprice.
Which likewise the king of Hungarie did send certaine
newes into Englande , and to haue some sufficient guide
to conduct the army homewards at the end of two yeres,
all which time he deteined the souldiers , vpon hope to
finde their Captaine, no news being heard of him. The
Kinge embarked them homewardes to greate Britaine,
with giftes and presents vnto the king of Englande, and
sufficient rewards plentifully bestowed vpon the mainye,
ouer and aboue the due payment of their wages.This the
liberalitie of the king , profited him not a little in other
matters of great importaunce , as you shall vnderstande
in this history. The knights thus shipped redy to depart,

were

were néere in number 20000. In fewe daies they coasted
Fraunce, and enteringe in the narrowe seas, with a good
winde they landed in great Britaine, where soone theire
hanging countenaunces, gaue testimonie to the heauie
newes they brough. Which thing so sore appalled ꝑ whole
realme, that of a long time after their comminge, there
was not vsed any exercise in armes : and the Quéene
dyed also, adding to this myshappe, a newe corsie. This
Quéene lefte behinde hir a daughter of young yeares named Oliuia, so renowned for hir beautie, that she well
wanne to be loued and serued of ꝑ most loyall knighte of
all the worlde. She was brought vp, as being enheretrix
to the state, with great care by the king hir father.

¶Clandeſtria deuiſeth with the Princeſſe Briana how
hir ſonnes might be brought vp in hir company.
Cap. xiiij.

HE Princeſſe Briana liued no doubte better
contented after hir deliuerie of the ij. faire boyes,
which she thought had bene Prince Edwards,
& yet as I say, verie religiouslye, as it had bene
in a cloyster for the reason so often alledged . Now yet
somewhat there was which impaired this contentation,
which was the absence of hir children. This she thought
to repaire again by bringing them vp in hir owne lodging
and hauing broken it vnto hir gentlewoman Clandeſtria,
whom she desired to finde the meanes for it. Clandeſtria
after conference had with hir mistreſſe, one day sayd vnto
hir, that she had well foreséene the meane. The Princeſſe
then vrged hir to vtter it, which Clandeſtria deliuered in
this speach. Madame, that which I haue thought in this „
matter, is like. That one day whē I shal come from ꝑ ci- „
tie of Buda, you shall demaunde of me what newes is „
there. I will aunswere you among other thinges, that a „
sister of mine hath two sonnes borne both in one daye, so „
excel-

" ercellently faire,that al the lookers on,do not a little com-
" mend so goodly creatures.They are borne morcouer with
" notable tokens , which they bring from theire mothers
" wombe . You madame hearing this may say ÿ you haue
" great desire to see these straunge children, and may will
" me to procure the bringing of them into this monasterie
" with their mother, that here in your company they may
" be broughte vp, for that in such children you maye take
" some solace, thereby to forgette part of that which sore
" annoyeth you. In this manner neither your gentlewomen
" nor any other person shall vnderstande our secret . Clan-
    destrias counsell seemed so good vnto the Princesse , that
" embrasing hir many times, she said vnto hir .My faith-
" full and loyall Clandestria,whē shall the day come wher-
" in I shalbe restored vnto the first ioy and estate which I
" was wont to holde,and in which I may reward the good
" seruice thou hast done to me? Go thy way and put in ef-
" fect that which thou hast deuised for mine ease. Madame
" sayd Clandestria, if my seruice may in any wise aswage
" your griefe, which I so sore pitie : I thincke it sufficient-
" ly rewarded,considering the dutie wherein I stand bound
" vnto your highnesse, and assuredly no lesse is the pleasure
" which I receiue by the acceptacion of my seruice , then
" that which you haue by the fruition of it . But sith my
" counsell liketh you so well: I will make no tarying : go
" you madame to your gentlewomen and I wyll presently
" to ÿ citie. Go in Gods name sayd the Princesse, & so she
    toke hir to hir gētlewomen,Clandestria being in hir way
    towardes the citie . When Clandestria had perfourmed
    vnto hir sister that which the Princes had commaunded,
    not long after she came to the monasterie , at such time
    as the Princesse was in the company of hir gentlewo-
    men. Clandestria entred into the chamber , making hir
    obeysaunce. The Princesse espying hir, sayde vnto hir
 . merely.
"   Welcome my Clandestria,how is it with the Quéens
                                                    my

my mother, and the young Prince Liriamandro my brother. They are all very well madame sayd Clandestria,
and the Queene your mother commendeth hir selfe vnto
you by me. Well said the Princesse but what newes haue
they in the citye, say they any thing of Prince Edwarde.
Of the Prince surely I heard nothing, aunswered Clandestria, but I haue newes if it so please you to heare thē,
me thincks ȳ straungest that you haue heard. Tell vs thē
sayd the Princesse, if they be such as you speake off, we
shall haue pleasure to heare them.

Knowe you then madame sayde Clandestria, that a
sister of mine, which is married and dwelleth in the
citye of Buda hath two sonnes of the age of two
yeares, both borne at one houre, in the toppe and
pitch of all beautie, so that their matches are not to be had.
They haue besides markes on their bodyes such as those
which haue sene them, cannot tel what to thinck of them.
The first borne of them hath on his lefte side the forme of
a face very beautifull and so bright, that I dare liken it
to the Sunne, which ouershadoweth the earth, and for
this cause the little boy is called El donzel del Febo. The
other little boy hath betweene his brests a Rose growing
in the fleshe, so freshe of hewe, and so perfectly coloured
that they which see him saye he beareth the badge of his
mothers bedde, as if he had bene borne in an arbour: for
this token, they name him Rosicleer, I tell you madame
so excellēt is their beautie that the best paynter in Hungarie, neede no other example to drawe out the picture
of beautie. The Princesse making a shew of great meruayle, and as it were mistrusting the report, bicause of
the straungenesse aunswered. Truly Clandestria you
haue brought vs matter of some meruaile, but I feare
me ȳ nærenesse of kin betwæne you maketh you to speak
of affection more then knowledge, I wolde ȳ by sighte of
them you would proue vnto vs that which you haue spoken, with this the Princesse gentlewomen, hungrye
                                                                    after

after nouelties , impoꝛtuned Clandeſtria to deale herein,
ſo that they all might enioy the ſight of thoſe two ſo rare
childꝛen . Clandeſtria tourning toward hir Lady ſayd, by
,, my faith , if my Lady the Pꝛinceſſe be ſo contented, I
,, will go to my ſiſter, and cauſe hir to come hether with hir
,, little ones. The gentlewomen then beſought the Pꝛinces
,, that ſhe would commaund them to be bꝛought thether.
The Pꝛinceſſe telling them that ſhe did it moꝛe at their
requeſte, then of hir owne good will, ſayd to Clandeſtria,
,, you were beſt do this , which your felowes require you,
,, my likinge you haue, foꝛ I my ſelfe woulde gladly be a
,, witneſſe of ſo great a meruaile. Clandeſtria toke hir leue
,, of them haſting towards the citie, where hir ſiſter dwelt
and declared hir meſſage foꝛ the bꝛinging of the Pꝛinces.
Hir ſiſters huſband was a verie good gentleman boꝛne,
though very pooꝛe, he & his wife made them rdy to come
befoꝛe the Pꝛinceſſe, with the little Pꝛinces, which by this
time were of ſome groweth, being two yeares olde, hauing
both goodly lockes, ſtanding as it were vpon a iuſt tempe-
rature of grauitie and pleſaunce. When they were come
to the Pallaice, Clandeſtria firſt entred into the lodging,
of ẙ Pꝛinceſſe, being as yet in ẙ company of hir gentlewomen, ther ſhe led in by the hand the faire & gratious
Roſicleer. So ſoone as he was ſeene of the gentlewomen,
they beleued him to be no leſſe then an Angell of heauen,
and that wherein Clandeſtria had befoꝛe enſtructed them,
ſhe had nothing deceaued them. The Pꝛinceſſe not hauing
ſeene hir childꝛen ſince hir firſt bleſſing of them, and now
ſeeing the height of Roſicleer with his beautie aboue hir
hope, ſhe made ſuch ioye as might haue well bene diſcer-
ned by hir countenaůce, but hir gentlewomē moꝛe attentiue of ẙ beautie wherwith God had indued ẙ youg Roſicleer, were not ware of it. Clandeſtria made the little boy
bowe his knees to the Pꝛinceſſe , and whether it were
nature, oꝛ the beautie of his mother, oꝛ both, ſo ſoone as
he beheld his mother, he left the other gentlewomen. The
mo-

mother taking the little boy in hir armes, kissed him many times, shedding vpon his faire chœkes great abcun-
daunce of teares, for the memorye which thee sonne
gaue hir of hys Father, and for the great ioy she had, in
hauing him so nœre vnto hir. Not longe after, ther entered Clandestrias sister to hir husband, leading by y hand
the fairest among y most faire, Donzel del Febo . At the
sight of him the gentlewomen repented them of their former iudgment as concerning Rosicleer, that there might
not be his like in all the world, in the ende, the question
arising of comparison, to part the striefe they agrœd, that
as the one moued euery one to loue him tenderly by hys
gracious behauiour, so the other by his modest iestures
made them to feare him with reuerence. The difference
onely put in this, that the one had more maiestie, y other
more mirth and delight in his countenance. The princesse
hauing Rosicleer in hir armes, when she sawe hir other
sonne before hir vpon his knœs to kisse hir hande , with
gladnesse she raysed him from the ground, and with Rosicleer in one armie, tœke him on the other, kissing him vpon
his chœkes, and in dœde rather obeying the loue she bare
vnto hir sonnes, then regarding the feare she was wont
to haue for bæing discouered, albeit to say the trouth, the
Princesse was of the better hand, for all the good will she
shewed, hir gentlewomen imagined to procœde of their
beautie. And yet to take all suspect away, she could very
wisely moderate hir passions. Clandestrias sister the supposed mother of those children, and hir husband by name
Armaran, kissed the Princesses hands, where she in token
of good liking entertained them as hir seruants, from thence
forth to remaine with hir, as their sister Clandestria did.
On this wise the Princes were nourished in their mothers presence, without that any knew the right parentage whereoff they came, & they so enticed the gentlewomen to the liking of them, y there passed not one houre,
without playing and daliaunce with them. This ioy en y

Princesse part was vnspeakable, I dare not say, able to countermaunde hir foreconceiued griefe, but the worst was, it was not durable. For fortune euer mutable chaū, ged hir copie and became so contrary, that the date of hir ease bæing out, there succæded disease and mishap, so that hir death shoulde not haue bene halfe so yerkesome as hir life was dolorous. This shall you heare off, in the next Chapter.

¶ Donzel del Febo was lost by misaduenture. Cap. 15.

NOwe the creator of al things minded to manifest the worthy dædes of ỹ valiant Donzel del Febo, which as yet lay hidden in the armes of the delicate gentlewo, man his foster mother, and therefore in such sort, he orde, red the celestiall influences, and powers of the planets, that scarcely had the young gentleman fully reached vnto thræ yeares of his age, when he was carryed from the princely graces of his vnknowne mother (leauing hir pensiue, and sad) into a large & maine Sea whence, bæing tossed with waues, and almost weatherbeaten, at length he escaped. Such an argument god left vs of his prowesse to come, sith in so tender age he enabled him to subdue the most raging element that is. And you which reade this history, may be brought by good reason to giue cre, dit to this my report, sith you your selues are witnesses of the euident presence of the Almightie in so certeine a daunger. And as the learned well know, Achilles hath his Pallaice in Homere, and Aeneas his Venus in Vir, gill, Goddesses assistaunt vnto men in their daungerous conflictes, Homere and Virgill meaning no other thing, then the care of God towards his, why may not we be, lieue, that if it so pleased God that this infant had the se, cret direction of Gods mightie hand in al his enterprises.

But mine Author willing to entreate somewhat of
him

him,fetteth it downe thus. That in the ende of a yeare,
thefe two beautifull boyes bæing bzought vp in the mo∙
naftery of the riuer,with great pleafure of the Pzinceffe
and hir gentlewomen,one day in the moneth of May,the
comfozt of the funne there enfozcing them to come abzoad
and fæke their folace vnder græne boughes . The Pzin∙
ceffe & hir gentlewomen leauing their lodging,went into
a large & fayze ozchard excædingly well caft in one part
of y monaftery,there they tœke vp their feates at a wels
mouth,ouerfhaddowed with træs , that the heate of the
funne could not annoy them,and fpozting with the little
Roficleer,who was femewhat moze giuen to play then
his bzother Donzel del Febo,they fo much delighted in
Roficleer that they tœke no hæde of Donzel del Febo,
fitting not farre off . The little one being very ycung,
yet greatly difcontent to fæ the fmall accœnt they made
of him,in a fume rofe from the place where he was fette,
and by foft paces got from them,without bæing efpied by
the gentlewomen,fauing of his mother fo called,whiche
loued him no leffe then hir owne felfe. She rifing from
the place where fhe was fet,followed him and tœke him
by y hand laughing a gœd to fæ y choler wherin he was,&
walking among the træs fo long with him,that fhe came
to a large and dæpe water running thzough a part of the
great ozchard,where hard by were great ftoze of træs,&
wether the Pzinceffe bicaufe the place was very pleafant
often refozted with hir gentlewomen to reioyfe hir felfe.
When they were there,the little boy fæing the water,
was defirous to playe with it. The nourfe,though other∙
wife willinge to haue contented him , yet fearing the
daunger of y water went farther,to finde fome fure place
wherby to come vnto y water,& taking a little boat at the
banck,which y gardeiner vfed,in comming into y ozchard
put hir felfe in it,and the child with hir. The boy leaning
his bzeaft vpon the bzimme of the boate , troubled the
water with his handes & tœke vp fcme to wafh his face,

a while after the water bæing calme and plaine, he loked in it againe, and sæing his shadowe there, he began to play with it, and stroke it with his handes, now bicause it would not giue place, but did that which he did, waxing angry, he prayed his mother to giue him a rod which lay vpon the land to beate the babe withall. It was a good pastime for hir to sæ the displeasure which he had conceiued against his owne shadow, and leauing him thus, she lept vpon the land to reatch him the sticke that he required. Bæing thus on land, either with the force she put to the side of the boate, in aduaunceing hir selfe out of the boat, or els bicause it was the will of God that ye little boy should then be prest to trie the hasard of his constellation. So it was, that the boat bæing vntyde, it showed from the shore: The nourse not perceuing it before she tourned againe, then was it more then two yards from the land, and not hauing whereby to take holde, it bare so swiftly downe the streame in a little time, and so farre off, that she lost the sight of it. When she sawe the daunger wherin the little childe was, not hauing power to succour it, she rent hir garmentes and tore hir haire, and fell to the grounde making suche mone, that the Princesse and hir gentlewomen sitting aboute the well, heard it, and much abashed rose from the place to knowe what the noyse meant. When they sawe the pitifull dealinges of the nourse vppon the grounde, quickning their pace, they gate nære hir, and demaunding the cause of hir great lamentacion, they founde hir so sorowful that shæ coulde no speake to them, but rather the more shæ was comforted by them, the more shæ outraged in crying, as that they iudged hir to be distraught. So longe lasted these hir cryes, that the Princesse disquieted, went towards hir, leauing Rosicleer with one of hir gentlewomen: as ye princesse came towards hir, ye nourse knew hir, & not hauing the boldnesse to shew how it fell out, in respect of the griefe ye princesse would take for ye losse of hir sonne,

before

before the Princesse came at hir, she ranne & lept into the
water with full entent to drowne hir selfe, the which she
had done, had not hir clothes borne hir vp, & the gardener
hearing ÿ great outcries she made, waded in the water for
hir, and brought hir to land all wet and bloudy with the
blowes she gaue hir selfe in the face. This caused such pitie and compassion in the princesse and all hir gentlewomen that all astonished, they abode onely to see the nourses
demeanour. In the ende at the instance of the princesse
she declared how Donzel del Febo was got from hir, for
the which they imparted with hir griefe, and especially
the princesse benommed of all hir senses suncke to the
ground with no more colour and breath then if shee had
bene quite dead. The gardener entering into another boat
there which he had to fish withall, pushed vp the streame
amain with his ower to ouertake ÿ boat in which Donzel
del Febo was caried, but all his trauaile was lost, for either by diuine promission, or by Arte Magicke, made by a
learned man, as shall be tolde you hereafter, the boat rode
faster then the violence of the streame might driue it, & in
short time it entred into the great sea, where it followed ÿ
mightie waues more then an 100 miles in a short space,
so that neither the gardener nor who els followed them
might in any wise atteine vnto him or bring newes of
him. When the princes was reuiued, and remembred the
chaunce of Donzel del Febo, she powred out so many
salt teares from hir faire eyes, that like as out of foun-
taines or springs the water gusheth out abundantly, so
from hir face streamed downe floods of water, issuing
with sobs and sighes as would haue broke hir heart in a
manner, such as commonly the fall of the water maketh
from the steepe mountaines. But for that she would not
be hearde of hir gentlewomen, she tourned hir selfe and
went towardes hir lodging, where remayning alone with
Clandestria she gaue a fresh onset to hir former complaints
on this sort.

C.iij.   D

,,   O mightie and souereigne Lord, wherefore doth thy
,, highnesse suffer the Princesse Briana to liue this long, see-
,, ing she doth roll on this life with such sorow and care? O
,, Lord, wherefore gauest thou me a husband in this world
,, so valiaunt, seeing that so soone as I had lost ý name of a
,, maiden, thou madest me an vnfortunate widow? Where-
,, fore gauest thou me sonnes with so straunge tokens at
,, their birth, if with so soodine misfortune I shall lose the
,, one of them, why did I reach to so great estate, in which
,, I must liue with sorow? and why gauest thou me beau-
,, tie, not to enioy it? Alas poore woman that I am, I see
,, that each thinge enforceth my paine, for Fortune the
,, mistresse of mishap, despitefully throwing downe those on
,, whom she frownes, hath tourned hir backe on me, which
,, desire to liue without ý compasse of hir wheele. Ah seely
,, woman, the longer I rub out this life, the more my griefe
,, encreaseth. When I seeke to mollifie my griefe, then my
,, care redoubleth, and one sorow surceasing, ther succedeth
,, an other, as one billow followeth on the others neck in
,, the maine sea. O thou Lord which hast created me, take
,, me out of this deceiptfull world, if by death onely the in-
,, tollerable misfortunes may take ende which dayly awaite
,, me. These and other wordes spake the Princesse Briana, much agreeuing therewith hir gentlewoman Clandestria, who a little altering the course of hir aunswere from
the platforme of the others complaint, droue with ý princesse vnto these conclusions. First that there was hope
inough to recouer hir losses, the reasons which lead hir
therunto were these. Albeit, saith she, Gods workes bee
vnsearchable, yet thus bolde may we be with them, not
medling with the causes to compare the euils together,
and then surely the whole course of worldly things sufficiently teach vs that God createth not such excellent
personages but for excellent purposes, and not as in
dombe showes vpon a stage, where the players onely present themselues and passe awaye. Againe, sayth shee, you
are

are altogether vncerteine of their death,and why not in
so doubtfull a case,should hope be as ready as rare,oz perhaps you thinke as sone happens the woze as ꝩ better,
yet the auncient pzouerb is,that he which naught hopeth
fo2,ought to dispaire naught,fo2 hope and misgiuing are
in the same subiect . Therefoze sayth she,you may well
hope. The second was,that she should comfozt hir selfe,
in the beautifull Rosicleer,who was then in hir kæping,
fo2 saith she,he alone suffiseth to counteruaile al ꝩ harmes
which haue chaunced you. Fo2 J dare warrant if god pze-
serue him,that you may name your selfe mother of ꝩ best
knight in the wozld. With these,& many other gwdly coun-
sels,Clandestria dayly laboured ꝩ pzinces to giue ouer hir
griefe,but fo2 al this,if God w his mightie hand,had not
helde hir vp it had gone wzong with hir. Fo2 he pzouided
hir of comfozt by a man very wise and well learned in
Arte Magicke,of who shal be made mencion in this historie. By him God permitted that the pzison of ꝩ Emperour with other appurtenaunces should be discouered,foze-
sæing by the signes,planets,& other naturall operations,
that which sæmeth impossible vnto vs. Thus the truth is,
that this wise man knowing the great sozow and care
wherin the Pzincesse liued,& wel perceiuing that vnlesse
she had moze succour at his handes then she had earst
by other,bicause of that which befell hereafter,it shoulde
be impossible to maintein hir life: determined in himself
to comfozt hir,& so one day as she sate alone very sozow-
full wæping with great aboundaunce of teares,nære vnto ꝩ well where hir two sons were begotten,he appeared
to hir in ꝩ shape of a Nymph in ꝩ clære & chzistalin water,
with ꝩ haire lose,& shedding vpon ꝩ greatest part of ꝩ body,& with a face so beautifull ꝩ the pzincesse abashed to sæ
hir,& in some feare fo2 ꝩ she had not sæne the like befoze
would haue fled fro thence. But ꝩ Nymph called vnto hir,
saying,if ꝩ knewest noble pzincesse who J am,& hew wel
J know thy great thoughts & passions,ꝩ wouldest not flye

,, from me but rather ſtay and talke with me. Now bicauſe
,, the time affozds me no leaſure to tarrie with thee, and to
,, diſcourſe at large all the loyaltie I beare vnto thee, and
,, the deſire I haue to ſerue thee, in a word I pray thee take
,, good courage vnto thee, to ouercome the great aduerſities
,, which may come, and ere it be long are like to come vnto
,, thee, ſo ẏ thou ſhalt be left altogether cemfoztleſſe. I giue
,, thee yet to vnderſtand that Pzince Edward is not nowe
,, liuing, and that in the time wherein thy diſpaire ſhall bee
,, higheſt, thou ſhalt obteine thy huſband againe, as ſafe and
,, ſcund as he departed from thee, and he ſhall acknowledge
,, thy childzen, and ſhall ioy in their vertues, ẏ the ioy which
,, thou ſhalt haue hereafter ſhall ſurmount the paine wher-
,, in thou remaineſt at this pzeſent. Aſſure thy ſelfe there-
,, foze that as all ſhall come to paſſe which I haue fozetold
,, thee, ſo were it good to keepe it in memozie, thereby to
,, ſtrengthen thy courage, the better to reſiſt the malice of
,, thy aduerſary Foztune: whoſe wheele as it is rounde and
,, in continall motion, ſo perſwade thy ſelſe when it is at the
,, loweſt muſt needs tourne agayne vpwardes, and reſtoze
,, thee thy damages. Farewell, and hope no moze to ſpeake
with me till all be accompliſhed which I haue ſayd. In
this ſozt pzeparing the Pzinceſſe to the confliā with hir
aduerſitie, the fayze Nymphe baniſhed aſray, diuing down
into the depth of the well, and the Pzinceſſe demuſing vpon
this ſaying, was as it were beſides hir ſelfe, not ſully
knowing whether ſhe had heard theſe wozdes, oz dzeamed them. Foz as ſhe vnderſtode of the one parte, that
Pzince Edward was dead, & of the other, that ſhe ſhoulde
once againe ſee hir huſbande, ſhe was ſo confuſed in hir
theught, that ſhe knewe not what to iudge, and ſaid to hir
ſelfe, that peraduenture ſhe had miſtaken the Nymphe.
In the end reſting vppon the hope which ſhe had made
pzomiſe off, ſhe was ſomewhat comfozted, not doubtinge
the accompliſhment. Yet ſhe remained in the monaſtery
not willing to go out of hir lodging, and clothed alwayes
in

in blacke mourning apparell, and delighting in nothing so
much as in little Rosicleer. Rosicleer as he encreased in
yers so he exceded also in beautie, goodlynesse of body, & ex-
cellente qualities that a man might well prognosticate
thereby of his valiauncye. But bicause the historye shall
more specially talke of him, I leaue him for this time to
his nurse there to be instructed, till he shalbe called foorth
to greater matters. Nowe it is time to go to the succour
of Donzel del Febo his brother, who is all this time vpon
the riuer.

¶ The pedegree of the valiant Prince Florion. &
other matters as touching him.　Cap. xvj.

BY the most auncient and true records of the Assirians, it appeareth that in that time, when Theodoro predecessor of the great Emperour Trebatio ruled in the Empyre of Greece : there gouerned among the Persians the mightie Orixerges king of
Persia and Souldan of Babilon, for his great power a-
mong the Pagans much renowned and feared. This man
after he had lined in great prosperitie, dyed, leauing behinde him three sons, y eldest king of Persia, y secōd Souldan of Babilon, the thirde Lord of the Crimsin Ilande
which is in the red Sea, whence also it taketh the name,
bicause al y lād is died with y colour. This third brother
from his youth was very studyous and geuen aboue all
to Astrology, and other vnknowen sciences. In these he
became so exquisite y scarse in his time might any be cō-
pared vnto him. The greatest parte of his life time, he
dwelt in that Ilande chosing that place as most conuenient for his studie. The eldest of the three brethren, being
king of Persia dyed about xl. yeares after this distributi-
on of their enheritāce, hauing for heir a sonne of his xr.
yeares olde called Florion, a valiant and strronge knight,
bigge made and of a goodly stature. This Florion being

C.ii.　　a

a young man but of a great courage, putting in his roome a viceroy for his kingedome, wandred as a knighte arrant through the world to seeke aduentures, wher he did great and noble deedes of armes. At the ende of three yeares, after this his absence from his country, he stroke euer towards the courte of the Souldan of Babilon his vnckle. Where he remained sometimes very well welcomed and beloued of the Souldan, for he was a good knight. The Souldan had a little sonne and a meruailous faire daughter whose name was called Balisea, of hir Florion became enamoured & requiring hir to wife of hir father, she was graunted him, and the mariage celebrate betwene them with great solemnitie of feasts and triumphs. While he was thus within dores sporting, ther was worse newes abroad. For a mightie Pagan called Africano the brauest and boldest knight that euer was in all the coastes of Africke had transported ouer into Asia, and by his greate force in fewe dayes subdued the whole country of Media and two other kingdomes adiacente, belonging to two great Pagan Princes. These thus vanquished, after became tributaries, as subiects & vassalls. The fame whereof was bruted farre and neere, that there wer few kings in those parts which requested not his amitie, for al accounted him y lustiest warriour in the worlde: & soth it is that in all Asia was neuer borne so proude and fierce a Pagan.

But he was gainesayde by him, vnto whose courtesie not onely our liues and liuings, but we our selues stande thrall and subiect, otherwise he had in fewe dayes made himselfe Lorde of the greatest part of all Asia. This Pagan was a huge and mightie man, large lymmed of the bignesse of a Gyant, and so strong and weightie with all that the strongest horse which was, he coulde make to bowe betwene his legges, any peece of armour howe fine soeuer it were hee woulde bende and wreathe in his hads, as easely as if it had ben framed of waxe. This mã well knowing his owne forces and estate, and not con-

content

tented with that he had gotten in few dayes determined
to inuade the kingdome of Persia , to bring that also to
his subiection. Into it he entred,and in a little time he conquered many cities playning townes and castells,all this
while the Prince Florion being in Babilon . The Péeres
of his kingdome sent messengers vnto him, declaring the
whole state of the coũtry, how vnable it was to make resistance, without the leuying of a newe army, and some
forayne succours.

Then the Prince assembled the royallest army that he
might in the lande of the Souldan and shipped into Persia,
there to giue battaile vnto Africano,& to punish by armes
his enemies intrusion.But he reckened without his host.
For he had not rode x.myles in hys owne kingdome when
the mightie Africano came and pytched néere with his
whole army, and in the first fielde discomfited Florion the
most part of his people being slayne . The Prince Florion hasted into Babilon , for euer disparing to be reuested
in his segniories, and Africanos power was so great,that
he well wotte al the Souldans power to be of little force
to withstande him.The Souldan receiued him gladde
of his escape , but yet sorye agayne for his people
and disheritinge of his Nephewe in so noble a kingdome.

As they were thus sorowfull within a fewe dayes after came into the court the third brother Lyrgandeo, which
as the story sayth inhabited the crimsũ Ilande , at his
comming they wer much quieted, he bad them be at rest
and not take care for the kingdome of Persia for that
there was among the Christians a childe borne in the
happiest and most fortunate houre that euer knight had
bene borne in, the which by good aduenture shoulde be
brought to these parts , and by his noble valour and
vertue , shoulde delyuer the Souldan and the Princesse his daughter from death, or from perpetuall
                                              imprı-

imprisonment, & dispossessing the wicked intruder, should place the Prince Florion in his lawfull enheritaunce, to his owne great glory and the vtter confusion of his enemies. This done that Florion should enioy his kingdome in peace and tranquilitie all his life, vntill then he required them to haue patience, sith it is not yet saith he when these things shall happen.

Lyrgandeo was helde for a very wise man, and they all beleued his saying, for that at other times he had deuined of many things which came to passe accordingly: but yet they knew not who that knight might be so strong as to resist the force of Africano, for he was reputed the brauest & most valyant knight of the worlde, & they were very desirous euery day to heare of his arriuall in their lande. Now not a moneth after this the wise Lyrgandeo, counsailed with the Prince Florion in secret willing him immediatly at that houre to take xx. knights of the best he had in the court and himselfe, and to embarke themselues in a warre shippe, as it were to scowre the coasts. Wher sailing in the Sea Mediterraneum, Fortune should bring vnto their power two little boyes the most beautifull and excellent that euer he had sene, with these sayth he you shall retourne to Babilon, for these are the nurses of your good happe. The Prince glad to please his vnckle, chose out his knights, and tooke leaue of the Souldan, departing from Babilon, and passing through Asia the lesse, he came to a hauen in Phrygia, where he put himselfe and his mates in a ship well puruayed of vittaile, and lately rigged and trimmed for some such voiage. In this with a prosperous winde he sayled till at the ende of xij. dayes mounting on the tilbacke of the shippe to looke if perhaps he might behold the thing, of which the wise man had tolde him. It was so that he kenned a farre off a little barke in which the gentleman of the Sunne was driuing towardes them, and the waues rocking it on eury side. It might be that this beate defended the burten naturallye,

as

as onely following the course of the waues : But J rather beleue that God which had created him with so wonderfull marks , tooke this care and kepe of him , vntill
that Florion espying the barke comming righte towards
him, and the gentleman in it so beautifull and bright as
an Angell of heauen , no toungæ can expresse the ioy that
nowe he promised himselfe touching the perfourmannce
of that hope which Lyrgandeo gaue him to repossesse his
kingedome. His conceit also as concerning the beautie of
Donzel del Febo was, that some one of his celestiall gods
had begotten him on some faire Lady here on the earth,
and therefore as to a personage , which did participate
with the deitie, he bowed himselfe, honouring and embracing Donzel del Febo, & vpõ his knees thancked his gods
for ye grace they did him in deliuering into his hands one
w̃ whom they themselues might ioy. The beautiful yoũg
gentleman, which saw him so before him embaced ,feared
him not a whit although ye armour glittered,but with a
ioyfull and pleasant countenaunce colled him and clasped
his armes about his necke , as if he had knowen him a
long time. J doe not thincke that the desire of safety made
him so to fawne vpõ Florion,for they with whom he was
earst acquainted wore no armour. But the Prince Florion tooke him vp in his armes and kissed his white & ro-
seall cheekes as tenderly as if he had ben his owne childe,
making him to eate of ye most delicate meats which he had
thẽ on boarde. The little boy which was very hungry fed
very well,and from that time foorth loued the Prince Florion more then any other:as it is natural in man to preferre those of whome they receiue benefites . When the
gentleman of the Sunne was well satiffied, the Prince
Florion entred againe into his owne shippe and hoysed
sayle toward Phryga with a good winde.

¶ Prince Florion in his waye homewardes findeth
by aduenture the young gentleman Clauergudo
sonne

sonne to the king Oristeo of Fraunce and bringeth him
with the gentleman of the Sunne to Babilon. Cap.xvij.

The second day after the Prince Donzel del Febo,
had bene thus taken into Florions shippe, they tourned about towards Phrygia whence they first departed
and escried at three of the clocke in the morning right a-
gainst their ship, e an other the tallest & beautifultest shyp
that they had euer seene, which the faster it sayled, the nerer it approched to their vessell. For the Pilot directed ther
course straight vpon Florions ship, and in short space they
ioyned together. This ship grappling with the other, by
and by a Chefetaine getting vpon the hatches commaunded all in the other shippe to yeelde as prisoners. Then
the strong Florion not knowing who they were, toke a
heuy & well steeled battell axe, & getting vpon yshipbord,
made him auswer on this wise. What art thou knight so
arrogant, which without knowing who we be, wouldest
,, make vs thy prisoners. What may you be sayd the knight
,, that you can acquite your selues from the terrible Mam-
,, briniano which commeth in this shippe, now except you
,, do this that I commaund you, all the world is not suffi-
,, cient to make you a way to escape his handes. Untill this
,, day there was neuer borne a man which hath made lyke
,, effusion of humaine bloud in this Sea. Then fayne would
,, I see this braue knight aunswered y Prince Florion, and
,, scarcely had spoke these wordes, when the diuelish rouer
armed with a very great & heauie armour, & a battell axe
of fine steele in his handes, ioyned to the Prince spedely,
and without God spede you, layde at him such a a blowe
vpon the headpeece, as might haue clouen his head in pe-
ces. But the Prince was deliuer and quicke, and seeing
the battell axe descending, the ayre beare before it, he stept
aside & the blowe fell vpon the planckes of the ship, which
made a great peece thereof to fall into y water, quite shutting him, from hope of a second blowe. Then the bolde

Florion

Florion closing with him, gaue him a buffet with his
swozde, vpon his great and fine helmet that he made him
bowe his knæs, and with the great weight of his body
scarsely might this rouer arise, but he tearned himselfe
with great paine to ffrike the Prince. There beganne a
braue and teribie battayle, either of their knights much
amased in beholding ȝc. Now wel fare thy hart thou valyant Florion, for thou much disappointedff Mambriniano of his enterprise, ƫ madff him confeffe that in twentie
yeres robbing on the Sea, of so many as he might finde,
he had neuer met knight which had put him in so great
daunger, noz sought with one of so great force. Thus they
fought halfe an houre ƫ no man might iudge who should
haue the better. The great rouer ffrake with all his fozce
at his enemy, (but the finall houre of his owne life nowe
edging nære him) so it was that the couragious Prince
auoyded it, ƫ as he was already entred into the good suc-
cceffe of his voyage, hauing in his power the gentleman
of the Sunne, so fired all with wrath, his colour (as a
man might say) betwraying his choler, he gaue the rouer
with both hys hands such a blowe vpon the head that he
he felled him to the grounde, and befoze the rouer might
get on his knees, he gaue him another betweene his helmet and his neckepeere, and layd him flat vpon the planks
of the Shippe. Ther the wretched Mambriniano with his
gluttonos defire spitte out his ffincking and cozrupted
spirite, and the noble Florion reffed not heere but with
a braue and ffoute courage entred in the Shippe and
layde about him on both sides. The knights of the ro-
ner to reuenge their Lozds death wounded him on all
all parts, but by and by there bozded them the twentie knights of the Prince, all chosen men of war ƫ helped
their Lozd in suche wise, that in shozte time the grea-
teff parte of their enemies were flayne, and the reffe
seeing their fall, yeelded themselues to his mercye. The
battaile thus eased, the Prince would see what was

iii

in the shippe for he beleued that there was within great
riches according as the dealings of ẙ rouer had ben. Ther
was much treasure found, but searching euery place of it,
they found in a cabbin a knight of an indifferent age, clothed with rich garments, and by his graue countenaunce
seeming to be of good account, and nere vnto him a young
gentleman of foure or fiue yeares olde, very beautifull &
seemely arayed in cloth of golde and about his necke a col-
ler of golde set with rich and precious stones. The young
gentleman was so gratious in behauiour, ẙ if Florion had
not before seene the gentleman of the Sunne he had beleued him to be the fairest and properest gentleman that
euer he had seene, and desiring to know who they were, he
saluted them courteously , willing the knight to tell him
who they were. He which had already knowne Florions
great vertue in the battaile that hee had with the rouer,
rose with the young gentleman from the place where he
was sette, and vsing an humble ductie to him aunswered.
» Syr knight I am a prisoner to the rouer, Mambriniano,
» which toke me and this young gentleman at a place nere
» a hauen of the Sea, and sith G D D by Fortune hath
» bene so fauourable vnto you, that in a righteous battaile
» you haue slaine him, we remaine now for yours to doe,
» With vs that which shall seeme best vnto you, and we haue
» good hope that with a knight of so great valour , there
» cannot happen vnto vs so much euill as with him which
» toke vs prisoners. The Prince accepted well that which
he sayd vnto him, and prayed him to go on in declaringe
who he was, for that by lacke of knowledge he might
foreslacke to doe to them the honour that they merited.
Albeit nowe the knight wished that he might dissemble it
for the daunger which might ensue, yet in the ende, put-
» ting his affiaunce in the Prince, he sayd vnto him. Sith
» it lyketh you sir knight to know who we be only to please
» you I will tell it you, though I would gladly haue sup-
» pressed our names till Fortune somewhat more friendly
vnto

vnto vs ſhould haue betwꝛayed it . But knowe you that ,,
this young gentleman is called Clauergudo, and is the ,,
ſonne of the king Oriſteo, king of Fraunce, onely inheri- ,,
tour and ſucceſſour of that great kingdome , and J haue ,,
to name Armineo, being bꝛother to the king Oriſteo ,,
vnckle to this young gentleman. The whole oꝛder of this ,,
miſfoꝛtune was in this ſoꝛte. One day foꝛ to ſpoꝛte our ,,
ſelues in the company of many other knightes , we rode ,,
to a fayꝛe foꝛreſt nære vnto the Sea, and the knightes ,,
which came with vs, the moſt of them delighting in hun- ,,
ting, ſeuered themſelues foꝛ their diſpoꝛt, in ſuch manner ,,
that the young gentleman and J with onely x. knightes ,,
were left in a freſh and fayꝛe harbour about a well, nære ,,
adioyning vnto the Sea. In this time while our knights ,,
followed their game, this great Rouer Mambriniano ,,
whether eſpying vs, oꝛ by chaunce taking lande foꝛ freſh ,,
water, wæ knowe not, but with moꝛe then xx . knightes ,,
he beſet vs, and although wæ defended our ſelues ſome- ,,
time, in the ende, this gentleman and J were taken ,,
pꝛiſoners, and our x. knightes ſlayne and ſoꝛe wounded ,,
befoꝛe the other knightes which hunted in the foꝛreſt ,,
might vnderſtande of it . He carryed vs to his ſhippes ,,
where it is moꝛe then a moneth ẏ wee haue ben in this ,,
maner as you haue ſæne vs, cloſe pent vp in this cage. ,,
Foꝛ my ſelfe Sir, as J neuer hope foꝛ libertie, ſo J re- ,,
ſpect not my impꝛiſemnent, but foꝛ this fayꝛe young gen- ,,
tleman, my heart is ſoꝛe wounded. J had rather ſuffer x. ,,
deathes, then any ſuch miſfoꝛtune ſhould happen to him. ,,
Bicauſe that when ſuch newes ſhall be repoꝛted to hys ,,
father, he will beare it moꝛe impatiently then his owne, ,,
& that which woꝛſt is, to me onely will he attribute this ,,
fault, ſith hauing committed his onely ſonne to my gouer- ,,
nance, J haue giuen ſo ill account of him, vnto theſe woꝛds ,,
ẏ knight lent many a teare ſlyding down his face, which ,,
well ſhewed ẏ griefe he boꝛe in heart. The pꝛince Florion ,,
in great compaſſion comfoꝛted him, pꝛomiſing libertie of

F. retourne

retourne into his countrey when he would, but by and by
remembring the wordes which the wise man his vnckle
had sayd, he called it backe againe, and in steede of his first
promise, he tourned his tale to the narration of his owne
" mishaps, being on this wise. I thanck you hartely for your
" courtesie, in recounting to me the whole discourse of your
" imprisonment, and of this young gentlemans captiuitie,
" and I call ý high Gods to witnesse, what paine your mis-
" fortune hath caused in me , and howe ready my power
" shalbe to remedy it when I may. For I meane to giue
" you libertie of retourne, and with my men to conduct you
" homewardes into Fraunce, thus much occasioned in mee
" by the deserts of your estate. But Fortune hath bene so
" contrary to me, that except your retourne be delayed , I
" my selfe shall want my necessary helpe, the whole state of
" the matter lying thus, if it so please you to heare, I am by
" name Florion, king of Persia, my father deceasing whiche
" was king thereoff, & so by iust title as to his onely sonne
" and heyre, ý crowne of ý kingdome descended to me. This
" charge I susteined in mine owne person a good while, but
" being young and lustie, and in good age to followe armes,
" I was desirous to wãder in ý world. So leauing a gouer-
" nour in my kingdome I trauailed through diuers coûtries
" vntill ý ende of three years, at which time I tooke ouer in-
" to Babilon, where I was matched with ý daughter of the
" Souldan being mine vnckle. Whether came ambassadors
" from my subiects, certifying me ý the king of Media the
" stowest Pagan in al ý heathen cõstrey, w maine force had
" intruded vpon my kingdome: I for to remedy it, gathered
" a great host in ý Souldans land, & trãsporting into Persia,
" at ý first battaile ý I had with ý king of Media, ý greater
" part of my people being slaine, my selfe was ouerthrown,
" & with great griefe by secret bywaies recouered Babilon,
" wher I could willingly haue dyed for paine anguish. But
" one mine vnckle, a very wyse & learned man in Art Ma-
" gicke, recomfort me saying, that the time should come, in
which

which I should be restored to my kingdome with great »
honour,& y for this it behoued me to await on y sea, till »
I met w two little boies of excellent beautie:with whom »
I should retourne to Babilon,for that they should bee the »
principall cause of my redresse,and so giuing credit to hys »
word, I thus put my selfe in aray,for this aduēture,where »
thanckes be to the Gods,all hath succeeded as y wiseman »
forespok it,for within this three daies I lighted vpon one »
being alone in a little boat, hauing in him according to »
my fancie,the very pride of all beautie,and the other must »
needes be this young gentleman Clauergudo y fairest be »
side him y euer I knew,so as I haue good hope hereby to »
reēter into my kingdom. For this cause I haue in charge »
to bring these two to Babilon,& now ūr knight I beseech »
you to take it in good part,for he shal be as wel entertai- »
ned in y court of the Souldan as in y court of the king his
father,& when my good fortune wil y my seat shal be esta-
blished,he & you shall retourne into Fraunce w my ships,
& my people,& my selfe also if it be so conuenient. When y
prince had here stayed,Armineo was wel contented with
his talke,taking him for a knight of great prowesse, & al-
thought y long stay y y prince Clauergudo should make in
this countrey grieued him : yet with hope to retourne in
the ende,seeing it was not in his power to doe otherwise,
he subiected his will to the princes commaunde,& with
courteous woordes rendred him thanckes for the storie of
his aduentures,& for y offer he had made thē, y pith of his
aunswere being in few words this.Be it as you haue said
syr,for I denie not but y gentlemā Clauergudo shal gaine
very much by his bringing vp in yours & your vnckles so
noble a court.With these profers to and fro,Florion toke
Clauergudo in his armes,& entred in his own ship, Armineo following him,when Armineo had beheld within
Florions ship the young Donzel del Febo , you must not
meruaile though hee blessed himselfe,for there was none
whiche had had but a blushe of him within his tender

yeares

yeares, but tooke him rather to be a celestiall Seraphin, then an humaine creature, and beleeued that this might not be done without some great misterie, as if ye younge gentleman shewinge in hys infancie the comelinesse of stature, and other excellent qualities wherewith he was endued, besides the straunge findinge him alone in the rage of the tempest, dyd well foreshewe his nobilitie in time to come. But when they sawe him naked and the portrature of the Sunne, with the brightnesse that it gaue to the beholders, it was so straunge that they called to minde Phaetons fall out of heauen, comparing thys younge gentleman with Phaeton as if he had bene Phœbus sonne, like as Phaeton was, although somewhat diuers, agayne in this for that Phaeton taking his fathers chariot, for his presumption was drenched in the Sea, this younge gentleman was preserued in the Sea, as betokeninge some greater secrecie in Nature. Armineo was best apayed to haue the companie of so excellent a gentleman for the Prince Clauergudo. Now by ye way this may you learne, ye although they could not tell Donzels name, yet by the tokens he had vppon him, they named him the gentleman of the Sunne, somewhat in other tearmes in the Persian toggue, but in signification, all one with the name that his mothers gentlewoman gaue him in Hungary, beeing worth the markinge that both Persians and Hungarians shoulde so iumpe in naminge him. But to make hast homewardes they tooke the way to Phrygia, and with a good winde ere.xv. dayes they landed there, and comming a shore, they sente harbengers aforehande, as well to aduertise the Souldan and Lyrgandeo of the Princes comming as to puruaye by the waye, of lodginge for the estates. The two young gentlemen being not a little welcome vnto Florions two vnckles, as you may reade in the next Chapter.

Prince

¶ Prince Florion with the two young gentlemen entered into Babilon, and were there honoura-bly receiued by the Souldan.   Cap. 18

He prince Florion néeded not to haue giué intelligence to ye Souldan of his comming, foz ye wise Lyrgandeo opened all which had chaunced, as well as if he had bene a partie in the doinge of it. So when the Pzince was in lesse then an halfe dayes iourney from the citie, the Souldan and hys wise bzother Lyrgandeo, issued out with a great traine to receiue him, and comming nære, the wise Lyrgandeo espying Florion with ye gentleman of the Sunne on his hozse befoze him, in great ioy rode a pace, & taking him in his armes, spoke these wozds. O ye souereigne Gods, immoztall thancks be giuen vnto you foz the high fauour you haue shewed vnto vs, in bzinging into our power this rare gentleman with whom you haue imparted of your most secret graces. O that mine armes coulde once merite such an heauenly burden. O how well may Babilon reioyce sith he is thether bzought, whose glozy shall no lesse glister thzough the earth, then the bzight Sunne shineth in the wozld. Who deserueth to haue his biding amonge the demigods foz his valour and mightinesse. O how he shal „ race out the memozie of Ninus and Xerxes, and all the „ pzide of the Asirian monarches. From hence fozth „ Asiria, foz bæing onely the cradell of this gentlemans „ nourserie shall be famous thzoughout the whole wozld: „ from hence fozth men shall haue so much to doe, to put in „ wziting the wozthinesse of this gentleman, that all the „ monaments of our aunceftozs shal quite die, and this man „ onely shall be our tabletalke. The wise man thus as it „ were rauisht, and vttering his conceiptes in greate gladnesse by interbzeathinges, the beautie of the chylde sometimes amasing him, and his diuinitie astonishing the hearers, he kissed the young gentleman & held him in his

F.iij.   handes

handes till the Souldan drew néere, as ý Souldan approched, he deliuered Donzel del Febo vnto him, & tourned
hunself towards Clauergudo embzasing him gœdly but in
moze modestie of speach oz lesse delight, he said vnto him.

" You are welcome noble and soueraigne prince, I know-
" ing howe well knowne your name should be in ý wozld,
" had great desire to sée you, albeit, it shall be some griefe
" vnto your parents not to enioy your presence, the time
" shall come when you shall giue them greater comfozt and
" pleasure. In the meane time, you shall not lese any thing
" in béing bzought vp in the company of this gentleman,
" whom you shall loue so excéedingly, that his loue shall of-
" ten extinguish the remébzaunce of your parents. Armineo
which was not farre off, gaue him great thanckes in the
behalfe of the Pzince. Then they two rode together deuising of many things, and many courteous wozdes of
gœd entertainement passing betwéene them, vntil ý Souldan fell in talke with the young Clauergudo & Armineo
to whom he shewed a friendly countenaunce in token of
great gœd loue. These things thus done, they all held on
their way to ý citie, & passing thzough towards ý pallaice,
there they were receiued by Balisea, pzincesse and wife to
Florion, making semblaunce of great liking to Donzel del
Febo, whose excellent beautie and comlinesse she wel noted, and already concluded in hir thought foz a companion to hir sonne now of thzée yeares olde very large and
beautifull called Brandizel: Which in déede after pzoued
a knight so gœd, as fewe better, béing strong made, somewhat higher then his father, & of moze puissaunce. These
thzée gentlemen by the Pzincesse Baliseas deuice were
bzought vp altogether in like suites, and like exercises, &
so from their youth their friendship encreased with their
yeares, that in the ende, as they themselues were at their
full growth, so their friendship waxed so firme, ý neither
the diuersitie of thir pzofessions, noz the distaunce of their
coūtreys might in any wise enfringe it. These young gentlemen

tlemen thus brought vp in Babilon, Armineo which in al
things was very wise & well learned,taught Clauergudo
the liberall Artes,and instructed him in the true & perfect
lawe of God:in such manner that although his education was among the Pagans,yet the Prince was alwaies
a good christian. The wise Lyrgandeo likewise carefull
of the gentleman of the Sunne,& of Brandizel,read vnto
them diligently what was conuenient,saue that as he was
a Pagan , so hee acquainted them onely with Pagansie
in their religion: Which errour notwithstanding afterwarde they both renounced . This was the tray-
ning vp of the young princes in the court of the Souldan,
as .hædfully looked vnto, as if it had bene in their parents courtes . But as their yeares multiplied , so they
exceeded, all others inferiour in iudgment ,wit, discretion , goodlinesse of stature, actiuitie, and all that which
was requisite to such princes , but especially and aboue
all his equales , Donzel del Febo surpassed . For atteining to the age of r.yeares, hee sæmed to bee more
then rb.both for witte and strength , courage and pol-
licie,and by the bignesse of his body(bæing withal well
featured)men gathered vndoubtedly of his might. They
made their argument thus.If he be so strongly set in his
youth at r.yeares,what will he bæ at rr. And truely although his father the Emperour Trebatio was big of body,as the historie hath already specified,bæing.biii.foot in
height,yet Donzel del Febo ouerreached him somewhat,
& with al this mainteined ꝑ prerogatiue of his proportiõ.
So ꝑ I thinck our painters as well Grecians as Assirians had neuer the perfect knowledge to drawe and finish
ꝑ true proportion of man,before they had the biew of this
knight . His picture was sent into sundry parts as ꝑ no-
blest painter ꝑ ere was wrought.Besides this,ther appe-
red in his face a maiestie so graue & princelike,ꝑ it stroke
a feare of him into mighty Princes.For all this,he was
yet of behauiour affable & somewhat familiar,ꝑ he which

knew him

him well, albeit his mortall enimie could not but highly
commend of it. What shal I say? as the Adamant stone
draweth to it the hard and sharpe yron by his hidden
vertue, so likewise this knight procured the loue, as well
of foes as of friendes, and of as many as knewe him and
were conuersant with him. And so this younge gentlemen Clauergudo and Brandizel, and other younge gentlemen which were his playfellowes were so gladde of
him, that they could at no time be without him. Nowe
bicause we haue more perticulerly to descende into this
storie hereafter, and to describe the manifolde graces of
this knight, for these matters we will let them passe at
this time, and remember you of his age of xii. yeares, at
which time there happened that which shall appeare in
the Chapter following.

¶ The deliuerie of the Souldan by the gentleman of
the Sunne.   Cap. 19.

MAny times the Souldan and the Prince Florion, with
some other knightes for their recreations, rode on
hunting into a thicke wood standing in a faire forrest seated somewhat néere the Sea, and plentifull of all kinde of
game, especially of wilde boares and such like beastes.
Nowe when the young gentlemen could sit their horses
and were able to endure some trauaile, they tooke them
with them, and furnishing them with boare speares in
their handes, they appointed them to the chase. Some
game ther was killed before them, wherin they toke great
pleasure: but especially ye gentleman of ye Sunne, which by
himself wearied a wilde beare, & two beares so fierce as
might haue frayed a right good knight. His practise was
alwayes to hunt alone, to haue no mans helpe to the
encounter with any wilde beast. And it was so, ye one day
the Souldan would go to the same forrest to delight himselfe, there for certeine dayes taking with him the Princesse

ceſſe Baliſea his daughter, and the traine of many Ladyes
and gentlewomen and the moſt principall Lordes of his
courte, bicauſe the place was gallant and delectable, and
repleniſhed with varietie of game, being as I ſayd hard
vpon the cliffes of the Sea. For this cauſe there were re-
red vp many pauilions there, and there was puruayed
of other prouiſion neceſſary for the houſholde. He made
his owne tent to be pitched in a flouriſhing medowe next
to a goodly fountaine. Ther reſted he one day ſolacing him
ſelfe among his knights, for the firſt day they wente not
out to ſœke their game. The next day early in the morning the Prince Florion, the young gentlemen and the
moſt part of all the knights tooke their way through the
forreſt climing vp a ſtœpe hyll, and parted themſelues into diuers companyes, ſome to rayſe the game, and others
to be at the receipte. The Souldan and the Princeſſe with
hir Ladyes, and only xv. knights remaining in their tents
as vnmindefull of any daunger if any ſhoulde happen.
The Sunne being almoſt at the higheſt, and his beames
more direct, the Souldan with the Princeſſe his daughter and hir gentlewomen lefte their tent and came to the
fountaine the water being clœre and the place well ſhadowed with trees, there in the quyet ſhade to abide the
comming of the Prince Florion and the young gentlemen to dinner. In the meane time the gentlemen ſewers
prepared the cupbœrde and the cœkes made ready for dinner. The tables being ſpredde vpon the greene graſſe and
euery man attentiue to his function, the officers to their
charge, the knights to their game, and the Souldan with
the Princeſſe and Ladyes to refreſhe themſelues in the
cœle ayre: there came in place a mightie and wofull Gyant, with more then twentie knyghts after him. The
Ladyes ſcrœched out, but ther was no remedy. For the
Gyant with his knights tooke the Souldan, the Princeſſe,
and moſt of the gentlewomen and conuayed them into a
chariot drawne by ſtrong horſes which they brought with

F.v.   them

them for the same purpose, with the outcries of the Ladyes the knights which were in the tent issued and séeing
their Lord and the Princesse with hir Ladyes so carryed
away perforce (albeit this they did more for shame then
through hardinesse, yet) they made towardes the Gyant
with their swordes and began to compasse him about, but
they so ill perfourmed their duetie that in short time them
selues were either wounded, slaine, taken, or put to flight,
and their Lord for larke of rescewes was bound and fettered. The Gyant hauing his praye withall the hast he
might toke towarde the Sea, where he had a good shippe
in redinesse. The lamentable noyse which the Ladyes
made was such that it beat through ye ayre vnto ye skyes
and yet could not penetrate so farre as to Prince Florion
or his knights, either that they wer so eager in the pursute
of their wilde boares that they marked it not, or that the
crye of the hunters was so lowde, that it drowned the o-
ther. But the young gentleman of the Sunne, losing his
company, and well mounted vpon a lyght horse with a
borespeare in his hand, being also clothed in a húters wéed
of gréene cloth of golde, and a hat to képe downe his yelowe haires, roade roming about the woode to séeke some
beast vpon whom he might try the stéele of his boarespere,
and taking this way and that way without staying in a-
ny place, he mette with a knight sore wounded by the Gyant, which roade piteously to call the Prince Florion and
his knights for succour to the Souldan & the Princes. As
Donzel del Febo saw him thus arayed he asked what he
,, ayled. Alas gentleman of the Sunne said ye knight, ye Soul-
,, dan our Lord and the Princesse are taken prisoners by an
,, vgly & monstrous Gyant, & by the hast he maketh, I gesse
,, he is already néere vnto the Sea. The gentleman of the
Sunne much lamented such newes, & with a noble & he-
royrall courage which by nature nowe enforced it selfe
foreward, he prayed ye knight to guide him on ye way, towardes ye Gyant. The knight thinking it an vnfit match &

besid?

beſide his purpoſe to turne back with him, for he thought
him to young for ſuch an enterprice would not ſtaye, but
rode on faſter. The gentleman moued with this that the
knight ſet ſo little by him yet ſaid nothing, but not tarying
for more company broched the horſe with his ſpurs, ẙ he
made him ſpin ẙ ſame way in which he had ſene ẙ knight
before. The haſt he made is incredible, for before ẙ Gyāt
had recouered ẙ ſea, he ouertœke him in a playne amongſt
his knights ẛ the chariot in ẙ midſt. The Gyāt was hund-
moſt on fœt, with a great battell are of ſtæle in his hand
ſo ẙ it might haue diſmayed one to ſæ his fierce ẛ cruell
demeanour. When ẙ gentleman of ẙ ſunne had got a ſight
of him with greater force then before he ſpurred his horſe
making way through ẙ græne medow as faſt as if he had
bene driuen by the rage of tempeſt ẛ thunder, and crying
aloude. Stay, ſay. The Gyant and his knights hearing
the noyſe that he made and the ſound of the horſe fœt gal-
loping in ſuch haſt, turned their heades aſide to ſæ what
it ment, ẛ amongſt the reſt ẙ Souldan likewiſe lœked behinde him, and eſpying him to be ẙ gentleman of ẙ ſunne
with only a boareſpeare in his hand, he much pitied hys
caſe , for he thought ſurely Donzel ſhould neuer eſcape
death or duraunce. The lothſome Gyant wondring at the
young gentleman comming toward him, with great fury
lifte vp both his hands to his head, and there ſtaying on
fœte as he was, made a fierce and ſterne countenaunce of
diſdayne till the young gentleman approched . But the
noble ẛ valyant Donzel del Febo borne for the achieuement of greater aduentures, with a furious mœde as it
had bene thunder drew nere, and with his boareſpeare in
his hande being very ſtrong, ſharp, and well ſtæled with
all his force he ſhoued it into ẙ breaſt of the Gyant, that
although he had a breaſtplate of fine ſteele a finger thicke,
yet the ſpeare entred, and iſſued out at ẙ ſhoulder all be-
gored with bloude. Thus the Gyant fell downe deade
on the grounde to the greate abaſhement of all thoſe
                                                    which

which saw him, iudging that Donzel del Febo had bene then let downe from heauen to doe this feate, for in their fancies, not the thunderbolte which by the renting of the cloudes driueth the windes before it, might euer giue a more sodayne or more forcible blowe then that which Donzel del Febo gaue the Gyant, especially the knights of the Gyants retinue not witting who he was, vnagined that their owne gods had sent him downe from the heauens for the more notable chastisement of their Lordes crueltie. Now some of the knights hearing a rushing, a farre off in the woode, and thincking it to be the Souldans people, their maister thus flayne, without hauing care of chariot or prisoners, toke them to their heeles with more haste by halfe then good speede. For one letting the bridell slippe, and for feare not able to guide his horse, by the stumbling of his horse had so sore a bruse, that his horse rising, he laye still on the grounde tormented with the fal. And those which got to the Sea, themselues being past daunger nothing sorowed at the death of the Gyant, for they hated him, & serued more by compulsion then with good will. This trouble in the Gyantes men made the gentleman of the Sunne make no account of them. Wherefore alighting from his horse, he went towardes the chariotte where the Souldan was, with the Princesse and Ladyes and vnbounde them. The Ladyes when they sawe him, were no lesse gladde of the prowse of armes in Donzel del Febo, then of their owne deliuerie. But the Souldan embrasing him & kissing him with great loue, sayd vnto him.

,, Oh my sonne now I know assuredly that the mightie
,, gods highly fauour you, & that onely by miracle you haue
,, ben brought to Babilon as to giue succours to me & to my
,, children. Now doe I firmely beleue my brother Lyrgan-
,, deo, who long before prophecied of the great merueiles
,, of your valour, sith that being so young and tender and
,, in the maydenhead of your strength, it being neuer before

tasted

tasted vpon an enemye , you haue begunne so well as I ,,
haue knowne no knight in his perfection machable. And ,,
truly this is the accomplishment of your first aduenture, ,,
as my brother forecasting it tolde me, that you shoulo re= ,,
scew me ano my daughters from death or imprisonment, ,,
and I hope as well in the immortall gods y the second ,,
shalbe lykewise finished,that is, the kingdome of Persia so ,,
long withhelde by a false vsurper, may by you be redeli= ,,
uered to the Prince Fiorion. My Lord aunswered Don= ,,
zel del Febo, I haue not as yet done the thing in your ser= ,,
uice neither in my lyfe may hope to compasse which may ,,
counterpaise with my good wil in this behalfe,and truely ,,
the duetie which I owe to your good grace my Lorde, to ,,
the Prince Florion, and to my Lady the Princesse your ,,
daughter, dayly so augmenteth as more then that duetie ,,
I cannot owe vnto my father, to the discharge whereof, ,,
notwithstanding I stande bourden to your goodnesse,not ,,
onely of courtesie but in conscience,and so humbled him= ,,
selfe before the Souldan : but the Souldan againe embra=
ced him and they two helped the Ladyes out of the cha-
riot.The Ladyes were desirous to know who the Gyant
was,¶ what should be the cause why he so assayled them.
Therfore the Souldan and the gentleman of the Sunne,
made toward the knight of the Gyant which was falne
to the grounde , and as they toke of his helmet to giue
him ayre , they fetcht him out of his sounde and setting
him on his feete they demaunded of him who the Gyant
was and why he came to take them prisones.The knight
seing it behoued him to say the troth made aunswer short= ,,
ly thus.You shall vnderstande my Lordes that this Gy= ,,
ant was called Brandasileo Lorde of the toured Ilande, ,,
which is in the great Ocean , at the mouth of the redde ,,
Sea. This Ilande is so stronge and inuincible that being ,,
within, he needs not feare all the worlde if they had bent ,,
their force against him, ¶ being proude vpon the safetie ,,
of this Ilande he did much wrong to the nations round ,,

about

,, about him spoyling and robbing all Arabians, Aethiopi-
,, ans, Aegyptians, and the Garamants of Inde, and finally
,, so many as he might come by in the great west seas, and
,, so the Ilande of Traprobne, and by long continuaunce in
,, this trade of rouing he is become so rich of captiues and
,, treasure that no Ilande is comparable with his. Now the
,, cause wherfore he came into this your lande was, for that
,, in the time ẏ the mightie Orixerges your father reigned
,, in Persia the father of this Gyant called Briontes then be-
,, ing Lorde of the toured Ilande, by occasion of Briontes
,, euill life, your father and he fell at variaunce, wherefore
,, the king your father sent out his whole nauy to subdue
,, this Ilande but being not able to conquer it, he gaue them
,, notwithstanding in charge to lye in the outcreekes awai-
,, ting when he came forth from the Iland ẻ so to set vpon
,, the. One time ẏ Gyant making a road out for a lyke che-
,, uisaunce a farre off from his owne Iland, the king your
,, father dogged him with his shippes, and as he retonrne d
,, met him in ẏ halfe tourne ẻ (for all the hauocke he and
,, his made of your fathers souldiers) in the eude killed him.
,, This Brandafileo his sonne then being a childe of tender
,, age, yet so soone as he was of yeares to be made knight he
,, greatly longed after ẏ reuenge of his fathers death, ẻ bi-
,, cause he coulde not worke his mischiefe on ẏ king Orix-
,, erges being then deade, at the least it would ease his sto-
,, macke, if he might wreake himselfe on you his sonne, and
,, for this cause many times he hath sente spyes into your
,, lande to be aduised by them when he might haue oppor-
,, tunitie of vẻgeãce, ẻ learning of your cõming to this for-
,, rest for your disport, he hath now layne more then a mõth
,, in secret expectatiõ of so good lucke as to take your persõ.
,, This time he had found to his contentation had not thys
,, gentleman bene, who now hath made sufficient paye to
,, Brandafileo for his months hire. This is all my Lorde
   which I can tell you as to your demaunde, and it is truth
   which I haue tolde you, as I certeinely beleue, that if euer
                                                              he

he had cleane carried you from hence you should not haue
escaped from death or bondage, for so he had determined.
The Souldan mused at ẏ which ẏ knight had told him, and
waying ẏ great daunger wherin he was like to haue faln,
he ceased not to giue thancks to his gods & to the gentle-
mã of ẏ sunne for his safetie. At this time Prince Florion
came with more then .xxx. knightes running their horses
so fast as they might, bicause already they had heard the
newes, & comming where ẏ Gyant lay dead, tiewing well
the wide & mortall wound, they highly commended of it,
and coulde not iudge by whom he had receiued it: but uery ioyfull to see ẏ Souldan & his Princesse out of daunger,
leaping from their horses they came towards them. Then
Florion excusing his long absence by ẏ ignoraunce of the
fact, desired to knowe who he was which had so gently
bayled them from ẏ Gyant . The Souldan annswered on
this sort . Ah Florion Florion, now we know your vnckle ”
Lyrgandeos diuinations, as touching this gentleman of ”
the sunne to be sooth and stedfast, for we haue well apro- ”
ued his valour, & know you ẏ he alone, being ẏ only man ”
which came to succour vs brought to grounde the Gy- ”
ant Brandafileo by one only blowe with his boarespeare, ”
riuetting as you see his coatearmour, and ridding vs ”
from so daungerous a foe, making his entrance to knight- ”
hood ẏ strangest ẏ euer was heard. Florion giuing back ei- ”
ther as woodring or not credeting his vnckles speach, was
still vrged by ẏ Souldan who tolde on foreward as Bran-
dafileos knight had cõfessed. Floriõ yet as it wer halfe in
a mãmering which part to take betwen ẏ gẽtlemãs youth
& his courage disputed rather ẏ impossibilitie by means of
ẏ hugenes of ẏ Gyant, his strong armour, & the number
of his knights, in ẏ ende he ouercame himselfe, by remẽ-
braunce of Lyrgandeos report, & thancked the gentleman
on this wise. O my right noble & beloued sonne, I graunt
that not my force , but the mightie windes and swelling ”
waues by the . ordinaunce of my Gods , haue gyuen me ”
                                                    power ”

,, pow:r ouer you, fo2 that by your foueraigne bountie the
,, wronge which is done to me by the tyrant shalbe re=
,, uenged and J shall recouer mine owne kingedome.O how
,, happy was the day and the houre fortunate in which J
,, found you,sith my gods haue reserued you fo2 so great be=
,, nefites towardes me and the relefe of mine bnckle,with
these and many other wo2ds Florion wept fo2 great plea=
sure to thincke of Donzels magnanimitie . And in this
tune the other young gentlemen his companions came ri=
ding from hunting , and sawe the fierce Gyant lye dead
by the way they enquired after the manner of his death
and hearing it to be as you haue heard,ŷ one tœke great
pleasure in it, and the other with an honest emulation of
the fact wishing it to himselfe,acco2ding to the diuersitie of
the gœd will they bare bnto the gentleman of the sunne.
Then they came altogether to their tents , where they
made but a ħunters b2eakefast, fo2 ere dinner was halfe
done the Souldan commaunded to ho2se to retourne to
Babilon, and so they all on ho2seback the P2incesse and
hir gentlewomen on their palfrayes, & the lustie knights
on their sturdy Rounceualls,tœke the way towards the
citie,laying the mightie Gyant bpon a ho2se,his head and
fœte trayling on the grounde.

When they were within the gates of the citie , all
that which had happened being published, all the citizens
and other of the courte wer in contrary arguments about
the hugenesse of the Gyant and the courage of the gentle=
man of the Sunne thinking it an impossible matter to be
b2ought about by one of so few yeares . But from that
tune fo2th, (although befo2e likewise they loued him)yet
nowe they made much mo2e of him,and the Souldan with
the P2incesse and all the courtiers helde him in great ac=
count alwaye. Notwithstanding the repo2t of men, and
the high extolling of his actes to his owne face , the gen=
tleman of the Sunne kept the same tenour of life,not bea=
ring himselfe any thing bpon his gœd fo2tune, but rather
as

as the windes encreased which promised him safetie & honour,and as his fame was more blased, so he stroke hys sayles & became more lowlier. This his humilitie made him much more to be loued, as the sprinckling of water augmenteth the flame in a smithes forge: Clauergudo at this time egged on by Donzels good hap,and bæing of of riper yeares sued to be made knight. But the wyse Lyrgandeo foreseæing somewhat, and to haue him kæpe company with Donzel del Febo,and Brandizel withstood his purpose for that time. Clauergudo was but about.xiiij or xv. yeares of age,but he was so comly and nimble in all feates of armes, that there was not a knight in all the court which outpassed him. In this manner were these two gentlemé brought vp in ẏ Souldans court,with great magnificence as if they had bene in their fathers courts, & aboue all,they were so throughly enstructed in learning,that ther were none able to come in controuersie with them,al this equal to both,notwithstanding the difference of belæfes which shall be a like ere it be long. Clauergudo which was guided by Arminco his vnckle, was a christian:and the gentleman of the Sunne belæued in the lawe of the gentils, as the wise Lyrgandeo had taught him. Lyrgandeo himselfe bæing bred and brought vp in the same errour by his father,for all his great cunning was not able to finde out the vanitie of hys false Gods . O the prouidence of God howe much be wæ bound to thæ, and howe ill doe wæ acknowledge thy great goodnesse in suffering vs to be become christians, when thousandes wise men and myghtie monarches dye in ẏ lawe of the gentils,not all their power auaileable to saue their soules,and their learning not worth a rushe for the displaying of the falshode of that lawe, wherein their Fathers haue nousled them. And shall wee Christians thincke that our knowledge can pull vs out of hell, if not the wysest of the earth , I meane the learned gentils could once reproue their owne lawe

G.   and

and knowe the onely and true God. As for example this Lyrgandeo was so wise and well learned, that not Artimedoro, nor Rogel, nor Turke, nor Sarasin, nor Iewe nor Christian came euer nære him, and yet bicause hée had learned that lawe from his cradell, and wanted the gifte of God for the true vnderstanding of his will, he wallowed still in his errour, as ÿ sowe doth in the myre, till God hauing a regard of the gentleman of the Sunne, and minding to make him a true christian, did by his meanes conuert the wise Lyrgandeo to the knowledge of his will, and poure out his grace aboundantly vpon the whole kingdome of Persia, according as more largely shall bée recited. But to retourne, the two younge gentlemen, albeit contrary in professions, yet in friendshippe and good will were conformable, as shall bée declared in this storie.

¶ An aduenture in the court of the Souldan, which befel to the young gentleman of the Sunne. Cap. 20.

THe Souldan and the Prince Florion with all the knightes of his courte, greatly prayed their Gods that the gentleman of the Sunne might come to his full age to bee made knight, for that onely they stayed their voiage into ÿ kingdome of Persia, for his cause as willing to haue him with them for ÿ great prowesse which rested in him, and they thought their stay not ouerlong, sæing it was not vnlikely that whiche the wise Lyrgandeo prophecied of him, that he should bee a valiant knight, and that without him their enteraunce into Persia were to small effect. For this cause, they employed their care in the aduauncing forwarde of the gentleman of the Sunne. This gentleman now being of the age of xvj. yeares, was so high and well fashioned that he wanted little in stature of any man. One day Prince Florion with many other knights being abroad at ÿ riuer to flye at a fowle, the young gentleman staying in the pallaice

laice . The Souldan with many of his knyghtes and
gentlewomen toke their pastime in one part of his great
pallaice where entred in at ý gates sire auncient knights
with white beardes hanging downe to the gyrdlestoedes,
and all armed saue the headpæces , compassing on eache
side a gentlewoman fayre and young,clothed al in mourning apparel,and hauing a crowne of golde vpon hir head.
This Lady was led by a knight great of body well and
strongly proportioned , and armed at all pointes with a
rich and strong armour. This knight lifting vp the visor
of his helmet,shewed himselfe to the Souldan,where they
perceiued his face to be very foule and fearefull , of co-
loure more tawnie and sunburnt, then cole blacke . hys
eyes flaminge in his heade,his nostrels wide and large,
broade lipped , and his sharpe fanges issuinge out of his
mouth like boares tuskes , and reaching to his chinne ,
so that there was no man liuinge but might haue bene
afraied of hys fierce semblaunce . But besides this, hee
was so highe that there was not any in that place
whom this knight exeæded not two spanfulles at the
least, and in makinge of his body he was so large and
well quartered,more them the compasse of two knightes.
Hauinge thus entered and sette himselfe to viewe , those
which were present had inough to occupie their eyes,
either on the vglinesse of the Gyant, or the beautie of the gentlewoman . But the gentlewoman kneeled before the Souldan to haue kissed his hands.But the
Souldan taking hir by the hand , raised hir vp dinge hir
the honour hee thought it conuenient, in that she appeared to be a Lady of greate byrth. Shee with teares di-
stilling downe from hir beautifull eyes , and wateringe
hir crimson cheekes, spake vnto the Souldan on thys
wise . The heauenly and immortall Gods mainteine ,,
and encrease thy highe estate most puissaunt and mighty ,,
Souldan of Babilon.Know for certeintie ý vncerteine for- ,,
tune neuer constant to any,hath in such maner shewed hir ,,

G.ij.   selfe

„ felfe cruell and aduerfe to mee, that fhæ onely not fuffifed
„ with the death which my father and mother, and many
„ of their fubiectes haue receiued for my fake, fhe ceafeth
„ not dayly to afflict me, and to bring me to fo lowe an eb,
„ that being defeated of mine owne inheritaunce, I am yet
„ faine to wander through the courtes of mightie princes
„ to finde fome good and pitifull knight, which bewaylinge
„ my mifhap, will eafe me of the great trauaile I dayly take
„ to faue my honour. For if you will fuffer me to lay open
„ my cafe, the whole ftorie is thus. I am right enheretrix
„ of ÿ Iland of Cypres, where my predeceffors reigned long
„ time with much ioy, vntill that their good hap was hin-
„ dred by my beautie. For hauing brought me into thys
„ world, with ÿ beautie wherin you fee me, which I would
„ to our gods had either perifhed when I firft was fwad-
„ led, or els had neuer bene knowen, that none might haue
„ taken delight in it, fo foone as my beautie was founded a-
„ broade, this knight heere prefent, king of the Zardians,
„ Lord of the Iland of Zardia called Raiartes, hearing of it
„ came to fée me, and fo foone as he came, he was taken with
„ my loue, and demauding me for wife, was denied it of my
„ father. Wherfore very angry retourning to his Iland of
„ Zardia, with a great army of knights he came againft
„ my father, & at the firft field killed him and murthered al
„ his people, and in fhort time became Lord of Cypres, my
„ mother féeing my father dead, and hir land wafted, dyed
„ for griefe. I remained alone without company till fuche
„ time as Raiartes came to the pallaice where I was. I
„ knew to whofe power I was become feruaunt, & fearing
„ that he would haue forced me, determined by endinge my
„ life to make my felfe frée from his fubiection, eftéeming it
„ farre better to die with my parentes, then aliue to be-
„ waile their deathes, and hauing no better leafure nor
„ meanes to achieue my purpofe, I leaped vp to a window
„ the higheft in all the pallaice, thence to haue throwne
„ my felfe downe, if Raiartes feing me in this plight had not

prayed

prayed me not to doe it, promising if I forbeare that, to „
doe the thing that I commaunded him. I resoluing vpon „
death told him ý vnlesse he graunted me one gift, I would „
be mine owne executioner: he to saue my life, promised it „
wherby I left off from putting ý in practise which I had „
contriued in my thought. By this meanes Kaiartes had „
me in his power, & hauing the whole Iland at his com- „
maundement, bee carryed me contrary to my will into „
his owne countrey, with these aged knightes my nære „
kinsmen, there he requested me of loue, and praied me to „
accept of him for husband. What should I doe he was „
importunate in his demaund, & I remained in his daunger „
so that to put by the execution of his desire, I had none o- „
ther remedy but to aunswere him that so soone as he had „
performed the promise which he made mée, I woulde „
satisfie his whole entent. This hearing he was wel con- „
tent, and so I tolde him that bee should carry me for the „
space of a xij. month into all places whether I would, & „
if in the meane time I founde a knight to defende my „
right by fighting against him, he should graunt the bat- „
taile with condition, that if my knight vanquished him, „
I should be frée frō his demaund, and my land at quiet, „
otherwise if he had the vpper hand, I from thence forth „
to be at his commaundement, and he doe what euer liked „
him. This knight most noble Souldan, counselling with „
his strength, and thincking all mens vertues inferiour to „
his, tooke vpon him the quest, glad by such meanes to „
manifest his power, and so he carryed me from the I- „
land Zardia, more then halfe a yeare past, in which time „
yet I haue not founde a knight to vndertake my qua- „
rell, and yet I haue bene in the courtes of mightie kings, „
and other great Lordes: Now séeing the terme sette be- „
twéene vs is more then halfe expired, for my laste re- „
fuge hether am I come to thy court to proue if hære my „
good fortune should be such that I should finde in it that „
which I haue so long sued for in other courts. Here she

ended

ended with sighes and sobs out of measure, thereby vttering the sorrow she had in hir heart, and the griefe for to
loue such a knight, which moued great compassion in both
Souldan and others of his companie. But there was no
knight which would aunswere for the Princesse Radamira, that was hir name, and yet there were many in the
Souldans presence. Then in great pride and with a fierce
,, looke this terrible Raiartes spake vnto hir. What knight
,, is there in the world so foole hardy and presumptious Ra-
,, damira, which for thy cause durst enter listes with me, yea,
,, be it that both right and iustice were right and clære on
,, his side, and art thou not quite deuoide of reason to leue
,, vndoits, that which I besæch thee besides balewing thy
,, bæutie with my brauery, and thy pride with my puissance,
,, I shall sæme to set to lowe a price on my selfe if I enioye
,, thæ, & if ther be any knight here which will say y contra-
,, ry, I wil sœne make him recant his folly. Raiartes hauing
said thus, knit his browes and made such a grimme countenaunce that all they feared him which behelde him, and
ther was not a knight ther so hardy as to aunswere any
thing in the Princesse Radamiras behalfe, as if it had bene
mære sinne in a gentlewoman straungers right, to hazard
their person vpon a diuell rather then vpon an humaine
creature. Euery man was still to the no little griefe of the
Souldan in that his court receiued such disgrace, but the
gentleman of the Sunne sitting by and moued with compassion towards the gentlewoman, arose on his fæte, and
,, made aunswere to Raiartes, saying. Sir knight it is a
,, great blasphemy to knighthœde, to say that in the whole
,, world there is not a knight which dare fight with thæ.
,, Thy lye is loude, and thou doest against all reason enforce
this princesse to marry thæ. Be thou sure that if I were
a knight, I would suffer a thousande deathes rather then
,, such reproch should be offered to a gentlewoman. For thy
browne beautie is not fitte to be hir playfellowe, and
,, sayinge thus hee set himselfe downe agayne. Raiartes
madde

madde angry fo2 these wo2des, tourning towardes him, and rolling his eyes with greate rage, aunswered . If theu wert as stronge as thou art foolishe, theu weake younlinge, I woulde make thy life and thy wo2des ende at one time. But they say commonly, that women and those which are not able to weare armour, are p2iuiledged fo2 their speach : and maye talke without controlment, and so Raiartes lefte him . But the couragious gentleman not bæinge able to beare that contumely, in his anger rose from where he sate, and comming to the Souldan knæled befo2e hun besæching his grace to graunte this, one suite, the firste which in his life time he had made . The Souldan little thinckinge what he would aske , and louing him so well, that what thing he demaunded, it should haue ben graunted, willingly sayd, yea, and bad him say on what it was that he desi2rd. The gentleman of the Sunne sayd, my Lo2d, ÿ which I require is, that you make me knight, bicause it is highe time that I receiue it. I doe not thincke my selfe so young as to put vp w2ong at any mans hande . Those which were p2esent, were much troubled at the request of the gentleman of the Sunne, fo2esæing the ende which was to aunswere the bolde Raiartes, ‡ the Souldan was greatly so2ie to haue bene so rash in making p2omise befo2e he had knowen his suite, wherefo2e he sate still without speakin1, yea, o2 no, diuising onely, how to satisfie the young gentleman, and to quite himselfe of his p2omise. The gentleman of the Sunne doubting least the Souldan woulde linger and delay the time very angerly sayd vnto him. If I can not obteine this at your hands my Lo2d, I sweare by the high Gods that during my life I shall not bæ merry, and I will goe serue some other Lo2de which mo2e liberally will consider of my requestes. The great Souldan loth to disquiet the gentleman of the Sunne whome hæ sawe attent vppon this matter, albeit is p2omise græued him much , aunswered him thus sayinge.

„ Aſſuredly Donzel del Febo, if you had demaunded any o-
„ ther thing of me moꝛe pꝛofitable foꝛ your ſelfe, doubt you
„ not but you had bene in poſſeſſion of your deſire by thys
„ time, yea, had it bene the greateſt part of my kingdome.
„ But bicauſe J ſee you are of tender years, & that the time
„ is not yet foꝛ you to ſuppoꝛt the burthen of armour , J
„ would wiſh you to refraine and let fall your ſuite foꝛ this
„ time, oꝛ if you will not otherwiſe be perſwaded, holde
„ you, J yæld vnto you, watch this night in your armour .
„ and to moꝛrowe at day bꝛeake J will giue you the oꝛder. The gentleman of the Sunne tooke him at ẙ woꝛd,
& very ioyfully kiſſed the Souldans hand foꝛ his gracious
fauour. Then frõ thence by ſoft paces, cõming to Raiartes,
„ he ſayd vnto him. Nowe ẙ J haue licenſe to parle with
„ thæ as a knight, J will aunſwere thæ Raiartes, to the
„ woꝛdes which thou haſt ſayd vnto me, and ſo J tell thæ
„ that if the Pꝛinceſſe Radamira, will put hir quarell into
„ my handes, J will defend hir right, and take the battayle
„ vpon mæ, and be it that the Pꝛinceſſe Radamira dare not
„ commit hir right vnto me, yet J ſay, that to be auenged on
„ thy repꝛochfull ſpeaches which thou haſt blowed foꝛth,
„ J will fight with thæ, and make thæ to knowe that thou
„ art moꝛe vniuſt and fooliſh, then valiant and courteous,
„ as knightes ought to bæ. The gentleman of the Sunne
here ended, and the grimme fier Raiartes began a laughter
„ with theſe woꝛdes. In dæde if all folly were foꝛce, many
„ knights were couragious & ſtrong, foꝛ moſt of thẽ are to
„ to ventrous, and if thy ſelfe wert of as great habilitie as
„ thou art of foꝛwardneſſe, the Pꝛinceſſe Radamira ſhould
„ ende hir quarell by to moꝛrowe night, but theu deceiueſt
„ thy ſelfe , and albeit J am halfe aſhamed to take the
„ battaile againſt a knight neuer befoꝛe acquainted with
„ armour, yet bicauſe thou ſhalt not want due coꝛrection
„ foꝛ thy follie, J accept the battaile which thou offereſt,
„ as well foꝛ the one cauſe as foꝛ the other. As this talke
was at the hotteſt betwæne them, the pꝛinceſſe Radamira
beheld

beheloe the gentleman of the Sunne very earneſtly, noting as well his yeares as his perſon, and albeit he was
then beardleſſe. Yet ſhe thus conceiued of him that
he was of noble courage, and very ſtronge, and beſides
this ther appeared in his face ſomewhat which ſhe iudged moze then manlike. And as ſhe was wiſe, ſo hir heart
gaue hir that this younge gentleman had ſome diuine
blonde in him which ſhe thought to haue diſcended from
ſome of hir falſe Gods. So neither lightly noz wanton-
ly mouing but with great diſcreation and wiſedome ſtanding in ꝑ ſame place, ꝝ muſing what ſhe ought to do in ꝑ
ende, no other knight anſwering ꝑ challenge foz hir, not
altogether out of hope, ſhee agrœde to put hir quarrell into his handes by deliberate counſayle, conclu-
dinge, if hee were murthered hir ſelfe to followe after,
and ſo ſhe ſpake to the Gyant on this wiſe. Raiartes ſithe „
this gentleman with ſo good will pzofereth himſelfe to „
maintaine my right againſt thœ, I am very well content „
to put my quarrell into his handes, and from this time „
fꝏzth I will not ſœke other knight. The beautifull pzin- „
ceſſe Radimira doing thus, the fierce Raiartes was ſoze „
moued to ſœ that ſhe made ſo little account of him, and
ſo much truſted the boldenes of the young gentleman, and
foming at the mouth lyke a wylde boare he was not a-
ble to ſpeake one wozd foz the fury and choller which boy-
led in him. The gentleman of the Sunne thancked hir
gꝏly foz the acceptation of his paines in hir name. In
this manner the battell was put off till the next day, but
the gentleman of the Sunne was not ſo glad, to haue occaſion offered to be made knight, as the Souldan and
his friends were ſozrowefull, to haue him fall into this
daunger, which they imagined to be to tꝏ ſure, bicauſe of
the ſtrength of Raiartes, and the youth of the gentleman
of the Sunne. They thought it a deſperate caſe foz him
to wage this battayle, with the ſauegarde of his honour.
Then the young gentleman Clauergudo being of moze

yeares

yeares then Donzel del Febo was, repented that hée had
not annswered for the Princesse, both bicause he thought
it a blemish in his honour to haue excused himselfe from
such a matter, and his age was more then Donzel del
Febos was, and so might better acquite himselfe against
the force of Raiartes, & especially fearing the perill of his
friende, he would néedes haue taken the battayle out of
his handes, but perceiuing the vnwillingnesse of the gentleman of the Sunne he would speake no more in it. At
sunne set Florion came from hunting, and hearing of the
battayle which was appoynted he was very sad for Donzel del Febos sake, bicause of Raiartes force, and Donzels weakenesse, and so he tooke vpon him to perswade
Donzel del Febo to giue ouer the battayle, and put it vppon some other in his right if it so pleased him. But Florion & Clauergudo wer both beguyled in Donzel del Febo,
albeit either of thē wer such knights as of ý one hath ben
rehersed & of ý other shalbe shewed you hereafter. Raiartes
was strōg as his lyke scarcely among ý Pagans, & it might
be it woulde ill haue proued with them two, as a man
would haue sworne it only by ý tencur of Raiartes countenaunce, no man beholding him but wyth the same good
wyll which they beare vnto the Diuill. And if Florion
and Clauergudo desired this battayle it is to be thought
it sprang of theire loue towardes Donzel del Febo
rather then of any comforte theire courage gaue them to
winne honour in the battayle. But the day was spente,
and things necessary for the battayle were in prouiding.
At night Lyrgandeo the wise comming from the red I-
land, tooke landing at Babilon, and méeting with the gentleman of the Sunne he told him ý manydaies had passed
since he knew of the conflicte betwene Raiartes and him
and therefore had brought certeine armour for him, and
so he commaunded his squiers to vntie their two packets,
out of the one packet Lyrgandeo tooke a white armour
wrought with beames of golde descending from his helmette,

mette, wherein was grauen a face so faire and shœne, that
it shedded out beames as the Sunne, and scarcely for the
brightnesse might a man beholde it , and out of the same
he tœke out a sworde all garnished with golde and embossed with precious stone, ȳ pomell, scabard & chape being
so rich and curious , that none there was which praysed
not the workemanship. Out of the other packet he drewe
out an other white armour pounced with Floure de Luces
of golde , and an other sworde , both which he gaue to
Clauergudo, bestowing the other vpon Donzel del Febo.
With these gœd armours the two gentlemen were well
apayde , especially the gentleman of the Sunne , which
more esteemed of this gifte then of al the segniories of the
earth. And so he continued hys charge for the morrowe
battayle, very confident on his owne parte , but te the no
little dismaye of his friends, chiefly of the Princesse Balisea which woulde not hys destruction for all hir fathers
landes . The Princesse Radamira, in the meane time not
fully settled in hir thought droue out ȳ night neither merrely nor dumpishly, but very heuily as abhorring nothing
so much as ȳ company of Raiartes. Hir flesh would tremble often & quake for feare , mistrusting Donzel del Febos gœd Fortune for ȳ perfecting of his charge, his yeres
being cleane contrary to al gœd hope.

¶Donzel del Febo is dubbed knight, and ouercommeth
  Raiartes.   Cap.xxj.

The next daye in the morning , the gentleman of the
sunne, with hys rich harnesse buckeled about him,
was brought before ȳ Souldan & all the knights & gentlemen in ȳ court. When he was thus brauely armed he shewed greater and stronger then he dyd vnarmed, & none of
them which saw him would haue iudged him of so young
years. And when he came before ȳ Souldan thus accompanyed w all ȳ principall knights & gentlemen of ȳ court, the
                                                  gentle

gentleman of the Sunne knæled downe, and humbly craued to be made knight. The Souldan with teares flowing
from his eyes embraced him, greatly reioycing to se him
so comly in armour, then taking ye rich sword which ye youg
gentleman helde naked in his hande, he gaue him three
blowes on the creste of his helmette, and so sheathing it
againe, gyrded it about Donzel del Feboes loynes, and
with these wordes blessing him. (The high Gods defend
thæ with their mightie hande) he bad him arise knyght,
and then made hym sweare to the obseruaunce of all the
orders of knighthoode, which done the young gentleman
kyssed the Souldans hande, and all the hall range with
the noyse. Our gods defend the Souldan.

This was in the morning but before dinner was
cleane done and ye tables taken vp, the houre was neere
wherein they ought to perfourme the battayle, and
Raiartes richly armed and mounted vpon his horse tra-
uersed vp and downe before ye pallayce, wher the Ladyes
which were bestowed in the windowes to beholde the
fight were afrayd, for in their seeming by the hugenesse
of his body and his fierce countenaunce he was the bra-
uest knight in ye world, & his harnes couered in him ye de-
formities of nature. The Princes Radamira in hir mour-
ning weede accompanying the Princesse Balisea, was in
a great bay windowe, and seeing Raiartes so great, strong,
and well horsed, she chaunged hir colour without hope to
remoue Raiartes loue, and there fully appoynted wyth
hir selfe rather to murther hir selfe then to be in his power, for his filthy and vgly shape was such, that what
gentlewoman in the worlde could haue asseured hym
for loue?

When the Souldan and other knights toke their seats
as iudges of the field the Knight of ye Sunne departing
from the pallaice, was conducted by diuers knyghtes to
his tent and there sitting vpon a lustie courser he praunced a whyle before the Souldan, hys horse was all couered
with

with rich harnesse, in which were enchased sundrye precious stones, all both horse and harnesse of the Souldans gyfte, himselfe being clad with his bright armour his vmberere pulled down, and a mightie speare in his hande, so bigge as they all meruayled at his good making. When Cheualiero del Febo stayed, Raiartes drewe nere, and with a proude voyce sayd vnto him. Thou presumptious „ knight, what wouldst thou giue now not to be here alone „ with me: doest thou not thincke it no wisedome to aduen- „ ture thy body wher ther is no hope of safety. Assuredly Ra- „ iartes aunswered the Knight of the Sunne, hetherto I „ haue not sene the thing wherefore I should repent me of „ my enterprice, and hetherto I haue had more experience „ of thy vayne and foolish wordes then of thy great and ba- „ lyauntprowesse. Raiartes was sel angry at this (the foame storing through his visour) would haue runne vppon the knight, but being awarded by ỹ Iudges to the lists while the trumpetts sounded, he groned out thus muche to him selfe in the cursing of his Fortune. Oh how doth Fortune enuie my felicitie in prolonging the time thus that I cannot so soone as I wold dispatch this wretched knight saying this and somewhat els the trumpetts stayed, and with great rage he ranne towardes the Knighte of the Sunne, but the knighte bearing his shælde before him, with his speare in his hande met Raiartes with all his force, with the violence of this course, the grounde shooke vnder their horses, and this first iourney brast their great speares into small shiuers. Raiartes with the strong encounntry of the Knight of the Sunne, doubled and fell ouer the arson of the saddle, his horse carying him out of the prease, to blush without company for neuer in his life time had he receiued the lyke blowe. But when he recouerd his seate, and saw the Knighte of the Sunne not stirred in his saddle, and now with his sword in his hand comming toward him, he drew out his sword which was broad and heauy, in great choller to receiue him, thinking

for

for a suretie with the edge of his sworde, to supply that which had failed in the poynt of his speare. Both of them madde angry, Raiartes to amend that which he had mard in breaking his speare, and the knight of the Sunne to reuenge the prowde wordes which Raiartes had spoken, their first blowes were such that their pauises wer hewen a sunder, and fell to the ground the other part they after threwe from them and griping their swordes in both their handes, they hitte eache other such blowes vppon the helmette that flakes of fire issued after them. By this time neither of these knights were well pleased with the other, and they let dryue so each at other that in shorte space they made plain their singuler mãhods, & they which sawe it iudged it to be the brauest battayle which they had euer seene betwẽen two knights. The valiant knights with malicious eies sorrowing each at others welfare, because their armour was so good that no sword would enter, were much more woode laying about thẽ without order, and caring not where they hit, so they might see the bloud spin as fast as the sparcles encreased.

It was now halfe an houre since the battaile began, and Raiartes well feeling the courage of the knight of ẏ Sun, in that he had gotten none aduauntage ouer him in all ẏ time. Nowe with what courage foughte he thincke you, beeing besides himselfe for the desire of the Lady, at that time he doubted whether this were the gentleman of the Sunne, whom before he had continued, and if it wer not he, yet he meruailed in himselfe who this valiãt knight might bee, in the meane while ẏ Souldan & Florion with all the beholders of the battaile were estonished at the great prowesse and valour which the knight of ẏ Sun shewed against Raiartes. They thought truely ẏ he would proue the best knight of the world, sith in so tender years he was of great vertue. The Princesse Radamira which loked on this battaile before, halfe against his wil for fear, now viewing how wel hir knight had behaued himselfe a-

gainst

gainſt hir enemie, with greater ioy and hope ſhe gaſed
on him & often prayed hir gods to graunt him ẏ victory.
But as I tolde you Raiartes ſæing his aduerſary ſo vali-
antly beare himſelfe againſt him, and not being able to
gouerne his ill will he liſte him ſelfe vp in his ſtirops and
lent the knight of the Sunne a blowe with all his force,
that although he could not cut his fine helmette, yet he
made him bowe his head to his horſenecke, being blyn-
ded with the continuall ſparkes of fire which came out of
his headpæce. The worthy knight of the Sunne comming agayne to himſelfe and ſitting ſurer in his ſaddle,
retourned the lyke blow to Raiartes,ſo that Raiartes loſt
his memorie and receiued an other blowe on his bulke a-
gaynſt the ſaddle bowe, which made the bloud guſhe out
of his mouth and noſtrells,and the knight of the Sunne
followed him to haue vnhorſed him. But Raiartes recouered, and ere the knight of the Sunne coulde hit him,
he gaue him on the leſte ſhoulder a mightie blowe, that
with the weight thereof he had falne to the grounde but
for the embracing of his horſe necke.Againe Donzel del
Febo repayed him with a plus vltra, the ſurpluſage more
then an ordinary intereſt, and they wounded each other
mangling themſelues pitifully,& the claſhing of their armour was ſo great,that it rang lyke bells in all the citie.

This was the ſecond houre of the fight,and the mach
was equall not being knowne whe had the better hand.
Raiartes not greatly pawſing, but in his anger reuiling
his gods ſayd vnto himſelfe. Oh immortall gods, howe „
little is Raiartes beholding vnto you if a man is able to „
reſiſt his might? why? if the report of my valyant dædes „
and noble proweſſe made knowne in the heauens cauſeth „
you to maligne my ſtate,come you downe and fight with „
me, for I had rather be vanquyſhed by your Deities „
then to be yelded to mans ſtrength. But what can I „
thincke, either then that this knighte is one of „
you, for the loue of Radamira to take hir ryghts „

in

,, in hande , o2 at the leaſt ſome finde of hell in lyke▪
,, neſſe of a knight minded to quell me . But ſeing this is
,, the iſſue that if I loſe the day, I muſt looſe Radamira al-
,, ſo , let him winne hir and weare hir, fo2 be he what he
,, may be, he ſhall get no honour at my hands, and ſo ſaying , he ſtroke his aduerſary ſo ſo2e on the b2eſt, that he
b2uſed his curaſſe and put him in great daunger. Cheualiero del Febo not a little abaſhed at the great fo2ce of Raiartes this being the firſt battayle that euer he had fought,
thought in himſelfe that if all the knights in the wo2lde
were lyke him he ſhould get but ſmall p2ayſe , and there-
fo2e to embolden his courage he rated himſelfe on thys
,, wiſe. Am I he of whome the wiſe Lyrgandeo hath fo2e-
,, told ſo much? am I he without whom ẙ Babilonians dare
,, not ſet foote into Perſia? am I he fo2 whome they haue
,, thus long time wayted ? Certaynly if this be all which
,, I ſhalbe able to do, ſhal not all happe̅ co̅trary to ẙ which
,, the wiſe man hath ſayd: ſhall not ẙ Babilonians be moc-
,, ked of their hope: hath not one only knighte much enda-
,, maged me: what ſhall ẙ whole multitude of the Perſians
,, do, ⁊ the puiſſaunce of ẙ G2ants which ſhal come to aſſiſt
,, them: Had it not bene better fo2 my credit not to haue
,, bene bo2ne with ſo great fame as the Aſtrologers haue
,, fo2 ſhewed, then in ſo ſho2t a time ſo much to be troubled.
,, O Souldan of Babilon and you others which are Iudges
,, of the fieldе, are you not aſhamed of me that in my firſte
battayle, and the firſt fruites of my knighthoode, I am at
·: the poynt to become recreaunt. But recreaunt I wyl ne-
· uer be, and ſo as it were blowing the coales of his anger,
when he was on a lightfire he ſet Raiartes in ſuch a heat,
⸱ with his thicke and mightie ſtrokes , that the vnlacing
of his helme and the vnmaylig of his armour could ſcare
· giue him b2eath inough . Raiartes then thought that his
enemyes ſtrength encreaſed, yet not altogether ſown-
dered, he aunſwered him as well as he coulde, that the
battayle ſeemed to be mo2e fierce at that time then at the
be-

beginning.The houre clock hath smitten thrice,since they
entered the listes,all much mervailing how they were a-
ble to endure so long.The Souldan said to Florion ꝭ to ẏ „
wise man which sate by,certeinly if I had not seene it w̄ „
my eyes,I should hardly haue beleeued ẏ a knight of so „
young yeares,as this knight of the Sunne is,might haue „
had the force so to endaunger a worthy knight,for you „
knowe howe ẏ houres are passed since they began ẏ com- „
bate,and how yet he abideth many blowes,ꝭ still seemes „
as fresh as he was whē he first came forth.The wiseman „
aunswered,yea my Lord,but if you knew with whom he „
doth fight,you might with more reason mervaile at it.For „
Raiartes is one of the strongest ꝭ worthyest knights that „
is among the Pagans,and his pride is so great ẏ he alone „
would not refuse to ioyne with all C.knights,and would „
well thincke to haue the mastery of them all,before hee „
would be taken. Thus the bench was not idle,ꝭ the prin- „
cesse Radamira very busely attended vpon hir knight,and
watched euery tourne,more then halfe ioyfully,speaking
thus vnto the Princesse Balisea standing by.I beleue for „
a certeintie Princesse Balisea,that our high Gods now at „
length closed with my mishaps,haue prouided this knight „
for me,for in respect of his beautie ꝭ great bountie he see- „
meth rather heauenly then terrestriall. Yea,so I thincke, „
then aunswered the Princesse Balisea,and that not onely „
for your succour,but to ayde me and my cause ẏ gods haue „
sent him hether,for by him I looke to be Queene of Persia. „
Do you so madame said Radamira,now I pray our gods „
that he well escape this battaile,to fulfill your hearts de- „
sire,and truely if he become victour,not onely I shall bee „
auenged on him for my fathers death,but I will make „
account that I am nowe risen from death to life , for „
sooner had I purposed to kill my selfe , then to lye in Ra- „
iartes armes. „

　But all this while the good knights plyed the combat, „
fighting couragiously till they were sorewearied, euery

one misconstruing the euent. For Raiartes seeing that the longer the battaile lasted, the farther he was from ý victo= ry, with all the force he might, he stroke the knight of the Sunne such a blowe on the helmet that his sences were bereft him, & had he not taken holde of the saddle bow, he had kissed the ground. So the fray was renued, but the knight of ý Sunne gaue Raiartes an other blow as strong which bewitched his vnderstanding, for his horse carried him about the field, tossing him on the pomell of his sad= dle as if he had bene dead. The knight of ý Sunne think= ing it no glory to smite a man halfe deade, pursued him not, but Raiartes reuiuing his face all bloudie, with both his handes, hit the knight of the Sunne vpon the head= peece, that if the helme had not bene the surer, it had riuen him to the belly, but the stroke amased him, & the goare bloud ranne out of his mouth and nostrels, and his horse feeling part of the great blowe carried his master from thence, the good knight lying vpon the crouper of his horse in an extasie as if he had bene quite dead. Raiartes hasted to haue giuen him an other blowe , those which sawe it were very sad, but none were euer so wofully begon, as was the princesse Radamira who with great griefe tour= ning hir selfe from that sight, and fel on weeping bitterly. But Raiartes had not followed him iiii. paces with his horse, when the good knight start vp, and feeling his face wet with bloud, in great fury spurred his horse, and met Raiartes with such a blowe, ý the fine helmet could not denie him passage, but that he cloue Raiartes head in sun= der. Heere ý shute of ý peole & the princes Baliseas calling hir awaked the princesse Radamira as it had ben out of a sound sleepe, and little looking for so good newes : and the good knight, (Raiartes being dead) put vp his sword into the sheth, and demaunded of the iudges if ther were ought else to do to make the Princesse free . The Prin= cesse hearde this gladly, and the iudges aunswered hym noe, for that suffised which hee had done . Then with
the

the noise of instruments, and much honour, the iudges led the knight of the Sunne from that place to the pallaice where with great ioye and pleasure of the Souldan and Florion, hée was well receiued, they shewing as muche good wyll to him, as if they had neuer inoughe in making of him. The gentlemen, Clauergudo, and Brandizel, glad of their friends conquest holpe to vnarme him. Then ye princesse Balisea came & the princesse Radamira, owinge hir duetie to the knight of the Sunne, and as not able else to requite the curtesie he had shewen hir, shée offered to him both hir landes and hir person the better to serue him. Thus they tooke their rest many dayes, and the good knight was much honoured of them all. And there was a great feast made, and diuers iustes and turneys there proclaymed, for the dubbing of Clauergudo and other gentlemen knightes. At this feast, the Prince Clauergudo behaued him best, so that all men iudged him to bée a valiant knight. And after this, the Princesse Radamira minding to retourne, desired a safe conduct of the Souldan, who sent with hir an hundred knights, and other men of warre which sawe hir safely landed in hir countrey, and in full possession of the crowne. For after they knewe that Raiartes was dead, willingly they gaue hir place, and the Princesse remained Lady of it, although not very frée of hir thought from the knight of the Sunne whom she loued so well that in long time she forgate him not. And it fell out so that in the ende shee pleasured hym, wherefore hee gaue vnto hir a myghtie Prince for husbande, as shall bée declared héereafter.

¶ Africano king of Media and Persia, inferred warre vpon the Souldan of Babilon. Cap. 22.

The historie hath tolde you before ye the strong & mightie Africano transporting frō Africk into Asia by his force & valiaunce made himselfe Lord & king of Media, and after entered into the kingdome of Persia, conquered it, and ouerthrew Florion comming to succour his owne people, after which time ý prince Florion reculing back to Babilon, there remained very sorowful, and without hope to recouer his kingdome. Now the story retourneth to the same Africano, and saith, that when he had appeased the people and brought these two kingdomes in quiet subiection, (as this is an inbecilitie of mans nature, euer coueting to amplifie and enlarge cur possessions) so this stoute and proud Pagan not content with that which he had already got by disorder and rapine, he aduentured yet farther to winne Babilon, with all the kingdomes of the Assirians bordering in those parts, reckening himselfe already in possession of them, for the power of the Souldan was in sufficient to repulse his forces, hoping moreouer to ad his dominions, all those countries lying in the coast of the middle earth sea. For this cause he assembled his power as well Medians, as other his subiects. Hauing this great army in a readinesse, yet trusting more in his owne person then in all his people, he tooke the way toward Babilon, minding not to stay till he came nære to Babilon. This was some dayes after the combat which the knight had with Raiartes. And as it fell out, it was at the same time as the Souldan and ý Prince Florion were deuising of ý order which they should take for to recouer the kingdome of Persia, that the newes came how the puissant Africano was on his way with a huge army toward Babilon, for which cause they were cast into double doubts, seeing that the enimy whom they purposed to finde abroad, came to sæke them at their owne dores. Well with greate care and diligence they began to prepare all things necessarie for the welcomminge of such a ghest, by gatheringe his people out of all partes of the kingdome, raysinge the walles hygher, and fortifyinge the towers once builded by Semiramis, all whiche woulde little haue

helped

helped the great Babilon againſt the power of Africano, if the puiſſant arme of the young Greke, had not defended it. But thus the Aſsirians were almoſt at their wittes ende, not knowing howe to repell him, for the bruite of his fame was greatly noyſed. The Souldan of Babilon well experimented in warfare, commaunded all whiche could beare armour to come to Babilon that his forces béeing vnited, hée might bée of greater power agaynſt his enimies, Africano ſtayed not till hée came to the very walls of Babilon, where he gladly beheld the citie, bicauſe of the fame it had to be ſo great & ſo well peopled, he highly commended of the ſumptuous edifices & high wals encloſing it, which enflamed his deſire to the Lord of it. Preſently he made to pitch his tents in a large field, enuironing the wals as farre as he might, for it was impoſſible to compaſſe them round about with two of Xerxes armies, he had in his camp. 20000. knights, &. 30000. horſemen, & two ſtrong giants beſide, the one of them called Herbyon, & the other Dardario through whoſe force hée thought to haue ouercome the Aſsirians. So ſoone as he had trenched round about his camp. and prouided for the ſafegard of his army, before he would enterpriſe any farther, he ſent a meſſenger with a letter to ẙ Souldan, conteining this that followeth.

J the great and mightie Africano king of Media and Perſia, ſend gréeting vnto thée Souldan of Babilon, ſon of Orixerges. Know that the report of thy citie of Babilon, hath procured me to cut the ſeas, & to arriue in this countrey, rather with deſire to haue it as mine owne, then for any pleaſure to offend thy perſon or moleſt thy people, for thy father and mine during their liues wer great friends, which friendſhippe J would willingly ſhould endure betwéene vs, if ẙ wilt as willingly ſatiſfie my deſire, albeit J am content in recompence thereoff, to giue thée ẙ kingdome of Perſia or Media, chuſe thée whether. Nowe thou knoweſt my whole meaning, faile not to accopliſh my deſire

Africanoẜ letter.

ſtre,foʒ vnleſſe I haue it with thy good wil, I wil foʒce thée therebnto maugre thy ill will. Farewell.

The meſſenger comming to the gates of ỹ citie was let in, and being bʒought vnto the pallaice,he deliuered ỹ letter to the Souldan in the pʒeſence of Pʒince Florion, and the other knights of ỹ court.The letter was read,and they all ſaid that in great pʒide the Pagan had ſo wʒitten,but biꝰ cauſe pʒince Florion ꝉ the moſt part of thoſe which were there,knew the ſtrength and power of Africano in ỹ batꝰ tailes foʒepaſſed,they would not make anſwere noʒ ſpeak a woʒd vntil they had heard ỹ Souldans minde.Bæing in this oʒder all huſht,the knight of the Sunne roſe vp,and demaunded liſence of the Souldan to giue anſwere to the meſſenger.The Souldan graunted it him,then the knight of the Sunne adnauncing his voice that it might be heard

” ſpake to the meſſenger thus. Retourne to thy Loʒd,foʒ it
” is now to late to aunſwere his letters,but in ỹ moʒning
” my Loʒd ſhall call his counſel ꝉ ſhal ſend thy Loʒd an anꝰ
” ſwere by one of his knights,to whõ he muſt giue credit in
” this behalfe.Thus ỹ meſſenger diſpatched from ỹ Souldan

went to his Loʒd,who little delighted in the foreſlowing of the Souldans anſwere,foʒ he leſſe waied the Souldans power.Therfoʒe he determined in few daies to deſtroy ỹ great citie,burning ꝉ waſting all,foʒ al that,that he wiſhed rather to haue bene owner of it by exchaunge oʒ couenant then by raſing and batterug the walles which were ſo goodly.The meſſenger auoiding the pallaice, ỹ knight of the Sunne directed his ſpeach to the Souldan in this wiſe.

Sith your excellencie wel vnderſtandeth ỹ arrogancie and

” high diſdaine of Africano,ꝉ hath giuen me in commiſſion
” to deuiſe ỹ aunſwere, I humbly beſæch your grace to be
” content therewith,if to moʒow in ỹ moʒning I alone take
” vpoñ me this meſſage to ſatiſfie him as ſhal ſæme beſt vnꝰ
” to me,ꝉ accoʒding as his pʒide deſerueth. When ỹ knight

had ſo ſaid,ỹ ſute which he made grœued the Souldan veꝰ ry much,although ỹ great exploites which he had already

done

done,and which were diuined to be done by him somwhat
abated his griefe,yet gretly preferring ý valour of Africa¿
no aboue ý which he had heard of al ý princes Paganes,for
there might none be compared to him,he put of ý knight of
the Sunne for that time with this answere,ý he would
not haue him to hazard himselfe in such daunger,vntil he
had growen to more ripe yeares.But if ý Souldan was in
any perplexity for loue to ý knight,much more was prince
Florion troubled which had had experience of Africanos
puissance,¿ had sæne Africano in his own person,demene
himself so lustely in ý battaile betwæne them,ý he thought
him to be vnparagonized for manhood,¿ therefore he was
more then vnwilling ý the knight shold alone dele in this
matter,albeit he had well ¿ worthely acquited himselfe a¿
gainst Brandafilco ¿ the strong Raiartes,for it was not a
thing couenient in his iudgement,ý he being as yet of ten¿
der years should proue his body vpon Africano.But were
it that ý Souldan ¿ the prince Florion were leth of this,as
at the first it appeared,yet they thought it best to dissem¿
ble their conceipts,least ý knight should take displeasure at
their little account of him,¿ therfore in the end,after some
consultation had with Lirgandeo,w a milde countenaunce
the Souldan agræd to ý knightes request,saying.That he
would put into his hands,both his honour ¿ the cause,to
the end ý he should aunswere Africano as best should like
him.The knight of ý Sun would haue kissed ý Souldans
hand,but ý Souldan imbraced him,¿ there it was solemp¿
ly enacted that the next morrow,the knight of the Sunne
should be ý onely messenger.Clauergudo,¿ the prince Flo¿
rion lay at him earnestly to beare thē in his company,but
he shifted them of with this,ý it behoued him to be alone
for the aunswere which he should giue to Africano.

The knight of the Sunne,maketh answer to *Africano* as to his letter.
                          Cap.23

At the day pæpe before the gray morning,the valiaut
   ¿ worthy knight of ý Sunne got him vp,in ý means
time while he ought to execute his charge,he armed him
                          H.iiij.   selfe

felfe with that armour which the wife Lyrgandeo had beſtowed on him,& ſo ſtaied a great while vntil it was paſt
bzoad day,euery minute in this time ſæming an houre,&
euery houre.xl.foz his magnanimus ſtomacke alwayes
coueted to put himſelfe in pzaiſe,where to exerciſe his valoure,and ſo when it was now time,caſting a faire hozne
about his necke tipt with golde,and hauing a hozſe vnder
him the beſt that the Souldan had,(as the night befoze he
had taken his leaue of the Souldan and the other knights
of the court), ſo he pziuely put himſelfe on his iourney,
without bæing ſæne of any of the courte , and makinge
thoſe gates of the citie to bæ opened which were ſhutte
to Africanos campe,hæ rode thzough, and by ſofte paces
comming within a bowe ſhot of Africanos owne tent,he
winded his hozne ſo loude, that it was eaſely hearde, in
both the enimies campe,and the citie of Babilon. Imme-
diately,the Souldan,the Pzince Florion,Clauergudo,and
other knightes cryed Alarme,and iſſued foorth of the gates
in battaile araye to ſæ what the good knight of the
Sunne woulde doe, and by and by the walles and highe
towers were full fraught with as well nobles as com-
munaltie. The king Africano in his tent buſied about o-
ther matters , hearing the ſhzilneſſe of the ſound was
ſomewhat diſquiet not thincking any knight to haue had
the hardineſſe to ſumon him to the battaile,and deſirous
to know who he was,he called befoze him one of the two
Gyants which came with him named Herbyon a ſtrong
man and king of the Camarians,a little region adioyning
,, to Media,to him he ſayd,take thy hozſe and armour,and
,, ride toward that knight which hath winded his hozne,
,, and faile not foz any entreatie to bzing him befoze vs,here
,, in our pzeſence to declare his meſſage.The grant hauing
his charge,delayed no time,but haſtely arming himſelfe
with fine ſtæle,he tooke a ſtrong ſpeare in his hand, and
rode toward the knight of the Sunne,who in the mydſt
way aboze his comming very glad,when he ſawe ſo great

a

a Gyaunt come against him, as desirous to purchase honour vpon his lykenesse. But the Gyant sayd vnto hym. What art thou knight so bolde and venturous, that hast in such wise disturbed our campe, wyth the noyse of thy hozne. The Knight of the Sunne replyed. I am a knight of ∫ Souldans which come to the king Africano to make him answer to the letter by him sent vnto the Souldan. Now returne you backe and tell him, I am here to dce my message, and if he will heare it bidde him come armed and well hozsed foz otherwise I will not make him answere. The Gyant very scoznfully tooke vp a great laugh≠ ter, and giuing the knight a litle sowce on the helmette with his gauntlet he sayd vnto him. Now I tell thee, that that thou arte the maddest knight in the wozlde to chal≠ lenge him to battayle, at the only hearing of whose name the greatest part of al Asia doth tremble, and if thou wert not a simple fole thou wouldest not in such soz diſcouer thine impotencie. If thou hast any message to the kynge Africano from the Souldan come with me and thou shalt be bzought to his pzeſence, foz he is not ſuch a one as to come into the fielde agaynst one ſely knight. The kynge Africano himſelfe muſt hear my meſſage ſayd the knight of the Sunne and he muſt heare it armed, foz otherwiſe I will not open it. The strong Herbyon was angrye at the knights wozdes and thincking him to be but as other knights were oz amongst the meaneſt he offered to haue ſet the knight beſide the ſaddle and ſo to haue dzawne him perfozce to ∫ king, ſhewing herein no leſſe pzide & diſdain then the greedy Fawlcon doth in the purſute of the ſim≠ ple Pigeon to carry it to the ayze among the young ones. But his lotte was farre otherwiſe, foz the knight perce≠ uing his entent tourned the poynt of his ſpere and strake him so strongly on the cheſt, that though his armour was god it entred a lyttle and left him windleſſe foz a time. Herbyon thought himſelfe now not well at eaſe, and therefoze retourning to himſelfe, he neuer studyed at

Y.b.   the

the courtesie of the knight in sparing him in his traunce,
but taking one part of the field and brochyng his horse
with the spurs, his speare being in the reste with deadly
rage he ranne against the knight of the Sunne, who was
nothing slow in the receipt. Their shocks were such in
their meeting that the heauy speare of the strong Herbyon brake into shyuers in ye fine helmet of the Knight of
the Sun, not diseasing him. But the knight of the Sunne
hit the Gyant with such dexteritie that he ouerthrew him
and the great wayght of his body made the Gyant weare
his necke on the to side lyke a fidler, which was no little
payne vnto him. Yet he gate vpon his feete rising with
,, much a doe. Then the Knight of the Sunne finding him
,, vprisen bad him defend himselfe. The Gyant aunswered
,, that he could not, therefore doe with me what you will.
,, The knight of the Sunne sayd. No, but retourne to the
,, kinge Africano thy Lorde and tell him that a knight of
,, the Souldans doth awayte him here to make aunswere
,, vnto his letter, and if so be he be minded to heare it, will
,, him in his armour to come foorth, for in no other order
will I vtter it. The Gyant answered he would doe it,
and not being able to sit on horsebacke, he was compelled
to go on foote through the campe, driuing in his thought
the remembraunce of the knights prowesse, so that hee
was perswaded that not twentie knights Assyrians could
haue done him so much harme as this one knighte had
done. The Souldan with the Princes Florion and Clauergudo wer no lesse amazed in their contemplation to beholde the euent of the first welcome, and they gaue great
thanckes to their gods for sending them so good a knight.
Herbyon came before the king Africano his Lorde, and
without fayling in any part declared to him that which
had chaunced with the knight, and the message which was
sent by him, moreouer telling the king that he thoughte
that knight to be the strongest knight in the worlde, for
that with these two blowes which he had giuen him, hee

had

had throwen hỳm to the grounde, and might haue killed him.

The king Africano not a lyttle ſorỳ to ſẽ ỳ ſtrõg Herbyon ſo ill entreated and abaſhed at the force of one only knight, would therebpon haue put on his armour to haue bene auenged on the knight and to heare his meſſage. But the other Gyaunt then in preſence called Dardario, and much about Herbyons pitch, being of no leſſe value then the firſt, in his choller menacing the knight, ſwore a great othe that he would bring the knight bound hand and fote vnto the king, wherfore taking a great horſe he paſſed through the campe and approching nẽre the Knight of the Sunne, he would not ſalute ỳ knight, but as his anger was throughly kindled, with a great ſpere as big almoſt as a Pyne trẽe, he prepared himſelfe for the carier. And the worthye Greeke knowing the Gyauntes errande dyd the lyke and ſpurring his horſe he came vnto the cloſe. The greate ſpeare of the Gyant was thought to haue perced the harneſſe of the knight, by reaſon of the few ſhyuers that it made but it did not ſo, and contrarywiſe the knights ſpeare couched with great derteritie entred through the body of the great Dardario a great parte of the ſtaffe appearing at the ſhoulders.

By this meanes the monſtrous Gyant fell dead from his horſe with ſuch a grone as the tall Cedars of Libanus make, being rent vp by the rote. The Babilonians reioyced exceedingly at this: but Africano was all enflamed wyth choller to ſẽ his Gyaunt ſlayne wyth one only blowe and knowing that to himſelfe alone this baſe was bidde, in great rage roſe from the ſeate where hee ſate, without ſpeaking a word, & entring into his tent armed himſelfe with ſure armoure, and choſe him a very ſtrong ſpeare, not tarying for ſquyer or page to helpe him.

In this anger he was ſo terrible that none of his people durſte come nẽre him, and ſo with a moſt fierce and cruell coũtenance he armed himſelfe. So ſone as ỳ Pagan had

had buckeled on his armour, immediatly ther was brought him a horse such a one as could haue carried tenne armed knights, as I thinke of the same bredth whereof the horse of Troy was. The trappings of the horse aswell golde as the stirops and all his armour set with precious stones, that he might well seeme a great Lord which was mayster of such armory, but this was the straungest sight that Africano set vpon so mighty a horse made him notwithstanding to bow & double vnder him. But to go forward Africano taking the greatest speare which might be had, rode with a softe pace towards the knight of the Sunne. The knight of the Sunne saw him come from amongst his people and thought presently that he was the kynge Africano aswell for his rich armour, and his horse so curiously barbed, as the talnesse of his personage which he very well noted to be not farre dissonant from the common report: so he beseeched his gods from his heart to be fauourable vnto him agaynst so strong a Gyant. Africano well biewed the knight of the sunne his stature and making, and vpon these premisses inferred thus much, that well might he be a man of much force which so well shewed it in his exteriour countenaunce, and much more in his dædes and balour. But comming nærer vnto the knight as his custome was little to regarde the whole worlde, so with a proud & disdaynfull boyce, he spake vnto y knight.

" Thou miserable & wretched knight, thou sayst thou art a
" messenger & bringest a message vnto me, thou hast slayne
" the Gyant Dardario and almost y strong Herbyon, which
" two had ben sufficient to haue bet downe y walles of Ba-
" bilon, I swear vnto thæ by my gods y if al y world were
" giuen me for thy ransome thou shouldst not escape y death.
" The knight of the Sunne embasing his boyce mildelye
" aunswered. If I haue had to doe with thy Gyants Afri-
" cano, they were occasioners of it themselues, for I came
" not hether to other purpose but to make the aunswere in
" the behalfe of the Souldan, and if I came onely to seeke
the

thæ thou oughtst to haue bene first which should haue presented hunselfe to mæ, and to haue heard what I would
haue fayd, and to haue heard mee as a messenger, and not
to attempt my death as a knowen enemy. Now that thou
art come Africano, I tell thæ why I am come, heare it if
thou wilt. The gods which haue preserued me from thy
Gyants haue reserued me to fight with thæ. But listen
on &c. Here the rage of the Pagan stopped the course of his
talke, and the mightie Africano smiting his hande on his
thighe for anger liste vppe his other hande also to haue
buffeted the knight, but a better minde ouertooke him that
he thought it reason to heare the Souldans aunswere before he should condempne the messenger, and so staying,
he bad him tell on quickly, for I will well punish thy offence whatsoeuer aunswere the Souldan sendeth mee.
The Knight of the Sunne wishing the battayle with all
his heart said. Then know thou Africano that thy letter
being receiued and reade in the presence of my Lorde the
Souldan, after consultacion had, my Lord sendeth thæ this
aunswer by me. Albeit before this time thou art notori-
ously defamed for a tyrant in that thou hast falsely & fraudu-
lětly enchreched vp many kingdoms, yet he neuer thought
thou wouldest haue enterpryfed the vsurpation of the
most sacred Assyrian Empyre, an Empyre consecrated to
the gods, and claymed by them as their right, and in their
righte gouerned by my Lordes auncestours as Liefete-
naunts to the gods and their Feefarmers, and therefore
though peraduenture the open wrongs done vnto men, the
gods doe often pardon and winke at, yet seldome leaue
they vnreuenged the iniuries offered to themselues, and
as it is to be thought so manifest a contempt of their deuine power shall not escape them. Besides for the citite
of Babilon, he letteth thee to vnderstande that thy selfe art
not ignoraunt that it is his and that he hath right to it as
heire to the king Orixerges his father on that part of his
laiewode, and that thou hast no title nor colourable shewe

fo

,, to demaund it . Wherefore if it be so ẙ thou wilt take
,, it against all reason from him, hee telleth thee that he can
,, no lesse doe then defend it from thee & the whole world,
,, for hauing right and iustice on his side , hee little feareth
,, the inuasion of man, deliuering his message in this forme
of words, the knight of the Sunne sayde. This is the
Souldans aunswere, and pausing a while, he began againe
,, thus. And I, Africano craued of my Lord to be the mes-
,, senger, for I would thou shouldst know how daügerously
,, thou offendest the diuine Gods in entering vpon ẙ king-
,, dome of Persia, and disenheriting the Prince Florion, the
,, legittimate and onely Lord of that kingdome. Now ther-
,, fore thou shouldest well doe , to surrender thy claime
,, into his hands, and contente thee with the reuenues al-
,, ready receiued, & the iniust deteining of his right so long
,, time. If thou wylt doe this not for my sake , but for the
,, high gods agaynst whom thou hast hainously trespassed,
,, thereby thou shalt pacifie the Gods and lose the name
,, of a tyrant, so odious and so detested amongest men. If
,, thou wylt styll perseuer in this thy tyrannicall obstina-
,, cy, I vtterly defie thee to ẙ death, and certifie thee ẙ either
,, I will slay a tyrant , or vpon a tyrant I will be slaine.
.Whilest the knight of ẙ Sunne amplified at large vpon
this point. Africano albeit very angry, yet marked him
from top to toe, waying with what confidency he had discharged his charge, sometimes quietly admonishing to a-
mend, & otherwise threatening & defying with a fierce semblaunce. But as he cared neither for God nor man, so he
swallowed vp ẙ knights words, reputing the knight for a
foole, for he thought his name only to able to afraye any
,, knight, thus he replied. Wer thy hands foolish knight as
,, good to fight, as thy tongue is fine in preaching, I would
,, not meruaile though thou hadst ẙ hardines to defame A-
,, tricano. But I wil curtal thy copie w this currish answer.
,, Prepare thee to ẙ battaile, & take this promise at my hand,
ẙ if I be ouercome, I wil leue to Florion not onely ẙ kingdome

donie of Persia but also all that which I my selfe haue of „
possessions in Asia, & so saying Africano made against the „
knight, but the knight of the Sunne wisely to order „
his affayres aunswered him saying. Stay a little Africa- „
no and heare that which I say. Thou knowest that alre- „
dy this day I haue twise fought with two of thy Gyants, „
and am forewcried, if now I fight with thee and thou sub- „
due me, what honour shalt thou get thereby? will not men „
say that thou tokest me at the aduantage, when I was „
hurt before or weryed as I am? Appoynt that our com- „
bat be to morrow, and that assurance be had of this con- „
dicion on either parts, & say thou the same before the prin- „
cipall of thy army, that if perhaps I should slay thee in „
this battayle, y Souldan should not neede to haue a newe „
skirmish with thy people. This deuise of the knight was „
sore against Africanos minde, for he would willingly haue
purged some parte of the choller which he brought with
him boiling in his stomack: but seing this auoidance could
not be at this time made with the warrantie of his honour, he graunted to the condicions, and thus aunswered
him. Let it be so as thou sayst, foolish knight, I wil do thee
a pleasure in delaying y time of reuenge of my knights
and thy foolish words, but sith I may not refraine my anger hauing thee before me, retourne hastely to y citie and
I will to my tent, & with this he tourned y raynes of his
horse & came to his pauilion wher he fed vpon melancholy
all the day, not speaking to any one. The Knight of y Sun
deffered y battaile till y next day, not for y he was wery,
but to aduertise y Souldan of y which was agreed vpon,
now y rather to assure himselfe retourned to y citie, wher
he was receiued w grat ioy & pleasure of all his friends,
& being within y pallaice he told y Souldan to what issue
he had brought y matter, he was very ioyfull by reson of
y wise Lyrgadeos prophecies which he hoped thee to be accomplished, & partly doutful of y succes, bicause prince Florion knew Africanos stregth was such, as few wer able to

resist it, he would haue had him not to deale in this aduenture alone, and requested him to ioyne vnto him some other companions, namely Prince Florion & Clauergudo, which themselues laboured greatly, but hee gaue them thanckes and excused himselfe with this that it was so decreed, but sayth he ther may be a time wherin you may employ your forces. For he knew the people of Africano to be so hardy that if perchaunce their Lorde shoulde be slayne or be in daunger, they would either succour theire Lord, or worke his reuenge vpon the conquerour. Therfore he willed them to bee in a readinesse . So these two knights gladly accepted that charge, and all that day chose out of the people , those which should the next day keepe the fielde with them to be at hande for succours to the knight if any treason should be compassed agaynst hym. The Knight of the Sunne tooke his reste merely till the day wherein he prospered as you shall now heare.

¶ A cruell battayle betweene the Knight of the Sunne and Africano, with the discomfiture of Africanos hoaste. Cap. xxiiij.

SO soone as the day appeared the noble Greeke arose from his bedde, and he being now ready to arme himselfe, the Souldan, the Prince Clauergudo , Florion and other knightes his friendes came into his chamber, which all helpped to arme him. When he was all armed, the wise Lyrgandeo came in also with a helmette in his handes, the richest and most precious that euer was seene and the strongest also & the best wrought that euer came on knights head, for that the wise man had made it by obseruation of signes and planetts in such aspects that no sworde how good soeuer, might enter into it , and he had bene more then twentie yeares in making it to haue the true coniunction of the celestiall bodyes which were apte for the operation of it , besides all which , he had fetched

from

from farre countries, the stuffe whereof it was made, for
it was no common mettall. This helmet was for workemanship
so exceeding, as for it onely Lirgandeo wan hys
spurres, and was commended aboue all the learnedst and
wisest Magicians, for none other hauinge not attained
to the lyke perfection in Astronomy or Arte Magicke
coulde haue euer made it . Nowe as I sayde cumming
into the chamber, where the knight of the Sunne, the
Souldan, and the rest were, and shewing his helmet , hee
droue them all into a wonder at the beautie and richesse
of the helmet, for although they knewe not the hidden vertue
of it, yet for the brauerie of the stones they iudged it
valuable with a kings delight. He bare in it a féeld Azour
of the liknesse of the element in most quiet and peaceable
manner, not troubled with winde or cloudes, in the chiefe
there was a Sunne guilded spreading his beames al ouer
the helmet, as it were the mantling, somwhat besides good
armory I thincke, but well fitting for so gorgious a péece
of armour. The Sunne shined so bright, that it almoste
dazeled the eyes of the beholders . This helmet christening
him now by the name of the knight of the Sunne,
as the Sunne in his left side named him, the gentleman
of the Sunne when he was first founde in the Sea by
Florion . The wise man came vnto the knight and tooke
from him the helmet which he had already laced on, & put
this other, saying. My Lorde you goe to fight with one so
strong and valiant a knight, that neither may I report it
for the straungenesse, neyther can you giue credit vnlesse
you haue tryall , nowe though the helmette yeu haue
is very good, yet béeing hacked and brused with the terrible
blowes of the stronge Raiartes, it is not suche a
one as maye resist the weightie strokes of Africano , but
this which now I giue you, make much of it, for I knowinge
that this battayle ought to bée foughten by you
in the right of my nephewe the Prince Florion, haue this
xx. yeares and more bused my selfe aboute it, and ful

ly finished it, not paſt a yeare ſince. The knight of the
Sunne triumphed nowe to be made the maſter of ſo
rare an helmet, and in ſo needfull a tune, ſaying to Lyrgandeo in thanckfull wiſe, that he accepted better of that
helmet then of the whole worlde, if it were giuen hym.
„ You doe not amiſſe in ſo doing, aunſwered the wyſe
„ man, for I tell you the time will come when you ſhall
„ make exchaunge of it vnto a knight ſtraunger farre borne
„ out of theſe countryes, and I doe not meruaile thoughe
„ you ſhall then make merchaundiſe of the headpœce which
„ nowe you ſo highly regarde, for at that time you ſhall
„ ſell the moſte precious thinge that euer you had, for a
„ worſe thing which ſhall bringe you to the ieopardy of
„ death a M.tunes, and neither ſhall wit nor might, cun-
„ ning nor courage helpe you to auoyde this chaunce. The
knight of the Sunne ſtood looked vpon þ wiſe man, as not
witting to what ende thoſe wordes tended, and ſtudy-
„ ing a long time, he thus gaineſayed it. Of thinges to
„ come, I haue naught to ſay, but to referre ſuche thinges
„ to the prouidence of our Gods, but of thinges which are
„ alreadye come, thus much I ſaye, that I knowe nothinge
„ in the worlo for which I woulde loſe this helmette gy-
„ uen mœ in ſo good oportunitie. But the morninge bœing farre ſpent they left off for that time, and departed
all from the pallaice towards the Souldans army, & ſetting
their people in order, they paſſed out of þ gates with all
things prepared for to kœpe the field. The knyght of the
Sunne accompanied with the Souldan, and the other two
Princes Florion, & Clauergudo, Armineo & the wiſe Lyrgandeo rode to the place appointed for the execution of þ
conditions concluded vpon. The great Africano was in
place before expecting his aduerſary, whom when þ knight
eſpicd, he rode againſt with onely two knightes, of the
moſt principall in the Souldans hoaſt. The knight of the
Sunne ſaluted Africano courteouſly, but Africano bœing of a ſtubburne and diſcourteous nature, gaue hym
the

the refalutation in this manner. Thou oughteſt to haue
come earlyer into the fælde , to the ende our battayle
might haue bene ſœner diſpatched, but tell me nowe
quickly the articles of the agrœment to bœ made , and
ſpende no moꝛe time leaſt we take an other daye of reſ-
pite . Naye there is no moꝛe to doe , aunſwered the
knight of the Sunne , but that of thy parte, two of thy
knightes bœ iudges,and foꝛ my part theſe two knightes,
Clauergudo Pꝛince of Fraunce,and his vnckle hœre pꝛeſent ſhall ſit with them , befoꝛe them take an othe foꝛ
the perfoꝛmaunce of that whereoff thou madeſt mee
pꝛomiſe bœing alone with thœ. I am well contented with
this ſayd Africano,and now I ſweare the ſame,that if I
bœ either ſlayne,oꝛ yelden the kingdome of Perſia ſhall
be redeliuered to Florion,& this I commaund my knights
to ſœ auouched. So ſœne as hee had ſayde this hœ gaue
backe,and the knight of the Sunne did the like , the
iudges aſſigning a place foꝛ the combatte , Nowe are
the two couragiouſeſt knightes of the woꝛlde. lefte the
one agaynſt the other with ſo fierce and manly countenaunces that it might haue diſmayed the ſpectatoꝛs.
When the ſounde of the trumpette had ſommoned them
to the battayle,the two ſtronge knyghtes gyꝛdinge theyꝛ
hoꝛſes with their ſpurres,rode the one agaynſt the other,
with ſuch vyolence as if the cloudes had rente a ſun-
der by the outbꝛaſting of the thunderbolte. Their great
ſpeares bꝛoken vpon their armour flew in ſmall ſhyuers ,
and they rode one by the other as quietly as if no ſhocke
had bene made . Africano the Pagan not acquainted
with ſuch encountries , and alwaies wont to vnhoꝛſe all
knyghts whome hœ mette ſœing the knight pꝛepared foꝛ
ẙ ſecond iourney meruailed much who this ſtrong warriour might be,whom befoꝛe this time he had not pꝛoued,noꝛ
yet euer heard off. But lightly caſting theſe thinges in
his minde,as at a ſodeine he dꝛew out his ſwoꝛd & tourned
towardes his enemy which was then ready foꝛ him.

They strake each other such heauie blowes that warding them on their shaldes, although they were of pure steele, yet they cleaued them in the middest, and their swoordes lighted on their helmettes driuing out great sparcles of fire before them. The great Africano gaue the knight of the Sunne vpon his helmette such buffettes and with such force that euery man would haue iudged it had ry, uen the headpæce. There the cunninge of the wyse Lyrgandeo wel appeared, for it was not possible for yron, steele, or Adamant stone, but to haue yelded to that stroke. But what thincke you y the knyght of the Sunne did, when he thought that he had cleane lost his hearing by it, and sayde to himselfe, that not without good cause Africano was greatly feared amonge the Pagans? Nay, to the no lesse meruaile of both hoastes, the knight of the Sunne let driue at Africano with such force as it was to the no small admiration of all men that he hewed him not in pæces. But you must learne that when Africano passed by sea from Afrike into Asia, it was his chaunce to saile by Lemnos where Vulcans forge was. There he heard of Vulcans caue where his storehouse was, and enteringe into it he achieued straunge thinges, not here to be recounted, and gayned Vulcans armour wrought with his owne handes, the best in all the land. This when Africano tryed often times to be very good, whereoff he was well pleased, from that time foorth he neuer fought with other but with that. Nowe albeit this headpæce was well framed from bæing cut, yet the knight of the Sunnes blowes were so heauy y oftentimes Africano wist not where he was, & recouering would say vnto himselfe. What is this? I belæue the strength of the whole world conspireth with this knight against me, & if it be not so that he is of the offsprigs of our Gods, yet am I sure y he is no man. But among all the great blowes which y knight of the Sunne lent to Africano there was one at the fore end of the battayle vppon y top of Africanos

canos helmette, the ſwoꝛde not enteringe but ſlidinge
downe vpon his ſhoulders with ſuche foꝛce that it made
him leane all his body vpon the hoꝛſeneck, wherreoff if he
had not taken hold he had fallen to the greund. Then the
Pagan ſure enough yet in his ſaddell and his foꝛce redou-
bling as his anger encreaſed ſmote at the inchaunted helmet that he made the knight confeſſe in his thought, that
his helmet was his good boꝛrow . The blow ſounded
thꝛoughout all the fœlde, as if it had bene a bell, and the
knight of the Sunne with the weight of the blowe, neither bowlt vpꝛight noꝛ full declining, but ſtaying vpon the
arſon dꝛouped as halfe dead. But the bloud guſhing out
of his noſe fetched him againe quickely ere that Africano could come within him. Nowe ſeeing it time to defend himſelfe from his aduerſary, he ſtode vpꝛight in his
ſtirops, and with both his handes ſtrake at Africano, ſo
ẙ if the woꝛkman had not bene moꝛe to blame, the blowe
had made peace betwœne them, but foꝛ all the woꝛkmans
craft, the weight of the blowe bꝛuſed the helmet whiche
was the cauſe of Africanos ſpœdier death. Africano benummed of his ſences, the bloude ſtrayning thꝛough the
ioyntes of the helmet and he ſitting in his ſaddle as halfe
dead. The hoꝛſe ſoꝛe daunted with the blowe, ſtode ſtyll
till Africano reuiued, and in the gathering of his ſtrength
outbꝛayed thus much in his thought . O infernall furies
are you not all hyꝛed againſt mœ? oꝛ is it creadible that
either Iupiter, oꝛ Saturne, oꝛ Mars, oꝛ all the Gods maye
haue the like foꝛce as this young mans . But Africanos
heart fayled him not, albeit his woꝛdes outraged, foꝛ
he followed the knyght of the Sunne who attended hym
ſpeadely . Then the Pꝛince Florion ſayde to the Souldan his vnckle, wœ make great account of the trauayles
of the auncient Aſſirians our foꝛefathers , and of the
Grecians with whome our countreymen ioyned at the
erpedition of Troy, but I cannot thincke that euer two
ſo ſtrong warriours haue ben as Africano and Raiartes.

I.iij.   You

„ Pou may boldly iuſtifie that, aunſwered Lyrgandeo,
„ for there was neuer vntil this day a battaile betwene two
„ knights ſo valiaunt and ſharp as this is, nor yet euer two
„ ſo hardy drew ſwords againſt eche other, although things
„ before done carry a greater burden of authoritie then that
„ which we our ſelues can teſtifie. But the iclouſie which
Clauergudo had ouer the knight of the Sunne was not
a little, to be iudge of ſo valiant behauiour, not that he had
an ill eye towardes his friendes good Fortune, but either
wiſhing to himſelfe the like tryall, or deſiring to aduenture with his friend, although not many dayes ended ere
he had his fill to his contentment. Africanos people looked
euer for the victory, greatly forethincking them that any
one knight ſhould make reſiſtaunce to their Lord, as hauing experience in themſelues, which al ſpoke for feare to
ſee him angred. Now was it more then two houres ſince ye
battaile began, and then fortune alwayes fickle & vnſtable
which had of a long time gone euen with Africano, now
played hir part in hir kinde, and as already weryof hys
companie tourned hir tale, and ſtroke in an other waye,
deſirous to ſhewe the great ſwiftneſſe of hir euertourning
whæle, and minding ye ſodeine ouerthrow of thoſe which
to much truſt in hir. For Africano deſperately determining to breake vp the fight one way or the other: once
againe hit the knight of the Sunne vppon his Magicall
helmet that he tooke quyte his memory from the knight,
the ſwoorde and the raines falling from him. Yet the
ſwoorde hanging by a longe ſtringe at the pomell was not
out of his reach, but the horſe hauing the libertie of the
raines, and fæling his part of the blowe flange vp and
downe the fælde with his maſter, the ſtronge Pagan fol-
winge to haue vnhorſed him. But howe dare was
this blowe to Africano for it coſte him no leſſe then hys
lyfe, for the valiant knight of the Sunne neuer ſtayned
in fight, became woode madde for hys hurte, and in great
rage tooke his ſwoorde in both hys handes, and repayed
the

the borrowed blowe so surely vpon Africanos heade that
not Vulcans well tempered steele coulde forbid the passage, but that it quartered the helmette and made the
braines sprinckle on the grounde. Nowe sounde yee
trumpets, for in this wise is the great Africano brought
to grounde, ending his life in such sorte as is fatall to
tyrantes, whose death commonly is cruell and bloudy.
This the Souldan and those of his part seeing, made such
ioye as cannot bee tolde, but on the contrary side Africanos people made great lamentation, and reckening little
vppon that which their Lord in his lyfe time had commaunded, bicause they were more in number then theyr
aduersaries, they ioyned together on heapes sine discre-
tione, and without a guide made an assalte vppon the
knight and his adherentes. But they not taken at vnawares receiued them accordingly. These were the
Souldan, the Prince Florion, the Prince Clauergudo, and
Armineo with the knight of the Sunne, in whose company they were the bolder, and comming to the foreward
in the formost rancke, they finde of the stowtest and prin-
cipallest knights that Africano had. These foure encountred them and vnhorsed as many as they came against,
& breaking through to the thickest thronge, they wrought
wonders, especially the Prince of Fraunce desirous to get
honour in the first heade of his knighthoode shoued into
the middest, beheading some, and mayminge other some,
making as it were a lane before him to passe throughe,
so that the wise Lyrgandeo sayd openly that now his outwarde sight dyd well witnesse the selfe same thing which
his Arte had shewed him in casting the constellation of this
Knyght, for hee was a valiant knight, and the slaughter he
made was nygh hand comperable with that of the knight
of the Sunne. Vppon the left winge prince Florion tryed his
manhood hauing neere vnto him the Souldan. Where (be it
that otherwise to a stronge Gyant as Africano was he
was inferiour,) yet amonge the other people hee was

as proude as a rauenous wolfe amonge a flocke of sheepe: The Souldan and the good knight Armineo did their part, but what would all this auailed, vnlesse the knight of the Sunne had bet the waye before them with his sharpe sword slaying so many as it was easy for the followers to keepe the troden path. And now at this time y Souldans army appointed for the gard of the knight of the Sunne came to the battaile, and finding Fortune so courteous at their comming, they refused not hir gentlenesse, but following hir commaund, made it a bloudy conflict for the aduersary. But yet a man may rightly say, that y knight of the Sunne deliuered that daye the Babilonians from death or bondage, for if he had not ouercome Africano, not the high walles of the Queene Semiramis could haue kept Africano out from enioying the Citie . But their Lord bœing slayne and they left without an head , theyr courage was so quailed that ere two houres passed , the greater part of thẽ was slaine likewise, & of those which remained on liue, the most part fledde by one and one, the Assirians pursuing them till the Souldan commaunded the retreate to be blowen, fearing to be ouertaken by the night, by this meanes some escaped to their countrey, most of them bœing inhabitantes of Media , where also was the abode of Africanos son called Brandimardo, not being able for yeares to be made knight , and therefore goinge not out with his father to y warre. These so sœne as they came home crowned Brandimardo and incensed him to the reuenge of his fathers death , for although he was of yeares younge and tender, yet was he very stronge and of a lusty body, bœing lyke vnto his father as well in stature as in qualities, and in deede bœing continually layde at by his fathers subiects, passing into Greece, he behaued himselfe manfully as shall bee shewed you . Well the Souldan and those which were with him as you haue heard, retourned in ioy and pleasure, and highly magnifying the noble knight of y Sunne, so as this discourse as an

argu⸗

argument of greate good will canuaſed betwéene theſe
knights and Princes brought them ere they were wel a-
ware before the pallayce gate, where the Princeſſe Baliſea welcomed them with torch light, the firſt whome ſhee
embraced was the knight of the Sunne to whome ſhee
ſayd on this wiſe. Syr knight we haue great cauſe to giue ,,
thancks to our gods for your hether ariual. Firſt you de- ,,
liuered my Lorde the Souldan and me from death, & now ,,
you haue ſet all vs frée from ſorrowfull captiuitie. But ,,
madame aunſwered the knight of the ſunne, to my Lord
the Prince Florion and to theſe other knights you ought
to attribute this, for they are thoſe which haue deſtroyed
Africanos hoaſt. Then the Princeſſe tourned to Clauergudo and thancked him lykewiſe for his paynes in the
defence of hir fathers citie, and ſo to the reſt in that order which beſt lyked hir. After this they ſupped in the
great hall, continuing there their ſports till bedtime, as
lykewiſe the citizens wel ſhewed their good lyking of the
victory by bonfires and other reuelling ſport. The nexte
day they ordeined that which followeth.

¶ The Knight of the Sunne, the two Princes Florion and
    Clauergudo, with a great hoaſt enter into Perſia and
    there put Florion in poſſeſſion of the crowne.
    Cap. xxv.

THe next day after dinner, the Souldan himſelfe
entred into the counſayle chamber, and other affayres being layd a part, ÿ wiſe Lyrgandeo made
this oration. It is apparantly knowne vnto vs ''
all how bountifully our high gods haue dealt with vs as ''
wel touching my Lord the Souldan as the Prince Flori- ''
on, and the whole nation of the Aſſyrians in bringing to ''
this court, the knight of the Sunne and the Prince Cla- ''
uergudo : who by their notable vertues not onely haue ''
kept this citie from ſacking, but alſo as we make account, ''

» haue left the realme of Persia naked for resistaunce, not-
» one speare remayning to be tossed agaynst vs. For the at-
» tayning of either of these thinges we are not ignorant,
» how weake and vnable we were, that were it not for
» these two young gentlemen, not onely our homebredde
» power but also thrice as manye of forreyne succoures
» coulde not haue hindered Africano from his purpose.
» Wherefore I thincke it conuenient, that sithe the Gods
» haue graunted vs this victory, and that we haue the winde
» at our backes that we followe our good Fortune while
» we haue hir, least by ouerslipping the opportunitie, we to
» late repent our to much daintines. My meaning is y with
» such speed as may be, y Prince Florion & these Lords de-
» part the realme into Persia, there to make claime of his
» right by armes, whilst euery man is occupied in complay-
» ning on his owne harmes. For although as yet there dare
» no man stande against vs, yet for a certeintie there is a
» king of Media Africanos sonne, which ere it be longe
» wilbe our heauy neighbour, he is not yet made knight,
» but his desteny foresheweth vs that if he once come to
» boord in Persia we shalbe no lesse disquyeted w his company, then we were with Africano his father. The wise
Lyrgandeo made an ende of his oration, knitting vp hys
matter with this clause (that it was not out of the way to
aduise themselues) notwithstanding for good reasons this
was his iudgement.

They which would neuer contrary him in any poynt
toke no further respite, but consenting to the effecte of
Lyrgandeos oration concerning the conqueste of Persia
toke this order. That Prince Florion, the knight of the
Sunne, Clauergudo and Armineo his brackle, with fiftene thousande knightes, and fiftie thousands footemen,
within tenne dayes should prepare themselues for this
aduenture, the Princesse Bahsea abiding with the Souldan hir father, till the kingdome were well setled from
tumulte, and the prince in peaceable fruition of y crowne,

Thus

This they dealt in effectually, for within the compasse of the dayes limitted they lefte Babilon, the Sould. and and the Princesse onely comforted with the hope which I yrgandeo made promise off.

The fiftene thousande knightes with the footemen by long iourneyes entring into Persia, and comming nere vnto one of the chiefest cities of the kingedome, there in the plaine vnladed their carriage to erect their tents there. But the citizens hauing vnderstanding of Africano death by the fugitues in the last discomfiture of Africanos hoast, and thinking it not safetie for themselues to rebell agaynst their liege and naturall Lorde Florion especially he hauing the aide of the whole floure of Babilō, set their gates wide open for hys armye, & sent of their worthyest knightes to Florions tent to inuite him to his owne citie, and to craue pardon for their former reuoulting, in that time when they were lefte destitute of mans succour, not being able of themselues to withstand the force of Africano. And also excusing themselues that they had neuer a guide to conducte them into the fielde, agaynste so strong an enemye, hauing in his power the greatest part of all Asia.

The Prince lightly excusing their fault easely condiscended vnto their requestes, and being gladde of so good enterteinement at the firste, the next daye rode into the citie, with the ioyfull acclamations of the whole multitude. There he resumed the crowne and scepter, and being in quyet seyzure, the subiects of the realme by the fame of his thether arryuall, came from all parts to do hym homaxe, so that in halfe a yeares space all the principall Cityes of the kyngdome submitted themselues, and there was lefte no more memorye of the vsurpers name.

The kinge Florion seyzed of hys lande in such a fryendly manner, nowe tooke counsayle how to haue the Queene his wyfe conuayed thether, and for that it was
                                                              requi-

requisite that the king himselfe should tarry behinde for
the appeasing of all tumults if any should arise in so raw
a possession, he gaue the charge of fetching the Queens
with all reasonable pompe , vnto the knight of the Sun
and the Prince Clauergudo they to take with them 200
knights for their safetie. They tooke it gladly, and frayted their shippes with necessary prouision and other furniture for war, determining to trauayle by sea the sooner to
come vnto their iourneyes ende. When euery thing was
in a readinesse the knights tooke their leaue of ye king Florion and the wise Lyrgandeo . But the wiseman not refrayning from teares, and louingly embracing the knight
of the Sunne, burst out into these speaches in such sorte
as the Sibilles in auncient time were wont to read mens
,, destenyes. Noble and worthy knight, you are determined
,, to see Babilon, but you are vncerteyne whether euer to
,, see it, or to retourne to Persia, and as little know I what
,, shall befall. For truth it is, that all the heauenly sphæres
,, warrāt more vnto you then to any knight, what that is,
,, it is kept from me, I cannot finde the entry therebnto
,, wherefore I am in doubte of your hether retourne. But
,, if the fates, or otherwise the course of the starres
,, which impose a necessitie to man, carrie you beyond the
,, compasse of your will into a farre country wher ther shall
,, be greater neede of your presence, grudge not at it , but
,, giue thanks to our gods. For all shal redound to your ho
,, nour and the magnifiyng of your lignage . This I tell
,, for a suretie that you shal neuer doe the thing in your life
,, whereof you shall take lyke pleasure as in your two first
,, aduentures vndertaken for two knightes straungers,
,, whome notwithstanding you shall not know till time and
,, place discloseth them vnto you. Of your lygnage I wyll
,, report nothing for it is ordayned by the gods that by the
,, mouth of one of these two knights of whome I haue spo
,, ken your whole parentage should be layde open , before
,, which time you shalbe at most ll defiaunce. For the shutting

ting vp of this fpeach,the remainder onely is that I make „
offer of my feruice vnto you,whereof I hope it fhall bæ „
nædeles to make a profeffion in words, feing I am ther- „
vnto bounden by your manifolde friendfhips towards my „
kindred. In a worde Lyrgandeo fhall neuer fayle you in „
the thing, wherein either his wealth or wifedome maye „
ftande you in ftæde, and the day fhall come wherein you „
being in the countrey wher you were borne,and amongft „
your owne parents , fhall account them all for enemyes „
and yet no man fhall take your part but only Lyrgandeo, „
which for that time fhall fane your lyfe,and I hope that
this feruice fhall not be the laft in account, or the leaft in ”
value which I wyll doe vnto you. The wife man ended, ”
and they all which were prefent wondrred to heare hym ”
fo diuine of things to come. But the Knight of the Sun ”
not vnderftanding the tenour of this prophecye , wifely ”
referred all things to Gods prouidence,thanking the wife
man for his great care ouer him.

Nowe when on all partes all courtefies were perfourmed and that the king Florion had commended them
to his gods, they embarked themfelues , and fpredding
their fayles followed the waye towardes Babilon as the
chapter following fhall declare.

¶The Knight of the Sunne and the Prince Clauergudo being in their way towards Babilon, were
deuided by a fodayne aduentue.   Cap. xxvj

AS already the noble and knightlye dædes of the
Knight of the Sunne did bud out and were likely to florifh more hereafter, fo now not onely the
celeftiall influences , but the confluences of the
tempeftuous windes alfo, and the Sea it felfe became fo
carefull for his aduauncement that ther fayled nothing of
that which mighte worke his preferment , for fo it is
that whē any thing is forced by the ftarres as to fuccæd
prof-

profperoufly vnto a man, albeit mountayns of aduerfitie
impugne & affaile him, yet can they neuer expugne his good
fortune, but in the ende he recouereth his quyet refte
maugre the malice of mifaduenture. And fo the iffue declared in the knight of the Sunne. For the ix. daye after
that the knight of y Sunne, Clauergudo, and thofe which
wer to them had failed in y Perficke fea, y night attached
them ouercaft with darke clouds without any ftarres appearing whereby the marriners conftrued the roughneffe
of y wether on y inorrow, & therfore guided towards land
to caft anchor in fome good herberowe till y ftormes ceafed. Eare the dawning of the day they difcouered a docke
not farre from the continent in their feeming very commodious, but in deede very daungerous as it proued. Entring the docke, they fcarce had leafure to throw out their
anchors but two other fhipps ioyned with them to feeke
fome fafe roade out of the tempeft. Thefe which laft got
to the port were very defirous to knowe what the other
might be, and therfore an armed knight fo huge and
great as if he had bene a Gyant mounting on the fhippe
borde called aloude vnto them to aunfwere him. Some of
the other fhippe hearing him in this wife crying, leapte
vpon the hatches faying. What is it fir knight that you
would haue? Mary I would know aunfwered the knight
" what you are and whether you will. One of the company being ftoute and of ill behauiour, and fuppofing thys
knight to be fome Gyant of that countrey minding to fet
" vpon them, made him aunfwere thus. Retourne to thy
" dwelling, and bee not carefull to knowe them which
" knowe not thee, otherwyfe affure thy felfe heere are
" knightes which will chafe thee hence in fuch forte as it
" fhal wel grieue thee. The ftrange knight ftomacking this
rudeneffe, fayde agayne. Affuredly knighte thou arte
" fome bilayne borne or of bafe byrthe, fithe in fuch order
" thou rewardeft me demaunding onely vpon courtefie, but
" feing I cannot learne it of the with thy good will, I will

com-

compell thee therebnto with thine ill will, and saying no
moze he dzoue at the knight so strongly that he claue both
shielde, helmette, and head bnto the eyes. O what a
mischæfe doth ill speach bzeed bnto man, & how incrusa-
ble was it in this knighte when he redeemed this franke
speach with his owne lyfe, and solde to make payment the
lyfe of many others. An other knight seing his fellowe
slayne, stept into his rowne, and smote at the straunger,
where by the clattering of theyr harnesse, the dinne was
so great that it raysed the people on both partes by clust-
ers. And there was a great fray betwixt them, the knight
of the Sunne noz Clauergudo witting of it, till the great
knight had ouerthzowen and put to death fiue oz sixe of
those knightes which came nærest to hande.

The Knighte of the Sunne seing his knightes so destroyed, especially by this greate knighte leauing the o-
thers bent his force agaynst him, and strake him a blowe
ouerthwart the headpæce making him to abate his courage. The great knight aunswered the loane, and the battayle was verye hotte betwæne them, for thoughe the
night was darke yet they knewe where to hitte aswell
by the flames which spzang out of their helmettes as the
clashing of their armour. Clauergudo put himselfe a-
mongst the thickest and at his first godmozrow slew tenne
knights and then not finding with whome to fighte, hee
lepte into his enemyes shippe with his vncle Armineo
where he felled moze then rrr. knightes, and the skirmish
beganne a fresh either part willing to helpe theirs, and
the foure shippes grapled together, so that the fighte
would haue ben dangerous if it had lasted lōger, but halfe
an houre & a little moze ouerpassed, ŷ tempest which befoze
thzeatened to appeare now outraged, & the pozt not verye
sure, the iiii. ships were deuided by the stozme euery one
withdzawing himselfe to sæke succour. Now in the ship
wherein the knight of the Sunne and the great knighte
foughte there were no moze knyghtes but they two,

for all followed Clauergudo into the other shippes. The two knights left alone were so earnest that they tooke little keepe either of the tempest or of their daunger. The succes of ẙ battayle was doutefull, sometimes enclining to ẙ one part sometimes to ẙ other, neither part quailing, but gathering their strengthes to them by the emulation of each other. For ẙ knight of the Sunne verely beleued that excepte his enemye had bene some such as Africano was he could neuer haue abid these mortall strokes: and the other knighte thought aswell that no mans force could be macheable with the knights, and either of them both had better cause to thanke Lyrgandeos kindenesse, especially this strange knight at this time, for had not his armour kept out ẙ edge of ẙ other knights armant swoord eh could not haue prolonged ẙ battayle till day lyght, yet at ẙ time he was so ouermatched ẙ if a sodayn aduēture had not broke vp their fight, he had ended his lyfe in that place.

But when it was broad day by this the battayle surceased, that the straunge knighte knewe the deuise of the Sunne vpon the knight of the Sunnes helmette, which when he espyed letting his swoorde fall, and lifting vppe his beuere, he cast himselfe at the knights fēte with this
,, speach. Oh my Lord the knight of the Sunne pardon I
,, pray your friende who by meere ignoraunce, hath made
,, vpon your person, and who acknowledgeth in you suche
,, souereigne vertue as may not be in other but in these to
,, whome our gods haue imparted of their goodnesse. For if
,, the day had lyngred, or that the morning had not bene
,, somewhat cleare I should haue receiued a full payemente
,, for my rashnesse: and saying this, he would haue embraced Del Febos knees. Now the knight of the Sunne so
,, sone as ẙ others bisour was pulled vp knew well that he
,, was the Prince Brandizel whom his father not willing
,, to make knighte before his yeares were more, had lefte
    with the Souldan in Babilon. For he was scarcely righ-
                                                        tene

tene yeares of age, yet being in armour he was as byg
as you haue heard off, and taking courage vpon his stature, in his fathers absence hee laye at the Souldan
his graundfather to be dubbed knight, thincking it longe
till he were with his father, and his great friendes the
knight of the Sunne, and the Prince Clauergudo. So
after y͡ he had obteined his sute of his graundfather he demaunded licence of departure of the Souldan and the princesse Balisea his mother to passe into Persia, which was
graunted him, and two shippes charged with ij.C. knights
to conuaye him thether, where after the fourth dayes
sayling that chaunsed to him, which the historie hath recounted. But to retourne, as soone as the knight of the
Sunne knewe his deere friende the Prince Brandizel very glad to haue found him so valiant and hardy he embraced him hartely, and so they communed of their owne
affaires, and the desire that each had to see others. But as
they began their seuerall stories by enterchaunge of
speach, first one and then an other : The Marriners cryed that the shippe rent in peeces. So some lepte into the
water, and other threwe out planckes to saue themselues
by, and the knight of the Sunne finding the cockeboate
neere vnto him, let it downe into the water by a cable,
& calling the prince Brandizel, he lept into it first himselfe.
Thus muche is ordinary in the course of worldly
things, but that which is to come is beyond the credit of a
storie as it were an extraordinary myracle . For when
the knight of the Sunne lept into the beate, the cable
rent in peeces, and with the force of the iumpe, and the
rage of the windes together, the boate launched into the
depth, that the Prince Brandizel coulde not followe
hym, but gotte into a little boate whiche the gouernour
of the shippe had before taken . But by and by after
these Princes had thus escaped, the shyppe wherin they
had bene, tore in peeces wyth the storme . Some being drowned, and other some in no little daunger, as

the waues began to swell, so euer prognosticatinge of their owne deathes. The knight of the Sunne saylinge alone in the vessell, and in such feare of destruction was not so stoute harted as to contemne the sencelesse element, but confessinge the imbecilitie of mannes power subiected vnder these weake thinges as fyre and water, besides casualties infinite more, hée commended hymselfe vnto hys Gods by earneste prayer, not yet onely for hymselfe, but also for his friende Brandizel, not beeing able to diuine of his deliueraunce. Sittinge thus in the boate all pensiue, till the wyndes were somewhat alayed, and the Sea wared more calme, afterwardes hée loked about hym and sawe that hée was out of daunger, with other two thinges whiche made hym more to meruaple. The one was the great foyzon and plentie of all victualles, sufficient to a man for many dayes, the other was the swyftnesse of the boate in the Sea, hauinge neyther sayle nor oare to rule it, and musinge of this in his thought, hee coniectured presently that it should be done by Lyrgandeo, and therefore as very glad of suche a mans friendshippe in so needefull a time, hee gaue hym thanckes as hartely as if he had seene hym there. In thys order hee was vppon the Sea many dayes wythout knowing whether the wynde woulde dryue hym, tyll that from out of ý Persians Seas he came into the Occean, and so coastinge the whole countrey of Asia, lying vppon that sea, he was carried into Africke, which stretcheth vppon the wyde West Seas. In which countrey the historye leaueth hym tyll an other wynde serueth, nowe it proceedeth with the storye of hys friendes, Brandizel and Clauergudo, who were on the Seas tossed in lyke manner. Clauergudo as the storye tolde you boorded his enimies with fiftie knyghtes in his companye and made greate hauocke of them, so that he had not left any of them aliue if the storme had not risen so greatly. For the windes were so outragious betweene
them

them, and when they coulde stande no lenger on shyp-
boorde to trye it out, they lefte not off, to aske who each
other was, the one party sayde we are Babylonians, and
the other, we are Persians, all this happened in good time,
for when they knew each other, they fel not agayne to qua-
relling, but they agred to emptie their ships, thereby to a-
uoide the daunger. So Clauergudo hauing new leasure
to looke about him, the battaile being ended, and not En-
duig the knight of the Sunne, nor the Prince Brandizel,
withall remembring howe he had left them twaine in
fighting, was greatly afraide least that the knight of the
Sunne should endaunger the prince, before the one should
know the other. Therefore he besoched God like a good
chrithian to deliuer them both, & to make them know each o-
ther, thereby to make greater account the one of the other, &
it is to be thought that this his prayer was heard, for the
second day following the storme slacked, & the ship wherin they sayled arriued to a porte, not farre from a place
where they were newly rigged. There they had not staied an houre, but that they sawe the boate in which the
Prince Brandizel was. The mariners in Brandizels boat
not being perfect in the hauen, woulde not venture to take
landing there, but coasting a longe they passed by the shyps
to finde some more safe place to land in. The prince was
ascried by his men in his ships, & therfore they made signes
vnto the gouernour to stere towards them, so the gouernour vnderstanding the tokens, guided thether. The prince Clauergudo & his vnckle Armineo, standing on the hatches redy
to welcome the Prince Brandizel, betwene whom there
were shewed tokens of great good wil, & each made much
of other as two faithful friends. But questioning about the
knight of the Sunne. The Prince Brandizel declared the
manner of their parting, & the daunger wherin he had left
him. This caused great sorrow in them, for they loued him
as derely as any father his childe or any wife hir husbad.
And to asswage their griefe, Armineo remembred vnto them

the

the wordes which the wise Lyrgandeo had spoken to the knyght of the Sunne at his departure . Whereby they were perswaded that his departure by such a chaunce was but for the achiuement of things more worthy of him alone, and for whom enely they were reserued . Now hauing stayed in this hauen two dayes to repayre their shippes, when they were in a readinesse they sayled towardes Babilon where they were goodly receyued of the Souldan and of the Queene , both very ioyfull of the newes as touching Persia, and the king Florions peaceable possession , and agayne as sorrowfull for the losse of the knight of the Sunne, and the perill of death wherein Brandizel sawe him last. But in short time after there were letters recciued from Lirgandeo, conteining the certeintie of hys safetie, the manner of his escape, & the affaires wherein he was employed. Which last point bred a great desire in Clauergudo, & Brandizel to stray through the world, and to exercise the feats of armes. And a while after they had rested themselues in Babilon, they brought the Queene to Persia by land, for they woulde no more aduenture the Seas, especially hauinge the Queene as parte of their burthen, and the historie bryngeth them on their waye as farre as Persia, whence it retourneth towardes Hungary to matters of lyke importaunce, wherein the younger sonne of Trebatio had to deale, whose prowesse is no lesse worthy my paynes , then hys brothers valoure is worthy of your remembraunce , for hœ surpassed all other knyghtes in loyaltie and might, bœing equall to Donzel del Febo in all pointes, as hœereafter you shall hœere.

¶The Princesse Briana discouered to Rosicleer secretly that he was hir sonne.　　　Cap.27.

T HE story left the Princesse Briana straungely afflicted & tormented with the double losse, both of Prince
Edward

Edward hir husband, & Donzel del Febo hir sonne, which griefe no doubt had quickly killed hir, had not a Nymph giuen hir comfort at ye well in the orchard as it hath bene shewed. But yet it somewhat eased hir melancholy that she had the fayre and courteous Rosicleer, in whose onely company she was wont to beguile hir mishappes, and by his meanes to forget hir miseries. For he was so gracious, as that he was beloued not onely of his mother, but of the other gentlewomen also which might not one minute spare his company, as if he had bene childe to euery one. This Rosicleer when he atteined to the age of.rij. yeares, remoued out of the monastery to a house hard by, where his nourse Leonardo kept, whom he thought to be his father. Here he was diligently enstructed in all good literature, and in the exercise of armes, both to be able to be a good counsailer in peace, and as good a warriour in battayle, ouer and besides the knowledge of the tongues, wherein Leonardo was very curious as hauing trauayled for his knowledge through the most parts of Europe and Asia, being thervnto both wise and wel learned. Rosicleer was of such pregnant wit, and so ripe of capacitie that he little néeded the helpe of a teacher, and to ye which his nourse read, he added by his owne industry somwhat, that he became so profoud in these studies, as if he had ben studyed in them all his life time at Athens. But remayning thus, vnder the gouernaunce of his supposed father till he was riiij. yeares of age, he then was so highe and big made that fewe in that countrey were so tall, and being at this age, he was able for strength to doe that whiche thrée knyghtes together were vnable to doe. The Princesse knowing of his strength forbad hym hir fathers court, and would not suffer him to forgoe the monastery, for she feared least ye king hearing of his towardnesse should enquire after him, & so reteine him in his seruice. For this cause Rosicleer thus kept in at this age, and thus strong became very sad, for his so straight enclosure as if he had professed already a vowe in some cloyster, and his minde euer ranne vpon his desire to be made knight, to the ende he myght experiment the aduentures of the worlde, & learne by proofe that which he had often heard by rehearsall . Hereunto hauing no hope nor helpe by this restraint it abated his cheere & encreased his sadnesse. Leonardo his nourse marking in what plight he was, ofté demaunded the occasion of his heauinesse, but could by no meanes wringe it out of him, and so one daye talking with the Princesse, hee tolde hir that vnlesse she founde a remedy for hir sonne, his thought would anoy him. The princesse very pensiue at that which Leonardo had told, commaunded Rosicleer to be brought before hir presence. Rosicleer comming into the presence of the Princesse, knéeled downe, and humbly asked what was hir graces pleasure . The Princesse bidding him stande vp, spake

,, thus. Rosicleer, thy father Leonardo telleth mée thou art
,, neuer mery, nowe therefore open to me the cause of
,, this thy heauinesse , and if thou wantest ought whiche
,, thy father can not supply, vtter it frély, and I will pro-
,, uide thée of the remedy to haue thée contented . Rosicleer
hearing the wordes of the Princesse , knéeled downe
,, againe, and sayde. Madame I kisse your hande for the
,, souereigne grace you shewe mée in hauinge suche com-
,, passion on my griefe, and I am well assured that if it were
,, for any thing wheroff I haue néede, your Ladyship would
,, furnish me of it, as hitherto you haue done , but if I bée
,, sadde or solitary for any thing which grieueth me , it
,, is not for néede of any necessarye prouision, for I
,, thancke your goodnesse, I haue had it hetherto aboundant-
,, ly considered by your highnesse without my speakinge.
,, But it is for that in respect of my age, the lyfe whiche
,, I now leade, is more lyke a gentlewoman then a young
,, man, which made me desire to be dubbed knight, & to wan-
,, der abroad for to seke aduentures. Now for ÿ I know your
,, Ladyships pleasure to be ÿ contrary, as neither willing to

de-

depart without your lifence, no2 daring to vtter my defire „
vnto you, I cannot doe leffe but be fo2rowfull, fo2 I want „
the remedy of fatiffying. When Roficleer had thus fayd, „
the p2inceffe fœling already in him ý heroicall ftomack of
his father P2ince Edward(as fhe thought)and calling to
minde the continuall cafualties of knights arrant, burft
into teares in great aboundaunce, which occafioned great
ruth in the young Roficleer, but ý he durft not demaund
the reafon. After a while the P2inceffe to withd2awe hir
fonne from his thought, o2 by fome meanes to remitte his
griefe & to côfo2t him, ftretching hir armes ouer his neck,
faid vnto him. O my fonne Roficleer, already thy valiant „
heart doth manifeft that which fo long time fo2 mine hone- „
ftie fake I haue concealed, this is that thou art the fonne „
of my Lo2d and lawful hufband the p2ince Edward, begot- „
ten in wedlocke, but my parents vnwitting thervnto. Thy „
fathers likeneffe in other qualities thou doft wel refemble, „
albeit his fauour is cleane out of my rememb2aunce. „
Thou canft not be content with the lyfe which thou „
nowe leadeft, voyde of all daunger, but coueteft to bœ „
made knight, and to ieopard thy perfon in the fearch of „
aduentures as thy father did. This if thou doeft fo that „
I maye not beholde thœ euery day, from that time make „
account of me as dead, fo2 my great miffo2tunes toge- „
ther, with the double loffe both of thy father and thy „
b2other, in that o2der as thou haft knowen, hath by thy „
onely p2efence bene bo2ne out and fuppo2ted, and nowe „
dep2iued of this fuppo2te mufte I not yelde my backe „
to the burthen of continuall woe and myflykinge? Be- „
holde then my childe the extreame griefe wherein thou „
findeft mee, and fo2 that as yet thou art younge of yeares, „
doe awaye thys affection fo2 a time, and hœreafter „
when thou fhalte bee of mo2e ftrengthe and better a- „
ble to vndertake the enterp2ice of armes, I wyll fo „
trauaile with the kinge my Lo2d, that he fhall dubbe thœ „
knight, and thou fhalt haue ho2fe & harnes at my charges „

B.iiij.   confo2-

conformable to thy eftate. In the meane while refte thǣ hǣre, foz it may fo bǣ that I fhall in that time heare fome newes of the Pzince Edward oz of Donzel del Febo, which if it fo fall out, then fhall thy abfence be leffe grieuous vnto mǣ, when Roficleer heard ẏ fecret which the Pzinceffe his mother bewzayed vnto him, he was well apayed as touching his thought of bǣing made knight, befoze the bafeneffe of his fofter father hanging in his light, and now bǣ reckened the rather to vndertake the higheft exploytes wherfto his heart dzaue him, and knǣling downe befoze hir, he kiffed hir hand foz the fecrecie which fhe concionated with him touching his true oziginall. His mother by the outward ioye he made, fuppofing his fozmer thought to be put out of conceite was very glad, but ẏ Pzinceffe was deceiued in him. Foz Roficleer hearing himfelfe to bǣ named the fonne of fo mighty pzinces, if befoze he wifhed to be made knight, either of a wanton delight oz foz fome greater occafiõ, now he thirfted grǣdely after knighthood, as thincking himfelf bound in confcience to aduaunce his lignage in the right of his parentes, and his care encreafed howe to fteale from thence. This care he couered the beft wayes ẏ he might, & ftayed with his mother comfozting hir in all that he coulde, vntill that the Pzinceffe went to hir lodginge, and he retourned with Leonardo who onely hearde that which the Pzinceffe had declared. But from that tyme foozth, as I faye, he canuafed in his thought to and fro, the fercete meanes of hys efcape, which he thought (though perhaps at firft it might wzinge fome teares from fo tender a Pzinces,) yet in pzoceffe of time woulde as well dzye them vp, his valour making amendes foz his fodeine departure.

¶ Roficleer departed from the monafterie of the
ryuer without the knowledge of the Princeffe
his mother.   Cap. 28.

Eight

Yght dayes after Roſicleer knewe himſelfe to bee the ſonne of the Princeſſe his Lady, he aboue with Leonardo caſting how he might conuay himſelfe from thence without the knowledge of any man. In the ende one night all the houſholde being on ſlæpe, his lodging ſtanding in one corner ſeuered from the gentlewomens chamber, he tæke a ſword which his nurſe had giuen him, and out of a windowe læking into the gardeine he vaulted downe, and cõmmng to the porters lodge he requeſted an horſe of him, whereon ſometimes before he had ridden, ſaying vnto him that his Lady the Princeſſe had ſent him on a ſecret meſſage. The Porter beleued him, and ſadled an horſe commending Roſicleer to God, who from thence rode ſo faſt that by the morrow he was beyond hew and crye. Before nœne the Princeſſe ſente for him, but he coulde not be founde, then the Princeſſe geſsing what it might be, was ſo ſorrowfull that it little fayled of hir death, which aſſuredly ſhe had not auoyded but that there came to hir remembraunce then that which the Nymph had foretold hir in the fountaine of hir loues as concerning hir loſſes, and ſo with ſome lyttle lyngrmg hope for the retourne of Fortune baniſhing all delyghts ſhe ſhut hir ſelfe vp cloſe in the monaſtery, more lyke an obſeruant vowleſſe then a ſtately Princeſſe, whence alſo ſhe neuer departed vntill that God had permitted hir to recouer hir huſband, as ſhalbe tolde you.

But to retourne vnto Roſicleer, being neither ſicke nor wel at eaſe betwene the conceit of his mothers griefe, and the hope of being made knight by ſome aduenture. He gaue him ſelfe vnto the queſt of ſeking Prince Edward ſ Donzel del Febo his brother, and therfore his entente was to paſſe into great Britaine to ſæ the king Oliuerio his grandfather as he had hearde, and by ſome gœd hap to be made knight. In this iourney he made ſo greate haſt, that in ſhort ſpace he entred into Almaine, and ther trauailing by the ignoraunce of the way, one daye he loſt

himselfe amongst the mountaynes which wer thicke of
tall woode, and other lower buske, seming to be no waye
vnto him, and he strayed so long not finding his way that
the Sunne was set ere he knew how to get out, wherefore hauing no other remedy he clymbed vp to the toppe
thereof to take a view of the place on each side, and hee
saw beneth him a deepe and large valley as it wer a mile
from thence, enuironed with steepe and high hilles in
which there wer some castells and other buyldings very
faire and goodly. Now that it was nighte and that this
was his onely refuge, he made his horse easely descende
the hill, at the foote whereof he espyed a sauage Beare
running from the towne with a childe in his mouthe of
two yeares olde. The childe cryed so pitifully that Rosicleer tooke great compassion of it, and seeing it euen at
the poynt to be deuoured, he ranne his horse with great
fury towards the Beare. The Beare nothing afrighted
at the noyse of the horse, stoode still with his praye in his
mouth, and he so glared with his eyes setting his formost
pawes for his defence, that although Rosicleer spurred
him, his horse yet would not approch neerer. Then Rosicleer alyghted and fastening his horse to a tree, with
his sworde drawen went towarde the Beare, and the
Beare seing him so make towardes him, lette the young
childe fall vpon the grounde, and began to buskle himselfe
to the fight with such a loude grone that he mighte haue
feared a right good knight, but Rosicleer as it were dedicated to greater purposes then to be murthered by a bear,
was nothing appalled at this, but whe̅ y̅ bear snapped at
him to haue griped him betwen his arms, he gaue y̅ bear
a blow crosse y̅ raines of y̅ backe, y̅ the Beare almost hewen in sunder fell deade to the grounde. Rosicleer by and
by wiping his sworde in the grasse put it vp in his sheath
and to the child he went which lay crying on the ground
being also in his seming both beautiful and plesaunt and
therefore lykely to haue bene taken from some of those

castells

castels in ẙ valley. By ẙ time Rosicleer had ridden a myle in the valley he saw therein situate many castels and edifices so nære together as that ẙ valley semed to be wel peopled, and taking his way to the nærest, hee sawe two young men and an olde man with battayle axes in theire handes & in their armour ride in great hast as somewhat disquyeted, as they came nere to Rosicleer & sawe ẙ childe whom they sought for, they were very glad, and well eying his good proportion and beautie sayd. God reward you faire gentleman for you haue ridde vs of a great part of trouble which we shold haue suffred in seking this child, and we praye you on your fayth howe you came by him. Rosicleer saluting them courteously tolde them, that the childe was caryed by an vgly Beare, and that hee was fayne to set the childe frē by slaying the Beare. The men more amazed at this, gaue him great thancks & certefied him ẙ the most auncient in that company was ẙ childes father, and that the other two were his bretheren, and that they walking on the battlements of their castle, the childe stode at the porch, from whence the Beare had caryed him, and neighbours espying it had tolde which way the Beare ranne, vpon this wee prepared our selues, although we are sure that if you had not succoured him before, we should haue come to late for refcetwes. Rosicleer then deliuered the childe to his father, whome the father kyssed with so great loue as if he had sēne him newely rayfed from the dead.

Then ẙ aunciēt man making his preface with a great sigh sayd. Beautifull gentleman if you know how plen- ,,
tifully God hath bestowed his blessings vpon vs on ẙ one ,,
part, and how iustly he hath scourged vs for our offences ,,
on the other part, you would not so highly commende of ,,
the frutefulnesse of ẙ soyle, as greatly bewayle ẙ misery ,,
of the inhabitaunts enduring such torments, as were ne- ,,
uer greater in ẙ land of Pharao. What great visitation is ,,
this said Rosicleer, you make me muse on it. This plague

" replyed the olde man is so insupportable that diuers times
" the indwellers haue forsaken their countrey, and aban-
" doned themselues to winde and weather, to auoyde the
" inconuenience of this place, but for that all my lyuing
" lyeth hære and in other places I haue nothing whereby
" to mayntcine my degræ, I driue out my dayes hære in
" sorowe. The valley of it selfe is fatte, delectable, and
" holesome and so large that it conteyueth more then 2000
" Castells and other houses all deuided as you sæ. But I
" pray God our fulnesse of bread be not our iust vndowing as
" it was to the Sodomites. For we haue a Prince and
" Lorde ouer vs in times past good and gratious, but as
" God hath prouided for our misgiuing, in our time very
" cruell and vicicus, he hath to name Argion, who accor-
" ding as his power by reason of his exceeding wealth which
" the country yeldeth, is not to be contraried, so I beleue of
" lyfe he is the most peruerst and wickedest vnder heauen.
" For among other his diuelish & detestable customs which
" he ordinarily obserueth, & besides the impouerishing of his
" poore tenauntes racking them shamefully to enhaunce his
" tresory, and besides the dayly raunsoming of his neigh-
" bours lyues and goods at his pleasure for euery lyttle dis-
" pleasure conceiued against vs. This is one ẏ most vngodly
" of al, ẏ euery weke he enioineth vs to finde him a gentle-
" woman for his carnall liking. This vse he hath frequen-
" ted this foure yeares so ouerawing vs and murtheringe
" such as make denyall that now there are none to make
" resistaunce, and hys fad new growen vnto an habite by
" our patience perforce, and his force in spight of our pati-
" ence is nothing straunge vnto vs, that now all of vs obey
" his heast in being bawdes vnto our children, so that it
" would riue a mans heart a sunder to heare the faire dam-
" zells curse the lyght into the which their parents brought
" them only to fulfil the shameleffe lust of so tragicall a ty-
" rant. And to my share it is falne that hauing one onely
" daughter the fayrest in all this valley, since she hath bene
fisiæne

fiftене yeares of age I haue euery day expected hir sen ,,
ding fo2 . If I ought coulde remedy it I would either ,,
murther my daughter o2 banish hir my countrey to releaſe ,,
hir of ſo great an infamy: but Argion is ſo wicked and ,,
diuelish, that this will not ſuffiſe him, but rather if he be ,,
defrauded of his bargaine , wee ſhall all dye fo2 hir ,,
ſake.We2e ṗ aucient man was ſo ouertaken with griefe "
that he might not vtter a wo2de mo2e,his name was Ba
lides.Roſicleer angred at the heart to hear of the mallice
of the w2etch Argion, would haue giuen away the peſſi
bilitie of his lyuelode to haue bene made knight, onely
to haue ſet the lande free from ſo intollerable ſlauery, and
therfo2e he appoynted with himſelfe when he were made
knight in England, to retourne hether and to wage bat
tayle with Argion . And ſo ſtill deuiſing of ſuch things
he came to the caſtell of Balides, where he alyghted and
was frindly entertayned by the auncient mans wife, and
the young gentlewoman their daughter named Lyuerba,
both greatly p2ayſing Roſicleers good fauour and feature
of body, but much mo2e his courage when they vnder
ſtode that he had delyuered the childe by killyng the
Beare. Roſicleer ſeing the gentlewoman faire and p2o
per, and yet very ſad fo2 that Argion had ſent hir wo2de
that he ſho2tly loked fo2 hir,was greatly moued, and the
rather fo2 ṗ he knewe not how to acquit hir . Balides at
his firſt comming in,commaunded the ſupper to bee made
readye , in the meane while taking Roſicleer a ſide to a
window opening into the valley, and queſtioning with
him of his birth and of the aduenture which b2ought him
thether . Roſicleer aunſwered, I am bo2ne in Hungary, ,,
and I am to trauaile about my affay2es into great Bri ,,
tayne, and being on my way this mo2ning I loſt my ſelfe ,,
in the wode, which was the occaſion of my hether com ,,
ming. In good time came you this way ſayd Balides,fo2 ,,
by you I haue recouered my ſonne , and talking of ſuch
lyke matters they paſſed the time till ſupper was readly.

Ro-

¶Roſicleer in Lyuerbas name ſlayeth Argion, and remoueth the Iewes. Cap.XXIX.

The ſupper being reaDy Roſicleer, with Balides his wife and children ſate at the table.but there was little diſcourſe at the boꝛd ſaue that the beautifull Lyuerba felt ſo great griefe in ẙ remembꝛance of Argions paſſage that in lieu of meat ſhe fed on teares,and hir parents helped to bere a part with their ſighs,which made it a very melancholicke ſupper vnto Roſicleer. And in the necke of this, ere the cloth was taken vp, they hearde great rapping at the gate, and loking who they were , they ſaw moꝛe then xx. knights & other ſeruingmen, with toꝛckes in their handes at the gates.Theſe of the houſe demaunded what they would, one of them aunſwered . Tell Balides that Argion our loꝛd hath commaunded vs to bꝛing Lyuerba by and by,foꝛ he tarieth foꝛ hir to haue hir company this night. O how vnwelcome was this arrant vnto the parents , and how pitifull vnto the gentlewoman, which ſwounded at the hearing of Argions name,and all the houſholde wepte bitterly. Roſicleer foꝛ company moꝰued to great pitie,with the beſt courage that he migḥt to giue remedye vnto this outrage, deuiſed a pꝛeſent ſhifte and bid ſome of the ſeruauntes to tell thoſe which were without that they ſhould ſtay a while vntill the gentlewoman were in a readines,and after that,that ſhe ſhculd be ſent vnto them . Then he made the coſtlyeſt apparell which Lyuerba had to be bꝛought vnto him , and clethed himſelfe with all,making foꝛ his head a periwicke of Lyuerbas haire,& binding it with a little chain of gold,ſo that being thus readily arayed he was ſo beautifull as no gentlewoman thereabouts might parage him foꝛ grace oꝛ fauour.His hoſte & hoſtes wer amaꝛed in beholding him ſo well bere out ẙ credite of a gentlewoman, in his diſguiſed habite,neither yet knowing what he ment therby noꝛ yet minding to learne it of him vnles he firſt declared it.But

ſo

so sœne as he was throughly arayed in this wise, he soft‑ „
ly rounded his hoste in the eare saying . My friende your „
mishap & the thraldome of this lande hath had such force „
ouer me y hauing hope in God which brought me hether, „
I wil take vpon me to be Lyuerba and wil go with these „
knights to the castle of Argion. When I am alone in his „
chamber, I will behaue my selfe God willing, that I will, „
frée you from this mans tyranny, Or although I be slain „
in the execution of this enterprise, yet it were a small da‑ „
mage in respect of so great a cure. But I would haue you „
Balides, your sonnes and your other acquaintaunce and „
friends to arme your selues lykewise and lye couertly a „
little from the castle, where if you sée that I make you a‑ „
ny tokens by the lyght at a window make accounte that „
Argion is slayne, and be not afrayed to come nœre the „
gates which I will set open for you & so with little adœ „
we shall make our selues Lords of his castle. When this „
is done we wil publish it abroade to the inhabitaunts of „
the valley, which being certein of Argions death will rise „
to our succour. Balides loked wistly vpon Rosicleer and „
wondred at his courage, for he being so young, it was
in his fancie the boldest match which he had hearde off,
yet, thoughe it was impossible as he thought to come to
their purpose, for that he saw how willingly Rosicleer had
made this offer, he consented to call his friendes , este‑
ming it farre better to dye in such a quarrell then to sée &
suffer so great a mischefe. The gentlewomā Lyuerba being
made priuie therebnto by hir father knœled downe before
Rosicleer, & shedding aboundance of teares sayd vnto him.
The God which created both heauen & earth graunt you „
faire gentlemā so god hap y both this land may be acquit „
from this tyranny, and I delyuered from this bilayny. „
The knights which were without hasted to haue the gen‑
tlewomā with them, & so Rosicleer putting a sword vnder
his kirtle closely and surely that it coulde neither be per‑
ceiued, nor fall from him, hee toke his leaue of Balides,

his

his wife, and his daughter. Balides wishing him well and commending him to God, accompanied him to the gates where the knights were attendant, and there peured out so many teares to the outward sight as if it had bene his daughter. The people without hauing a glimps of Rosicleer by the lyght of the torches, tooke him to be the fayrest gentlewoman which they had euer seene, and verye glad to bring so good tidings vnto their mayster, they set him vppon a palfray prouided for the purpose, only they were agrieued at the time which was so short that they could not sufficiently gaze on hir. Their whole talke by the way ran vpon this that it were for Argion more conuenient to detaine hir for wife, then euery weeke to seeke a new, and laughing at their owne deuises they came to Argions Castle, being very great and of buylding the most sumptuous in the valley as it had bene a kings pallayce. In this they entered and helping the fayned Lyuerba from hir horse, they led hir vp a payre of staires into a chamber, where Argion awited hir comming. Rosicleer keeping a demure and sober couutenaunce, droue Argion into a great amaze at his beautie, that gredely beholding him he arose from the place where he was sette, and embraced him in these termes. You are welcome hether my Lyuerba for you make me right gladde to haue your company, and for that your beautie is more then the rest, I wyll do you more honoure then to others. The fayned Lyuerba countenaunced out his counterfait with graue behauiour, onely firing his eyes vpon the grounde, without aunswering a worde, sane that he thought vpon his purpose which he knewe would be somewhat daungerous in that Argion was strong, fowle, and fierce of looke more then he had euer seene any. Argion tooke him by the handc, and placed him next himselfe, demaunding first how hir parents did, and from thence he fell to more amorous delights, stil staring on Rosicleers beauty which throughly kindled his lust, and he desired hir to vnclothe

hir

hir felfe,and to come vnto him into the rich bedde. This
fuppofed Lyuerba framing a fhamefaſt and bafhfull looke,
with a lowe voyce gently aunfwered him, that vnleſſe
he commaunded his feruaunts to auoyde the chamber,
and the doores to bée faſtened,fhe would not be féene naked in that company. Argion taking it to bée an argument of great honeſtie did of his clothes firſt, and lepte
into his bedde,commaunding his people to goe out, and
fhut ẙ doores after them.They lighting a great candle fet
on a candleſtick of filuer went out,& ther remained onely
this Lyuerba with Argion,leiſurely vnclothing hir felfe
to delay time, and that the feruauntes fhoulde miſtruſt
naught by hearing a buſtling in the chamber, firſt fhée
put off hir vpper gowne, then to hir peticoate,and fo
fhe ſtayed a whyle, Argion callinge on hir to difpatche
quickely,as if the greateſt part of his delight had bene to
come. Roficleer thincking it nowe time to difcouer hir
felfe, and that the houre was already come wherein
God almightie woulde the wicked Argion to bée chaſti-
fed,caſt of his long garment,& tourned himfelfe into his
doublet and hofe,and hauing his fwo₂d d₂awen,he came
to Argions bed fide,faying,come out of thy place where
ẙ art thou foule letcher,& come to reioice thée of Liuerbas
loue,fo₂ very bitter fhall this nightes reſt bée vnto thée.
Argion which beheloe him rofe vp lightly,and taking a
fwoode which hong at hys beddes head,went towards
Roficleer to haue catched hym in his armes, but Roficleer with his naked fwo₂d watched him fo ẙ he fmote
the necke from the fhoulders,the heade beating agaynſt
the wall,and the body falling headleſſe to the grounde.
This done, Roficleer quietly fate downe in the fame
place,and thus remained till the greater parte of the
nyght was fpent.Balides nowe in this time had not fo₂-
gotten his charge,and hauing talked with mo₂e then xx.of
his friends, as concerning their entent,he eafely perfwaded them to this enterp₂ife,fo hauing thē in his company

L.

withɔ

with his sonnes he lodged nære to Argions castell, onely looking for a signe which Rosicleer should make them out at a windowe, which when Rosicleer had for a time neglected, they suspected ý vnlikelihod of the fact, & had retourned closely to their homes, if ý Rosicleer had not thē taking ý light in his hand, opened ý dores of the hall & shewed the torch out of a windolv. Then they knew lvhat had happened, & went ioyfully tolvard the castel. Rosicleer cōming dolvne, opened the gates, so that they all entered, & lighting many torches which they brought with them they cast themselues into seuerall cōpanies to serch euery corner & ranging without feare, throughout the castel when they knew that Argion was slaine, & killing so many as they found that in dæde though there were mo then an. I oo. knights and other seruaunts within the castel, yet all were slaine before they could puruay of armour, or thinck of remedy, in such sort that in the castel ther was not one left to take Argions part. At Argion may the stout Lords & vntamed tyrants take example of their endes, & make it a benefit of his fall, for although God sometime forbere the wicked giuing them space of amendement and repentaunce, yet when they can in no wise be reclaimed, his iustice must of necessitie correct them in the manner that both their bodyes repaye in this life their trespasses with cruell death and perpetuall deshonour, and their soules in the other world receiue dubble disgrace and horrour of conscience for their misdædes: Howe many great Lordes & tyrants haue we read off to haue bene in the worlde, and howe felve or none haue we heard off vnpunished which can be no other thing but that the diuine prouidence hathe so ordeined it, some to be chastised for the misgournment of themselues, and other some to amend by the terrour of others destruction: Well, the tyrant Argion thus being slaine wth all his people, Balides and those which came with him for his great prowesse in killing Argion, sued vnto Rosicleer, to acknowledge them for his subiectes,

as they all would willingly obey him for their Lord. But
he feuerally making femblaunce of great loue to euery
partie made them to rise, aduifing them on this fort. That
for their deliueraunce they ought to attribute it vnto
God with harty thanckes: for it which by his goodneffe
had prouided ý the euill luft of wicked Argion fhould laft
no longer. But for that they called him their Lord, he faid
he would be their friend, and neuertheleffe fith they requefted him therevnto, ý he would not refuse their proffer,
not for himfelfe, but in deede to giue order to that whiche
fhould fucceede for the quiet gouernment of the feignorie.
This done, Balides fent for his wife and his daughter
Lyuerba, with his houfeholde, they comming before Roficleer gaue him thancks for this great good tourne in procuring their fafetie. He receiued them with great pleafure, and they made meery all that night. The next daye
they deuifed for the publication of Argions death, which
Balides made to be knowne to the moft principall in the
valley. They all very defirous of fuch newes came to the
caftell, where knowing the manner of Argions ende,
much prayfing the ftrength and boldeneffe of Roficleer,
with all feeing him fo well fauoured and of fo younge
yeares, they ceafed not to giue hym thanckes for the
good which he had done, fo that Roficleer fomewhat blufh-
ing at it forbad them to fpeake more of it, but to attend
their owne affayres, for the valley being fo replenifhed
with dwellers all of them were not founde, but for feare
or fauour were Argions clawbackes. Thefe they had
to dee with all, and in the ende fubdued them, after
wanting a gouernoure they befought Roficleer to a-
byde wyth them and to take othes of their allegy-
aunce towardes him, for fith that by him they haue
bene refifored to their auncient lybertyes, they thought
him to be an able maynteyner of they franchifes, but
Roficleer made them aunfwere, that at the fute of
Lyuerba, Argion was flaine, and that hee moued with

L.ij. pitie

pitie vpon hir,had enterpꝛiſed it foꝛ hir ſake,if therefoꝛe he had deſerued ought, he wiſhed them in reſpect thereof to make Lyuerba miſtreſſe of it,and foꝛ the eſtabliſhment of hir poſſeſſion to match hir vnto the chiefeſt inheritour of land and fee amongeſt them. This if they did foꝛ hꝭ ſake,he ſhould account it not onely a ſatiſfaction on their partes foꝛ the pleaſure he had done them:but alſo a bond foꝛ a further good tourne if it ſo lye in his power . They debating vpon this matter were all contented with it and pꝛomiſed all their habilities to doe his commaund,ſo a-mong them there was a knight called Brandidonio, the chiefeſt of all the valley,a pꝛoper and honeſt gentleman, Loꝛd of thꝛée great caſtels,and beloued of al the countrey foꝛ his bountie and courteſie , him they choſe to marrie with Lyuerba their Lady,Roſicleer very wel pleaſed with this gentlemans noble diſpoſitiō,concluded vpon ẏ marri-age,ſo that in foure dayes the Loꝛde Brandidonio ẑ the ſhire]Lyuerba were created Loꝛd ẑ lady of the valley,and in ſtoken of obedience toke the othe and aſſuraunce of their ſubiectes , where they liued longe time in quiet-neſſe, their ſubiectes as well at eaſe to haue ſuch go-uernours.

¶Roſicleer departed from the valley of the mountaines, meeteth with two Princes chri-ſtened,& by aduenture is carried from them againe. Cap.30.

ROSICLEER remayned foure dayes in the val-ley of the mountaines,foꝛ ſo it was called, to ſolem-nize the marriage betwéene Brandidonio and Lyuerba , whereat the tenauntes of the valley béinge pꝛeſente, and féeinge his perſonage ſo tall and goodly, and ioy-ned with ſo good grace and gentle behauieur, iudged him a perſon rather celeſtiall then moꝛtall , and belée-ued that God had ſente him foꝛ their deliueraunce, from

the

the miserable subiection wherin Argion had holden them,
so they reuerenced and honoured hym, as if they had
seene in him some vndoubted Image of immortalitie. But
Rosicleer, this marriage being finished, hauinge no more
to doe, made to assemble the greatest of the countrey, vnto whom he said, that he had vowed a voyage which might
not be left off, and therefore now at his departure, he praied them to accept well of his so short tarrying, and in his
absence to doe thée honour diligently to Brandidonio, and
Lyuerba, which was due vnto their liege Lord and louing
Lady. They ouercharged with griefe for the lacke of hym
who they loued as their nigh kinsman, layd to stay him by
giftes and other offers, but when it booted not, they swore
faith and obeysaunce towardes their Lord, and for a remembraunce of their loue, they forced vpon Rosicleer an
horse which was Argions, a very fall and strange horse
which he refused, not as being very commodious to trauaile with, and then after this tooke his leaue of Lyuerba, hir father and mother, and Brandidonio hir husband.
Being ready to mounte on horsbacke, a younger brother of Lyuerbas called Telyo, throwing himselfe on hys
knées before Rosicleer, besought him to graunte hys
sute, which Rosicleer willingly promised, bidding hym
saye on, Telyo then sayde. Syr sith you are to tra- „
uayle alone, and haue none to serue you by the waye, „
maye it please you to shewe me the fauoure as to re- „
teyne me for your squyer. Rosicleer well pleased wyth „
the good affection whiche Telyo bare towardes hym,
embraced Telyo with muche loue, and thus made
aunswere. Telyo thou art before hande wyth me, for „
I haue geuen thee thy requeste, so that I maye not „
excuse my selfe of my former promise, althoughe I „
woulde aduise thée rather to tarry at home in the de- „
lights of thine owne nation, then to put thy selfe in „
daunger in a forren and vnknowne countrey. Telyo „
glaober of this then of a good purchase, prepared all

L.iij.   things

things ready for their iourney, and tooke his leaue of hys
Father, Mother, and kinsfolke, who were nothinge
miscontent of his choyce, for that the company was suche
as euery one coulde haue wyshed his roome. Rosicleer
and Telyo tooke on their waye, neyther speakinge to o-
ther, for the thought of theyr so louynge partinge from
their friendes, whiche as yet stake freshe and grœne in
their remembraunce. And sooth it is, that within a
whyle after Rosicleers departure, to the ende the straungenesse of their deliuery might be renued by their posteritie, and no age should leaue to speake thereoff, they founded an house of religion wyth a fayre Temple, wherein at the one side of the hyghe Altar they erected a pyl-
ler of marble very fayre and curious, bearinge the true
counterfette of Rosicleer, wyth the hystorye of Argion,
the frœing of Lyuerba, and all that consequently followeth in that storye, so that in longe time after thys mo-
numente of restoringe the inhabitantes, was founde by
our age in the pursute of aduentures in that countrey.
Brandidonio, and Lyuerba hœre ruled long time in peace
and tranquilitie, and from them descended all the Lordes
whiche since haue had the gouernaunce of that valley.
But from thence to followe Rosicleer on hys waye, the
historye sayeth that wyth hys squire Telyo hœ trauayled so longe thoroughe Almaine that hœ came to an
hauen of the Sea, in a manner directe agaynst greate
Britaine in Picardy, where there were two great and
fayre shyppes taryinge for the wynde to coaste ouer into Englande. Rosicleer hearinge of this in hys Inne,
wente out of hys hostrye to the hauens mouth, there
to speake wyth the master of the shyppe for to become
a passenger, and comminge thether hœ sawe manye
knightes and other seruauntes by lykelyhœde of some
worshipp passe to and fro which made him thincke it was
no marchaunts vessell, but yet he entered the ship, & there
espying two knights younge men, richly apparelled
and

and placed in two seuerall seates, to whome the other
knightes in the shippe made their obeysaunce he tourned his face to haue gone out agayne. But the young
knightes sæinge Rosicleer and greatly delighted in
his beautie and comlinesse of personage, called to him.
Rosicleer tourninge towardes them made lowe reuerence as vnto so greate estates. The knightes receiuing him with as greate courtesy, demaundinge
of him gentelye what countryman hee was, and
what he sought there. Rosicleer looking vpon them sadly, and soberly aunswered. I am come my Lordes „
from the valley of the mountaynes, and I am desi- „
rous to sæ greate Britaine, for my affaires whiche „
lye in that countrey, whether as I haue learned by o- „
thers, your shippes are prepared, I am therefore to be- „
sæch you to do me the pleasure, as to graunt me passage „
in your company. They well contented withall, for „
that he was a younge gentleman excellinge in beautie all those which they had sæne, tolde hym they were
willinge therevnto, and that if he næded ought vnto „
this iourney, they woulde minister vnto his wantes. „
Rosicleer gaue them many thanckes for this their courtesy, but they demaunded farther howe he was called,
and of what linage he came, to the first Rosicleer aunswered, that his name was Rosicleer, and mindinge to cutte „
of the rest, he desired them to spare him for the other at „
that time, and to content themselues with this that hee „
nowe came from the valley of the mountaynes, wherefore
they belæued that he was naturally borne there. By this
means Rosicleer was entertained with these Lords, and
grewe farther in acquaintaunce wyth them, that hee
knewe the one to bæ Bargandel the Bohemian cosin
Germaine to the Emperour Trebatio, and eldest sonne
to the kynge of Bohemia, the other to bæ the Prince Lyriamandro brother to the Princesse Briana, both of them
of his nigh kinne.

L iiij.

The Fortune which linked and conioyned thefe Pinces in this amitie, was this. The king of the great Britaine called Oliuerio, confidering that the loffe of the Pince Edward his fonne, noifed through his Empyre for.xv. yeares fpace had fo appalled the courages of his knightes that neither feaftes were made, nor turneys proclaymed, nor any difportes vfed with gentlewomen in his countrey, whereby to fyre the heartes of younge men to the deedes of armes. But that either all of them ouercome with griefe, and mourning ftill for his fonne, forfooke to weare armour, or els fuch as their owne good natures pricked forwardes to try aduentures, departed out of hys realme, in other regions to become famous, fo that the kingdome of England was very naked of able Knightes to defende it, wheras before it was beft knowne in all the world for knighthood and chiualrie. The kinge I faye, wifely cafting of thefe thinges, did not nowe fo muche lament the lacke of his fonne, as fearing the inconuenience which might enfue by the want of good fouldiers, if any enimy fhoulde arife, prouided againft this mifchiefe on this fort.

First taking the aduife of his counfell therein, he caufed to bee proclaymed through euery fhire and markette towne. That fuch knyghtes his fubiectes as either were already departed, or nowe were in minde to depart the realme, for to ferue in other Pinces courtes, fhoulde retourne to their homes by a day prefixed in the fchedule, vppon payne of his high difpleafure. This proclamation diuulged abroade by the found of a trumpet, as many as heard of it, either by their friendes letters, or by the rumour fpred in other countries, retourned fpeadely, fo that the king in a folemne triumph, taking the mufter of hys fpeciall knightes, founde himfelfe fufficiently furnifhed. Nowe the fecond care was, howe deteine them at home, and for this he cruifed with his counfell to make a highe feaft in the Citie of London, with iuftes and turneys, for

all

all knights aduenturous both Engliſhmen and ſoꝛreiners, and to oꝛdeyne ſuche pꝛices as might inuite noble Pꝛinces thether . This thus agræd vpon the king Cluerio a yeare befoꝛe that theſe feaſts ſhould begin directed his letters to all Pꝛinces Chꝛiſtened and otherwiſe as farre Turkey certefiyng them that he had appoynted iuſtes to be holden at his citye of London and pꝛices foꝛ the beſt doers , and that thether it ſhoulde bee frée foꝛ all knights to come and try their foꝛces . The pꝛice was a maſſy crowne of golde al ſette with pearles and pꝛecicus ſtones valued by al mens dæming at the pꝛice of a great Citie . The newes hereof by the kings letters ſpꝛedde ouer all countryes entiſed theſe two Pꝛinces lykewiſe being but of young yeares to craue to be made knightes by their parents, & to trauayle towardes England. So hauing obtayned their purpoſes either of them pꝛepared foꝛ his iourney, and mette together at one time in this hauen neither of them knowing other , noꝛ of theire intentes, Whereafter they had knowledge each of other, and had concionated about their enterpꝛice, they determined to go together as friendes, and had ſtayed thꝛée dayes foꝛ the winde ere Roſicleers comming, whom good foꝛtune dꝛoue vnto the ſame coaſt, there to make an aſſurance of perfect friendſhippe betwéene theſe thꝛée, lyke as ſhe had earſte done betwéene Donzel del Febo, Brandizel and Clauergudo. This knot betwéene thꝛée being the moꝛe inſonable as both it hath moꝛe hope of ſucour by the greater number, and repꝛeſents in my fancy the figure of the triangle in Geometry, wyth this poſy. Euery way the ſame. This amitie by degrées encreaſed as their acquaintaunce augméted, foꝛ Roſicleers conuerſation was ſo good ẏ they wer very glad to haue his cōpany, but they left him, ere they had thꝛoughly founde him , and as no pleaſure in this woꝛlde may dure : ſo at the time when theſe two Pꝛinces moſt ioyed in Roſicleers company, their pleaſure was ouerturned and their delyght conuerted to mourning.

For the next day the winde blowing very calme the mariners hoysed vp the sayles, and plyed their tacklinges so
merily, that with great lyking of them all, they rode easely yet not so as they could attayne to the hauen, in good
spæde, but that one euening when the Mone shone bright
and the waues of the Sea were still and quyet, the two
knights with Rosicleer betwæne them, leaned ouer the
sides of the shippe reioycing all thræ at the brightnesse of
the starres in the firmament, & at the delicate rombling,
which the winde made in the bottome of the water. This
was so pleasaunt vnto them as that in this contemplaci-
on they spent the third parte of the night, about which
time they heard the cry of a gentlewoman as it might be
in some distresse. Then they loked about them, and e-
spyed a little crayer comming towardes them, in which
there was a wilde man for making a Gyant, fierce of
countenaunce and all hairy of body, of manners sauage,
and cruell, hauing in the one hande a knotted club wyth
pikes at the ende of Iron, so heauy as a lesse man coulde
not lyfte it: and in the other hande haling a faire gentlewoman by the haire, hir face all bloody with the blowes
he gaue hir, and punches with his fæte. The Gyant still
cryed. Tourne thy boate thou false and trayterous en-
chauntresse, or I will make thy lyfe to aunswere it mæ, in
that thou hast kepte me so long from it. The gentlewoman neuer aunswered him, but continually prayed vnto
God for succours. This they both heard and sawe easely
by Moonelyght, for the boate approched to their shippe,
and the two other gentlemen were much abashed to sæ
so wilde a Gyant nære vnto them, for they had neuer
sæne his lyke before. But the noble ccurage of Rosicleer
coulde not be so countermaunded by the Gyants hugenesse, as to suffer such vilany towards any gentlewoman,
& therfore setting his fote vpon the side of ye ship & taking
his swoorde in his hand, he leaped into the gentlewomans
boate.

Nature

Nature as it wer willing to manifest hir owne workes
and to discouer the secret graces, which shee before had
couered in his comely personage. For so as if he had long
time experimented the daunger of conflicts, boldely hee
tooke vpon him this aduenture. At his first comming into
the boate he strake not the Gyant, but with great mode-
ration and more discretion then was needefull (but that
he was verye circumspecte and in all things lowly,) hee
sayd vnto the Gyant. Leaue of Gyant to entreat thys ,,
gentlewoman in this sort, and way well, that it is great ,,
shame to a man for to laye his handes vpon a woman. ,,
The great Gyant lyttle respecting this courtesie, left the
gentlewoman to haue taken vp Rosicleer, & to haue throwen him into the water, but Rosicleer perceiuing him,
put his naked sworde poinaunt before him.

The Gyant rashly ranne vpon the sworde, that it entred a lyttle, and therefore madde angrye at his wounde,
he gaue backe, lyfting vp his greate batte with both hys
handes to driue at Rosicleer. But Rosicleer as destenyed
to greater exploytes, watching the blowe starte aside, and
closing with the Gyant thrust his sworde into his guttes.
Rosicleer pulled out ye sword hastely to haue giue him an
other blowe, but the Gyant fell vpon the planks gasping
for breath: then Rosicleer stept vnto him, & with mayne
force tombled him ouer shipborde, wher he lay drenched
in the Sea.

All this the two Princes beheld and wondred at the
great conrage of Rosicleer, but not a lyttle diseased in that
they coulde not helpe him. For when he leaped into the
gentlewomans boate, they cryed a loude to theire
knightes, to lette downe theire shipboate into the water,
but it coulde not bee, before that the valyaunt youth had
drenched the Gyant in the Sea, & that the gentlewomans
boate rode with such swiftenes as in short time they lost
the sight of it, with so much griefe vnto both these Princes as they might scarse speake the one to the other.

For

For when they compared together the shortnesse of time
in which they enioyed him, & in that short time the great
prowesse which he had shewed before them, they coulde
not easely asserteine themselues, whether they had dreamed of such things or seene them waking. But if so bee
they were not beguyled either by a dreame, or some
fantasticall illusion, I dare warrant they thought that in
regarde of that which God had wrought by him, he could
not be, but of noble estate. Well, when ther was no hope
of following, they haled vp their boate againe to keepe
their course towardes Britaine, hauing hope to meete him
ther, otherwise appoynting with themselues, if they ther
fayled to go in quest of him.

I may forgette to tell you of his squire Telyo but you
may easely thincke of his paynes, by the loue he bare hys
Lorde, and I will leaue him to your seuerall consideratĩ-
ons of your selues in lyke cases, being farre from your
country, and farder from your friende whome you haue
preferred before your country, the rather to accompanye
these noble gentlemen vnto the coast of England, which
in their waye still kepte on their former dittie, euer talking of Rosicleer, either cõmending his good grace, or bewaylinge his departure, or blaming their own misfortuns,
or extolling his strength, and euer the fote of their sõge
was, what should the swiftnesse of y̆ boate meane & our
sodayne acquaintaunce. Unto the depth whereof bicause
they coulde not reache, thereby to quyet themselues, their
sorrow redoubled by misiudging the worst. In the ende
the winde was so good that it sette them on lande in the
great Britaine not farre from London, where the kinge
was resiaunt. Where as soone as they came one shore,
before they presented themselues to the king they dispatched out one of their shippes with some of their knights
and Telyo Rosicleers squire to coast the same way which
Rosicleer was gone, to the ende if Fortune were so fauourable to bring some tidings of him. Afterwards them

selue

felues with the maieftie that doth belong to fo greate
Princes, tooke towards the great citie, viewing on euery
fide ý great affembly of people, all ý fields & high wayes
befides townes and hamlets taken vp for knights, afwell
ftraungers as naturall, and an infinite number of Ladies
and gentlewomen, comming onely to fæ the tournayes.
The two Princes fent two of their knights before hande
to giue vnderftanding vnto the king of their comming.
The king glad to haue the prefence of fo noble Princes
at his high feaft, with a great trayne of knights mette
them without ý citie, & comming towards them, embraced them with great loue. The ftorye leaueth to recount
the words of courtefie, which paffed betwæne them, and
fayth that they entred into the pallaice with the king, and
were lodged in one quarter thereof, himfelfe kæping his
newe guefts company that night, and talking with Liriamandro as concerning his daughter in lawe. At whom
he learned the whole ftate of Hungarye with the appendices as touching that matter, which in fome refpect made
him very forowfull to heare of the continuall affliction
wherwith Briana tormented hir felfe in the monaftery of
the riuer. And he was as greatly abafhed to heare that
in Greece they knew as little of the Emperour Trebatio,
as in England he heard of the Prince Edward.

Then Liriamandro efpying the king fomewhat inqui-
fitiue, procæded farther with his talke, in declaring the
aduenture which had ioyned him & Bargandel, and how
that they two mette at the hauen with a gentleman called Rofícleer and fo confequently of the battaile with the
Gyant, the king hearing of fo many vertues in Rofícleer,
as Liriamandro did his vttermofte to fette them forthe,
greatly wifhed to haue fæne him. Hære the ftory leaueth
the king and thefe Princes to the prouiding of thinges
neceffarye for the tilte, & goeth on with Rofícleer, whom
thefe Princes lefte vpon the mayne Sea.

Cer-

¶ Certeine accidents which befell Rosicleer after
his departure from the two Princes. Cap. 31.

ROSICLEER made an ende of the battayle with
ẙ Gyant, ʒ the gentlewoman so wel reuenged by his
meanes kneled down before him to haue kissed his hand
ʒ to giue him harty thācks for his his gret friendship shewed in working hir deliuery from the terrible Gyaunt.
Rosicleer tooke hir vp, and demaunded of hir what shee
was and by what aduenture she was broughte into the
Gyants hande. The gentlewoman aunswered : Knowe
„ my Lorde that I am named Calinda, daughter to the
„ wise man Artemidoro of whome peraduenture you haue
„ hearde speaking before this time, inhabiting in an Iland
„ not farre from hence in the midst of the Sea, which may
„ neuer againg his will be sene of any body. This wyse
„ man my father hauing sent me on a message in this boat
„ to a friend of his, Lord of an Iland not farre hence, my
„ fortune was such, that when I retourned by this Gy-
„ ants Iland there entring on lande for fresh water, I was
„ espyed by this Gyant, who made to me to haue taken me,
„ but I fled towards my boat which I could not recouer
„ so sone, but that he entred with me. But as he shoued to
„ land, my boat droue backward into ẙ streame ʒ had losse
„ the sight of his Iland. The cruell Gyant seing this, and
„ thinking that I had done it by my knowledge, woulde
„ haue killed mee, and entreated mee in such sorte as you
„ saw. Now as for the lyghtenesse of the boate sir, I be-
„ leue sayth ẙ gentlewoman, ẙ it is guyded by my fathers
„ Arte, and that we are on the way towarde his Ilande.
„ Whereat gentleman I beseech you take no thought, al-
„ though you haue lost your company, for I doubte not but
„ that by my fathers cunning you shalbe ioyned, ʒ then my
„ father shall serue you loyally, for the mercye you haue
„ shewed me.

Ro-

Roſicleer much wondꝛed both at ẏ gentlewomans ſpech, and at the Gyants crueltie without good occaſion, and eſpecially at the incredible ſwiftneſſe of ẏ bote, laylyng in the Sea, faſter then a birde flyeth in the ayꝛe, which made him iudge Artemidoro to be a very wiſe man, in that he had ſo great authoꝛitye ouer the Sea. And therefoꝛe he reioyced himſelfe vppon hope to ſæ the wiſe man at whome he might demaunde ſome newes as touching Pꝛince Edward his father, and Donzel del Febo his bꝛother. And foꝛ that he queſtioned with the gentlewoman many thinges as concerning hir father, of whome he lerned many things.

Nowe as they talked of theſe thinges, the boat ſtode ſtill as it had bene ſanded. Roſicleer much abaſhed thereat loked on euery ſide what it ſhould be that ſtayd it, and gaged the water with a poale, but he perceiued nothinge, wherfoꝛe he thought ẏ peraduenture vnder the bote in ẏ place ther laie ſome Adamant ſtone, of ẏ vertue whereof he had red befoꝛe times that it dꝛaweth vpon vnto it, and ſtayeth the ſhippes which ſayle ouer it. And as he was much perplexed in his thought, not knowing how to remedy it: he ſawe befoꝛe him a lyttle Ilande, the freſheſt and moſt delectable that in his lyfe he had ſæne, and the boate alreadye faſtened to the bancke. Then the gentlewoman bad him not to feare, but to come out on lande, foꝛ the Ilande which he ſawe befoꝛe him was hir fathers Ilande.

This was ſtraunge vnto Roſicleer, to ſee the lyquyde Sea ſo ſone conuerted to ſclide earthe, but he made not ſtraunge to come on lande at hir bidding. Where by and by the wiſe man met them, a man by ſæming very aged, his bearde all white and reaching to his waſt, with a little white rodde in his hande, as ſome token either of his honour oꝛ profeſſion. The wiſe man foꝛ the greate pleaſure hee had to ſæ Roſicleer, ſayd vnto him on this

wiſe

,, wife . Right noble and most woppthy Rosicleer, you are
,, welcome vnto this my country, foz by your comming I
,, haue bene moze at my hearts ease then during my lyfe I
,, haue ben, and many yeares past haue I longed foz your
,, prefence. Foz although I knew foz a certeinty that hether
,, you should come, yet the time when, I knew not, which
,, hath hetherto bene concealed from moztall men, and on-
,, ly made knowne to God himselfe . I knewe lykewyfe fo
,, fone as my daughter Calinda was boznc, that she should
,, be fette free from cruell captiuitie and perpetual dishonoz
,, by you onely, but the manner howe , was not reuealed
,, withall , onely that it should be when the pzouidence of
,, God directed by his wyll, committed the execution there-
,, of to Foztune. Thus may we men foz all our cunninge
,, neither alter the course of things appoynted by destenye,
,, noz yet finde other remedy then is permitted by the foze-
,, knowledge of God . As this my daughter coulde neuer
,, haue bene faued, but onely in that same manner as you
,, gaue hir fuccour . The reafon was , bicaufe my know-
,, ledge coulde not wade fo deepe as to fozfée euery thinge
,, concluded by destenyes, the felfe same thing being fubiect
,, vnder the lyne of destenye, that I should not perceiue it.
,, So my daughter went on lande vnto the Gyants Iland,
,, which I neither fozefawe to pzeuent, noz could haue pze-
,, uented if I had fozeféene . Yet that which was in my
,, power I fo ruled the boate that it came to your shippe,
,, thereby to haue reliefe at your hands foz my care . This
,, haue I tolde you at large the inhabilitie of our cunninge
,, agaynst the influence of ý stars, wherby you may perceiue
,, how much I am beholding vnto you, the rather to make
,, bolde vppon my feruice, if in any refpect either my Art oz
,, my armour may doe you pleafure.
,,   Rosicleer attentiuely lyftening vnto the wife mans
discourfe, in the ende gaue him great thanckes foz his fo
lyberall offer, pzomifing lykewife the feruice of his body,
foz other thing had he nought, to do his commaund in any

matter reasonable. With this the wise man toke hym
by the hand, and lead him towarde a great and beautifull
pallaice seated vpon the shore. Rosicleer with a curious
eye gased on each part of the pallaice, so situate in an vnknowne Iland, and was neuer content, for in dæde y͏̔ sub-
teltie of y͏̔ workmanship surpassed y͏̔ far craft of masonry
in our daies. But here he abode ij.daies with Artemidoro, serued of delicate viandes and strange deuises, able to
quicken a dead mans stomacke, bæing hære better pleased with his entertainment then he was euer otherwise.
One day sittinge at the boarde with Rosicleer, the wise
man espying hym ouercupped in his thought about hys
iourney to England, sported wyth him in this sorte.
Rosicleer, I sæ wel this coūtrey brædeth not such things ,,
as may content your appetie, and I holde you excused, for ,,
your desire coueteth after Mars and Martiall feates, ,,
wherefore as my learning sheweth me, your lust carrieth ,,
your stomacke into England, ther to be knighted. Truely ,,
faire sir you haue gꝏd reasō therebnto, for the time is at ,,
hande wherein your knighthꝏde muste bee manifested. ,,
But for to doe you honour I my selfe will attende you ,,
thether, in respect both of your friendship paste towardes ,,
my daughter Calinda, and other greater matters to ,,
come which I hope shall bæ accomplished. I knowe ,,
not in dæde the time when it shall bæ, neither the man- ,,
ner howe, but this I knowe, that by your meanes I ,,
shall once escape the death. Nowe as well for your ,,
owne sake bæinge for the very moment of your byrth ,,
illumined with more then mortall graces, as I haue ,,
already engrossed the dolorous lyfe of the Princesse ,,
Briana, so wyll I be also the regester of your actes, to ,,
enroll your memory in the recordes of fame, that it ,,
shall bæ maynteinable agaynst all counterpleas, and ,,
forged euidences. Thys will I doe for you besides the ,,
perpetuitie of my seruice in other matters, and for ,,
your brother Donzel del Febo he hathe already found a ,,

M.   croni-

„ cronicler(meaning this by Lyrgandeo)such as his wor-
„ thinesse meriteth.Roricleer tickeled at his talk,touching
„ his brother Donzel del Febo,bowed himselfe thanckfully
„ and requested him to goe on,sayinge. Ryght honourable
„ Syr , seeinge you haue entered into thys discourse,I
„ praye you continue it , for I knewe naught as pertay-
„ ning to this my brother, saue that he was loste in the
„ Sea being very younge , and I haue hitherto thought
„ that hee had bene deade, and sith nothing is hid from
„ your knowledge,I pray you likewise satiffie me in y e same
„ manner as concerninge the Prince Edward my Fa-
„ ther, that I maye seeke hym if there bee hope of findinge
„ on this earth . Most noble Prince aunswered the wyse
„ man, you drawe me vnto a longe tale, and in some
„ poynt nothinge pertinent to you . But knowe for a
„ truth that the gentleman of the Sunne your brother is
„ aliue already knighted , and for hys first prises he hath
„ achyued suche meruaylous deedes of armes , as that it
„ standeth you in hande to bestirre your selfe if you
„ mynde to be matchable , beinge the onely man as yet
„ vnparagonized through the worlde. Hee is nowe in
„ a countrey where wythout knowledge of hys estate,
„ he is notwithstandinge muche praysed for his perso-
„ nage, the regyon so farre dystant from thys our cly-
„ mate,that if you put your selfe on the waye to seeke
„ hym, your payne shoulde bee infinite and as I can
„ learne needelesse, for ere that you passe out of thys coun-
„ trey hee wyll come to seeke you heere . Nowe as to
„ your demaunde touching the Prince Edward whome
„ you call your Father . I doe you to wytte that hee
„ was deade before that you were begotten, and that
„ the royall Princesse your mother nowe destitute of an
„ husbande,shall in tyme recouer hir lawefull husbande,
„ and you shall knowe your Father,for the greatest and
„ mightiest Prince christened . Furthermore bycause
„ it is forbidden mee to discouer of the greate secretes of

God, vntyll it be his pleasure that all men shall knowe „ it, J maye not aunswere you , but the euente shall „ witnesse wyth my prophecie . Nowe wyll J make ready for your passage into Britaine, for there muste bee shewed the first flowre of your manhood. Rosicleer was greatly confused in his vnderstading, at the words which ẙ wyse man spake bœing yet plaine & easy, and he able to make English of euery woorde, but the cause was, for that he was vnable to finde out ẙ true sence which this diui= nitie carried, bœing repugnannt to hys former belœse. So hacking and gessinge about it to make lykelihoodes of impossibilites, and examining euery point by it selfe, yet coulde he neuer bee setled nor make good construction of it. For his mother tolde hym that prince Edwarde was his Father . The wise man deliuered the con= trary . And if his Mother knewe his Father , then howe coulde his Father be dead ere he was begotten, and howe coulde his mother recouer hir lawefull hus= band bœinge dead , and howe coulde his father become such a monarch after his discease, and so foorth . Nowe if he gaue credit to the wise man , yet no man better knoweth the childes father then the mother . So that for reuerence of the wyse man , and to reconcile hys mothers woordes with the wise mans rœde, he framed to hymselfe for that time a newe article of beliefe that one thinge myght be, and not bee . Yet time founde out a better solution of this sophisme . For thys time see= ing it was no reason to importunate the wyse man vppon this matter , it contented hym to knowe for a truth that Donzel del Febo his brother was yet a= lyue, and hee gaue hym hartye thanckes for the cour= tesie hee had shewed hym herein. But for his voyage into Englande , hee lefte that to hys direction, sith hee perceiued his meaning therein . The wyse man sayde it should be so prouided for, as best beseemed his honour. The third day after when al things were in a readinesse,

M.ij. Artemis

Artemidoro brought out of his armory a riche armoure and gaue it to Roſicleer. The armour was framed ſo cunningly, as for workmanſhippe, coſt, and ſecret vertue, it excelled all that I haue ſæne. It was cloſely wrought, couriouſly engrauen, enchaſed with precious ſtones, and aboue all this efficacie, that it reſiſted the edge of all mettall, this effect procæding either from the ſtones, or the examination of the aſcendentes in the forginge thereoff. The colour of the armour was all whyte, well fittinge for a newe knyght. Artemidoro gaue at the ſame time to Roſicleer a bay courſer ſtrög & wighte of limb, which hee had bought for that purpoſe in the countrey of Spayne where the beſt bræd of ſuch horſes were. And after all things ſet in order thus for their iourney, taking men wt them for their neceſſary bſes, they ſhypped thēſelnes in a faire Bark, ſayling with great ſwiftneſſe, as the wyſe Artemidoro had by his ſkyll directed it, in which iourney the hiſtory leaueth them tyll theyr ſodeyne approche bnto the lyſts, within great Britaine,

¶The great feaſtes began in Oliuerios court. Cap. 32.

IN the freſhe and pleaſaunt moneth of May, when the græne boughes and ſwæte ſmellinge flowers renue ioye and gladneſſe in the heartes of young folke, the great Citie of London and wyde fieldes ther eaboute ſæmed not leſſe couered with armed knight sthen if the mightie hoaſtes of Darius and Alexander had thether aſſembled, for the great feaſts and iuſtes were ſo diligently publiſhed in euery region & countrey, & the priſes which the kinge had ſet were of ſuch balour, that there came thether from diuers farre and ſtraunge lands ſo many knights & ladies as that the number of thē was infinit. Now that ỹ eſpecially drew youg princes & men of great name thether, was this. The king Oliuerio had a

daugh.

daughter named Oliuia the onely enheritrix of his kingdome, of ÿ age of xiiij. yeares, a beautifull & delicate dam-
sel, as not hir lyke might be found in all ÿ quarters. For
ÿ fame of hir singuler beautie, thether came many noble
princes & worthy knights to win hir liking, each of them
wearing so rich and quaint deuises, that their brauery in
short time exiled the longe mourning which had continued in great Britaine . The myrth which they made,
much delighted the kinge Oliuerio, and it ioyed hym
much to see hys courte and countrey so well stored of
knyghtes and Princes to whome hee gaue honourable
entertainment and countenaunce of good wyll , as woll
of his owne subiectes as straungers, and all were well
content with it highly commending of his courte , for
magnificence and courtesie . The kinge at thys time
was a wyddower, and therfore he sought much the honour of the Princesse his daughter . But to come to our
matter amongst ÿ knights straungers: The two Princes
Bargandel and Lyriamandro bare the greatest stroke:
next Don Siluerio Prince of Lusitania a younge knyght
and valiant in armes, already enamored vppon the fayre
princesse Oliuia, for whom he had bene a longe time syter
in the kinges pallayce, presuming vpon his byrth & liueli-
hood that she should be graunted vnto him, & as it fell out
ÿ princesse vnderstood some part of his desire, but she was
of an hautie heart and hyghe minde, makinge no more
account of Don Siluerio in respect of that demaund, then
of an other ordinary knight, or the refuse of other . For
amongest all which were already come, she thought none
merited to be a peere and match for hir beautie, beeing (as
my authour saith , suche in hir owne conceite as if no
Prince were worthy of it). But the truth is that ÿ blinde
boy shooting at randon had ouerreached his marke as appeared in the second shot at the comming in of Rosicleer.
In ÿ third place there came into this triumph the Prince
of Ireland called Argiles, & Don Orgiles prince of Scot-

land ⁊ Allamades king of Cornewaile, all thꝛéé vaſſals ⁊
ſubiectes to ẏ king Oliuerio.The fourth rowne was aſſig-
ned to Don Brynco Pꝛince of Numidio in Africk bꝛinging frō his countrey many valiant knightes richly armed,
⁊ with the Albalaxes king of Mauritania a Pagan ẏoūg ⁊
luſtẏ.Ther came thether alſo two gyants of an admirable
height ⁊ fiercenes,being ſuch a terrour to ẏ pooꝛe cōminal-
ty enhabiting ẏ villages nere to London,ẏ the pooꝛe mans
feare made them the moꝛe inſolent to commit diuers ry-
ots and other treſpaſſes befoꝛe the feaſtes began . This
was the ſeuerall countenaunces of the knyghtes of moſt
account,but to make ſhoꝛt, there came beſides many o-
ther knightes both Chriſtians and Pagans vnder the
kinges wꝛit of ſafeconduct whiche himſelfe gaue out.
That neuer England moꝛe flouriſhed of knightes , noꝛ
neuer nation was lyke to England . But nowe the firſt
daye of the iuſtes befoꝛe they ſhould ryde to the tylte,
the kinge Oliuerio inuited all the kinges and Pꝛinces
to dinner in his pallaice,where they were feaſted royal-
ly and with great melody . After the tables taken vp,
the knyghtes went to arme themſelues , and the kinge
conducted by the auncient Loꝛdes and Barons of hys
court tooke vp his ſeate in a windowe ouer the tiltyarde,
and vppon a ſcaffolde befoꝛe him reared foꝛ that purpoſe,
he commaunded the pꝛices to bée put,whiche were dy-
uers,foꝛ vnto the crowne befoꝛe ſpoken off,hee added a
choller of lyke valure , and many other iewels able,foꝛ
the honour of atteininge them and the woꝛthineſſe
thereoff, to animate a daſtard knyght to ſuch an enter-
pꝛiſe. After this the Pꝛinceſſe Oliuia comming foꝛth of
the great pallaice with an 100.ladies and gentlewomen
mounted vpon a ſtately ſcaffolde very richly hanged . A-
mong theſe Ladyes ther was ẏ pꝛinceſſe Siluerina daughter to the king of Scotland,⁊ Rodoſylua pꝛinceſſe of Luſitania ſiſter to Don Siluerio , and many other Ladyes
daughters vnto the great Loꝛdes of Britaine.

But

But in the middeſt of theſe the fayꝛe Pꝛinceſſe Oliuia
ſhewed not leſſe maieſty then the freſh and fragrant roſe
doth among the bꝛiers and ſtinking nettles, which not-
withſtanding haue their commendation foꝛ their græns
and liuely verdure. But the ſcaffolde bœing filde with ladyes and gentlewomen, there came the knights in place,
moſt of them young and ſhining in their bꝛight armour.
The firſt that pꝛicked himſelfe foꝛwarde to iuſte was
Allamades king of Cornewaile, a very gœd & tried knight,
againſt whome there came to encounter an other abled
knight an Almaine ſet vpon a ſtrong courſer. In theyꝛ
ſhocke their ſpeares flew in ſhiuers, & the king Allamades
ſomewhat ſtaggering in his ſaddle vnhoꝛſed ẏ Almaine,
after him there came.x.other knights ſtraungers moꝛe
bolde then ſkilfull in feates of armes, all whiche the
valyant Allamades ouerthꝛewe, with great pleaſure to
the kynge and all his court. Then the kinge called foꝛ
hys knightes, with this Allamades to gyue them place
voyded the lyſtes, and there entered Argiles Pꝛince of
Ireland, which with eyght ſeuerall courſes bꝛake eyght
ſpeares, and ouerthꝛewe eyght knyghtes. After hym
Don Orgiles Pꝛince of Scotland came, whom when Argiles eſpyed, not mindinge to diſturbe hym, hœ rode vnto the lyſtes ende, Orgiles wythout bœinge moued in
hys ſaddle caſt downe twelue knyghtes, and then followed hys fellowe Argiles. By and by Don Siluerio came in wyth a guilte armour goꝛgious to beholde,
and his hoꝛſe barbed wyth clothe of golde cutte vppon ſiluer Imagerie, bœinge a luſtye and baliaunte
knyght, and as the thoughtes of the Pꝛinceſſe Oliuia
emboldened his courage, ſo beſides the hautineſſe of hys
ſtomack contemned all other knightes in reſpect of hymſelfe. In his iourney he diſmounted xx.knights within leſſe
then halfe an houre, ſo that many thought be would wyn
the honour of that day. But ſtraight waye there pꝛeaſed
foꝛwarde the two Pꝛinces Bargandel and Liriamandro,

hauing in their company moze then 200.knightes,wyth
their haraldes crying befoze them, Bohemia, Bohemia,
Hungaria,Hungaria. The two Pzinces rode vpon fayze
and strong coursers,richly armed as became their estates,
their lustinesse bæinge enflamed by their loues, foz since
their conning to the English court, they were espzysed
with loue . Bargandel of the Pzincesse Syluerina , and
Lyriamandro of the Pzincesse Rodasylua , and hauinge
obteined the gwd fauoures of their Ladyes, they payned
themselues to be as boulde as the bzauest. So findinge
the tylt emptie by Siluerios departing,they pzaunced foz
warde till other knightes came agaynst them . And ey
ther of them in their turnes,befoze they left the listes,o
uerthzew at the least 30.knightes a pæce,so blasing their
pzowesse by the force they shewed,that the kynge and o
ther beholders chaunged their opinion as touchinge Don
Siluerio . Upon this the two Pzinces glad of that dayes
trauayle, and vaunting themselues befoze their mystres
ses made rwme foz others to doe their endeuoures. After
these the valiant and hardy knightes of the Englyshe
court came in against the straungers of other countries,
where the Englysh men so behaued themselues as that
dayes honour was theirs . Nowe as the kinge was in
talke wyth his Lozdes aboute the glozye whiche hys
men had gotten,and euery man was attentiue to that
which was befoze hym . Sodeinly there was hearde a
great crye amongest the people on the backe side of the
listes,no man knowing what it meant. By and by there
came fozth a tall Gyant wyth a traine of moze then xx.
knightes vpon a stone hozse which groned in a man
ner vnder his weight . The Gyant commaundinge
his knightes to stande a side,went alone to the windowe
where the king was , there raysing vp his beueare and
fozcing out a terrible lwke, without other reuerence, hæ
,, spake on this wise.King Oliuerio J am Brandagedeon,
,, Lozde of the Jlandes Baleance, and am hether come bi
                                     au

cause of the prices which thou haste appointed for the
best doers, I am well knowne in all the heathen countrey,for by the power which my Gods haue emparted
with me, there is no mortall man that may gaynstande
my puissance, and for that this day thou shalt haue some
triall of this truth, beholde before the night be shutte in,
there shall no knight of all these which are heere keepe his
saddell , vnlesse he keepe himselfe from me . And so in
great pride, as you may presume by ȳ course of his speach
he vttered this , and pulled downe his visoure . Then
with a great speare in his hand, he tooke the one ende of
the payle . This his comming was nothing pleasaunt to
the king, for since his arriuall in that kingdome, hee had
done many outrages to the poore subiects of the land.And
the king feared least the knights of his courte,should not
be able to maintaine their honour againste him . Nowe
this monstrous Gyant had not stayed there long , but
that a valyant knight a Britaine called Brandaristes made
a signe vnto him.

These two ranne together, and in their shocke Brandaristes with his horse fell to grounde : but the Gyant
nothing diseased,held on his way toward an other knight
by name Brandidarte, a Britaine to, a braue knighte and
as bolde as Gawayne , but the Gyant welcommed him
lyke as the other,and thus in shorte time the Gyant pro-
uing himselfe vpon moe then an I oo knights of the har-
dyest both straungers and Englishmen, he made them all
to descende from their horses , that the kinge Oliuerio
was much disquyeted hereat,ȳ wold haue bought out the
Gyāts presēce if he might,for moe th London is worth
euen for ȳ pitie which he had vpon his knights, not possibly able to withstande this Gyant.The king Allamades
beholding the kings countenaunce sadde and gessing the
cause , woulde needes aduenture the honoure which hee
before gayned vpon the vanquish of such a Gyant , and
taking a fresshe horse with a choyse speare from the ratler

M.b.   he

he rode to Brandagedeon whome the Gyant mette so
forcibly that Allamedes lay on the ground, and Brandagedeon dressing himselfe in his saddle passed on. By and by
Orgiles Prince of Ireland sette vppon the Gyant, which
somewhat estonished him: but neuertheles Orgiles happe
for himselfe was in no other manner then his fellowes.
Then came in done Don Argiles to take Orgiles parte,
and fiercely encountred the Gyant, but to ꝑ same purpose.
Now was Don Syluerio ashamed before the Princesse
Oliuia to haue taryed behinde so many good knights, and
therefore forcing his courage to please his Lady vppon a
lyght courser he ranne against Brandagedeon, & his Fortune was so good that he made Brandagedeon to lose one
of his stirops and the raynes of his bridell, but Brandagedeon quitted this with more then a tollerable vsury, for
he carried him beyond ꝑ crouper almost a speares length,
which disgrace before his Lady Oliuia made him woode
angry, and willyngly would he haue challenged the combat, if both leysure and place had bene conuenient. Not
long after the Prince Bargandel gathering his forces at
the beholding of the Princesse Syluerina went to encounter the Gyant, either of them being well heated, but di-
uersly, as arising of diuers causes, but their strengthes
encreased by their heates, made their shocks so terrible
as neither parte had great aduantage. The Gyant fell v-
pon the crouper of his horse and rode the length of a caryer ere he might arise agayn. Bargandel fel to the ground
with his horse vnder him. This made him hange his
heade, and styred vp his friend Liriamandro for his succours, who caused Brandagedeon to embrace the saddell
bowe, himselfe being cleane lefte out of the saddell by
Brandigedeon the Gyant, and Liriamandro layeon the
grounde to complaine him of his mishappe before his mistres Rodasylua. After these ther was none left so hardy,
as to dare encounter Brandagedeon, which caused ꝑ king
and other Princes to looke rufully, & the Gyant to beare
him-

himselfe as insolently, for when there was none lefte he „
lyfte vp his voyce in these termes . Come forthe, come „
forthe, ye knights of the hreat Britaine, & either knowe „
what the force of Brandagedeon is , or if you dare not „
appeare, sende me the prices presently, for to none of the
worlde they doe so rightly apperteyne as to me , and this
saying, he gallopped vp and downe in the place, expecting
either some knight or the prices . The king seing none
come to aunswere his challenge was verye angrye
and would haue giuen his best town to haue had a knight
which coulde haue quayled the Gyants courage , and for
very griefe he tourned himselfe from the windowe , tyll
the sodayne showte of the people , caused him to looke out
agayne.

Then he espyed the people flocking together towards
one corner of the lyste, and in the midst of them an aged
man with a long white bearde riding softly on a Mule,
and bearing the countenaunce of a very wise man . After
him he sawe a knight well harnessed in white armour,
richly besette with precious stones so that no man in the
place had the lyke, his helmette had a fine plume and his
horse the lyke, the pomell of his saddell of Goldesmithes
caruing, and the seate all embroodered with golde and siluer . Euery thing belonging to the knighte so braue and
lustye, that none nowe but gazed on the straunger. After
him a good distaunce there rode a gentlewoman an easye
pace vppon a palfraye driuing before hir a sumptuous
horse.

The gentlewoman comminge nære vnto the pallaice
alyghted, and vnlacing hir male, spreode a faire tente in
the playne , made all of clothe of golde, with suche
straunge deuises , that neyther kynge nor keysar in
the worlde but myghte haue vouchsafed it for hymselfe . But that whiche was most commendable, was
the most excelent and braue conceits with nædeleworke
which could neuer haue bene wrought but by an exquisite

seme

semſter, as in déde ý wiſe Artemidoro was the workeman. Now to make ſhort worke, when the pauilion was pyghte , Artemidoro leading Roſicleer with him vnto the king, ſpake on this wiſe.

" God encreaſe thy royall eſtate king of the great Britaine, & aduaunce the credite of thy whole courte. Witte
" you moſt puyſſaunt Prince, that from mine Ilande I am
" hether come with this young gentleman , that he may be
" knighted by your owne hands. And albeit ý ſo greate a
" courteſie neither he nor I haue merited of your maieſtie,
" yet vnderſtande worthy king that for his lygnage hee is
" ſuch a one as not without reſon he may craue to be dub,
" bed knight of ſo mightie a Prince as you are. And I dare
" warrant moreouer that it ſhall not be yll beſtowed on
" him, as your ſelfe ſhall teſtefie in ſhorte time , althoughe
" you ſhall not throughlye enter into the conſideration of
" his valour, till that his death be publyſhed by reporte of
" his drowninge , and that much bloode ſhalbee ſpilt to the
" greater prayſe of his proweſſe, to the contentacion of your
" perſon, and to the profite of your royall eſtate, and bée it
" my tale ſéeme incredible yet I beſéech you to remember it
" well, for I wil auouch ý euent as I haue told you . Re
" tayne him therefore ſir king in your courte, and beléeue
" that the time ſhall come wherein you woulde loſe the beſt
" part of your kingdome to haue him néere you . But to
" the ende, this ſtory now auerred by mee , maye carrye
" more authoritie with your worthy perſon . Knowe that
" this reporter is Artemidoro of whoſe knowledge you
" haue hearde before. For with my ſkill I haue done ſeruice
" to ſuch great Lords as you are . Artemidoro heere ma
" king a reaſonable pawſe, beganne agayne on this wyſe.
" Syr king with your maieſtyes leaue, we haue heare pit
" ched a tent in the name of the gentleman, as a challenge
" againſt all commers after you haue made him knighte.
" the firſt which ſhall vnhorſe him , ſhall enioy this tente,
" the value wherof may content him for his iourney , and

haue

hære ſtaying he ſayd. Sir king I haue done . King Oliuerio all this while not lending his eares idelly, as to a fable in a wynter nighte, but waying euery point, loked vppon Roſicleer , and well thoughte that his perſonage might agrée with Artemidoros commendacien , but yet as halfe in a doubt as touching himſelfe he made ẏ wiſe ,,
man this aunſwere. Aſſuredly Artemidoro with this demaund oꝛ any other which you ſhall require, I am verye ,,
glad that you take occaſion of cõming to my court, foꝛ ,,
by the bꝛute of your fame, I haue long time wiſhed to ſe ,,
you:but to ſende foꝛ you in dǽde, I was neuer minded,bicauſe as I hear,againſt your wil no man may ſpeke with ,,
you.And to make you anſwer, I am in purpoſe to ſatiſfie ,,
you, aſwell foꝛ your owne ſake, as foꝛ this gentlemans, ,,
whoſe behauiour ſǽmeth to be ſuch, as wout your repoꝛt ,,
he cõmeth ſufficiently cõmended vnto me.I pꝛomiſe you ,,
hære to make him knighte with mine owne handes, ⁊ I ,,
beſǽch God he pꝛoue no woꝛſe then you foꝛeſhew mǽ. ,,
Roſicleer and the wiſe man bothe bowed humblye on their hoꝛſebacks.

The king badde Roſicleer to alyght , which diſmounting from his hoꝛſe aſcended by a payꝛe of ſtayꝛes to a little ſcaffolde befoꝛe the kings windowe,where knǽling downe in the ſight of the whole multitude, he receiued the oꝛder of knighthod at the kings hands.The king demaundcd wher the young knight ſhould receiue ẏ ſwoꝛd, and the wiſe man aunſwered that he ſhould ſtaye foꝛ that till he could conquer it . Then after his ductie done to the king, Roſicleer retourned to hoꝛſebacke, and wyth a lyuelye grace ſo demeaned himſelfe vppon his hoꝛſe , as that it well pleaſed the beholders . Now foꝛ that which followeth you muſt entend that the wiſe man vttered his ſpeaches to the king in the audience of the whole multitude , many knyghtes and other compaſſing him about to heare his arraunt, ſo that felwe oꝛ none but were partakers of it . Amongſt them was Brandagedeon bearing.

ring himselfe within the lystes as proudly, as the Cocke
of the game doth in the Cockepit when the crauen is cha-
sed. Then hearing that the tent was put for a rewarde
to him which coulde vnhorse the young knight, when
,, he sawe time he cryed alowde to Rosicleer saying. In good
,, sooth new knight thou bewrayest thy folly and lacke of
,, experience, when thou sawest me stand in this place with
,, my speare in my hande to make that challenge , which
,, shall not be in thy power to maintayne so surely, but that
,, I wilbe the mayster of thy pauilyon, & yet Gods blessing
,, on thy heart for bringing so fayre a Jewell being in deed
,, fitter for me then for thee . Rosicleer whose courage ne-
,, uer taynted, aunswered as shortly. It shalbe thine Gyant
,, if thou winnest it, and there shall no man forbid thee the
,, possession of it if thou ouerthrowe me. And without more
wordes he toke a great speare from the ratler , and tourning his horse heade he rode softly to the place wher the
iustes were kept, In hys way thether, Rosicleer lyfting
vp his eyes to the scaffolde of the gentlewomen, he sawe
the beautifull Oliuia standing directly agaynst his face,
exceeding no lesse the other gentlewomen in brightnesse
then the Moone excelleth the starres in a frosty night. O
poore Rosicleer what a loke was that which locked thee
from thy rest, for with hir beautie thou wast wounded at
the heart, that albeit in time the skinne ouergrew it and
the flesh healed, yet the skarre remayned : & neuer knight
in the worlde loued more loyally then thou didst . For
though the sight was short and the blowe quicke, yet the
wounde was deepe and the smart curcles . O full many a
bolde enterprice diddest thou achieue ere thou gaynedst a
reasonable guerdon for thy greate good will . And thou
faire Princesse, being within the hearing of the wise mans
speach, diddest not spare to lende thine eares to an other
mans tale , and thine eyes to an other mans brauerye,
that thy succours being farre from thee, thy hearte had
not the power to repulse thy aduersarye , loue being the

onely

onely occasion of thy vnrest. But Lorde what alteracion both of you felte by the enterchange of your lookes, which serued lykewise for meisengers to tell your tales betwixt you.

And yet I cannot deeme but that this leue so enraged his courage against Brandagedeon as otherwise I maye thincke he had not done so well. But comming into the place, hee addressed himselfe towardes Brandagedeon, both of them now being in a readinesse. The kynge at this tyme very sorrowefull to see the newe knighte in his first battayle to endaunger himselfe vpon a Gyant, and woulde haue talked with Artemidoro about this matter, but the wyse man gaue no aunswere, and to the ende not to discouer more then was behouefull, hee conuayed himselfe out of the kinges sighte. So the kynge helde still his opinion of the young knightes weaknes, till the issue disproued his thought.

For in the caryer when the two knights mette in the middest of the tyltyearde, the Gyants speare burst vpon Rosicleers headpœce, no more mouinge him with the blowe, then if hee had stroke against a wall; But Rosicleer hurlyng at the breast of Brandagedeon ouerthrew him and his horse to the grounde, the horse in the fall, brusinge the Gyantes shoulder, that his knightes were fayne to carry him out of the prease, wherat all the standers by with great admiration behelde Rosicleer, euerye man being a Prophet as his heart gaue him, that Rosicleer woulde proue the beste knyghte in the worlde, seeing that at his first encounter in tilte hauing neuer had to doe with any knighte before he had ouerthrowen so mightie a Gyant.

The king nowe thought that Rosicleer had well amended the greate corsie whiche hee had taken at his knightes dysgrace, and the other knightes were glad to haue that huge monster ryd awaye, bolder and wyllynger valyauntly to aduenture themselues againste

Ro-

Rosicleer then againste a Gyant and their courage was
the more for the richnesse of the tent which had inueglco
their couetous mindes to venture the purchase. But as
the knights entred to iuste with him, he ouerthrew them
all, being more then an 100 knights, without that any
man was able to sit the seconde iourney. Then the kings
knights entred by name Brandaristes, Brandidarte, Allamedes the Princes Argiles and Orgiles, Don Brunio
Prince of Numidia and other, al which he threw down so
lyghtlye as that they mighte not tourne one course more
that daye. Some helde more tacke with him as you shall
heare hereafter, but by the way the king tourning to his
Lords, spake on this wise.

,,   Truly my Lords, if I had not my selfe sæne the va-
,, lourous dædes of this knight, I should hardly haue cre-
,, dited an other, so incredible the truth is that one shoulde
,, worke such masteries. I would the iusts were ended that
,, I might see this knight vnarmed to know him and honour him as is reason. True it is aunswered his nobles,
,, and for his valour there is not so puyssaunt a Prince in
,, the worlde, but that he shall haue cause to be glad of hys
seruice. This was a breathing time for Rosicleer, but
yet I am perswaded that it was no playing time although
no enemye appeared, for he had a greater conflict withiu
his bones then he professed outwardly, and therefore his
heart neither fully assured, nor yet in daunger, gased vppon the beautie of Oliuia. Wherby the fire entring closely by the vaynes wasted and consumed his fleshe, soner
then he felte the flame, or coulde thincke of remedye: but
better consideringe that hee was within the compasse of
loues segniorye, and that his matter was to bee tryed at
the great Assise in loues dominicn, he toke better aduise-
ment, to alter it to an action vpon the case of couenaunte
agaynst his mistresse, the matter arising vpon exchaunge
of lokes as you haue heard. And for this cause he entertayned Sergeaunt Hope to be his Lawyer, and keept

diuers.

diuers others to assist him, but master Dispayre an olde
stager had wonne the daye of him, had not the whole
bench, & especially the chiefe Iustice Desert, stayed vpon a
demur, which relieued much Rosicleers courage and made
him looke more freshly vpon hope to finde out better eui-
dence for recouery of his sute. But as Rosicleer thus
plyed his cause at the barre, so gentle Cupid attended
vpon his mistresse, faithfully seruing him, and beatinge
into hir head the remembraunce of his actes and the
beautie of his personage, that the wyndowes of hir desire beeing sette wyde open, she beloed hir fill wysshinge
yet to see his face, thereby to comfort hir selfe if hys
visage were aunswerable to hys vertue. Nowe Don
Siluerio with an enuious eye, mynding to interrupte
this medlea, prouoked Rosicleer to the lystes, whiche
Rosicleer refused not. Rosicleer shaked somewhat
in hys saddle, but yet withoute daunger of fal-
linge and Don Siluerio with his courser tumbled to
the grounde, so euill entreated as that hee was faine
to forsake the lystes. The Princesse Oliuia remem-
bringe his former importunitie was nothing agreeued,
thinckinge thereby hys sute to haue slaked, the rather
to delight in hir newe champion. By thys tyme the
greater parte of the afternoone was spent, and very fewe
remained in that place which durst ryde a course wyth
Rosicleer, albeit the number of knightes were more then
3000. But last of all Bargandel and Lyriamandro willing to proue themselues vpon the newe knight with
great courage, which the sight of their mistresses caused in them, rydde both against Rosicleer, and in theyr
waye as they two straue who shoulde be first, Bargandel
giuing the spurres to his horse ran against Rosicleer, Bargandel in his race hit so strongly that his speare flewe in
peeces, but Rosicleer knowing Bargandel, by a deuise that
he had, & mindfull of his former courtesie, when hee came
nere him, raised vp ye end of his speare, & rode by without

touch-

touching of Bargandel . Bargandel not fœling his aduer/
sary thought that he had missed his rest, and therefore
taking an other speare for the reencounter,he rode again
towardes Roficleer,but Roficleer did as he did before,
whereby he cleerely perceiued the knightes entent to
be for to spare him,and waxing madde angry he auoy/
ded the place , presently stepped in the Prince Lyria/
mandro, to whom likewyse Roficleer so behaued hym/
selfe as vnto Bargandel, albeit himselfe was well stur/
red with these shockes. Lyriamandro as madde as Bar/
gandel to finde a friende without occasion,and not know/
ing his meaning rode after Bargandel,where both of them
departed to disguise themselues thincking to beguyle
the knight,if peraduenture he had had some knowledge
of them. Not longe after the trumpettes blowed the re/
treate, and the iustes shoulde haue ended when these
two knightes entered wyth yelowe plumes and guyl/
ded armour,their horse trappings al of yelowe,& parting
company,the one of them ranne against Roficleer,whom
he mette so strongly that their speares flewe in pœces,
neither of them bœing vnhorsed , whereat all the peo/
ple were dismayde, for no knight that daye but was
ouerthrowne of as many as Roficleer had encountred.
But these two knightes rode againe the seconde time,and
as with more choller, so wyth fercer stomackes they
met,that Roficleer tourned with his horse more then iiij.
paces backewardes,hauing much a doe to bring him for/
ward,and the straunge knight lost his stirrops & fell to ye
grounde,w his horse ouer him . His companion tœke his
rœme & ran twise against Roficleer,neither of them lo/
sing their seates,but at the third encountry he fell to the
ground as his fellowe did , Roficleer a little diseased in
his saddle , recouered lyghtly . The yelowe knyghtes
thus ouerthrowen mounted on theyr horses to re/
tourne the way which they had come,fore displeasaunt
at the little harme they had done vnto Roficleer , but
they

they beſhꝛewed themſelues foꝛ the further attempting of
his acquaintaunce,and muſinge who it ſhould bée , they
remembꝛed themſelues of the younge gentleman Roſicleer and of hys greate pꝛoweſſe whereto themſelues
were pꝛiuy,thinckiug that perhaps it might be he,but yet
bicauſe of his younge yeares they remoued this thought
agayne,and coulde not well iudge who he was. Then
the king commaunded euery Knyght to leaue off , at
which the noyſe of the inſtruments were hearde ſo loude
that the whole place range of the ſounde thereoff . Oliuia nowe mynded to diſcende with the other Ladyes,
wherefoꝛe the knightes & other Pꝛinces flocked together
to giue their attendaunce, amonge whome Roſicleer as
foꝛwarde as the beſt in good will, pꝛeſented himſelfe vnto
his miſtreſſe,which pleaſed hir not a little.Entering into the great court of the pallaice they there alyghted,
where the king welcommed thē making ſeuerall tokens
of courteſie to euery one,& comming to Roſicleer he deſired him to be at hys appoyntment foꝛ that night , foꝛ
that he had greate deſire to ſée hym vnarmed , all the
reſt gladly obeyed,but Roſicleer with his beuere ſhutte,
requeſted his maieſtie of pardon foꝛ that it behoued
him to diſarme himſelfe in his tente , till the wyſe man
had permitted the contrary,and ſo ſayinge hée tooke hys
leaue of the kinge , enteringe into his tent where hee
found the wiſe Artemidoro , whiche with two pages a-
bided hys comminge , when Roſicleer was within,they
dꝛew the curtaynes ſo cloſe that Roſicleer was not ſéene
of any, and then helped to vnarme him . After the tables were couered and the boꝛde was furniſhed of all
delicacies whiche Artemidoro had thought on. The
wiſe man himſelfe beeing both Cooke & Cater. Roſicleer
ſitting downe gaue him harty thanckes foꝛ his good pꝛo-
uiſion,but in deede his ſtomacke was full with the Pꝛinceſſe Oliuia, which had ſo poſſeſſed his entrayles that
the daintie diſhes did a not whyt delight his appetie.

During this time the Princes and the knightes whiche supped with the kinge highly extolled Roficleers worthineffe, eache of them bæing defirous to knowe him, for they all iudged him to bee of highe parentage. Thus was this night beftowed till the daye came, wherein they were to expect frefhe matter of difcourfe and tabletalke.

¶An aduenture which chaunced in king Oliuerios court.   Cap.33.

The next daye after, diuine feruice finifhed. The king inuited to breakfeaft all the knightes, and that done tœke his place in that order as you haue heard before, lœking that fome ftraunge knight fhould iuft with the new knight. Now when the place was peopled with both gentle and vngentle, ¿ that the Princeffe Oliuia was placed on hir fcaffolde, in came Roficleer, mounted vppon his courfer, ¿ vaunted himfelf as ioyoufly before his miftreffe as if he had not feared the fkirmifh with.x.gyantes, but that which liked the Princeffe beft, was a conceit deuifed in the penfell of his fpeare, bæing a burning torche, the waxe dropping from it, fignifying thereby ý mifery of louers, with this pofy vnderneth in Romaine letters. Extinguo & Extinguor. After Roficleer was thus entred, many ftrong and baliant knights, fuch as had not iufted the daye before, defired to trye themfelues vppon the newe knight, efpecially Albalaxes king of Mauritania, who vpõ hope to be Lord of the rich tent, tœke a great fpeare, and with all his force ranne againft Roficleer, but Roficleer was not taken fo tardy in the receite but that hæ mette the baliant Pagan with fuch ftrength, as horfe and man tumbled to the ground. Roficleer rode on fomwhat troubled with this encountry, ¿ ere he was wel fet in his fadle, there ran againft him an other Pagan Lord of Bufia, but Roficleer finely vnhorfed him, and in the fame courfe

ouerthrew foure others that there was not a knight left
to dare him, at this time he tarried sometime awaiting
for newe comeners in, but there was none. Onely at a
corner of the listes, he sawe a huge Gyant in white armour vpon a great courser, with a hoarce and disdainful
voice, commaunding the people to make him roome. And
not farre from this gyant a gentlewoman vpon a palfray
in straunge attire much different from ours, hir face was
all bedewed with teares as if the gyant had vsed violéce
towards hir. The gyant approching to the place where
the kinge stode, made no reuerence, but the gentlewoman knéeled downe, saying. Know most excellent Prince "
that the renowne of this court hath brought me from far "
countries hether, chiefly for one cause, which the wicked- "
nesse of this gyant hath nowe made two, the originall of "
them both you shall héare nowe vnder one. In the far- "
ther part of the East nére vnto the great Cataya, there "
gouerneth a Princesse named Iulia, as yet but young of "
yeares, but not younge for handsomnesse, béing now as "
it were in the pride of all hir beautie. Hir father was "
a right cunning Magician enstructing hir so perfectly in "
his skill, as nowe therein there are fewe comparable. "
For since his death, she hir self diuined by hir knowledge "
that she shoulde be prisoner to two gyants, and shoulde "
be inlarged by one knight which should fight with them "
both. For the case should stand thus, that if hir knight "
were vanquished she should as perpetually captiuate be "
at their commaund, otherwise to be at libertie if they "
were yelden. Hir selfe foreséeing this, and not finding who "
he might be, hath prouided by hir knowledge not to bé "
beguiled. For by hir Arte she hath made this sworde, "
which no knight may euer vnsheth, but onely he whiche "
must fight wyth the two gyants for hir libertie, and be- "
sides the sworde is such as without it, it were an hard "
aduenture, but wyth it the knight maye boldely ven- "
ture on his foes. The sworde she made and kepte "

,, close till time thefe two Gyantes by night affailing hir,
,, got the Lordſhippe of hir perſen, after which tune by a
,, truſtie ſeruaunt ſhe cauſed this ſworde to be conuayed
,, vnto me with thys commaunde to trauaile for hyr ſake
,, in all Princes courtes, and to ſeeke out the knight which
,, could and ſhould maynteine hir quarell. Three yeares
,, are paſſed ſince I vndertooke this enterpriſe, and within
,, this three monethes landing in an Iland towardes the
,, Weſt, after a longe iourney to no purpoſe, it was my
,, fortune to meete this gyant Candramarte, there makinge
,, him pertaker of my ſute, hee requeſted to proue the ad-
,, uenture, which I graunted, but when he could not drawe
,, it out beinge ccuetous of the ſworde, he denyed it mee
,, agayne, ſaying. For ſo much as you goe to the kynge of
,, Englands courte, there to ſeeke ſome knyghte whiche
,, wyll doe his deuoure in your miſtreſſe behalfe. No man
,, ſhall attempt the aduenture of the ſworde, but he ſhall
,, firſt trye his forces vpon mee, and if by hym I be ban-
,, quiſht or ſlaine, let him take the ſword, otherwiſe I will
,, withholde it from all men, with this he promiſed to beare
,, me company, and I of two euils determined to chofe
,, the leſſe. Albeit at this inſtant I am in greater extremi-
,, tie, by reaſon of this Gyants wrong done to me, and my
,, miſtreſſe thraldome. This is the neceſſitie whiche
,, draue me hether, and I am humbly to beſeeche your
,, maieſtie, diſcretly to way my cauſe, and to giue remedy
,, by your ſubiectes as you beſte may. Candramarte all
this time ſtandinge by, in the ende auerred hir tale to
be true, and farther intimated to the knightes and
Princes that ſeeing he coulde not drawe out the ſworde,
there ſhould no man be maſter of it, but by the maſtery of
him: but ſayth he, I will defende it againſt any knyght
which ſhal demaund it. All the knights beheld the ſword
with the rich hangers as the faireſt which they had ſeene,
but the kinge ſomewhat angry at the Gyants rudeneſſe
towardes the gentlewoman, ſayd to him in this manner.

Can-

Candramarte thou haſt done ill to take this ſwozde from „
the gentlewoman, foz as it ſeemes Iulia made it not foz „
thee, & thy pzide is ouer great to ſuppoſe that none in the „
wozlde will demaunde it of thee . The Gyant anger= „
ly lꝏkinge vpon the king as though his eyen would haue „
flyen out of his viſage, ſaid to the king Demaund it then „
thy ſelfe Syz king, oz ſet any of thy knightes to aſke it, & „
I will then make aunſwere vnto thee howe raſhly thou „
haſt taken vpon thee to cozrect mee. Theſe ſpeaches were „
deliuered with ſo high a voyce by the Gyant, that all the
knyghtes whiche were in the compaſſe hearde it, but
no man ſpake a wozde, ſo that the kynges choller en=
creaſed both agaynſt the Gyant and his owne ſubiectes.
And I muſt beare with them, foz the Gyant was great
and tall, and as hardye as a Lyon , and no man liuinge
very neere matchable foz ſo good Foztune: but yet there
was within the lyſtes both a hardier and moze foztu=
nate knight, euen the good Roſicleer, which euer hearing
his vndiſcrete talke vnto the kinge, comminge neere vn=
to the Gyant, tꝏke him vp in this ſozte . Candramarte, „
content thy ſelfe, and learne to knowe vnto whom thou „
ſpeakeſt, foz I tell thee that kinge Oliuerio hath ſuche „
knyghtes in his court as can make thee amende thy ru= „
ſticitie, though thou wert moze vntaught then thou art, „
and foz that thou ſhalt not miſtruſt mee, beholde I am „
the laſt and the leaſt of them yet as one whiche deſires „
to ſerue hym with the moſte . In hys name, and in „
behalfe of the gentlewoman, I charge thee ſurrender the „
ſwozde vnto the gentlewoman, oz if thou wilt not that, „
do thou take that parte of the field which ſhall beſt lyke „
thee, foz in thys quarrell I wyll eyther kyll oz bee kyl= „
led. Wyth a terrible countenaunce Candramarte ſta= „
red vppon Roſicleer, as who ſhoulde ſaye , dareſt thou „
ſpeake ſo boldely, and perceiuinge hym to bee but a ., „
younge Knyght, whyche hee noted by hys white ar=
mour, in great ſcozne he aunſwered thus . I ſee well

foolish knight thou haſt not ben long acquainted with the
burthen of armour, foꝛ if thou wert in thy kinde and had
well wayed the ſucceſſe of Combatens thou wouldeſt
ſhake euery ioynt of thꝗ to beholde mꝗ. But thy ignoraunce makes thꝗ leape beyond thy laſhe, and thꝛuſteth
thꝗ foꝛward to thine owne decay. But ſꝗing thcu haſt
made choyſe thy ſelfe of thy deathſman, let vs go to the
battaile, foꝛ I woulde not but that thcu ſhouldeſt repent
thꝗ of thy foolishneſſe. So Candramarte bꝛoched his hoꝛſe
with the ſpurres, and Roſicleer did the lyke, whiche ap-
peaſed the kinges diſpleaſure, that he knewe not how to
recōpence his foꝛwardneſſe in doing him pleaſure, albeit
it may be if he loued Roſicleer, y̓ he ſomwhat miſtruſted
the euent bicauſe the gyant was byg and Roſicleer vn-
ererciſed in armes, and that whlch was chiefeſt without
a ſwoꝛde, but foꝛ remedy thereto, he cauſed a ſwoꝛde of
his owne to be fetched, wherewith he charged a knight
to deliuer it to Roſicleer, with this commaundemēt. That
ſꝗing in his name he hath ſo well fitted Candromarte
foꝛ his aunſwere, and foꝛ that cauſe was to take the battayle vpon him, nowe hee pꝛayed him to weare thys
ſwoꝛde lykewyſe foꝛ his ſake, whiche he would warrant
to be good. The knight dyd his meſſage accoꝛdingly, but
Roſicleer making his ercuſe gentely, retourned y̓ ſwoꝛd
,, with this aunſwere, I humbly thancke the kinges ma-
,, ieſtie foꝛ ſo high a pꝛeſent, the not receiuinge whereoff
,, commeth not of any refuſall but by a pꝛomiſe which I
,, haue made, as his maieſtie can teſtifie, neuer to weare
,, ſwoꝛd, but if I winne it, ꝓ therſoꝛe I craue pardon at his
,, maieſties handes foꝛ this diſcourteſie, otherwyſe I were
,, greatly to blame if I thought not my ſelfe honoured by
,, beeing girte in a kinges weapon. The meſſenger deliuered Roſicleers aunſwere in the ſame woꝛdes as Roſicleer had giuen it out. ſo the kinge ſomewhat lamenting
the knightes wilfulneſſe, as he thought, weaponleſſe to
wage battayle with ſo abled a warriour, muſed vppen
this

this and for the reſt commended him to God. All the ſtandders by were ſorp to ſée the new knight ſo couragious as to fight with a Gyant without a weapon, and eſpecially the beautifull Princeſſe Oliuia coulde not but bée an angred at the new knights ieoperdous aduenture, as if ſhe had had no ſmall title or clayme to his perſon.

¶ A daungerous battayle betweene Candramarte
and Roſicleer. Gap. 3 4.

As they prepared themſelues to the carrer, ý people gathered together to ſée this dangerous fight betwéen the new knight and the Gyant Candramarte, and they as glad to ſée the iſſue vpon their lyght courſers with their ſpeares in their reſtes ſo violently hurled agaynſte the other that the grounde yelded vnder their féete, the force of their ſtronge armes ioyned with the fury of their horſe in ſuch wiſe that the Gyant made ſmall ſhiuers of his greate ſpeare and conſtrayned Roſicleer to take his pillowe on his horſebacke, but the newe knighte gaue the Gyant ſo mightie a blowe that he made his ſtirops fall from him, and quickely cloſinge with the Gyant, he drewe him by force from the ſaddell, and threw him to the grounde ſo that he ſomewhat bruſed the Gyants ſhoulderbone, and preſently would haue tourned agayne vppon Candramarte to haue made a diſpatch of all, but that the Gyant being of greate courage, and enforcing himſelfe to endure the remnaunt, gotte on his legs, and addreſſing his ſhielde before him, with his Fawlchon in his hande awayted Roſicleer, for ſo ſoone as Candramarte was downe, Roſicleer then alyghted and ſent his horſe to his tente, Roſicleer now being on foote made towardes Candramarte. Candramarte firſt aſſayled Roſicleer with theſe wordes. What knight thinkeſt thou to fight with me without a ſworde? What if thou haddeſt a better then this which I weare of the Quéene

Iulias makinge, were all the Gods able thereby to warrant thee out of my handes ? No: and thou shalt deere-
ly repaye me the paine which thou haft put me to in this
fall. Rosicleer comming neerer aunswered. Candramarte
spare not to do thy vttermost, but ceafe thy reuilings ; for
God which gaue me might to ouerthrowe thee, wyll also
giue me power and ftrength without other weapon to
subdue thee, and although I bring no fwoorde with mee,
yet I hope in the liuinge God that thine shal profet me,
and serue my tourne. Then the Gyant was in fuche
a rage that the fury of his choller with the bluftering of
his breath iffued through the fightes of his equimas in
lyke fort as the smoke iffueth out of a fornace. And his
seconde affault was with his Fawlchon with both his
handes fetched compaffwife againft Rosicleer, which feing
the blow comming with fuch force, for ward lyft vp his
fhic'd therin to receiue ȳ ftroke, but ȳ blow was fo mightie, ȳ it hewed the shield afunder, & defcending vpon the
headpeece, made Rosicleer abate his lookes and bowe his
knees, for fauegarde to his fall. The Gyant doubled v-
pon him, but Rosicleer neuer yet daunted, and recouering
his courage almoft agaynft the hare ftepte afide that the
Gyants blowe was all in vayne, and being fomewhat
out of charitie with the firft, he determined no more to
receiue any fuche counterbuffes, fo that an halfe houre
after the combat had lafted the Gyant myght neuer hyt
him one blowe for all that he coulde doe. For Rosicleer
was fo diliuer and quicke that he lightly auoyded them.
Candramarte feing that Rosicleer woulb not abide by it,
chafed him vp and downe, and Rosicleer led the Gyant a
course lykewife : but fo, that the king and all the lokers
on iudged that if the battayle shoulde endure long, that
the newe knight might neuer efcape the death. Rosicleer
affayed many times to couple with the Gyant, and to pul
the Fawlchon out of his handes, but Candramarte was fo
wily and fo well aduifed of the woordes which Rosicleer
fpake

spake in the beginning of their battayle , that he either
kepte himselfe aloofe off, oz in his purfute bare the poynt
of his Fawichon befoze him:but by this meanes the battayle continued to the no little difcontentment of Roficleer . For although his armoure was fuch that no we-
pon might wounde him on his body,yet was he foze bzu-
fed with trauayle, and his bones were in a manner fof-
tened with the wearyneffe he had felte foz the lengthe of
the battayle . As the one gaue lyghtly fo the other pur-
fued as eagerly:, but as I faye neuer faftening a ryghte
downe blowe, but as he might ouerthwart and endelong
flipping his blowes , and in his pzide boafting out thefe
and fuch lyke fpeaches.

O knight howe coftlye fhall the challenge of Quéne
Iulias fwozde be vnto thee , if foz it thou muft exchaunge ”
thy lyfe? Haddeft thou not ben better neuer to haue bene ”
at this marte. But now know what balour Candramarte ”
is off, foz not all the wozlde are of that credite with mee ”
as to bayle thee cut of my handes. For the fitting of hys ”
action wherevnto he woulde fhake hys heauy Fawlchon
fo gallantly, and reare fo terribly : that euery man tooke
Candramarte, rather foz a Tyzant in a Tragedie , then
a Iefter in a Commedie . And Roficleers friendes with
their pitifull lookes bemened the pooze Roficleer , as if he
had already tafted of moft cruell and bitter deathe in his
gréene youth

Amongft them, the fayze and beautifull Pzinceffe O-
liuia although as yet altogether vnacquaynted with Roficleer, was a fpectatour , neither carcleffe noz curicus,
but as one withcut hope, fhe onely wifhed well to Roficleer,whofe bzufes were as dæpe fet in hir fides,as they
were impzinted in Roficleers flefhe , and euery wagging
of the moft huge and monftrous Candramartes weapon,
ftrake a falte teare from hir faire eyes, fc was fhe eftran-
ged from hir felf 7 altogether become an other mans : the
newe knight eying his miftreffe became fo defperate that
he

he fully refolued either to clofe with Candramarte and
wring his weapon from him, or to dye vpon him . And
watching the opportunitie, when the fawchon was ouer
the Gyants head, bending his body ſtept within the Gyant, the Gyant had no other refiſtance but to fel him to
the grounde with his elbowes. This was no great mif-
fortune to Roſicleer, for albeit he was fayne to bowe his
knées by the thruſt of the Gyants elbowes, yet couching
his bodye clofely, his chaunce was fo good as to faſten v-
pon the hilts of Quéene Iulias ſworde , which hee drewe
out, the ſcaberde remayning at the Gyants ſide . Roficleer nowe being feafed of the ſword ſtepte from Candra-
 ,, marte and called vppon him en this wife. Candramarte
 ,, nowe thou ſhalte fée who ſhall haue the worſte bargayne
 ,, of Quéene Iulias ſworde, ſith on euen hands we ſhall try
 ,, this combat, and with this remembring the Gyants former pride, he layed at the Gyant fo thick and fo fure that
in ſhort ſpace the blad ranne from the Gyante in more
then tenne places, for the ſworde was excéeding ſharpe,
and Roſicleer as fell and venemous . Nowe maye you
thincke that the mayden feeing the ſworde bared by the
knight, was the gladdeſt woman in the earth, and that the
king with other Princes and knights thancked God hartely , for prouiding Roſicleer of a weapon the fooner to
put ende to the battayle. But the Gyant aſſaulted fo fore
by Roſicleer and wounded fo daungeroufly, began wholy
to miſtruſt the prophecie of the ſworde , and to difpayre
of the victory, and as in fuch cafes wanhope is aduenturous : fo his armour being rente, the tabergeen trimay-
led, and all the riuetting out of order, for that caufe the
Gyant woulde needes put the tryall of the challenge vpon
one blowe . When this blowe was reached as farre
as the Gyant might, to haue defcended with more vyolence vppon Roſicleers headpéece, Roſicleer beinge more
quicke then hée, mette the blowe croſſewayes that he cut
off both the Gyants armes harde by the elbowes . The

Gyant

Gyant thus maymed, yelling out a lothesome cry, reuy-
led & railed on Rosicleer, as a man distraught, & y which
most encreased his payn, was not y tormēt of his disfigu-
red armes : but either the shame of the victory, or the
enuy at Rosicleer, but Rosicleer making little account of
him, tooke the scabberde from his side, and so lefte him.
Candramarte still followed blaspheming and cursing both
God and men, and when he coulde neither be his owne
executioner , nor procure an other to take the paynes,
sware, that for sparing his death, he would deuise all the
mischiefe he might againſt Rosicleer and that he woulde
practise his death also, if possibly he could innēt y meanes.
But truly, if I had bene in Rosicleers case, I should not
haue bene so straunge : seing, that bothe it shoulde haue
bene the Gyants last requeſt and so little encombraunce
towardes me . But the king, Princes and knights, were
so ioyous of the victory agaynſt the Gyant, as they bare
countenaunce of more ioy outwardly, then they had earſt
receyued, euery one openly deſiring to sée him vnarmed :
but chiefly Bargandel and Liriamandro, being in some ie-
louſie of y knight, whom they had found a friend ere they
loked for, supposing that peraduenture he was Rosicleer,
of whom the soddayne aduenture in the Sea had berefte
them . And Quéene Iulias gentlewoman seing the combat tryed and the aduenture of the swozde achieued, concluding therby that this was he for whom she had made
so long a iourney , saluted him courteously with this am-
baſſade . Now that it is euident noble knight , that you ,,
are the person, for whose helpe this swozde was framed ,,
by my mistreſſe, I am to certeſie that my Lady greeteth ,,
you by me, & giueth you warninge that for hir sake you ,,
muſt maintain y fight with two brane Gyants, iointly cō- ,,
battant againſt you only. For this she hath sent you this ,,
swozde, y commēdacion wherof, albeit not vnknown, lyeth ,,
in the continuall proofe which shee requeſteth you neuer ,,
to forſake, for it wil much furder you in your enterprises. ,,

Where-

,, Whereto I beseech you giue credite & deale effectually as
,, she hath hope in you. But now giue me the sword that
,, I may beare it to the king and the other Princes, that
,, they may iustifie the truth of my former auouch. So
,, Rosicleer deliuered the sworde into hir handes with the
sheath, which the gentlewoman brought before the king
and the knights then present, which all attempted the pulling out but coulde not doe it, as if the scabberde had bene
a peece of the same meitall whereof the sworde was, and
not seuered by edge or toole, which made them all confesse, that to the new knight it was proposed, and to hym
appertayned the fight with the two Gyants for the fran-
chising of Queene Iulia.

The king redeliuered the sworde into the gentlewomans handes, and bad hir yeelde it againe to Rosicleer,
which she did, & taking hir leaue of him receiued this for
answer. That he recommeded himselfe vnto hir good grace,
hartely thanking hir for so great care euer him, as to prouide a sworde, whereof he had nade as hir selfe can witnesse, and for the rest hee promised not to fayle hir as hee
was true knight to God and the worlde. The gentlewoman with this recommaunde gallopped away as fast as
hir palfray mighte carry hir, the whilest Candramartes
knights remoued their Lorde out of that place into hys
tent, whence afterwarde with greate griefe for his sore
mayme they conuayed him into his Ilande, wherein ha-
ning settled himselfe as mindfull of his othe, he neuer left
from immagening of crafty meanes, and coyning newe
pollicies to bring Rosicleer to the death.

When Candramarte was carryed into his tent, Rosicleer mounting vpon his horse, tooke a great spear in his
hande and stode at the lystes ende, thincking that some
knight woulde come against him, but they were all so scho-
led with the sight of this last victorye that neuer a knight
shewed himselfe. Wherefore the king commaunded to
sounde the trumpet to procede vnto the disposing of the

rewardes for their trauayle . An Heralde demaunding aloude who had done best, they all referred the prices to Rosicleer . The king woulde not contende with them, but sayth hæ, I will that my daughter haue the bestowing of them where shæ best lyketh as touching this tournaye.

She with much shamefastenesse which hir coloured cheekes bewrayed, accepted the charge, and taking the crowne with the choller in hir hande, she caused the new knighte to be called before hir, who burning in loue towardes hir, no lesse then shee was feruent in lyking towardes him, dismounted at the first call, and betweene the two Princes Bargandel and Liriamandro mounted vp the scaffolde where the beautifull Princesse was, before whom he appeared with greater feare arising of his conceit concerning his indignitie, then earst attached him in the fight with Candramarte without a weapon.

The two Princes comming before Oliuia, made their humble obeysaunce, and Rosicleer knæled downe. The Princesse with a good grace bending to euery one of them spake to Rosicleer. You knowe new knight what charge the king my father hath layde vppon mæ, although farre " more honourable then I am able to sustayne, yet by mæ " assumed, neither to resist his will nor yet agaynst my de " sire, for it is comendable of it selfe to be a commender of " vertue, & neuer to much may I commend it. The charge " is, that wyth mine owne handes I shoulde distribute " these prices accordinge as my own fancie leadeth mee to " deeme of euery mans trauayle and valyauncye . The " delyuerye of these Iewelles, were nothing harde nor " doubtefull,but the disposing is more then harde,bicause it " pertayneth to iudgement in deedes of armes, wherevnto " my sexe is not sufficiently abled. Neuerthelesse sir knight " as your paynes haue bene greatest, therto witnesseth this " whole multitude : so your prowesse in my iudgement, so " much assureth on your parte,that without doinge wronge "

to

" to any of thefe Princes and knights , I may with good
" reafon confer them vpon you . For this,if I knowe to do
" right vnto whome J ought, it is meete that you doe a=
" way your helmette, and fith youre deedes difcouer who
" you are,it is no reafon y you couer your felfe any longer.
When the Princeffe had thus fayd,Roficleer not hauing
power to excufe himfelfe, vnlaced his helmette which being put off, his face feemed fo beautifull by the heate and
trauayle of the armour, which rayfed a freth redde in hys
cheekes, that it ftroke them all in a maze , and none of
thofe which faw him, confidering his fayreneffe with his
age,but ratheriudged him an Angel of heauen,then a mor=
tall knight.
　　When the Princeffe Oliuia fawe him fo fayre, as al=
ready loue had made a wracke in the moft fecret part of
hir hearte by the viewe of his knighthode , fo nowe the
fame breache being made wyder by the feconde affaulte
in his beautifull lookes, loue entred with banner difplayed
and finding no refiftaunce, toke poffeffion wholly of hir
hearte, and fwore all that he founde to be his true pryfo=
ners . Thus loft the hir libertie, and yet with the befte
courage that a woman mighte,fhee framed out a counte=
naunne of great freedome in this manner . You needed
" not by your fauoure fir knight to haue bene afhamed of
" your face, and yet fuch as it is,it is farre inferiour to your
" manhoode,but this is beyond the compaffe of my commiffi=
" on, now come you neere and receiue at my handes the
" glory of your worthineffe, which your good Fortune yel=
" deth you. Roficleer approching very neere kneeled downe
and the Princeffe put the choller about his necke,and the
crowne vpon his heade. When the Princeffe had fo done
with a little ftaye betweene, Roficleer toke the crowne
from his owne heade, and as he was on his knees fayde
vntothe Princeffe .Moft excellent Princeffe for the foue=
" reigne grace you haue thewed me,J will remayne yours
" henceforth to ferue you loyally, as a poore recompence
"
　　　　　　　　　　　　　　　　　　　　　　for

foz so rich a benefit. And as I doe receiue this choller „
as the pzice of knighthoode in your opinion, so I beseeche „
you to take of me this crowne as a testimonie of your sur, „
passing beautie in my eye. With this he set ÿ rich crowne „
vpon the golden haires of the Pzincesse Oliuia, she be=
ing glad of this gift, although somewhat blushing at the
wozdes, he spake. The two Pzinces Bargandel and Liri=
amandro standing by and knowinge him to be Rosicleer
whom they had lost in the maine sea, when the cerimo=
nies were finished, went to him, embzacing him as goodly
as if he had bene their owne bzother yet courteously
challenging him foz his vnkindenesse in not making him
selfe knowen vnto them. The king Oliuerio abashed at
so great bountie in a knight of so young yeares, began to
thincke moze aduisedly of that which the wise Artemi=
doro had sayde, from that time he esteemed moze high=
ly of the newe knight, as you shall heare after this. But
now the noise was so great which the vyals made & other
instruments that one might not heare an other speake, at
which time the faire Pzincesse Oliuia with the riche
crowne vpon hir head, and in hir company ÿ knight Ro=
sicleer with the two Pzinces descended from the scaffold,
and in great pompe went to the kings pallace, the Pzin=
cesse leauing them ther to take hir own lodging, & they al
entring the chamber of pzesence where the king staied foz
thë, & after a generall welcome by name taking Rosicle=
er aside, he said vnto him. Sir knight Fether you are ve= „
ry welcome, foz I haue had great desire to knowe you, & I „
would to god by your stay I might as wel be acquain= „
ted with you, foz by you the honour of my court hath ben „
well vpholden. Mightie king aunswered Rosicleer, I am „
rather to be boznne withall if I desire to be your seruaunt, „
sith foz the same cause and foz to see your court I am come „
hether. The king kissed the knight vpon the cheeke as „
tenderly as if he had bene his owne sonne, saying. Rosi= „
cleer, I account moze of these wozdes then of ÿ wozth of „

my best citie, and aduise thée well of these speaches, for I
am to demaund them of thée if thou wilt not otherwyse
performe thy promise. So Rosicleer was retained for the
kings knight, and all the olde courtiers both Princes and
knightes of great name ranne to embrace Rosicleer with
great pleasure vnto thē to haue his company, except onely
Don Siluerio Prince of Lusitania, whō a ielous thought
bered as towardes Rosicleer for that hée had vnhorsed
hym in the presence of his Lady. But after this order
Rosicleer remained in the English court, where he rested
himselfe till this sodeine aduenture called him foorth as
shall be tolde you.

¶A gentlewoman came to the court from the
Princesse Briana, which made him follow Brandagedeon.   Cap. 35.

THe storie recounteth that Rosicleer abode many
dayes in king Oliuerios court, well liked and loued
of both king and nobles. In which time Rosicleer gaue
the king the rich tent which the wise Artemidoro had
wrought for him, wherein the king tooke great delight.
For although he had many other, both curious for making and costly for matter yet had he not séene in his life
any either so rich or of so cunning workmanship, so that
the kings good will towardes Rosicleer encreased by Rosicleers presence, and in that also for his company many
other great Princes and straunge knights remained with
ỹ king so long time after ỹ these iusts were ended, which
beginning of friendship betwixt Rosicleer and some of
these knightes grewe in the rude to such perfection by
his gratious and familiar behauiour, that neither faueur
of friendes nor dreade of daunger might wyth theyr
willes sunder them from this amitie. And if Rosicleer
had such power ouer knightes straungers, what had he
ouer the Princesse Oliuia being surprised with his loue, &
                                                      hauing

hauing engrauen his Image so deeply in hir immagination,ÿ he neuer departed from hir thought,but euermoze
there renewed in hir remembzaunce his knightly deedes
and great valour, whereby she made an euident demonstration of his linage as if naught els had bene enmy to
hir purpose . But this faire Pzincesse now so languished
with ÿ tozmēt of this amozous thought & pleasant liking
of hir loue Rosicleer, that nowe the conuersation of hir
gentlewomen was yerksome and to be solitarie did most
content hir,fozbearing withal, both hir rest in sleepe,& hir
sustenaunce in feeding.In which melancholy she was so
far gone without the feeling of hir owne disease,as ÿ nothing might ease hir highnesse but Rosicleers pzesence,
which bzed hir greater bale in his absēce,by ÿ griefe galling hir most to thinck that seing he was a straunger in
ÿ land,he would ere long retcurne to his own countrey.
One day casting hir selfe vpon hir bed, and tossing suche
like things in hir fancie,she sent out many a sozrowfull
sigh as ÿ fozerūners of this which followeth.O loue,loue "
how wel it eased me befoze times to heare louers mourn, "
to read their straunge fits,to see figured befoze me ÿ va "
riable successe of their attempts,with the fearful frights "
of thy subiectes and captiues . O how well at ease was I "
when being farre from the fire & out of daunger,I might "
laugh & loke on,& warme me by their flame.But now not "
so free noz clean deuoid of thought,I rue the little pitie "
I toke vpon their paine,& am therfoze scozched not with "
out desert. O loue,loue,by whem,not the feeblest onely, "
but the sturdiest also & stoutest are vnable to quench this "
fire,if it please thee to kindle it.Alas do not ÿ wisemen "
seine fooles,& ÿ hardy cowards if it be thy pleasure:& dare "
any man cōfesse ÿ truth in this his passiō,& are not al like "
sicke men beguiled,call sowze swœte,payne pleasure,bale "
blisse,griefe gladnesse,& the losing of their late libertie ÿ "
enlarging of their new franchise to cōtēt their fancies. "
And thou vnfoztunate Oliuia art thou Pzincesse of great "

O.ij.   Britaine, "

,, Britaine the daughter of king Oliuerio, the woman sued
,, vnto by so pliant petitioners both Princes and knightes
,, of great courage, whom thou hast all refused. So assu-
,, redly, but thou art some base and meane gentlewoman if
,, the sight of one onely knight not knowen vnto thee hath
,, so dimmed thy vnderstandinge, that reason is become
,, no more defensible. Where is thy late pride Oliuia,
,, where is thy auncient pleasure, where are thy hautye
,, lookes, where lyes the charter of thy libertie, where is
,, the estimation of thy beautie, where is the excellencie of
,, thy estate. O the miserable and euerchaungeable state
,, of man, lyke vnto the hearbes or flowers whiche the
,, morninges dewe refresheth, the noones heate opres-
,, seth, and the night shade encloseth in, as the graue doth
,, our bodyes: beeinge a liuely morrall of our mortalitie.
,, Alas Rosicleer, my father thinckes he hath made a great
,, purchase by thy being here, but I would to God I might
,, be as sure heire to this purchase, as I am otherwise cer-
,, teyne to repent thy comminge hether. And yet what-
,, someuer the euent be, my loue commaundes in me the
,, contrary. For is it not better for me to see Rosicleer, and
,, to acknowledge the goodnesse of God towardes man, in
,, inhablinge of him to the achieuement of suche won-
,, ders, whereby and by the enioying of his sight I receiue
,, suche pleasure, then neuer to haue seene him though I
,, lose the hope of augmenting my state. And truely befall
,, what maye in spight of Fortunes rancour, I wyll state
,, my selfe vppon this choise, and wyll not exchaunge it,
Uerie wyse was the Princesse Oliuia, and as the tymes
afforded very well learned, but yet these speaches proceeded rather of hir passion, then of aduised reason or good
readinge. And the lyke combatte to this of contrary
thoughtes Rosicleer endured, entertaining in his hearte
the counterfaict of the princesse in y secret contemplation
whereoff he was diligently occupied, immagining theroff
the brauorie of hir beautie, and the great desert in hir to
be

be best beloued. But as againe to the Princesse in all this
subiection to loue & his lawes, hir honesty is chiefly to be
noted, which for all that both ẏ remedy was aboue hir capacitie, & the paine likely to ouercome hir patéece: yet bare
out the bruntes thereof in such modestie rather by suffe-
raunce then striuing withall, that neither coulde Rosicleer euer assure himselfe of hir liking, nor any of hir
seruaunts wring it out by the maner of hir desease. Rosicleer was as close, which in him was the occasion of
farther trouble, for coueting to be alone the better to reioyce himselfe, and to enter more narowly into the serch
of his owne habilitie with the likelihod of his sute, hee
stumbled as in a blinde way vpon two blockes so placed
as that if he auoided the one, he must nédes hit his shin
against the other: for this was one. If he reuealed not
his griefe or not made hir priuie to his estate, there was
naught to preferre him before an other knight. Againe
ẏ other was, if he laid open his race, his supplicatio would
lacke succour. Nowe howe could hee with candlelight,
not hazard a fall vpon the one or the other. For he was
perswaded ẏ prince Edward, brother to the princesse Oliuia was his father, wherefore the néere kinred was to be
concealed if he loked for helpe, and yet the concealment
was the onely debarring of his hope. In this conflict he
did nothing but afflict himselfe, neither daring to discouer his malady, nor minded to dissemble it altogether,
by so much the more in worse case then ẏ Princesse was,
as the infirmitie of hir sere did lessen hir paine by yelding
at the first, and the magnanimitie of his courage to haue
the mastery, did in the end make the déeper impression in
his flesh, like as in nature the hardest fight is betwéene
the hardiest, & sooner shall the cannon shot deface ẏ high
towers, then breake through a rampier of wooll or flare,
and so the issue proued in him. But béeing one daye with
the king and the other noble Princes in ẏ great pallaice
to beguile his soléne conceits which ouercame his nights

reſt, he ſaw entering a gentlewoman well apparelled, which when ſhe came nære bowing humbly to the king,
" ſayd as followeth. God preſerue your maieſtie moſt no-
" ble king of the great Britaine. The Princeſſe Priana my
" miſtreſſe and wife vnto the Prince Edward your ſonne,
" with the remēbraunce of hir ductie, craueth to be certi-
" fyed by your good grace what you haue heard of hir Lord
" and huſband, for ſhe neuer ſaw him ſince his firſt arriual
" into Hungary. My Lady alſo by me grǽteth ẏ Princeſſe
" Oliuia you daughter, vnto whom ſhe commaunded me to
" deliuer a cofer of iewels, but cōming to land on ẏ Enliſh
" coaſt, I was ſet vpon by a great gyant, named Brandage-
" deon as I heare, who taking the cofer from me bad me
" come to this court, here to tel a new knight which ence
" vnhorſed him, ẏ he would make aunſwere to none but to
" him as concerning the coffer, and that for him he would
" ſtay at ẏ ſhore, there to make ſatiſfaction accordīg as he
" was charged. I beſæch your good highnes therfore to ſend
" that newe knight in your daughters quarrel againſt this
Gyant. Roſicleer hauing knowne this gentlewoman a-
mongſt thoſe which attended vpon the Princeſſe Briana
his mother in the monaſtery of the riuer, & that ſhæ had
to name Arinda was glad to haue ẏ oportunitie offred to
ſerue the princeſſes Oliuia and Briana, and therfore ry-
ſinġ from where he ſat he came before the king, to whō
" he ſayd. Sir ſæing it is Roſicleer whom this gentlewo-
" man ſæketh, and that Brandagedeon hath ſent for mæ, I
" beſæch your maieſtie to giue me licence to goe in theſe
" affaires, for it is out of reaſon to forſlacke ſuch wor-
" thy ſeruice to two ſo noble Princes. The king loth
of any occaſion at all miniſtred whereby he ſhould forſake the court for feare leaſt his retourne would not be
ouer haſtie, for he knewe well that he was nothing ad-
dict to idleneſſe, yet ſeeing his importunitie both to avn-
ſwere the challenge and to employe his trauaile, in the
name of theſe two princes would not gainſay his purpoſe

pofe,but wifhed him net to goe alcne fo2 that the gyant
was wel manned with about rrr.knights,fo2 this caufe
Bargandel & Lyriamandro,& other p2inces & knights offered to go in his company,but they could not p2euaile,fo2
he excufed himfelfe with this, p it fhould redound to his
difwo2fhip,if he fhould take mo2e company then the Gyant looked fo2. And by and by he craued pardon to depart
to his chamber ther to arme himfelfe. The gentlewoman
Arinda well knowing him,but fo2 that time fupp2effing
it,while Rofícleer bucled on his armour,went to deliuer
hir meffage vnto the P2inceffe Oliuia,vnto whome fhee
tolde that the cofer with iewels was intercepted by a falfe
barratour a Gyant named Brandagedeon,and that p new
knight had taken vpon him to fetc them againe,whiche
when the P2inceffe heard,although fhe was glad to vn-
derftand ought from the p2inceffe Briana,yet was fhe fo2-
rowful when fhe heard that Rofícleer would leaue p citie,and would go alone thether where the Gyant abode
him,fo2 hir minde gaue hir p fhe fhould not fæ Rofícleer
in haft,but tourning from this fhe demaunded of p gentlewoman many things in particuler touching hir Lady,
fo that the gentlewoman ftayed with hir till Rofícleer
being armed called vpon hir. Then the p2inceffe fayth,if
ther be no other remedy you may go with him,albeit tell
the knight frõ me,that J had rather the iewels were loft,
then he fhould put himfelf in fo great a ieopardy. Arinda
fayd fhe would doe hir commaund , and went downe to
Rofícleer being already on ho2feback with his efquire Telyo,fhe likewife toke hir palfray , and they th2ee rode
th2ough the Citie of London,muche gafed after by the
king and all the knights and Ladyes which ftode in the
windowes and battlementes of the pallace , and wyth
great fo2rowe pittied him to fee him goe alone, perfwa-
ding themfelues that if Brandagedeon were flaine o2 in
daunger,that his men would refcowe him.

O.iij.

¶ A cruell battaile betweene Rosicleer and Brandagedeon with his knightes.   Cap.36

ROsicleer being thus accompanied with Arinda and
Telyo his squier, willed the gentlewoman to guyde
him on the waye to the place where Brandagedon was.
Arinda knowing him well inough, sayde. Noble Roli-
cleer, J dare not so doe. The Gyant is fierce and strong
and hath with him many knightes, which if hœ haue
nœde shall helpe him, and then shall J see you in perill of
your life. Better were it Rosicleer that you should leaue
this enterprise and take the waye towardes Hungary,
there to comfort the sorrowfull Princesse Briana, which
since your departure from the monastery hath neuer ben
mery. Rosicleer perceiuing well that the gentlewoman
knewe him, casting his armes about hir necke, sayd vnto
hir. Why how nowe Arinda, how is it that you know
me and J haue not knowen my selfe since my comming
into this lande? But tell me gentle sister how we the Princesse Briana doth, my good Lady, for whose sorrowe J am
much agreeued, albeit to remedy it, there were no reason
in forsaking this enterprise which J haue taken in hand
to doe hir seruice therein. Besides that, J am determined not to retourne into Hungary before J can heare
some newes of the Prince Edward, whether he be deade
or aliue. No sayth the gentlewoman, but let this matter alone, for it were lesse losse that the two Princesses
shoulde want the cofer of iewels then that you shoulde
hazard your life in winning of it, and more acceptable
seruice shall you doe my Lady in going to visite hir, then
in seekinge out the Gyant to fight with him. The gentlewoman with all tooke holde of the brydle reynes to
haue ledde Rosicleers horse out of the way, whereat Rosicleer laughing a good, aunswered hir thus. Arinda, J
should get a good report in the court of kinge Oliuerio if
for feare of a battaile with this Gyant J should tourne
                                                            aside

aſide from this iourney which for the ſame cauſe I "
haue vndertaken . If I were certeine of more then a "
thouſand deathes I would not followe thy aduiſe herein "
Arinda, and ſo ſpurryng his horſe he kepte on his way. "
The gentlewoman woulde not importune him farther,
but leode him towardes the Gyant, where not farre off,
they mette an other gentlewoman on fate weping verye
piteouſly . At hir Roſicleer demaunded the cauſe of hir
griefe, which ſhe vttered ſtrayghtwaies in theſe wordes.
O ſir knight, Fortune, Fortune hath frowned on me, ſo "
that better welcome ſhould be the deathe then the daye- "
lyght . Roſicleer yet requeſted hir to ſpeake more playn- "
ly, and to tell wherein Fortune had wrought hir ſuche "
diſpite. I will gladly ſayth ſhe & for truth ſir knight I am "
a gentlewoman belonging to the Quane of Luſitania, "
which ſent me with a brother of mine a verye valyaunte "
knight, hether to bring certeine Iewelles for the Prin- "
ceſſe Oliuia daughter to the king Oliuerio, and for the "
Princeſſe Rodaſylua hir owne daughter . Now our miſ- "
happe was ſuch that entring the ſhore , wee hitte vpon a "
great and diueliſh Gyant, who examining vs whether we "
went and what we carried in our fardle, bicauſe my bro- "
ther made no aunſwere ſlewe him, and putting me from "
my palfray toke from me my horſe with the fardell , ouer "
and beſides with this commaund to go vnto the king O- "
liuerio and to the knights of his courte there to recorde "
my complaint againſt him. Thus haue I my Lord ſatiſ- "
fied your requeſt, now God be with you, for I will on to "
craue ſome remedye.

With this the gentlewoman parted from them , but
Roſicleer calling to hir ſayde.Gentlewoman, ſo it is that
my arrant is for ỹ ſame purpoſe to fight with the Gy- "
ant, for the lyke traſpaſſe by him committed agaynſt this "
gentlewomã here with me. If you wil retourne with vs, "
wee ſhalbe very glad thereof, and by Gods helpe I ſhall "
well quell that Gyants inſolency . What ſayde the "

gena

,, gentlewoman doe you purpose alone to fighte with the
,, Gyant. I in deede aunswered Rosicleer and haue hope to
,, reuenge this gentlewoman and your brother. God maye
,, well giue you power so to do if it please him sayd the gen-
,, tlewoman, but in respect of the Gyants strength it wyll
,, not sinke into my brest that a C. such knights as you are
,, can chastise him. Well sayd Rosicleer if you will go with
,, me you may at leasure when you see the euent deliberate
,, what to doe. If ye will not fare you well, for lesse shalbe
,, your hope of remedie in keeping your way as you nowe
Doe. Rosicleer helde on, and the gentlewoman viewing
his goodly personage, thereby perswading hir selfe that it
were but little losse to tourne backe with him, determined
to proue his good Fortune. And as she was not fully af-
,, sured in hir thought, she spake on this wyse . Be not
,, displeased with me but for the loue of God fayre knyghte
,, haue some greater regard of your owne safetie, not to cast
,, your selfe away for the recouery of my damage, it is no
great matter for me to take some paynes in goyng with
,, you : but it wilbe some griefe to retourne agayne laden
,, with a fresh complaynt of a new murder. And therefore
,, for Gods sake let the Gyant alone. Rosicleer sayd, I may
,, not, but seing you haue promised your company, gette vp
,, behinde my squire, and cast your care vpon God, which
,, will puruaye for your ease , as best shall lyke him.
,, So they foure trauayled towardes the place where the
Gyants abiding was, and comming neere vnto the shore
they sawe him harde by the water where he sate vpon a
great horse , and more then thirtie knights in a crayer
not farre off, as if they purposed to bord a tall ship, which
was on fleate in the Sea halfe a mile . Brandagedeon by
and by knew Rosicleer to be the new knight by the rich
armour he bare, the selfesame being worn by him in the
iusts, wherein he was hurled to grounde for which cause
preuenting Rosicleers salutacion, with a loud and hollow
voice he cried vnto him, Now Sir knight may I magnifie

mg

my gods for that I haue thee in such a place wher I may "
be auenged of thee at my pleasure for the despite thou hast "
done me, and all the word shall not rainsome thee from "
my hands. God of heauen shalbe my borrow aunswered "
Rosicleer, which also shall correct thy wickednesse & tread "
vnder foote thy intollerable pride and arrogancie. But to "
tell thee my message , I challenge thee for to make satis- "
faction vnto these gentlewomē of ý wrong thou hast done "
them, or to prepare thy selfe to mainteyne thy mischiefe. "
Brandagedeon spake no word, but signified his meaning
by his demeanour, for he tourned his horse head in great
rage and tooke a heauy speare with him, the other vnderstanding his signe, did as much. This first iourney brake
their staues & made them try the rest of the battayle on
foote. The Gyant being cleane vnhorsed, & Rosicleers horse
giuing backe, so ý he rusht agaynst ý ground, but ý succes
was diuers & vnequal in ý riders themselues. For Rosicleer keeping his saddel felte no harme in his body, & the Gyant thrown vyolently to the earth, was well shaken with
the fall.

But the combate is not yet ended, for Brandagedeon
being strong and mightie helde Rosicleer very harde , as
in deede it could not be otherwise, for betwixt them alone
the fight continued two houres, all ý meane time neither
part giuing ouer, nor making any semblaunce of discomfiture. In thende the knight hauing treble aduauntage o-
uer ý Gyant, first in Queen Iulias sword which byt sore:
secondly in Artemidoros harnes which held out the force
of the Gyants weapon : and thirdely the nimblenesse of
his bodye ready both to assaile strongly and to decline
as lightly from the others blowe, by whiche meanes hauing made a wide hole in the Gyants armour he wounded the Gyant at his pleasure.

The execution of this challenge to so little displeasure
on Rosicleers part , made Arinda thincke it long, till shee
shoulde blase it at home in the monasterye of the riuer:
but

but hir pleasure was soone ouercast , for there was ministred vnto hir a cup of colde water in steede of better lyking to alay hir thirst. Al this happening beyond hir expec-
tation, by ý Gyants knights, which seing their maister at
such an exigent although in no euident apparance of his
ende, in great fury came to lande, and at once all of them
with their swordes fell vpon Rosicleer . This was no
euen match, thirtie knights and a Gyant to set vpon one
silly knight, before almost tyred with two houres battails
against ý Gyant. But what thing may resist Gods ordinaunce? The Gyants knights layd on with such courag-
ges, that it reuiued the Gyant , for they were all chosen
knights , but I doubte not but that Rosicleer bestirred
himselfe, for so many as he mette , hee either maymed,
wounded, slewe, or threwe to grounde. And being ouerawed by number and fresh onsettes, he was fayne for defence to his backe, to withdrawe himselfe into the Sea,
there to stande in the water and receiue their blowes before him.

Nowe Telyo his squyre and Arinda the Hungarian
seing him forced to this extremitie were very wo begon,
but the gentlewoman Lusitanian as desperate of all succours by his meanes, gallopped from thence vpon hir palfray which stode by the shore, no lesse complayninge the
daunger wherein she lefte this good knight, then recurelesse lamenting the vniust death of hir brother. As she had
ridde some parte of hir way towardes Oliuerios courte,
there were two knights in hir iudgement very lusty and
armed at all poynts which made all the hast they mighte
to gette neere hir.

This gentlewoman comming within the hearing of
them, and minding to preuent other questions , cryed vn-
:, to them a farre off . For the passyon of God my good
,, Lords if all noblenes and vertue be not cleane buried in
,, you, make hast to succour a knighte the best in the world,
,, which is now enuironned with his enemyes being about
thirtie

thirtie knights besides a Gyant. The two knights with
these newes posted amayne, and by the same way which
the gentlewoman came, in short time got a sight of Rosicleer,
which at that time stode in the water against ri. or rii. of the:
for so many were left on liue of thirtie persons, those also
which then lyued being well nurtured by Rosicleers disci-
pline, that they woulde preace vppon him without good
warrantise.

Now by that time that the two knights came, Rosicleer had killed more then twentie, leauing a passage so
well trode as they might easely trace out his footesteppes.
At their first breaking in among the Gyants knights they
burst their staues vppon two of them ouerthrowing them,
and then drawing their swordes strake so lustely that the
assaylants were glad to leaue Rosicleer, and to defende
themselues against the two knights. Rosicleer hauing so
good helpe at hande, although he was stirred with the continuall heate of the foote battayle, would nædes be a partie player in the last act of this tragedye, and therefore
chose out Brandagedeon to deale withail, and with hys
sharpe sword gaue him so fierce a stoccadoe, that the bow-
ells trayled after the weapon, and the Gyant fell downe.
Now being thus put in possession of his desire, he came
to the two knightes vttering these or such lyke speaches.
I beseech you noble knights to lette me knowe at whose
hands I haue receiued so good maintenance, that I may ”
the better giue you thancks according to the state of your ”
degræ and your demerites towardes me. One of the ”
knights aunswered. You are not to thancke vs, for your ”
owne hand had wrought your escape before our cōming, ”
but neuertheles at your request we are contēt to discouer ”
our selues, and straight wayes they vnlaced their helmets ”
whereby Rosicleer knewe them, the one to be Bargandel
and the other Liriamandro his dære friendes. Rosicleer
after his presupposed thancks so happely stumbling on
his friendes helpe, fell to other matters, and first asked of
them

them foz what cauſe they came thether, they made aunſwer that the only feare they had leſt the Gyants knights
ſhould at once encloſe him, moued them to abandon the
court foz his reſcewes. And as this talke was intterrup-
ted by the comming of the two gentlewomen and Telyo
Roſicleers ſquire to demaund leaue of ſerch in þ Gyants
boate foz the cofer and fardell which had bene taken from
them, ſo after the gentlewomen with leaue obtayned,
departed foz to ſearch: theſe thzee knights began a dæpe
conſultacion of their owne affaires and what they ought
,, to do. Bargandel ſpake firſt in this wiſe. We haue this
,, moneth and moze loytered very idelly in kyng Oliuerios
,, court without exerciſe of armes oz armoure, therfoze it
,, wer not miſbeſæming vs knights if we ſhould foz a time
,, fozbeare our retourne to pzactiſe dædes of armes that our
,, good name & honour may enlarge our credit in this king-
,, dome, and be a meanes of the ſure ſettling of our memo-
,, ries in this lande, and the rather thereto am I ledde,foz
,, that I will not feare any diſwozſhip oz vanquiſh in your
,, company. I am content ſayth the newe knight with this
,, oz any other thing which you ſhall deuiſe. But what ſhall
,, we doe with theſe gentlewomen. Mary ſaith Liriaman-
,, dro, they ſhall retourne to the court with the dead body
,, of the Gyant,ther to pzeſent his carcaſe befoze the Pzin-
,, ceſſe Oliuia as a token from thæ Roſicleer and in part of
,, payment foz the great diſhonour which the Gyant hath
,, pzofered hir in witholding hir Iewels. They may lyke-
,, wiſe when they be there make all our excuſes vnto the
,, king foz our ſo ſodayne departure.

By this time the gentlewomen retourned with theire
owne carriadge, and what with the lengthe of the battaile, and other accidents, the daye was ſo farre ſhutte
in, that being verye darke they were conſtrayned altogether to tourne into a kæpers houſe nære at hande,where
they were welcome at ſuch warninge. Foz hee knewe
the thzee knights at the great feaſtes,wherefoze þæ en-
ter-

tertayned them as honourablye as he might. That night
not hauing wherwith otherwise to busie themselues, and
the opportunitie of the bearers putting them in minde of
their mistresses, they gaue themselues to enditing euery
man of seuerell letters vnto his loue and Lady Bargandel.
and Liriamandro deliuered theirs vnto the gentlewoman
of Lusitania, but the other not willing to make manifest
his choyse for that time toke Arinda a letter closely to
carry vnto the Princesse Briana his god Ladie, and afterwardes amongst other talke he required to sée the cofer of Iewelles which the Princesse Briana sent to Oliuia,
as if it had bene onely to haue séene the riches thereoff,
Arinda gaue him the cofer which he opened, and tosing
vp and downe as if to sée all the Iewelles, he secretly conuayed his letter to Oliuia vnder all the papers, and rede-
lyuered the cofer without being suspect. Well to make
an ende the talke had an end, & when ý rest went to their
reast, Rosicleer fel into his ordinary humor, driuing in his
thought, the whole order of the deliuery, and hir receite,
with hir manner of tourning ouer the papers to biewe
euery Iewell, this being but the first assay of the humor,
but when his fancie brought him to the finding of the letter, Lorde what a fight he sustayned, for the better vnderstanding whereoff, you must immagine a young scholler
but lately entred into schole poyntes ouerséeing of hys
theame before hée bringe it to the rebiewe of hys schole-
mayster, and beléeue mée in farre greater doubte hunge
Rosicleer of his Ladyes lyking then the boye doth of his
maysters. For in his reading of the blotted copie, as
distinctlye as if he were to gesse Oliuias coniecture vppon
euery syllable, god God vnto what a hard censure was the
poore paper subiect, as if euery sétence had bene then aray-
ned before him. For almost at euery lynes ende, he would
saye. Eyther this was to much, eyther this was to lyttle, or this is maymed, or this to rude and vnlearned,
or this was not well and finely penned, or that was not
playne

playne inough, o? this is faultie, o? this should be amen=
ded and to d?awe all into a summe, in euerye pare hee
woulde blame either the lytlle witte in inuention o? the
lacke of eloquence in the deliuery of the matter, but cheif=
ly his owne ouerboldenesse in p?esuming vpon so high a
P?incesse with so rude a discourse, and yet I dare say it
did him good to beguyle the P?incesse with this letter in
the colour of a Iewell, which she must receiue and reade
th?ough, ere she could learne the contents theroff, o? know
the penman. And beginning to recken a freshe after this
comfort, he stayed himselfe vppon these two poynts, first
that sith he was diseased, his remedye must begin by ma=
king his griefe knowne: second that his conscience tolde
him ther was nothing in the letter, the truth whereof he
durst not auowche as concerning either his owne person
o? the P?incesses, and this was his nightes reste as I
suppose.

¶ Rosicleer and the two Princes seeke aduen=
tures in the lande of Britaine, & the two gen=
tlewomen carrie the Gyants bodye to Oliue=
rios courte.   Cap. xxxvij.

NOT much out of the same manner was the other
knightes sleepe, d?eaming of their delights & other such
toyes, but the next day they arose and armed themselues
taking leaue of their heast and the gentlewomen. But
Rosicleer tarryed behinde to conducte the women a lyttle
on their way, and to haue mo?e secret conference wyth
Arinda about the P?incesse Briana, (the remo?se of his
conscience stinging him fo? stealing away so p?iuily from
the P?incesse) In the course of this talke he would some=
times name the P?incesse his Lady, sometimes his coun=
d?esse, by which name he requested Arinda to make offer
of his humble seruice with the best excuse it ce might fo?
his long absence, in that he had already entred the quest
 of

of seeking the Prince Edward or Donzel del Febo his
brother,and in such speaches hee brought them on their
waye, afterward taking his leaue wyth a friendly embrace, hee posted after his companye whome hee ouertooke in short time. Sre dayes these three knyghts rode
together without happening vppon any thing worthy the
recitall. The seuenth day in their way they sawe a farre
off a knyght very tall and bygge made vppon a fayre
steede, by seeming a knight of greate account. There
followed him two squiers,the one bearing his launce,the
other his helmette,for the heate of the daye had made
him vayle his headpeece, to put on a lyght Hat of taf-
fata,and comminge neere they sawe that hee was of a
good countenaunce,somwhat of colour dusky & blacke,but
in making both manlyke and of good proportion, hys
ioyntes well knitte and somewhat large wythall,which
foreshewed greate lykelyhoode of strengthe and courage. Thys knyght straunger firste salutiag these three
knyghtes rydinge by, spake vnto them thus. Tell mee
my Lords I praye you,whether you be of king Oliue- ,,
rios court or no, Bargandel aunswered him. Truely we ,,
are if we lyste, and so longe as our liking lasteth. But ,,
wherefore demaunde you thys. I wyll tell you sayde ,,
the knyght, sothe it is that I am a Tartarian borne in ,,
that parte of Tartary which bordereth vppon Europe, ,,
and trauaylinge to seeke aduentures I was caste by ,,
tempest of the sea vpon the countrey of Zeland. Where I ,,
heard that many knights should assemble in this realme ,,
at a great feaste and iustes proclaymed by the Kynge, ,,
wyth a safe conducte warraunted out vnder hys owne ,,
signet,for all knyghtes Christians and Pagans, or of ,,
all Nations else besides whatsoeuer, thether to come ,,
and proue their baloure. I am as I saye,a wandering ,,
knyght and haue no other erraunt but to see suche good ,,
knyghtes and to trye my selfe amongest them. Vppon ,,
the reporte hereof,as sone as my shyppe was rygged ,,
P.   and ,,

„ and trymmed, and that the winde ſerued foz my par-
„ poſe, J entered in my ſhippe to arriue in thys lande.
„ Nowe whether that the wape longe and daungerous
„ by the ignozaunce of my Pilotte ſhutte mee from my
„ hope,oz that the repozters miſtake the dape , oz rather
„ knewe it not. Since my conuminge to lande J haue
„ in many places bene aſſertayned that the feaſtes are
„ longe agone ended , and that the moſte parte of the
„ knyghtes haue taken ſhippinge and departed into
„ their countrpes, notwithſtandinge, leauinge behinde
„ them ſuche a good memozie in the mouthes of euery
„ man,as much it grǽueth me to haue loſte my laboure.
„ Foz thys cauſe laſte reinembzed, J am in purpoſe foz
„ one monethes ſpace to rpde thzoughe thys lande, and
„ to deale with all knightes commers to pzoue whe-
„ ther their credite bǽ not aboue their deſertes : where-
„ vnto J haue ſette thys condition, that if any of them
„ diſmounte mee oz make mǽ peelde, that then J muſt
„ faythfully accompliſhe all that whiche the vanquiſhour
„ ſhall wyll mee. But if J vnhozſe any of them oz
„ take any of them pziſoners, then the vanquiſhed ſhall
„ commende mǽ to the kynge Oliuerio , and make of-
„ fer of hys oz theyz liues and goodes at his courteſy as
„ a ſimple token of my great good will towards him.Since
„ this determination thzee dayes haue J iournped in this
„ lande,and J haue encountered ten knightes whome J
„ haue ſente accozdinglp to kinge Oliuerio . And my
„ Lozdes whether are you retapninge, to the Englpſhe
„ courte oz no,foz if you be J mape not bzeake my vow al-
„ though by your ſemblaunce & riding you ſhewe to me as
„ the beſt knights which J haue ſǽne in my lpfe.

This ſapde the knyght ſtraunger, and the other
thzǽ knyghtes were eaſely bzought to the allowinges
of the conditions . Wherefoze Bargandel whiche had
vndertaken to aunſwere, ſapd. Syz knyght we thancke
you

you for the large reconnte you haue made vnto vs of „
your hether comming, and as to your ouerlate arriuall „
and the condicions fet to the tylte, albeit I may not mif- „
like them beringe fo equall, yet for my parte, I aun- „
fwere and for thefe knightes that wee woulde not glad- „
ly deale wyth you vppon fo lighte occafion, for rather „
will wee honour ftraunge Knightes then in any wife „
be an incombraunce vnto them, but fith it is your ear- „
nett fute, and that therein wee fhall doe you feruice „
wee wyll not refufe you, and by the leaue of thefe „
my Lordes and fellowes, my felfe will bee the for- „
mott. But by God Syr knight, there is the Ladye „
Siluerina in the Englifhe courte, and if I fayle not of „
my purpofe I will make you kiffe hir white handes, ere „
you bee many daies elder. But Bargandel fayled in „
deede of his purpofe, for though he was a very valyaunt
knyght, yet was he but younge, and the Tartarian was
both mightie and well exercifed.

After the Tartarian had buckled on hys helme, and
Bargandel had obtained leaue of hys fellowes to bee
the firft in this aduenture, either of them clipped their
fpurres to the horfe fides, and their encountry was fuche
that Bargandel brake his fpeare in fmall fhiuers in the
fheelde of hys enemye, caufinge the Tartarian to lofe
the raynes and to wreath fomewhat in hys faddle. But
the Tartarian ouerthrewe Bargandel, horfe and man
to the ground, and wyth the tourne to recouer the raynes
dreffed hymfelfe in his faddle, paffinge forth gallauntly,
whyle Bargandel laye on the grounde very angrye and
defirous to haue had the combatte with the fworde.
Roficleer and Lyriamandro muche wondred at theyr
fhockes, Lyriamandro then tooke the nexte tourne,
and Roficleer bycaufe the ftraunger wanted a fpeare,
fente hys owne ftaffe vnto hym whiche peraduenture
if hee coulde haue forfeene the euente, hee woulde not
haue done, for by it Liriamandro was hurled to ground,

and the Tartarian almoſt vnhorſed, hys ſtyrroppes béeing bꝛoke and himſelfe caſte vppon the arſon of hys
ſaddle . The Tartarian knyght was much abaſhed at
the great force of theſe two knyghtes , foꝛ hée had not
thought to haue mette two ſo ſtronge knyghtes in all
this lande, and when there remayned none but one
knyght,and he lykewyſe without a ſtaffe to iuſte withall, hée came to this one and bydde the baſe to the
ſwoꝛde play,in theſe termes.

,,   Syꝛ knyght,ſith both of vs wante ſpeares to iuſte
,, withall,it ſhall be well to make vp this lacke wyth our
,, ſwoꝛdes., that you maye either reuenge the ſhame of
,, your companyons oꝛ elſe goe wyth them foꝛ companye,
,, and all thꝛee pꝛeſent your ſelues pꝛiſoners to the kynge
,, your Loꝛde. Whoſe courte notwithſtandinge J ſhall
,, highly commende off foꝛ the great vertue whereoff my
,, ſelfe hath had pꝛoꝛfe ſufficiently in your fellowes. Aſſu-
,, redly Syꝛ knyght (ſayd this odde man which was Roſi-
,,cleer) were it not foꝛ the duetie whiche J owe to my
,, companions,and foꝛ that you ſhoulde ill acqupte their
,, courteſies if you ſhoulde leaue me ſcotfree to ſcoꝛne at
,, their miſhappes, J woulde that thys combatte wyth
,, ſwoꝛds ſhould be excuſed,foꝛ that J am not accuſtomed
,, to fight foꝛ ſo ſmall a cauſe,but ſith that both my compa-
,, nions challenge thys at my handes , and that it is a
,, poynte of cowardlyneſſe to leaue the combatte, and al-
,, ſo that you will not haue vs to bꝛeake companyes. J
,, condiſcende to your deuyſe with thys pꝛouiſo, that if
,, by good Foꝛtune J ouercome you my companions ſhall
,, be fréed from your charge,& you ſhall goe in their roomes
,, to kiſſe the kinge of Englands hande, as J am ſure it
,, will doe you good to haue acquaintaunce with hys
,, grace.J am well pleaſed héerewyth aunſwerd the Tar-
,, tarian , and ſo ſayinge hée dꝛewe out a fine ſwoꝛde,
Roſicleer likewiſe dꝛawing his. Thus began the bꝛaue
combat in which they continued a long time,no aduauntage

tage being espyed on either part by the beholders, what
was within them, themselues best knew. But Rosicleer
rather delighted then afrayde at his enemyes courage,
deuysed by himselfe howe to winne that valyaunt
knight for friende and to leaue the combatte, for vppon
so slender a quarrell hee thought the hazarte would be
to great. Mary for all that he dyd his best, for when ye
felte the stronge buffettes hee coulde not but yelde the
like. The Tartarian knyght burning in rage, rather to
haue ŷ maistry ouer so valiant knights, rather thē for any
ill will he bare to Rosicleer, compassed howe by mayne
force to subdue his aduersary, & in this thought he strake
so furiously that with his charge and the others aunswere the noyse was so confused and great wythall, that
it was hearde vppon the toppe of hylles as the shotte of
Artilerie : When the Tartarian knight was so well
heated as you haue hearde, hee draue a blowe with both
his handes full at Rosicleers head, which lighting vppon
the fine and inchaunted helmette, notwithstandinge de-
priued Rosicleer of his eye sight & enfeebled his hearing
at that time. But Rosicleer could not so soone forgette
it, and therefore whyle it was freshe in hys remembraunce, he restored the lyke blow which in ŷ descending
missed the Tartarians crest, otherwyse it had put hym
in daunger. But alyding vppon his shoulder it was
so heauie that it made the Tartarian stoupe to his horse
backe. The next daungerous blowe which the Tartari-
rian gaue, made Rosicleer bowe vnto hys saddle both
the swoorde and the raynes falling from him. Eargandel
and Lyriamandro standinge by fell therewyth into a
straunge admiration of the Tartarian in that hee not
onely kepte Rosicleer play, but put him to his troumps, &
by this time I thinck their desire to fight with him was
well abated, seeinge they knewe nowe howe well hee
coulde handell his weapon. And Rosicleer hauinge got
greater courage through the griefe of his wounde, kept

no moze his seate , but ryſinge in his ſtyzroppes and recoueringe his ſwozd which was faſtened with a lyttle chayne vnto his ſaddle bowe,he hit the ſtrong Tartarian ſo great a blowe,that the bloud guſhed out both at his eares and noſtrelles , and hæ laye foz dead vppon the crowpe, the hozſe carryinge hym aboute the fielde tyll he rzuiued . After not without ſome abaſhment as one come out of an other wozld : the Tartarian when hæ felte the bloude iſſuyinge in ſuche meaſure, lyft vp his hande and callinge foz helpe on hys Gods, ſayinge . Aſſiſt mee D my Gods agaynſts thys fell knyghte , foz if J tarrye moze of theſe blowes my lyfe ſhall ſoone bee ended,and when he had ſo ſayde,as pur- poſed to make an ende of the fraye hæ tooke his ſwozde with both hys handes, and wyth all hys fozce follow- inge the blowe, he ſmote Roſicleer vppon the helmette to no greate harme on his bodye, but the weight there- off aſtoniſhed hym as muche as if a Towze had fal- len vppon hym , whereat Roſicleer waxed madde an- grye,and not rememb;inge that whiche befoze hee had pzemeditate as to ende the battayle in quyetneſſe, hee repayed the treſpaſſe wyth treble dammage to the Tartarian . Foz albeit the Tartarian myght well bæ reckened amonge the moſte famous knightes of elder tyme , bæing couered wyth a helmette ſo well tem- pered as any Pzince myght haue , yet liuinge in that age and encounteringe ſuche knyghtes, hys roome was but nexte the beſte . And when hee ſawe that terri- rible blowe ouer hys heade , hee coulde haue wyſhed a whole mountayne betwæne hym and it . But there needed no ſuche impoſſible meanes to auoyde thys miſſoztune,foz it was pzouyded by the diuine maieſtye of God that thys noble knyght ſhoulde dye a Chzyſti- an , and that greate friendſhyppe ſhoulde growe be- twæene theſe thzee knyghtes, and therefoze God ſo dy- rected Roſicleers hande,that it fell not right,but glaunce-

uig

ing downe vppon the shoulder, it netwithstandinge tourned the Tartarian from his horse, wyth so greate paine
on hys ryght shoulder that hee myght not ryse hymselfe vp agayne, wyth thys fall hys buckles brake and
the naylinges rente , and bainge then halfe vnarmed,
hee threwe hys swoorde frem hym , puttinge hys knee
to the grounde to gyue thanckes to hys vnmagyned
Gods for their deliuery from so furious a blowe , and
then tourninge towarde Rosicleer, he sayde. Noble and ,,
valyant knyght, the strengest and mightiest whiche I ,,
haue euer knowne , or haue beleeued euer to haue ,,
bene in thys courte or others , pardon mee my rash- ,,
nesse for I haue bene mysaduised when my wyll firste ,,
put me foorth to contende with you, onely your greatnesse ,,
of body and comlinesse might haue sufficed to teache ,,
mee that you were more valyaunt and stronger then ,,
I am, and sith I am nowe vanquyshed , and rather ,,
by greate myracle escaped wyth lyfe from your handes ,,
then by myne owne cunninge, saye on what you com- ,,
maunde , for I am preste to accomplishe all that ,,
whiche was agreed vppon before our combattte , and ,,
my duetie shall not bee slacked in any pointe , but I ,,
woulde rather fulfill more then all that, for to gayne ,,
the societie of your worthy person and your compani- ,,
ons, for I neuer mette with more nobler knightes for ,,
valoure and bounteousnesse, and so saying yeldes himself. ,,
By thys speach the furye and choller of Rosicleer was ,,
well slackte , and bainge gladde to see the knyght ,,
so humbled before him , hee aunswered . God knight ,,
I accepte in good parte that whiche you haue sayde, ,,
and it greeueth me muche to haue had the battayle ,,
with you, for vnto a knight straunger and valorous. I had ,,
rather be a meanes for procuring honour and ease, then ,,
their trouble and incombraunce, & as to the articles of the .,
couenaunt which you remember me off. Beleue mee I ,,
woulde not haue exacted them at your handes, and it shal ,,

he

" be yet in your chorfe whether you will fulfill them or
" no, and yet I feare not but that you shall well like of your
" feruice to the kinge Oluerio himfelfe, bæuing a good
" knight and a great honourer of ftraungers. Likewyfe
" we thre shall take it as figne of your good liking teward
" vs, if you make vs priuie to your name, that hereafter we
" may knowe you and doe vnto you that honour which fo
" good a knight meriteth. Sir knight, aunfwered the Tar-
" tarian, I haue great defire to goe and kiffe the hande of
" king Oluerio, as well to knowe him as to fatiffie that
" which I owe vnto you, and will not fayle to depart and
" take my way toward the king. But to your laft demaud
" I am as I tolde you before a Tartarian and my name
" is Zoilo Prince and heyre of that kingdome whiche I
" would with good will forbeare for fome time, if you and
" thefe knightes would vouchfafe your acquaintaunce and
" company, for I haue more defire to trauayle in thefe
" partes then in that countrey from whence I came, by-
" caufe there is no continuall affoorde of knightes and
" frefh accidentes as I finde in this kingdome, and I
" shoulde more highly efteeme of the friendshippe and fo-
" cietie of fuch noble and worthy knightes then of any
" riches in the worlde. And nowe for that I haue de-
" clared who I am, I shall thincke my felfe farther in
" your debte if you make your felues farther knowne vn-
", to me. Rofileer and his companions gladly heard of
his byrth & lignage, but much gladder of the friendshyp
whereto he requefted them, fo they gaue him manye
thanckes, & told him who they were. Diuers fpeaches of
great courtefy paffing betwæne them, whereby their a-
mitie was fo fure confirmed that it remayned vnto the
drath, euery one laboring to be found moft friendly. And
this done they appoynted that Prince Zoilo should gee
to the court, onely to haue a fight of the kinge, and that
Rofileer with his companions shoulde abyre hym there-
about, then they foure to trauaile together whether fortune

tune woulde carrye them . This being concluded, the
Prince of Tartarye tooke his waye towarde the courte of
king Oliuerio thinking long to finde the time for his retourne. They tooke the way towards a forrest where the
historp leaueth them, to intrreat of the gentlewomen in
the meane tyme , which broughte the bodye of the great
Brandagedeon vnto the courte of king Oliuerio.

¶The gentlewomen brought the bodye of Brandagedeon to the courte , and the Princesses receiued the letters of their knightes.
   Cap.xxxviij.

GReat was the griefe which the Princesse Oliuia felt
   by the absence of Rosicleer, that neither hir high e-
state nor the courtly disports suffised to make hir forget
hir care, or helpe hir to couer hir lyking, but in hir lodging she woulb be without company in the day and in the
nighte without slæpe ; euer wishing to sæ him agayne
whome she loued more then hir selfe , for hir minde prophecied to hir that she should not sæ him very quickely,
and as it is naturall for the patient to communicate hys
griefe with the Phisition, iudging this some ease where
the principall remedie wanteth. So the faire Princesse as
vnacquaynted and to beginne in such passions , not being
able at the first to counsayle hir selfe otherwise, thought
it best to discouer hir griefe to one of hir gentlewomen
named Fidelia the faythfullest and most secret of hir „
houshofde, the which many times had importuned hir to „
knowe the cause of hir sorrowe,and one night as she was „
alene with hir the Princesse sayde to hir . Thou kno- „
west my Fidelia how among all the Ladyes and gentle- „
womē which I haue,I haue chosen thæ only for þ faith- „
full treasorer of my secrets,& I haue not bene nor thought „
the thing which I haue not emparted with thæ , which „
hath come to passe enely by the loyall and good seruice, „
                                     where

,, wherein I haue alwayes found thæ plyant and dyligent,
,, with the like confidence vnto that which I alwayes haue
,, reposed in thæ, I will vnfolde vnto thæ a secret , which
,, none in the world my selfe except and thy selfe shall learne
,, at my handes, in the concealyng whereoff, vnto this day
,, I haue a thousand times endured lyttle lesse then deathe.
,, And the matter is such, that it is vnfitting for any one to
,, be a dealer therein but my selfe and thy selfe whome I
,, account as my selfe . At a worde my Fidelia that tyrant
,, loue which spareth neither high nor lowe , hath taken
,, possession of me by the great prowesse and beautie of the
,, newe knight, and I am sure that but my deathe, nothing
,, can sette mee frée : although I haue studyed all possible
,, meanes of my lybertie,and thereto haue sette the defence
,, of my honesty and great estate to withstande this conceit,
,, yet for all that I can doe, as longe as this knights race
,, is vnknowen I cannot case my selfe , my former reme-
,, dyes seruing me only agaynst the temptacion of the flesh,
,, and not to driue out the remembraunce of his personage,
,, whence my desire springeth . And truely I cannot per-
,, swade my selfe other, then y this knights offspring is right
,, noble, be being of so courtlyke behauiour and knightlye
,, prowesse the truth hereoff , being somewhat more incre-
,, dible, then the lying fables of our auncient Poets. Now
,, if he be a Prince borne , the onely hope to haue him for
,, husbande, my father and he being therwith pleased,may
,, yelde one some comfort , in the meane time while op-
,, portunitie serueth for the finall accomplishment. Where-
,, fore myne owne Fidelia séeing that I haue fully layde o-
,, pen the bottome of my heart, that which remayneth one
,, thy parte, is to trauayle with his squire or some other to
,, witte of what parentage Rosicleer is . Fidelia had lyste-
ned very attentiuely to that which hir Ladye had sayde,
and as shee was very wise, so perceiuing by the dryfte
of the speache, that neither hir mistresses maladye coulde
be remoued by counsayle, nor that she woulde accepte of

it

it if it were bestowed, besides that, that hir desire was
lawefull to match with Rosicleer, if there were no dispa-
rage in his stocke. She coulde not gaynesay hir mistresse
in flatte termes, but made aunswere, that sith hir grace
had layde that charge vppon hir she was contente to receiue, as also readye to offer hir seruice in any other thing
for this matter which she now moued, she sayde that sith
hir graces purpose was so good shee shoulde not nede to
remember hir farther in it, for that so sone as Rosicleer
shoulde retourne she woulde be in hande with his squyre
to boult out the truth of euery thing, and yet (sayth shee)
I cannot beleue by reason of his magnanimitie but that
he is descended from some noble progeny, which if it so
be I lyke verye well that your grace is so affectioned towardes hym, otherwise I dare not aduise you, but yet I
will tel you my fancie, it wer better for you to abide some
payne, then to make your head of your vnderlyng. The
beautifull Princesse was well apayed at this counsayle
so iumping with hir former determination, and it greatly
asswaged the mallice of hir passion, in that shee had bewrayed it to hir trusty seruaunt. The next day the gentlewomen entred into the pallayce, driuing a horse before
them loded with the Gyants body. At their entraunce the
hurly burly in the court was so great, euery man running
to see the wonder, that the king with all those which wer
with him and the Princesse Oliuia with hir gentlewomen ranne to their windows to see what the matter was,
and when they sawe the Gyant they knew hym, and as
newely abashed at Rosicleers vertues, they began to commend of him as of the best knight in the world. The gentlewomen presentlye were broughte before the king
which receiued them courteousiye, and they in order declared vnto him and the rest that which had chaunced to
Rosicleer since his departure from the Cittye. The
king lyked verye well of all, saue that when they tolde
hym that the knightes coulde not retourne presentlye

The Mirrour of Knighthood.

as minding to purſue aduentures . For the king feared,
leſt by being ſo much enclyned to knightly deedes , theire
good ſucces would carrie them farther off then ſhould be
for his pleaſure. But tye gentlewomen departed from the
king to do their meſſage vnto the Princeſſe Oliuia, whom
they founde in hir chamber with the two other Princeſſes in hir company . Comming before hir they deliuered
their meſſage with commendacions from Roſicleer and
the two Princes, which had ſent hir that Gyant ſo dead
as a ſatiſfaction in ſome parte for the detayning of hir Iewelles. The Princeſſe pleaſauntly laughing at that pre-
ſente , cauſed the gentlewomen to go on in that ſtorye,
and to make reporte of all occurrentes in their iourneye,
which they did ſo faithfully that the Princeſſe in the tellyng was not able to colour hir affection towardes Roſicleer . This tale ended, Arinda gaue into hir handes the
packette, which the Princeſſe opened , and tourning ouer
the Iewelles founde a letter, which ſhe put in hir beſome
taking it to be Brianas, and in lyke ſorte the gentlewoman of Luſytania made deliuerye of Bargandel and Li-
riamandros letters vnto their Ladyes, with the cofer vnto
Rodaſylua. The two Princeſſes, Syluerina & Rodaſylua
being great friendes, went both together in a cloſette to
reade without interruption their loues letters ſo eloquent
and ſo fraught with amorous ſpeaches, which much reioyced the young Ladyes to be beloued of ſo good knights
and not to breake off their ſeuerall commendacions of
their knights and Lordes , wee will ſpeake of the Princes Oliuia, who being left alone for ye company of ye two
Princeſſes diſpatched hir other gentlewomen into diuers
parts of the chamber, to haue a more ſecret ſuruay of Brianas letters.

When ſhee had redde on through that which was deliuered with the packet, ſhe tooke that other out of hir bo-
ſome , which ſhe had founde in ranſacking the pac-
ketts , and opening it ſhe ſawe in capytall letters R O-
SI-

SICLEER subscribed, wherby she knew it to be his, &
somewhat troubled she foulded it vp quickly agayne, minding to learne by what meanes that letter was hidde a-
mong the Iewelles. And therefore calling Arinda she asked if that any one had vnlocked the cofer, after that hir
Ladye had delyuered it vnto hir . Arinda supposing that
the Princesse had wanted something, aunswered. No truly Madame, for I haue alwayes kept the keyes , and no
body euer had them at my handes but Rosicleer, which
requested to see the Iewelles when we were in the kée-
pers lodge, and in my presence he shutte it, restoring mee
the keyes and not taking out ought whereof I can accuse
him. The Princesse smelling out Rosicleers shifte, and
somewhat smiling withall , to heare wherevnto Arinda
had construed hir meaning, replyed merely thus. I asked
it not gentle friende for that I thought there wanted any
thing in the cofer, for it was wholly lost when it was in
Brandageons power, but I asked it for that I meruayled it fell out so well, when Brandageon was the kée-
per. Arinda waxing bolde hereat. Nay mary sayth shee
with your fauour noble Princesse , Brandageon mis-
geuing in his minde how little time he shoulde enioye it,
toke litle care for the opening.

So thys question who opened it was concluded in a
laughter and little talke continued after . The Princesse
thincking long till she might alone reade Rosiclers letter,
and therefore somewhat earlyer then shee was wonte,
shee withdrewe hir selfe into hir bedchamber with
onely Fidelia in hir companye to sée hir in bed.
When the dore was fastened, shee drewe out
Rosicleers letter and not hauing power
hir selfe to reade it, shee gaue it
vnto Fidelia . The tenour
of the louing letter was
this, which héere-
after followeth.

¶ Vnto

The Myrrour of Knighthood.

That which is appoynted by God mightie Princesse,
maye not by mans power be altered or peruerted, as
in my selfe I proue it, for since that mine eyes first tolde
me of your beautye, and my iudgement gaue consent therto and that my will hath procured lyking thereoff in my
affection , I haue felte an alteration in mee so incurable,
that striuing with it both by arte and nature, I haue not
hetherto found my remedy : which thing good madame
I trust cannot seeme more vnlykely to, then it hath bene
to me in the feeling terrible . The clappe of the thunder
is the greater when it meeteth with the thickette able to
make more resistance, longer lasts y kyndled fire in y builded Oke, then in the parched strawe, and more vehement
is the fighte betwœne two enemyes , then when the one
yœldeth . What force loue hath as I coulde well wish
your Ladyshippe to consider in mee, or to fœle in your
selfe, so at least I besœche you to waye by others and to
belœue reporte, howe that with lyght assaults, he bea-
teth downe the stoutest courages , and with gentle cords
bindeth the biggest armes, that his force, neither the wisest nor the myghtiest were able to resist, that from his
subiection not Iulius Cæsar the greate Monarche of the
worlde coulde frœ himselfe : that he quelled the pride of
the mightie Carthagenian in the delyghts of Capua : and
fettered Mars and Iupiter two Gods of the Gentyles in
chaynes of Iron : that he transformeth men into sundrye
shapes, and as it were by sodayne inchauntment framed
the armestrong Hercules to the distaffe and spyndle : Ari-
stotle to be bridled and saddled : that he clymeth the highest toweres and stretcheth to the lowest valleye : that
hee deuydeth the harde rockes and bloweth throughe
the rasye passages : to conclude, nothing so strong and inuincible, but that loue can ouerthrowe, and doth what

him

him lyfteth. So that if I confeſſed my ſelfe yolden vnder ſo mightie a conquerour, I ſhoulde yet be blameleſſe for my cowardiſe. Yet what haue I not attempted? if either counſayle of friendes, or myne owne witte, eyther Phiſickes cure, or mirth of company might haue warranted my quyetneſſe. So God, good madame ſpæde my wryting as I ment not to trouble you with my letters. But the weake complayne, and the diſeaſed ſæke remedy, as what griefe is ſo greate or wounde ſo wide, but it hathe ſome redreſſe or other prouided in nature. To you therefore good madame thus boldely haue I diſcouered my vnreſt, that by your meanes whence onely I may hope for it I may receiue comforte. And ſo attending your highneſſe aunſwere eyther of lyfe or deathe, I humblye kyſſe your Princely hande.

The reſolued to loue or not to lyue,
Poore ROSICLEER.

Roſicleer penned this letter either not well in his wittes or els greatly perplexed in his thought, ſo harde it is to finde an iſſue, but I beleue rather that it came from heart to hand, and was ſo ſette downe, without farther aduiſe. Yet in the meane time that Fidelia redds the letter, the fayre Princeſſe broade awake to heare thoſe amorous wordes, and fælyng them in hir heart with the lyke loue wherein Roſicleer wrote them. When it was ended heaping out aboundance of ſighes vpon the argument of the letter, ſhæ ſayde vnto Fidelia. Ah Fidelia what force may a tender gentlewoman as I am haue for to reſiſt the tyrannye of loue, when ſo many famous and ſo mighty Princes coulde neuer cōquer him? How may I ouercome him, which hath had the mayſtrye of ſo many, tell mee Fidelia and counſayle me what I haue to do in this matter, for I miſtruſt my owne wiſdome, and very ſicke is the paſſyonates iudgement very ſure & requyſite. Fidelia
aoa

nothing wondring at that effect which loue had wrought
in the Princesse hir Ladie, for she rather wished hir selfe
worthy of so glorious pryne, aunswered hir thus. Madame to counsayle you arighte were to will you to defie
loue, and to abandon Rosicleers companye, and yet the
wordes of this letter leueth in me a doute theroff, if ȳ matter be as true as the wordes importeth. Next were to
desire you to haue an eye vnto your high estate, which yet
me thincketh is not necessary, for I knowe you to be so
wise, as that you will hazarde death rather then commit
a thing so preiudiciall to your honour. Nowe there remayneth onely to learne out Rosicleers lynage, that if he
be such a one as maye marry you without diswourshippe,
you may then beginne the redresse of both your wronges,
otherwise if he fayle in that poynt, the first counsayle
will be most conuenient to eschewe his presence, which
shall in time doe away this affection, as in time all things
are for gotten.

Héere the Princesse interrupting Fidelias speach, replyed in this manner. Ah Fidelia, you thincke me not such
a one but that although the loue which I beare vnto Rosicleer be such that it procureth me to will his presence, if
he fayle in gentrye, I will rather chastise his boldenesse
with perpetuall exile out of this lande, then giue him comforte to the empaire of my credite, and sooner will I dye
an hundreth times, then bestowe a countenaunce vppon
such a one. But this I iudge of Rosicleer by the pure and
loyall loue which he meaneth towardes mee, that it is
lykely he may merite me for wife, otherwise it is to bee
thought that in a knight so vertuous ther cannot lye hidden such impudencie as to moue a Lady vnto hir dishonour. In such lyke talke after the letter redde the Princesse and Fidelia passed the most parte of the nighte tyll
Fidelia tooke hir leaue, the Princesse notwithstanding stil
canuassing ouer the letter of Rosicleer, and euery swéete
worde which he had written, and she prayed to God with
all

all hir heart that he might proue such a one as was not
vnfitting for a Quænes marriadge.

¶Arinda the gentlewoman belonging vnto
the Princesse Briana tolde the bringing
vp of Rosicleer vnto the Princesse Oliuia.
Cap. 39.

Rinda remained a long time in ỹ court tarrying for such things as ỹ princes Oliuia made
ready to sende vnto ỹ Princesse Briana, vpon
which occasiõ as it happened one day, ỹ princesse Oliuia, Arinda, and Fidelia to be together, then
Arinda not so well aduised as she ought to haue bene
in the secrete affayres of hir mistresse, vnbryled hir
tongue and declared to the Princesse Oliuia all the lyfe
and doinges of hir mistresse the Princesse Briana as
farre as shee had any knowledge, and it may be that
she added somtime more then truth, amongst other things
in this tale she tolde of the little boyes which hade bene
brought vp with the Princesse Briana, reciting the meruailous tokens which they brought from their byrth, and
how that the sorrow of hir Lady was somewhat comforted by them, till Fortune brought one of them into a
barke nære a great and dæpe riuer running into ỹ maine
sea as you haue heard before, and that the other of riiij.
yeares, (the Princesse vnwittinge of it) stale away, after
entering farther she tolde that the same Rosicleer which
killed Brandagedeon was the same which departed without leaue when he was riiij. yeares olde, whome shee
knewe at the first sight, and had entreatie to retourne
into Hungary. When the Princesse hearde this, driuing
to the conclusion, she demaunded where the Princesse had
those little boyes. Madame sayd Arinda, in this shall you
sée the workes of God howe meruailous they be, whiche
from so base a stocke can rayse so worthy ympes, and

Q.   you

you shall vnderstand that they be sonnes to a knight named Leonardo not of the most noble, but of the meanest
knightes of the Citie, and for that their father hathe to
wyfe a woman, sister to a gentlewoman of my Ladyes
named Clandestria for hir longe seruice in great fauour
wyth hir grace: for hir sake the Princesse made the parentes of these childzen to nourse them vp in the monastery at hir charges vntill they were all lost as I made
mention. When the Princesse had heard Arinda in thys
sorte blasing the ofipring of Rosicleer, what sorrow may
be compared vnto hirs, for in that instant she could wel
haue yelded to death: and why? for that the onely hope of
all hir remedy was in the conceite of Rosicleers hyghe
estate, thereby meriting to be hir mate, which when shee
sawe to bee cleane contrary, she was in suche a case as if
hir soule had bene taking his leaue of hir body . When
Fidelia sawe hir colour so sone chaunged, as vnderstanding from whence this effect proceeded, she rose vp, & desired Arinda with the other gentlewomen to voyde the
chamber, for that hir Lady was newly entered into hir
sitte whiche oftentimes hath taken hir, and she hath no
remedy so present as to be alone. Arinda and the other
gentlewomen not mistrusting hir speach, conuaied themselues into an other chamber. Nowe Fidelia being left
alone with hir mistresse shut the dore, but Oliuia sancke
downe in a sound, whom Fidelia fetched againe . Afterwardes being well recouered, and seeing hir selfe without other witnesse, she sent out a deep sigh with $\tilde{y}$ company
of many teares as seldome as a stormy winde with-
out a showerof rayne: rufully withall making hir mone
vnto Fidelia on this wise. Ah my Fidelia didst thou not
heare what the gentlewoman of Hungary hath sayde
as touching Rosicleer? if thou dyddest heare it, why
dost thou not take part wyth mee in my insupportable
griefe? were it any meruayle at all if my lyfe shoulde
take ende with hir report? for sith the hope which he-
                                                    therto

therto hath maynteined my reſt is nowe ended, I would
to God my life woulde ende withall, and rather woulde
I dye not to heare ſuch newes whereby my hope de-
cayes then to be priuie to ſuch a trueth, and liue without
my comfort. Oh my Fidelia, come, come, and helpe mee
nowe either to ſet forwarde my miſhap with ſome deſperate ſhyft, or to lende me thy faithfull counſell and aduiſe the better to aſſwage my griefe and to forgette the
ſame misfortune which nowe aſſayleth mee. Alas I ſée
that it is not for my quyetneſſe to baniſh Roſicleer, and
if by the excellency of my eſtate I am forced to chaſtyſe
his ouerboldneſſe, in ſo dwing I ſhall both barre him from
the ſight & light of his eyes and make the ſtripe redound
vpon myne owne head, for who ſhall receiue greater
ſmarte by his abſence thē I ſhall. What a wicked world
is this, wherein men of force muſt neglect other mens vertues, and magnifie their owne nobilitie wythout deſerte:
were it not more reaſon to rayſe this man to the toppe of
honour ý in him his poſteritie may glory, then for lacke
of aunceſtors famous for like qualities, to ſuppreſſe his
vertue and kéepe vnder the magnanimitie of his courage?
When began my fathers & graundfathers to be nobles,
but when with the winges of vertue they ſoared aboue
the vulgar ſort, and if by their meanes onely I am aduaunced to be a Princeſſe, what thancke is there to mee
of my highneſſe? and thou Roſicleer if by thoſe rare & ſo-
uereygne vertues which flower and floriſh in thée, thou
doſt mount in credit, not onely aboue the baſer ſort from
whom thou waſt taken, but alſo aboue Princes & Lords,
whervnto thou art to make thy aſſent, art not thou worthy of greater renowne then we others whych clymbing
by vertue in lyke ſorte, neuer yet came to the poſſibyly-
tie of lıke worthineſſe? Is not this a forgery of the world
and a playne ingling wyth nobility, when we muſt make
more account of one which perhaps by diſorder of life de-
faceth ý honour of his race, then of one which reacheth vp

Q.ij.   the

the ignobilitie of his ſtocke, wherein conſiſteth nobilitye in the opinion of men, oz in bertue in deede? and do men inherit bertue as the chylde entereth vppon the Fathers lande beeinge lawfull heyze? No, heere wee receyue naught but what our ſelues ſowe, and hee that reapeth not maye be a loute foz all his Lozdſhippe, as in tyms appeareth, whiche iudgeth freely and wythout affection. And foz mee, if the eyes of my bnderſtandinge were not dymmed, I ſhoulde ſoone confeſſe leſſe merite in me to deſerue Roſicleer then wanteth in him to bee wozthy of mee. I am a Pzinceſſe by my Father, and my glorye reſteth in the reckening bp of a bed role of Pzinces, ſome of them dead a thouſand yere agone, which nothing perteineth to thys pzeſente age, but he maye be a Pzince by hys owne bertue, and his nobilitie aryſeth not by keepinge a tally of names, but by makinge iuſte pzoofe of his manhoode in defence of iuſtice euery daye, in ſuche ſozt likewiſe that not any of myne aunceſtozs bertues whereby they became noble, dare appzoch to bee tryed with hys in an euen ballaunce. And is there not many gentlewomen in the wozlde of as highe a calinge as I am? And is there any Pzince oz knyghte of ſo high renowne foz bertue and knyghthoode as Roſicleer is? Haue not the beſt knightes of both Chziſtendome and Paganſie, ioyned with him either at tylte oz tourney, and doth he not obſcure them all, as when the ſunne appeareth, no ſtarres dare come in pzeſence? And I ſilly woman hauinge not ſo muche as the refuſe in me of my pzedeceſſozs bertue, am notwythſtandinge by the iniurie of the times bonde to ſo greate folly, as that I muſt not thincke hym wozthy to equall me, which is muche my better. But ſith of fozce I muſt yeelde to the time and rather dye then acknowledge the contrary, ſith my Foztune is ſuch that I muſt liue by the immagination of other men, and ſith my eſtate may not be yoked with hys baſeneſſe, haue at it, I

will

will for euer shutte him from my presence for the saue-
garb of myne honour . But withall seeinge without
hys presence I cannot finde ease for this torment, I wyll
make hym amendes by endinge euer my life vnto the
enduringe of euerlastinge sorrowe. And i, it bee beste
so to doe, tell me my Fidelia my nurse , for I perhappes
am beguyled by my passion neither in deed haue I eyther iudgement or feelinge of ought but of griefe and
sorrowe. Fidelia hearde the wordes of the Princesse, and
takinge parte with the Princesse made vp this wofull la-
mentinge wyth hir sorrowfull speach , in this sort . Alas
madame howe much better had it bene that neuer the
knightly deedes of Rosicleer had bene manifested in
Britaine , for then without the sight of him you had neuer receyued thys wounde whiche nowe festering in you
for lacke of lokinge to will be very harde to be cured. But
the wyfeft saye , that in suche matters as are harde and
difficult a manne muft especially employe hys trauayle,
and that the successe is not so vnlikely, but that laboure
may reach vnto it, as for this griefe which nowe diftem-
preth you is not so greate but that you maye bee soone
whole, your selfe being thervnto willing. For in this, neither Nature worketh, neither Fortune, nor the stars, nor
the celestiall signes, nor any supernaturall influence as
you suppose, but onely the fancie and likinge of man, the
selfe same in effect with that which in the sicke is to desire to be whole and in the thirstie to drinck. And whosoeuer with the confente of his owne will attempteth the
breaking of these snares which hys fancy layeth to en-
trappe him in, may scape scotfree , and helpe others in
lyke necessitie . Otherwise if this loue were naturall to
all men, as all men then should loue by Nature, so should
they not forbeare it, either for shame or friendes displeasure, and if it proceeded from Fortune, or by grace inspi-
red, whereof the cause is not knowen, but the euente is
euident, then were our libertie herein irrecuperable, and

Q.iij. iij

in that the principall suite was wythout vs it might excuse the infirmitie of the pacient, whereas both experience proueth, that loue hath bene remoued by reason,
and we dayly chide their impotency which are not able to
resist the dartes of Cupid. It is therfore requisite madame that your selfe put to your hande and frame your
will to the obeying of that which may bringe remedy,
not onely for the loue which you presently feele, but for
that which you feare will hereafter happen by your yll
breaking off his absence .

And truely I am perswaded that seeing you haue with
your selfe resolued to exclude him from your companye
that the best is to put it in practise faithfully and effectually, least by forbearinge of this correction hee take
more courage to disturbe your rest, and yet am I not a-
gainst that which you haue confirmed with good reason,
that we ought to reuerence vertue rather then riches, and
in my iudgement that gentlewoman which shall matche
with Rosicleer may thincke hir selfe happy, for his rare
and meruailous deeds of armes make him to glister more
gloriously then al other Princes and knights whosoeuer.
And in times past when all thinges went not so ouerthwart as they nowe doe, he was the best of lignage,
whose prowesse was best knowen, and he best esteemed
which wanne his estimation by his manhood. And to this
purpose beholde the builder of Rome, by name Romulus,
taken from his foster father a shepheard, and in a manner
edified for ye erectio̅: although ther were many builders in
the world both before and after, but the difference of their
buildings lieth in ye excellecy of ye workemanship. Againe,
was ther euer one in such credit for honestie & wisdome
as Socrates, the senne of a base mydwyfe. Euripides
one of the rarest men that euer were in tragicall po-
ems, was borne of meane parentage. Demosthenes the
flower of Greeke eloquence was a Cutlers sonne : Ho-
ratius the Poet borne of a bondwoman which had bene
taken

taken prisoner, & yet all these preferred for their vertuous
qualities before kings & princes. Cicero could not dissemble his progeny, & yet was he lifted vnto the consulship
in Rome,& neuer proued other Consul so commodious for
the common wealth.Serramus & Cnimatus wise men,and
throughly exercised in their enimies land were Consuls
in Rome,& deliuered their countris from spoile & pillage,&
if for a matter perteyning to a kingdome,we had rather
take example at kinges : let vs see if meane estate hath
bene any let for men to aspyre vnto mighty kingdomes,
and by name let vs take a more perticuler suruey of the
thyrde,fourth,fiith,and sixt kinge of Rome . First Tul-
lus Hostilius had his cradell in a shepheardes cottage,
and his bringing vp in the wide fielde . Then the two
Tarquins were sonnes to a Marchaunt and exiled their
countrie. Seruius Tullius was sonne to a bondwoman
as his name importeth, all which notwithstanding in
their times were kinges of Rome,and if from thence
we take our way to other Nations round aboute, what
a flock of shepheards,surgeons,labouring men,founders,&
such like seruile occupations shall we meete which aspy-
red to the highest place of gouernment in their countries.
Alexander a crowned kinge was a gardeiners sonne,
Pertinax Emperour of Rome,borne of a slaue which lyued by thrashing of graine & selling of wood,Seuerus the
seuenth Emperour of Rome was bred and brought vp a-
mongst surgions,& these of the meanest sort.Agathocles
king of Sicile,sonne to a potter.Maximianus & Maximus
chiefe men of the Empire,the one of base byrth, the other
doubtfull whether a smith or a carpenter,and yet neither
barrell better herring.Vespasianus which was called the
good Emperour,rose from low degree,& by his vertue blotted out ye infamy of of his progeny,& to haue more notable
testimonies,who was father vnto ye great Cæsar Augustus
ye ruler of ye world.Virgil in a iest made him a bakers son
but his own minde misgaue him otherwise,as for a truth

D.iiij.

farre worse

worse be they which ryse to glorie from the mislikinge of their parents, like as Hercules, Perseus, & Iugurtha the kinge of Numidia, all begotten in aduoultry: and lykewyse mightie Alexander kinge of Macedon, as concerninge whom his father Philip on his death bedde denyed him to be his sonne by the reporte of his mother Olympia, for which cause after his fathers death hee woulde needes be called the sonne of Iupiter Ammon: Constantine the Emperour was borne of a younge mayde before lawfull espousalles: and Iepthah in the Scriptures was sonne to a harlot: Or if you will madame that for lyke examples we runne euer the histories wherbnto my witte can not carry me in so soddine speach, yet I remember that fewe yeares since there dyed in Spayne a stoute kinge of the Gothes called Bamba, which as I haue heard was a labouring man, and at that time when he was to be crowned king was faine to sticke his spade in the ground to receiue the scepter, beeing neither lesse feared then his predecessors, and not reserued by me to the last place, as one of least credite amonge others. Remember your selfe of the great king Arthur your progenitour, of whom (with your graces leaue) I doe not thincke that men of mallice doubted whose sonne he was: and we maye boldly speake of these and other thinges so longe a gone passed, without suspect of misliked affection. But why meruayle we at these thinges? doth not the wise man saye. That if our life were long we should see many kings become bondmen, and of many bondmen crowned kinges: the reason beeing the same as I haue rehearsed, that in elder age the onely Herolde to pronounce a man either noble or vnnoble was hys owne good deedes which aduaunced his good name and renowne aboue the inferiour deedes of kinges or Princes. But to paynt out the pryde of our tymes, let vs cast downe our eyes to y first root, from whence we al take our beginning, shal we not finde it all one for all men: Mary

in

in the body of this tree there are many braunches , some
higher and some onely waterboughes , from whome the
toppeboughes keepe of the comforte both of Sunne and
showers,yet no man I trowe wilbe so enuyous as to hinder the growth of the inferiour, if they be more faithfull
then the superiour , as not alwayes the tallest men doe
the best seruice, and the best borne for wealth or mighte
proue not the best alwayes for manners and worshippe.
Witnesse hereto the sonnes of Scipio and Marcus Aure-
lius, of which two descended two peruerse imps,far more
infamous then their parents wer famous.And ther ar infinit
moe lykewise to improue the succession of vertue , in the
succession of enheritaunce . And yet for all this long discourse, I cannot choose but reserue my former purpose towards you,for I am afrayde that the most parte will not
be of my iudgement. In a worde therefore , to make an
ende in that wherwith he first beganne,you must consider
both by what meanes and for what causes the times are
altered,and thereuppon take aduise according to the time.
And sith that for our sinnes God hath giuen vs euer to a
wrong iudgement in matters of high estate,rather to preferre wealthe then vertue, and sith you are newe fallen
vnto that time, wherein this errour generally hath ouer-
growen the truth, and is strengthened by consent of men
I would counsayle you to yeelde vnto the time,that is to
take it as you finde it,& to make the best of your chaunce:
for it were great folly for you, and no lesse daunger to resist a multitude. and you knowe your friends will neuer
be brought to esteeme so highly of vertue in a base personage, although a precious stone can neuer be but precious whether sette in Leade or Copper. You must forsake
him then, and that is the onely remedye, for according as
I haue reade and haue hearde the first remedye agaynst a
fitte of loue, is to exempt our selues from the companye
of the beloued,or to shunne and eschew the things which
maye bring it agayne to our remembraunce , the nexte

Q.v.
15

is to driue in our thoughts the things which be contrary therevnto : as to thincke with how many breaches of fleepe and with what continuall care we defire a thing eyther filthy,if vnlawfully coueted, or at the leaft wyfe tranfitory though neuer fo honeft, with all to fette before our eyes what harmes,what robberyes,what murthers, what madneffe it hath caufed in the worlo,whereof ther be to many hiftoryes:but yet from all this you may well acquite your felfe , if you will feperate from you your former conceit . And if none of thefe will fuffice, there is an other remedy behinde,which is to beftow your lyking vppon fuch a one as may be machable to your eftate. For as one naile driueth out an other fo men fay that the new loue difpoffeffeth g old, which remedy as I haue red was put in practife by Affyreus g kyng of Perfia. And this is my opinion, which it may be your grace woulde not miflyke,were it not fomewhat troublous,but if you haue an eye to your benefite, thereby I doubte not but that you wil wel ouercome the trouble,& I pray you fpeedely take fome way or other, but the beft I faye ftill is the former for to alaye the flame . The next is , to take awaye the wood, and fo to forgette loue, is to remoue from beloued, for otherwife that which you quenche in a moneth wilbe kindled in an houre.

Nowe the meanes to achieue your purpofe,is by writing your felfe to Roficleer to this effect , that hee aban don your prefence for euer , my felfe wilbe the carryer: althoughe I haue fome compaffion on hys payne . The Princeffe knowing the holefome counfayle , which hyr Fidelia as a faythfull friende had giuen hir,aunfwered louingly, but yet with fome confcience for hir owne fmarte in thefe wordes.

Thofe which are hole, can eafely giue good counfayle to g ficke, & euery remedy feemes to them eafy & poffible, as in lyke forte thou Fidelia not yet attaynted with loue, telleft me of many remedyes which not onely fame con-

uer

uenient vnto thée , but alſo ſo eaſye , that thou ſayſte it lyeth in my handes to make my ſelfe frée from the paſſyon which tormenteth me , I tell thée trulye that I knowe both that I am not worthy of Roſicleer: and that beſides it behoueth me to banniſh him from my preſence. This I knowe my Fidelia , but alas ſhall this be eaſye for me? Perhappes I maye make him auoyde the courte and countrey by the meanes thou haſte preſcribed : but what then? I haue a greater aduerſarye within my ſelfe which makes this match ſo not euen as thou wéneſt. I knowe that when Roſicleer ſhalt haue departed the land, that my lyfe will well nére departe my bodye , and I ſhall not eaſelye forgette mine owne choyce , But yet as thou willeſt mee I will aduenture to putte hym from his hope thoughe I beare parte of the ſmarte, and I had rather my bodye ſhoulde paye for it , then the ho-noure of the Princeſſe Oliuia ſhoulde bee blemiſhedde, nor neuer ſhall the force of loue be able to diſparage hir. In thys heate ſhée called for penne,inke and paper,which being brought,ſhe wrote to Roſicleer as you ſhall heare héereafter.

I cannot thincke that for all hir greate ſtomacke to to maynetayne hir honour agaynſt Roſicleers baſeneſſe , that ſhe coulde drawe thoſe cruell lynes with drye eyes, but when ſhe had made an ende, and cloſed vp the letter, as if ſhe had gotte ſome memorable conqueſt ſayth ſhée. Now dare I compare with ÿ Romaine Matrones which for the preſeruation of their honeſty ſacrifiſed themſelues, vnto their Gods,for what haue I done els, but in a man-ner ſacrifiſed my ſelfe to God,when for my honour ſake I haue bounde and lynked my ſelfe to ſuche a continuall martyrdome and perpetuall impriſonment,as the abſence of Roſicleer wyll bréde in me, and neuer more will lyue as a Princeſſe, but rather lyke a vowesſe . But holde Fi-delia take it, at which worde ſhee ſnet out ſuch a ſighe, and wept ſo bitterly as if hir hart had rent aſunder. Fidelia

pro·

promised to doe the message, and after shee had comforted hir Lady departed speedely. I thincke fearing left the
Princesse should reclayme hir opinion.

¶ Fidelia beeing on hir waye to carrye the
letter to Rosicleer was taken by sixe
knights, and from them delyuered by Rosicleer.   Cap. 40.

F Idelia hauing already taken leaue of the Princesse to
execute the cruell sentence pronounced vpon poore Rosicleer, was vppon better aduise called backe by hir Lady
and made stay till the morrow. The next day comming before hir Lady to giue hir warning of hir departure, scarse
might shee obtayne leaue to go or tarrie. And when shee
vrged ý necessitie of hir going, stil the Princes would stay
hir with some such speaches . Sweete Fidelia tarry yet,
yet a lyttle longer sweete Fidelia, tarry till my lyfe leaue
this carefull bodye, it will not be long my sorrowe prog-
nosticates of my ende, if thou tarry till I haue ended: this
my wery lyfe go in Gods name then to Rosicleer, it wilbe to some purpose to let him vnderstand that though my
body be dead, yet I mente mine honour should remayne
sure for him . Fidelia payned hir sefe to comfort hir Lady
and thinking it not best to enter any long talke, as if she
had gone of some other erraunt shee stale priuily from hir
mistresse in the company of other gentlewomen, the lesse
to be suspected, and mounting vppon hir palfrey. It is rode
through the citie of London, all disguysed, to seeke Rosicleer,

Ere long shee came to the keepers house , where the
three Princes, had lodged , at whome shee learned that
they were not farre from thence, so with great dilygence
shee hasted after them, and as their knightly prowesse left
behinde them the memorie of their being there so wher-
soeuer shee came, shee still hearde of them, ant wythin

cyght

eyght dayes after that shee had lefte the kepers ledge, she
came within lesse then one dayes iourneye of the place
where their abode was. That day passing alone through
the thickest of a forrest, there came out agaynste hir fire
knights, which tooke hir horse by the brydell, saying that
she shoulde go with them: which when she denyed and beganne to pleade for hir deliuery with words of courtesie,
one of them drewe out his sworde and sayde he woulde
slay hir, vnlesse she prepared hir selfe to their companye,
but whether she woulde or no they made hir palfraye go
by force with them towarde the forrest. Then Fidelia fering that they ment hærein some dishonour to hir perso-
fonage lept from hir palfray, and one of the knights perceiuing it, alyghted to sette hir vp agayne: but shee getting from him, ran thence as fast as she might & by hir good
fortune it came to passe that when the knight had ouertaken hir, and helde hir in his armes to put hir vp vppon
hir horse, that Rosicleer and the two Princes Bargandel
and Lyriamandro then passed through the forrest to seeke
the selfe same knights, and to be auenged vppon all the
euills, in which they had wronged that country. These
thrée hering the sæeches and outcries which Fidelia made
gotte nære the sounde, to knowe the matter: in the ende
they sawe that the knights woulde carry a gentlewoman
away agaynst hir will. At which (albeit Fidelia was so
well muffled that none of them knewe hir) they were
all displeased, and Rosicleer more angrye then the reste,
sayd. Syr knights what is the cause that you force thys
gentlewoman to go with you againste hir will. One of
them in great scorne sayde. If you will nædes be of counsayle with vs, I wil pricke you the cause vpon my spears
poynt. But Fidelia cryed. Ah my Lord delyuer me from
these false thæues which will leade mée away prysoner I
know not wherefore. Rosicleer hearing them both, without more to doe gaue one of them such a blowe vpon the
breast with his launce that it pearced him throughe, and
he

he fell dead to the grounde, the two valyant Princes ran
againſt two, and within ſhorte time ſlew them, the thrée
which remayned ſette vppon Roſicleer, but he clefte one
with his ſword and made the other two to gallope away.
The two Princes loth to lette any of them eſcape, followed them in ſuch ſorte, that they foure were now entred
into the thickeſt of the wood, Roſicleer being alone wyth
the gentlewoman. Fidelia now at lybertie and onely the
company of Roſicleer, ſtode in a doubte whether after ſo
great courteſie, ſhe might in hir miſtreſſe name declare
ſo vncourteous a meſſage, but remembring hir ſelfe to be
at an others commaunde, vnto whome ſhée had promiſed hir fayth in this matter: the time alſo ſo fitte for the
accompliſhing of hir Ladyes charge, ſhe diſcouered hirſelfe
to Roſicleer who preſently knewe hir, and much abaſhed
to ſée hir in that plyghte, alyghted from his horſe to embrace hir, and as it hath bene recounted, his ſpeach was
on this manner. What misfortune fayre gentlewoman
hath broughte you from that heauenlye courte, wherein
you were once acquaynted, to ſéke harborow among ſuch
vnciuill hoſtes as theſe knightes are. Fidelias aunſwer
was ſhorte in theſe termes. O noble Roſicleer, the an-
guiſh which Fidelia féeles is in déede greate, but yet it
onely ariſeth through the remembraunce of that meſſage
which ſhe hath in charge vnto Roſicleer, and with that
ſhe wept bitterly. Then ſomewhat amazed he ſayde vnto
hir. Tel on faire gentlewoman, and if your ſorrowe be
for my ſake let me beare part with you, and thancked be
God, I am not altogether a ſtraunger to miſhaps: yet
wiſt he not whereabout hir meſſage was, but hee being
very earneſt to haue ý meſſage told him, ſhe drew out the
letter out of a little bore, and put it into his haude with ſo
much payne that ſhe could not ſpeake a worde withall.
Roſicleer hauing the letter and deſirous to knowe what
was in it, opened it preſently, wherin he ſoone eſpyed the
ſet determination of the Princeſſe as touching his exile,
but

but before he had wel wayed of the contents, espying only Oliuias name in the inscription, as we say that mens
mindes misgiue them agaynst a mischiefe: so his hearte
throbbed, all his body trembled, and hee had much adoe
to force himselfe to endure the vttermoste . The letter
sayd as followeth.

¶ The high and mightie Princesse , the Princesse Oliuia, Princesse of great Britayne: vnto the most arrogant Rosiceer sendeth perpetuall disgrace for thy lewde attempt.

Eing no lesse iniuried by thy presumption the minding the punishment of thy folly I haue written
vnto thee. And know thou ẙ thy letter hath come
not to me in daylyght, nor deluered in thy name
lest I might iustly haue refused it, but in ẙ night time, ẙ ẙ
closely and by stealth conuayed in my cofer that I might
firste be beguyled, ere I mighte forethincke me of the de-
ceyte . The receiuing whereoff albeit so at vnawares,
hath somewhat blemmished my honoure, and the shame
thereoff if I thought possible to be rubd out, I would not
spare for Tems water being so nere my fathers pallaice,
But to make amends for my faulte , and least st take
some pride in thy impudencye, I am driuen now to an
other inconueniencye, that is to aunswere thee, whome
otherwise I woulde not haue vouchsafed in this respecte,
the courtesie of a good looke . In thy letter, the firste
poynte of thy pryde I finde, to bee in bending thy lyking
towards me. The seconde and greater, in daring to many-
fest it vnto me . The thirde and especiall in forcing me
by copy of wordes, and an olde tale of loues power to
giue some reliefe to thy heauinesse . Which thy intollerable pryde as it seemed rare and straunge vnto mee , so it
made me more narrowely to sifte and examining my selfe
throughly and in euery poynte , if eyther the lyghtnesse
of

of my lookes or my vnchaste demeanoure, or the lacke of
foresight in my speach, or the familiaritie of acquaintance
mighte giue occasion to so base a knight as to attempte a
Princesse. Wherein if I coulb haue called to minde a-
ny little ouersight, whereby thou mightest haue courage
of impeaching my honour, I woulde first haue punyshed
it in my seise as I am now purposed to amende it in thée.
Onely I remember, I bestrowed vppon thée largely: and
what then? Thou therefore as Lucifer hauing moze graces then thy fellowe Angells wilt pull G O D out of his
throne? Note that the staye of true vertue is humilitie,
and there is no glozy so cléere but pride maye darken it.
Bicause I humbled my selfe so much as to thinke of thy
meane vertues, woulbst thou venture this? Dyd my beautie cause thée to loue me, I coulb not my estate withholbe
thy penne but thou must challenge me foz it? I was a-
boue thy reach, and why diddest thou not feare thy ouer-
strayning, if thou mentest to compasse mée? God neuer pu-
nisheth the desire of things allowed by nature, but thou
shalte finde ocasion of smarte in thy disordered affection.
What if loue be so great as thou painest thy selfe to pzone
vnto me? Did not other Pzinces sée mee, from whome
yet the honest regarde of my greatnes shielded me, which
thou neuer entred into so abiecte a bzeast as thine is.
Yet forsooth and Hannibal, and Mars and Iupiter,
were ouercome with lyke passions. What euer good lyking I might haue had to them, I tell thée I lyst not to
heare Pooze Rosicleers tale. Thou wilt haue mée so to
vse clemencie towardes thée, as I shal therby to be cruell
to my selfe, otherwise thou byddest my losse. Then must
I haue regarde, and foz euer cease thou to trouble me in
lyke manner. Or if bicause thou louest mée, I musse
deale with thée accozdingly, I am contente, but to thy
greater griefe. Foz marke, the greater loue, deserueth
the greater chastisement: and greater is the faulte done
vppon pzesumption, then by ignozaunce oz infirmitye,

aa

as much lesse sufferable is the disgrace wrought by a
friende then by a foe, and the louers vnkindnesse is lesse
excusable then the straungers. Thou professest thy
selfe my friende and louer, and I protest and proclayme
my selfe nowe to be wronged at thy hande. Iudge thy
selfe howe I can beare it? For this iniury whiche thus
spighteth me, I charge thee auoyde this court, forsake
the lande, and if thou meanest good to me, get thee thether from whence neuer newes of thy name maye be
brought to England. This way shalt thou proue thy
loue, and els not, & so shee leaueth thee tyll doomes day.

¶Thy mortall enemy,
Oliuia.

When Rosicleer had read the wordes of the letter,
the contentes thereoff so galled him at the quicke, that
for very griefe his sences forsooke him and he fell vppon
ye ground, ther remaininge an whole houre wythout mouing foot or hãd & Fidelia departed: so soone as Fidelia was
gone, Telyo Rosicleers esquire came that way to seke his
Lorde, for he had departed from him before to fetch fresh
water at a fountayne hard by. Now when Telyo approched and sawe Rosicleer stretched in that manner vppon
the ground as if he had bene dead, he made the greatest
dole that euer poore creature made, and alighting from
his horse he plucked off Rosicleers helmet, casting water
in his face if perhaps hee might reuyue. In the ende
Rosicleer yelding foorth a grone as if his heart stringes
had burst withall came wholy to himselfe, and stretching
his ioynts vpon the greene grasse, began to speake in this
maner. O fell Fortune and euer spightfull, why hast thou
not made an end of my life which the end of my ioy, and
why lyue I sith that whereby my life is bereft mee.
Leaue me alone I praye thee and my griefe shall not
grieue me without thy company, aboue all welcome

R.   death

death the vndoer of my care, welcome my death, in what
manner J care not, suffer not a knight so vnfoztunate to
appeare amongst men, noz to receiue comunon sepulture.
Cato not to beholde the conquerours face, flewe hymselfe wyth his swozd, and Sophonisba poysoned hir
selfe to be free from bondage. Nowe what reason was
there in them by death, to flye common and ozdinarye
mishaps: Jf J mainteyne my lyfe to the abidinge of farre
greater tozmentes then are in death. And whence commeth this mischaunce vnto mee: from loue. O loue, loue,
farre moze outragious then fire and water, and farre
moze daungerous to deale withall then chaunce oz Foztune. Thou art straunge in all thy purposes, straunger
in the execution of them, and in the ende thereoff straungest of all. Howe commonly doe thy pzactises exceede the
wozking of Foztune, foz she neuer giueth paine but in
pleasure, neuer griefe but in gladnesse, and she neuer ouer-
thzoweth but at the top and pitch, so that ther is yet some
comfozt to haue bene high, but J which in true loue towardes Oliuia had neuer countenaunce of comfozt noz
pleasure of any height, am nowe so disgraced and haue
fallen so lowe as no aduersitie of Foztune can match
it. Artemidoro tolde me my kinred shoulde not let our
mariadge. But nowe farewell my friendes, by name
Oliuerio kinge of the great Britaine my louinge Lozde,
Bargandel and Liriamandro Pzinces inheritours
and my louinge companions, and Farewell, Zoilo
Pzince of Tartary as my last acquaintance. Foztune
did but shewe vs to eache other, when we hoped of great
acquaintaunce, and farewell all my comfoztes, foz
J will hence to some darke and cloudie country, that
not so muche as the light of the Sunne may bzinge tidings of my smart, this sayng, Rosicleer rose vp, & mounting on his hozse rode towarde the fozrest which leadeth
vnto the sea with full determination to leaue the country

pze-

presently,his esquire Telyo which both sawe and heard
his complaint,with great griefe followed him,not yet da;
ring to speake a word for feare of disquieting him.Rosi;
cleer in this iourney made great hast,& before night got
to a huge and hollow rocke about x.miles from the place
where he receiued the letter. There on he caste himselfe
tourning his horse lose vpon the clifts. Now being alone
as his maner was,he renued his complaints with many a
sicker sigh. In the morning whē y Sunne cast his beames
vpon the large sea,Rosicleer rose frō the ground to looke if
he might see any ship wherein he might put himselfe,whē
he espied none,he commaunded Telyo to ride vnto the
next hauen about two miles off,there to prouide a shyp,
himselfe promised in the meane while vnder that couerte
to abide his comming, Telyo presently did as his Lord
commaunded him & made as much speed as he might,not
to leaue his master comfortlesse. But ere Telyo had got
to the towne,it chaunced that Rosicleer hauing great de;
sire to be solitary mounted vpon his horse and rode a
contrary waye. In which waye he sawe a little shippe
makinge towardes the lande, and out of this shyppe
from vnderneth the hatches there appeared a gentle;
woman very high and big of body, but of a good com;
plection and straungely attyred as was hir countrye
guyse . This gentlewoman as sone as the anchors
were cast,caused the cockeboate to be let downe,where;
in shee entered,and comming to lande she toke hir pal;
fray to galloppe vp the sandes, but espyinge a knyght a;
lone whome by all semblaunce shee toke to bee Ro;
sicleer,shee framed a sorrowfull countenaunce , and in
greate ruth saluted hym to whome he rendered the lyke
salutations,demaunndinge what hir griefe was . The
gentlewoman styll counterfaytinge a showe of greate
sorrowe,stayed a tyme as not able to speake any thinge
tyll bæinge importuned by hym wyth much a doe she
as it were forced out these speaches.

Alas

Alas fir tell me if you can fome newes of a new knight
which hath wonne the prices at the greate feaftes in
London. Wherefore feeke you him fayde Roficleer, I
feeke him annfwered the gentlewoman, for that I heare
fo much of his glorie as that I am perfwaded y he onely is like to giue remedy to my trauayle, Roficleer to
make haft away for feare left his efquire fhoulde finde
them, opened himfelfe vnto the gentlewoman, faying that
he was the newe knight. The gentlewoman feeming to
be very gladde for to haue found him knæled downe, but
he lyfted hyr vp and defired hir to faye en prefentlye
what hir forrowe was, for he woulde willingly vndertake hir demaunde : the gentlewoman fayde on thys
wyfe . Sir knight, not farre hence there is an Ilande
where my Father dwelled, a plentifull land and auncient inheritaunce to our line . This lande my Father
gouerned a great time in peace and eafe, tyll that Fortune loth to preferue thinges in one eftate, chaunged hyr
copie, and that whiche grieueth mee mofte of all founde
meanes by me to worck y difcontentment of my friends.
For beeinge younge and marriadgeable, and my Fathers onely childe, it happened y I had many fuiters, but
to be fhort, my Father thincking it fafeft for the continuaunce of his line, and the peaceable gouernement of
his people whiche had rather haue bene fubiect to their
naturall countrey man then an Alian, matched me with
a lufty knight both beft beloued for his worthyneffe and
of greateft poffeffions in all that countrey. Now amongft
my other futers there was one of great liuelod, worthy
for his wealth to haue bene preferred before all the reft,
if himfelfe had bene as worthy, but this Lorde was
refufed by mee , and takinge it as fome part of difgrace
he kindled his choller and wrathe againft my parents
and me, and at a time conuenient which was not many
nights paft, and when we leaft immagined it, he burft in
vpon my parents, where he found but weake refiftance,
but

but I my selfe in the meane whyle stealing by the shore
side, recouered thys lyttle boate wherein I was scarcely
entered, when I sawe a farre off my parents & my husband ledde away prisoners. I thincke they can not easily
ghesse whether I am gone. But after that I was in
the boate I mette with manye which came from the
iustes at London. They saing my heauye cheere, demaunded the cause, and when they vnderstode it they
directed me to inquire after a newe knyght in the land,
for he alone say they is able to vndoe this iniurye. You
heare sir both the cause of my care and the occasion of
comming into this countrey to you sir, nowe sir knyght
if my ruth may work any compassion, or that you thinke
I haue cause to complayne, doe your best to amende my
harme, you shall doe double iustice in restoring the wronged, and in punishing the wicked doer. Rosicleer feelinge
a yerning in hys minde agaynst so vnlawfull a practise if
her tale were true, badde hir take hir boate agayne, for
he would hazard his person in hir quarrell. The gentlewoman desiring presently no other thinge, gaue hym
many thanckes, so they entered the boate, and the water
beinge calme they passed wythout any daunger. But
still Rosicleer haunted with hys auncient thoughts, now
seeing himselfe farre distaunte from the Princesse, and
wythout hope to retourne began a freshe to consider of
hys exile which thought so ouercame hym, that he wyshed hys soule to departe from hys body. But the Histozy leaueth hym on the Sea to recounte in the meane
tyme of his esquire, whych finding a shyppe in the hauen retourned to hys Mayster, but not meeting hym he
was soze abashed, and in greate sozrowe coasted ouer
the countrey to finde hym out.

After longe trauayle by lande to no purpose, hee
put hymselfe to the Sea in a shyppe prepared towardes
Almayne where after continuall wearynesse and not
hearing any newes of hys mayster he tourned for this

owne countrey in the valley of the mountaynes where
he was well welcomed by his brethren. There let vs
leaue him till time carry him from his fathers home
to meete with mayſter. Nowe telleth the biſtorye of
Zoilo Prince of Tartary which had trauayled towards
the court of kinge Oliuerio as hath bene recited. When
hœ came to the court, he founde in the pallaice hall the
Princeſſe Oliuia with the king hir Father, and diuerſe
noble Princes deuiſing and ſportinge of diuerſe matters, and eſpecially of Roſicleers worthineſſe which not
a little tickled the Princeſſe Oliuia for all that cruel ſentence which ſhe had giuen of him.

The Tartarian Zoilo enteringe the hall in godly
manner, to the great amaze of the knightes and nobles
which beheloe hym, after he had made hys humble o-
beyſaunce to the kinge, hœ ſpake as followeth. It maye
be noble and worthy kinge, that the greatneſſe of my
eſtate forbiddeth me to be ſo humble, but the greate
vertue whiche I haue founde in the knightes of your
Maieſties court hath enforced mœ aboue my wont to
doe you that honour which I woulde denye elſe to any
kinge or Emperour in the worlde. Nowe I beſœche
your maieſtie to accept of my ſeruice and to receiue mœ
into the number of your knyghtes, for I haue great deſire to belonge vnto your court if it ſo lyke you. The
kinge very well likinge of the maieſtie whiche the
knyghte bare. Albeit hee knewe him not whence hœ
was, of courteſie embraced hym gladly, and rayſinge
hym from ground, aunſwered thus. Sir knight you are
very welcome, for as your perſonage and god behauiour is aboue the credit of a meane man: ſo haue I great
opinion of your highe eſtate, and as to your requeſt to
be entertayned of my court, I receiue you willingly and
promiſe you therein my royall fauour, for I woulde lyue
no longer then to make of your likes, and I pray you ſir
knyght tell me who you are, leaſt peraduenture I ſhould

fault

in not honouring you according to your callinge . Zoilo aunſwered , moſte puiſaunt kinge , the repoꝛte of
your countrie aſſured me your good faucur befoꝛe I
demaunded it,and newe ſyꝛ vnderſtande you that I am
named Zoilo,ſeane to the kinge of Tartaria in that part
which boꝛdereth vpon Chꝛiſtendeme, and that I haue
ſpent many winters both on ſea and land, till that Foꝛtune caſt me en the Engliſh ſhoare, then comming out
of Ducklande After hære in your countrey, mindinge
as my vſage was to trye my ſelfe vpon knyghtes errants
it chaunced that I mette with thꝛee of your knyghtes
in a foꝛreſt,their names were as I learned of them,Ro-
ſicleer,Bargandel,and Lyriamandro,with theſe I iuſted,
and after that I had caſt downe the two laſt at the tilt,
I fought wyth Roſicleer at the ſwoꝛdes poynte , but in
ẏ ende I was vanquiſhed.Roſicleer,when I was yelden
hauing ſome lykinge of mee deſired me to come and bee
acquainted with your maieſtie and to kiſſe your royall
hand in his name.

All which I haue done as well foꝛ to offer my ſeruyce
to ſo myghtie a Pꝛince as foꝛ to accompliſhe the charge
of ſo valiaunt a knyght , neyther thincke I it any dyſ-
grace to bee vanquiſhed by him . Foꝛ beſides that hys
bountie and courteſy meriteth to be beloued rather then
enuyed hys valour and knighthoode pꝛomiſeth the conqueſt ouer the whole woꝛlde. He hath receyued mee foꝛ
a perpetuall friende and hys acquaintaunce doe I moꝛe
ſette by then the whole kingdome of Tartary my lawfull
enheritaunce.

Therefoꝛe bycauſe I hope the longer to enioye thys
newe friendſhyppe in your ſeruice,I haue bene bolde to
craue the name of your courte, which ſhall bee as well
welcome vnto mee as the tytle whiche you haue vnto
your kyngdome . The kinge was gladde to heare ſome
newes of Roſicleer at that time , and muche pꝛayſed
R.iiij.   his

his owne good fortune to haue lighted vppon him, for that by him his court had dayly encreased in worshyppe, and so tourning towardes the Tartarian, he sayd on this manner. Pardon me mightie Prince in that I haue not done you that honour which apperteyneth to a kynges sonne, but the litle acquaintaunce I haue had wyth you and the ignoraunce of your estate shall excuse me hence forwardes, if I amende not let me be without excuse. And with these same woordes the kinge led Zoilo to the Princesse, willing hir to welcome the knyght straunger. Zoilo comming before the beautifull Princesse Oliuia, kneeled downe before hir to kisse hir hande, which she refused, but gentlye kissing him she bad hym welcome, farther talke had she, not for the often naming of Rosicleer, brought to hir remembraunce the wrong which shee had done to hym, and hir heart was so great that she had no power to speake a woord, but crauing pardon she departed to hir chamber, this seemed straunge to hir father, but because hir colour was so pale it was thought to be by reason of sickenesse. When she was within hyr chamber doores she let hir teares flowe at libertie, which before she restrayned for feare of beeinge espyed. And thincking in what manner hir fathers court was honored by Rosicleer, and in what estimation he was holden amonge those Princes and knyghts, how glad they were of his friendship, and howe loth hir father was to lose hym, she burst out into aboundaunce of teares, and wyth the repentaunce of hir former fact, she began in this sort to repente hir rashnesse. Thou hasty and ouer credulous Oliuia what thinge dyd the poore Rosicleer craue of thee but the acceptation of hys seruice, and that thou wouldest become hys Lady, why dyddest thou not receyue him offered especially when so many puissaunt Princes and worthy knyghtes require to haue, and are refused, why wouldest thou not be Lady ouer him whom the best in the world woulde be seruaunt vnto. Where

was

was my iudgemente and the eyes of my vnderstanding
that I forethought me not of these things, now doe I to
much repent that which I hastely willed as touching the
bannishment of Rosicleer. Heere shee stayed hir speache,
and in great disease of minde,shutte hir selfe in hir closet.
Heere now wanted the faythfull counsayle of hir seruant
Fidelia for had she bene at hande she mighte haue slaked
hir mistresse sorrowe which in the ende grew so farre as
besides the losse of speach, and hir often sounding she fel
into a hotte burning ague , which left hir not of a greate
while,till more comforte came by meanes of an other letter which she redde of hir loues to his mother Briana.
Till that time we wyll helpe the two knights Bargandel
and Lyriamandro out of the woode,and bringe them from
the search of Rosicleer to the courte of king Oliuerio.

¶ The Princes Bargandel & Liriamandro retourning from the forrest, misse Rosicleer .
   Cap. 41.

THe great desire which ledde Bargandel and Liriamandro to pursue the knightes of the forrest made
them to followe on so longe , till they ioyned at a greate
and well towred Castle, standing at the one ende of the
sayde forrest. There before these two knightes could enter to saue themselues the two Princes had ouertaken
them and getting betwéene the Castle and them,they put
them to so great scath that the knightes vnable to resist
cryed amayn to those which wer within the Castle for suc-
cour:yet or they could côe they wer euerthrowen sore wounded,and as the Princes lyghted downe to make dispatch
of ten men issued out of the Castle well armed and comming néere layd at the Princes in greate rage , for they
wéened their Lordes to haue bene slayne: but this skirmish lasted not long betwéene them for the two Princes
were valyant and putting themselues in préace amongst

R.b.   the

the thickest in shorte time made riddaunce of the greater part, and those which remayned besought the Princes of pardon, which being easely graunted, the two Princes retourned to the two knightes which had bene felled but late before. These two knightes seing in what case they were, and pitying the destruction of theire people, yelded themselues to the will of the conquerour, promising that if they might enioy their lyfe and lybertie they woulde amende their folly, and make satisfaction to all gentlewomen, whereoff the Princes were glad & taking their othes for the performance departed in hast towarde Rosicleer as they thought, but he was not where they lefte him, wherefore they sought him out in all parts. This daye till nighte they neuer descended from their horse, at nighte they tooke their bed vnder a tree vntill the comming of the nexte daye, and they were verye pensiue, for that they knew not the cause why he absented himselfe, yet with some hope that the next daye they shoulde heare some newes of him they droue out that night, and on the morrowe mounted vp their horse agayne to finde him out but it was to no bote, for eyght whole dayes they trauayled through the country and hearde no newes of him in the ende thincking they shoulde meete with hym at the court they rode thether in the company of many knights, whether lette them go, whilest wee in the meane time beare the gentlewoman companye which had carryed Oliuias letter vnto Rosicleer.

This gentlewoman Fidelia as I told you, perceiuing aswell by the witnesse which his his eyes gaue of his outwarde griefe, as also by the sounde wherein she lefte him, as an argument of his inwarde sorrowe that he neded comforte, and yet not daring shewe him hope contrary to hir Maiesties commaundement strake hir palfraye and without more staye gallopped on hyr waye towards London whether in short time she came : but when she had entred the pallaice she would not presently make hir

com-

comming knowen vnto the Princesse, least hir sodayn retourne should worke some alteration, whereby the other gentlewomen might misdeeme of hir arrant. But when she had learned of the gentlewomen that hir Ladye was sicke she well wist whence hir disease sprang, and therefore wisely comming before hir mistresse she yet spared to name Rosicleer till she vnderstoode how well she woulde take his heauinesse.

The Princes now vncerteine in iudgement whether to commende of Fidelias faithfulnesse in executing hir deuise, if the letter were deliuered, or to lyke of hir good Fortune if some occasion had hindered the deliuery, being now alone stayed yet to heare eyther yea or nay, as touching the dispatch of hir message. But Fidelia aswell for hir owne compassion ouer Rosicleer as for sorrow to see hir mistresse in that plyghte by hir owne conceite, vttered neuer a worde, but burst out into weeping, whereby the Princesse more troubled then at the first with a feeble voyce spake vnto hir.

Tell me Fidelia what thou hast done in thy message, and doubt not but thy trauayle shall well please me, for although the loue I beare him feareth to heare thine aunswere, yet shall myne honour counteruayle the dreade, in which quarrell I will as I tolde thee earst venture my lyfe rather then yeelde my bodye to any opprobry. This saying she lent hir eare vnto Fidelias answere and fastened hir eyes vppon Fidelias lookes, as if no word should haue escaped vnmarked or vnaduysed of hir. Fidelias aunswere was short in these termes. For a truthe Madame I had soughte Rosicleer no little time ere I coulde finde him, and as it fell out I founde him when my selfe was not without daunger, as it were to participate of that crueltye towardes him wherein I was partly a dealer: but that which maketh me especiallye to repente my paynes herein, was that my deliuerye was wroughte by him. For at the same time I mette him, the knights

out

outlawes set vppon mee in a forrest, and had led me captiue away there to be spoyled of my honour: but that by my outcryes Rosicleer, with two other knights came thether none of them hauing any knowledge of me who I was. There in my presence he killed three of them, the other flying away were followed by the two knightes in Rosicleers company, by which meanes being alone with him, I there deliuered your letters. But I beleue that he had rather haue receiued his deaths wound, then that letter. Ere he opened it, his colour chaunged, and all his body shooke for feare, but after hee had redde the superscription, his eyes were filled with teares, and neuer man was so wo begonne as he: yet he redde it out, and as I remember with the last wordes he gaue a greate grone, and sancke to the earth. Whether he euer recouered or no I wotte not, for I durst not stay with him, therein to fulfill your graces charge which was not to receiue aunswere from him. This vnderstanding the Princesse, and that Fidelia had obeyed euery iotte of hir will so well, although she woulde that hir seruaunt had fayled in some small poynt of diligence in this matter, yet thinckinge to learne more at hir handes she demaunded what thing hee did when shee parted from him and what wordes hee spake, moreouer what she thought the euent would be. To all which questions, Fidelia aunswered at once, that she left him for deade vppon the grounde, and to deuine was not in hir skill. With this the Princesse wared angry and blamed hir very sore for not abiding the time of his recouery, whereto Fidelia excused hirselfe by hir commaundement but yet bicause the Princesse would haue it so, needs must Fidelia bee thoughte in a greate faulte and crime, for not doing so.

Now may you gesse that Fidelias trustinesse was lyke a cuppe of colde water to hir hir burning Ague, the more to enrage it, or lyke drincke to a dropsie man whereby his malady the rather encreaseth. For in lyke manner

as

as Roficleers heauines came by reading hir letter, fo hirs grew by Fidelia's report of his heauinesse. And albeit that we heare feldome time of man oz woman deade fo2 loue yet it is naturall fo2 euermuch griefe to abb2idge mans dayes. as now it was not loue which fo much afflicted the P2inceffe, but the iniury which fhe had offered Roficleer and the griefe which fhe conceiued by the difpaire of euer feing him, and this griefe had almoft w2oughte hir otter bane.

¶Roficleers departure is publifhed in the court of kyng Oliuerio, Oliuia after knowledge whófe fonne he was, reuerfeth iudgement paf- f d by a countermaunde in an other letter, wherecff Fidelia lykewife is the bearer. Cap. 41.

THe P2inces Bargandel and Liriamandro in the queft of Roficleer rode farre and nere and could onderftand any thing as touching him, till that hauing trauailed ouer a great part of that country they mette with people ftran- gers which certefied, that themfelues had féne a knyght in y fute of armo2 embarking himfelf with a gentlewo- man and after that a fquire fo2e weping entring into a fhippe to followe them, fo2 the which newes Bargandel & Liriamandro were very fo2rowfull, and fo2 nowe they were fure that he had fo2faken the kingdome, wherbpon they agréed to retourne bnto the court, and one daye as the king Oliuerio with the P2ince Zoylo and other wo2- thy P2inces and knights were gone out of the cittie to fo- lace themfelues in the fieldes, thefe two P2inces came to- warde the place where the king abode which had beheld them befo2e very héedefully, fo2 they femed bnto him to be two comly and noble knightes, and therfo2e he defired to haue a mo2e perfect biewe. But balyant Zoylo knew them by their deuices bppon theire armour, and fayde to

the

the king and to the other then in prefence, that he greatly meruayled why Roficleer came not with them, fo; faith
he when I parted from them they wer all th;ee together,
when the king knewe them to be the two P;inces, hee
caufed his trayne to ftaye till the two P;inces came a-
gaynft him, thofe he emb;aced with great loue & thancks
fo; theire retourne, demaunding withall fo; Roficleer.
They which I dare not fay knewe the righte caufe, but
conected fome lykely caufe by the ftrangenes it w;ought
in him, with greate griefe made a narration of each perticuler as farre as they knewe, both what befell him with
in the realme and in what maner he auoyded the realme,
as they had heard of others onely in the company of a
gentlewoman, and they added mo;eouer perhaps of their
owne heads, perhaps as I fayd befo;e vpon fome farther
knowledge that it coulde not otherwife be but that he had
fome great w;ong offred vnto him by fome perfon within the realme. The king excufing himfefe to the P;inces
fo; his owne dealing towardes Roficleer became verye
fadde and heauy fo; him, as alfo thofe which were nære
with him not being able to gheffe of his retourne: and in
dæde if they had ben certein of his long abfence, it would
much mo;e haue bene grieuous vnto them, fo rare was
the loue they all bare to him. But with fome little hope of
Roficleers fpædy retourne, the king with thofe P;inces
his friends tarryed fome dayes in the pallayce, till that bicaufe he was from them fo long, the th;æ P;inces Bargandel, Liriamandro, and the Tartarian Zoylo together
tooke vpon them to fæke him in which time they aduentured many ftraunge exployts as fhalbe fpecified hereafter
in this hifto;ye. But in the ende as the greateft parte of
thefe nobles and P;inces ftayed in England fo; the loue
of Roficleer fo his p;efence wanting that court dimini-
fhed fo faft, that in fho;t time there was not behinde remayning in the courte any knight of great account, but
the P;ince Don Syluerio vnto whome the loffe and ab-

of Roſicleer bredde no ſmall contentacion, as it wrought in the king Oliuerio to the contrary no leſſer diſpleaſure and diſquiet, as if the loſſe of Prince Edward had againe renued. For ther was no one in his kingdom which could and would advaunce his priuate credite and the honoure of his countrey by worthy proweſſe and by valyant deeds of armes.

But when all the kingedome beganne to bewayle the the loſſe of Roſicleer, What did that faire Oliuia which had abandoned him the country, and loued him more then any one in the worlde might ſhe forgette him one inſtant? No, but when ſhe wayed well that for the accompliſhing of hir charge he had forſaken the lande hir good will encreaſed towardes him, and in ſteede of the daylye viewe of his perſonage, in his abſence ſhee gazed at will vppon the counterfayte and portrature which he had emprinted in hir fancie. This did ſhe the oftener bicauſe ſhe founde not in hir ſolitarye contemplation anye other thinge to preſent it ſelfe. For amourous thoughtes are euer enemyes to company, and beeing alone, as commonly ſhee was by reaſon of ſickeneſſe, what was there to remoue this ſolytary thought and conuerſaunt companion from hir.

This companion ſhe ſtyll entertayned, which by vſe and continuance of time grewe to a ſetled ſentence, and hir loue waxed greater then it was before, and then encreaſed the flame which burnte more earneſtly then euer before it had bene. But as it chaunced, toſſing of theſe things in hir remembraunce, withall ſhe remembred that Arinda had tolde hir howe that Roſicleer had written vnto the Princeſſe Briana, and as the amorous are accuſtomed to buylde themſelues Caſtells of Hope albeyt ſometime without foundacion or ſure grounde whereon they may ſurely ſtande: ſo hir loue waxed ielous ouer him and ſhee beganne to caſt with hir ſelfe why Roſicleer ſhould write to the Princeſſe Briana being to hir no kiſſe

nor

nor kinne to hir, and so meane borne, out of which in the
ende she picked out this hope that out of doubt his birth
was as good as his bringing vp. In this matter therfore
she laboured Fidelia, secretly to steale that letter from the
gentlewoman Arinda hir bedfellowe, and talking about
this matter one certeyne time with Fidelia among other
things she sayde. Oh my Fidelia as I had the power to
bannish Rosicleer: the lande, so woulde I that I coulde
bannish him from memory, how profitable had thy counsayle bene then vnto me but what shall I do for that remedy is no more auayleable, since his absence woundes
me more then his presence, I graunt thee the sight of the
beloued to some encreaseth loue still offering it selfe to be
seene, and yet to other some againe the thing dayly seene
bringeth lyttle delyght but rather lothsomnesse as contra-
riwise sometimes loue is moued by discontinuance, and
sometimes mens desire encreaseth the flame albeit the beloued appeare not in presence. But this thou takest to be
impossible for thou art not touched with the lyke passions
and none knowes the bitternesse thereof but the experi-
enced, as appeareth by thee which hast ministred a medi-
cine not of force against my disease. But make me amedes
and once agayne venture for my sake, I remeber that A-
rinda hath a letter of Rosicleers to the Princesse Briana
to what purpose I knowe not, but I would gladly see it,
this steale from hir and bring it me that I may reade it,
I cannot say what good newes my mind foretelles me by
it, but sure I long to reade, as if there were some great
secret contayned therein, and quyet shall I not be till I
haue had it. Hereto Fidelia replyed briefly that this matter shoulde be lefte vnto hir to watche hir opportunitye,
and indeede when Fidelia and Arinda slepte together one
night, Fidelia espying Arinda fast on sleepe rose as softly
as she might, and taking one of the keyes which Arinda
had tyed to hir girdell, therewith she opened the caskette
and pulled out Rosicleers letter which she brought to hir
                                                        mistresse

miftreffe lodging whem fhe found waiting for fome glad newes. The Princeffe hir felfe would not open the letter but gaue it to Fidelia which vnfealed it and read as followeth.

¶To his good Mother the high and mightie Princeffe Briana.

IF my departure from your prefence procureth your iuft difpleafure, beleeue me madame, and my good mother, your fonne Roficleer can not be well pleafed therewith, forefoeinge the great folitarineffe wherein you remayned, and yet bycaufe this my iourney hath fo profpered with mee, I am the better contented and I befoech your grace to quiet your felfe vpon Gods ordinaunce, from whom I am perfwaded this motion in me proceeded. Befides the ftorye of myne owne good Fortune which Arinda maye fafely reporte, I haue heard newes as touching your felfe, the redeliuery of my Father, and the fafetie of my brother. For fince my departure I haue gotte acquaintaunce with Artemidoro a greate wife man of Greece, perhappes he is not vnknowen vnto you, of whom I haue learned that your hufband my father fhall ere longe retourne vnto you. That the gentleman of the Sunne my brother is aliue & already knighted, and for proweffe fo greatly approued, as not the knightes of elder time are thought matchable, that hee and I fhall knowe our Father for the moft valiaunt and worthyeft Prince on the earth, that we fhall haue a pleafaunt ende of our forrowfull beginninges, whiche God graunt. As touchinge myne owne eftate I haue bene brought by thys Artemidoro to the courte of king Oliuerio, where by his owne handes I haue bene dubbed knight, and haue receiued fuch honour as if I had bene his knowne nephewe, and had it not bene that your grace had commaunded the contrarye, not long

R.

our progeny to be knowne, I ſhould for this fauour haue
bewraied y truth at leaſt to haue giuen him ſome comfort
for the ſuppoſed loſſe of Prince Edward, but I will obey
your commaund. And theſe newes I thought to make
you priuie vnto, as not being ignorant of your beaui-
uineſſe, which I praye God leſſen to your comfort. Farther as touching theſe matters, Arinda may tell you of
the ſpecialities. The Almightie ſende you ſpedely your
deſired huſband. I take my leaue kiſſinge your royall
handes.

¶Your obedient ſonne
Roſicleer.

When Fidelia had ended the letter and the Princeſſe had well vnderſtode the ſecretes thereof, what
tongue may expreſſe the great ioye that entered into hir
ſorrowfull minde as if ſhee had but nowe recouered hir
loſt hope, and had ſhe not nowe counterpaized hir auncient ſorrowe with this late ſpronge ioye hir lyfe had
bene in daunger, for in no other thinge exceſſiue ioye
maye doe ſo much harme as in the hearts of true louers.
Amongeſt whome I can compare theſe two Princes,
Roſicleer and the beautifull Oliuia as the chiefeſt. This
Princeſſe nowe ridde of ſome part of hir feare, and as it
were brought into a newe worlde thought to make a-
mendes by puniſhing hir ſelfe for hir cruell letter, thus
ſaith ſhee. Oh how wel am I worthy of the paines which
I nowe ſuſtaine in the repentaunce of my former facte,
not onely for that which againſt Roſicleer I haue committed, but alſo for the little credit that I haue had of
his valorous perſonage, where were myne eyes & iudgement, when I did not proue his nobilitie by hys vertue,
howe great was my pride in that I would in ſuch ſorte
diſpyſe ſo worthy a knyght and banniſh him, not onely my preſence but thys kingdome alſo?

D

O inconſtant and frayle womankinde foʒ iuſt cauſe
lightly regarded amonge wiſe men ſith we are lyght in
beliefe,light in iudgement,and ouer haſtie in ſhewinge
the effect of our conceite : what occaſion had Roſicleer
gyuen me that I ſhould make erchaunge foʒ the greate
good will which I bare vnto hym with ſo cruell a ſentence as to diſpatche him from my pʒeſence , what had
he in his letter any diſhoneſt woʒde, any vnlawfull demaunde,oʒ dyd he moue mœ to the thinge pʒeiudiciall
to my greate eſtate . This hee deſired that I ſhould
knowe he loued mœ, why ſhoulde I bee aſhamed that
my inferiours loue mœ,and that hœ ſhoulde lyke of me
was the thing I deſired . Tell mœ Fidelia what is
thy counſayle foʒ to amende this faulte , mœ thinckes
we are in woʒſe caſe then befoʒe . Roſicleer is alrea-
die departed the countrey , and if I ſende to call hym
backe hœ wyll not regarde mœ,oʒ will it not be thought
lightneſſe,after that I had in ſuche earneſtneſſe refuſed
him as it were yeſterdaye , this daye ſodemely to alter
my purpoſe,beſides that when hee retourneth into thys
court,his gloʒie may encreaſe to my diſwoʒſhyppe,and
agayne if to beare out my foʒmer fact I let the matter
paſſe as it hath done,what ſhall then become of mœ I
knowe not howe to liue,he beeing banniſhed from my
pʒeſence whom I loue better then my ſelfe. But Fidelia
as thy part was in the firſt counſaile to banniſh Roſicleer,
ſo nowe put to thy helpe that Roſicleer maye retourne
agayne without the blemiſh of mine honour . Very ioyfull was Fidelia to heare the letter , and beeinge well
contente that hir miſtreſſe had kepte hir foʒmer con-
cluſion in this matter as touching the marriadge of
Roſicleer, if his parentage were not ſo farre inferiour,
ſoberly aunſwered.

Madame leaue off your complayntes,and be moʒe
gladde then euer you were,ſith God hath bene ſo fauourable vnto you as to make Roſicleer of ſo high eſtate ẙ he

S.ij.   may

may merite you. For in good sooth I stode in doubte whether of your paines were the greater, and I knewe no meanes howe to slake them. But sith nowe thys secret is disclosed, the remedy is in our handes, and not so difficult as you make it. For be it that you shall send vnto Rosicleer to demaund pardon of him for the offence which you haue committed againſt him, shall you thincke you doe your selfe any wronge therein in respect of your princely eſtate. No, for aſſuredly he loueth you loyally, & bicause he is of nigh parentage with you, you may therin beguile suspitious eyes, and after his retourne you may bolt it out of him, whether he loue you, yea, or no, if he doe without peraduenture you maye acquite hym, and loue of all thinges woulde be rewarded. I dare war-raunt that your loue shall detayne hym with vs, and to thys purpose, madame your hande and my heade whiche ioyntly committed the former facte, shall nowe together make the recantation and crye peccaui. The effect may be onely to will hym to retourne to your pre-sence, and my selfe wyll bée the meſſenger, and I pro-myse neuer to retourne into thys countrey tyll suche tyme as I finde hym, and haue deliuered your letter to hys handes. Withall sayth shée this ought preſently to bée put in practise, for by the griefe Rosicleer toke at the sight of your letter, I gheſſe that hee is eyther de-parted thys lyfe or auoided the countrey. The Princeſſe was very wel content wyth hir haſt as the thing which she moſt deſired, and so embraced she Fidelia gladly, and spake vnto hir.

Fidelia nowe I knewe the good will which thou haſt to serue me, and I confeſſe that I haue not made thée pryuie to my heauineſſe without great hope of com-forte at thy handes, therefore I beſéeche God once to rewarde thée as I wishe, but bringe me pen, ynke, and pa-per, for I will ſtraight way followe thy counſell héere-in. Fidelia brought vnto hir pen, ynke, and paper, where-

with

with the Princesse wrought hir reclayme wyth as many sugred woordes as the other letter had sharpe and
sower.

This letter the sequele wyll shewe vnto you,when
we come to the meeting of Fidelia and Rosicleer, but
before that time the letter wrytten after thys manner was deliuered vnto Fidelia,and it was agreed vppon betweene themselues that vppon the nexte daye
shee shoulde goe to seeke hym . This nyght they toke
theyr rest,the one for the better enduring of hir longe
trauayle which she shoulde sustayne, the other to make
satisfaction for hir broken sleepes . Ere broade morninge Fidelia was vp, and hauynge conuayed Rosicleers letter where shee founde it, shee went vnto the
Princesse to take hyr leaue of hir . When as they
were departinge. Oh my good Fidelia, sayde the Princesse,doe as much as thou mayest to retourne agayne
speadely,for if thou stayest longe I shall liue but small
whyle,there is nothinge that maye so soone shorten and
cutte off my dayes as to hope without successe , and
to dreade the worst. I tell thee that tyll thy comming
agayne my nyghtes well bee tourned to watchinges,
& I shal recken the clock hourely awaiting thy presence.
O God Fidelia when the daye commeth I wyll looke
for the nyght, then when as the nyght is ouerpassed I
wyll make accounte of the daye to come,and I wyll neuer leaue castinge of perilles tyll that I shall heare
thee bringe some tidinges of that good knyght . Fidelia was very sorrye to thincke of the cares whiche thy
Ladye was like to receyue, and principally for that shee
shoulde leaue hir alone wanting wyth whome to communicate hir payne . Wherewith beringe somewhat
troubled, and also foreseeinge the longe tyme of hyr absence,so shee departed wepinge in thys manner . Madame it is needelesse for you to charge mee farther in
these affayres,the paynes wherin I leaue you are insuffici-

S.iij.   ent

ent to haſten my iourney, I woulde to God my Fortune were auuſwerable to the deſire which I haue to
ſerue you in this matter. But bée of good courage and
hope for the cōming of your knight, or elſe looke not for
me, with theſe they broke off, & Fidelia wente to.hir fellowes vnto whome ſhée tolde that ſhée would ſoiourne
with hir parentes in the countrey for a ſeaſon, after
goinge to the Sea ſide, ſhée entered into a ſhyppe prepared towardes Almayne, wherein the hiſtorie leaueth
hir ſailing to recount of other things which chaunced in
the meane time.

¶ Roſicleer was betrayed into the Ilande of
Candramarte that Gyant whoſe handes
had bene cutte off before by Roſicleer.
Cap. 43.

Y Ou haue hearde howe Roſicleer departed from
the great Britaine in the company of the ſtraunge
gentlewoman neuer hoping to retourne agayne
into that lande, onely for the accompliſhinge of the
exile wherevnto he was bounde by hys Ladyes appointment. Nowe the Hiſtorie ſaieth that the gentlewoman with whome hée was in the boate was ſente by
Candramarte whoſe handes Roſicleer had cutte off before the kinge Oliuerio for Quéene Iulias rich ſworde,
and that ſhe was ſent vnder colour of a diſtreſſed gentlewoman to bringe him to hir Fathers Ilande, there
to be auenged of the hurte and ſhame which hir Father
had receiued. This deuice was thought fitteſt, both
for that Roſicleer as a noble knight pittied ſuche op-
preſſed gentlewomen, and that for other cauſe then to
ſhewe himſelfe Roſicleer coulde not be brought out of
Englande. In this Iland Candramarte had two young
Gyantes to hys ſonnes whome for that purpoſe hee had
knighted

knighted bæinge in making no leſſe then hymſelfe, be
ſides theſe Candramarte had foztie choſen knyghtes,
all which he armed to aſſault Roſicleer leaſt he ſhoulde
eſcape them . By this guyle the Ladye Oyanteſſe
daughter vnto Candramarte carryed hym to hir Father Ilande, wherein wythout any farther aduyce hee
aduentured hymſelfe foz very griefe of hearte whiche
hee conceyued to ſee hymſelfe abandoned hys Ladyes
pzeſence. But nowe ſire dayes haue they bene on the
Sea, at the ende whereoff the winde was ſo fauourable that they came within kenninge of the Iland, to hys
iudgement very ſtronge, and to the ſhewe very pleaſurable.

Thys beeing diſcouered by the gouernour, the gentlewoman ſaide that that was the place wherein hir
parentes and huſbande were taken, cryinge and tearinge
of hir haire as if the ſight of the place had redoubled
hir ſozrowe. Thys made Roſicleer to bæ moze earneſt in hir quarrell and to thincke it longe till hee were
landed, whiche his deſire beeing accompliſhed, the gentlewoman ledde hym vp vppon the ſhoare where Ro
ſicleer viewed at eaſe the whole ſight of the Ilande. In
the firſt entery vppon the lande there were two ſtronge
Caſtles as two bulwarkes ſituated vppon a ſtype rocke
as it were a bowe ſhotte diſtaunce ouer agaynſte the
other.

: Befoze the Caſtelles there was greate bzeade playne
ſhadowed with great Okes , and when they had come
nære vnto theſe greate Caſtelles , the gentlewoman
poynting to the one Caſtell ſayde to Roſicleer on thys
manner. If that Syz knight you will auenge my quarrell you muſte goe to that Caſtell which is on the ryght
hande, foz that is the traytoure knightes Caſtell whiche
hath taken my parentes and huſbande as pziſoners, and
vntill your comminge I wyll ſtaye heere in this little

S.iiij.   boat

boate we women are weake harted and fearefull, and aboue all J woulde not come into his power, for then would he for a suretie murther my parents and my husbande, whom now perhappes he entertaineth more gently vpon hope to winne mee. If you wyll, be it so aunswered Roſicleer, for your longe gownes are not fitte to fight withall, and your ſexe ſhall well aunſwere the challenge of your cowardiſe, with this ſpeach Roſicleer departed, and takinge his horſe mounted thereon to come to that Caſtle on the right hande, the gentlewoman toke hir ſhyppe agayne, and droue from land amayne. By and by Roſicleer hearde the winding of an horne at the one Caſtle, and preſently he heard an aunſwere at the other Caſtle, whereby ſuſpecting that this token was giuen of his comming, he tourned his head to ſee the gentlewoman whome he had left on the ſhoare. The gentlewoman houering about the bancke, nowe ſure of hys eſcape, and ſtrayning hir voyce cryed. Come foorth, come foorth, ſonnes of Candramarte for heere is the newe knyght which cut off our Fathers armes. Nowe wyſt Roſicleer by this horne and the gentlewomans outcries that he had bene betrayed, but as one careleſſe of his life as quietly as he could he prepared himſelfe, which hee certeinly looked for, his prayer was this. Lorde Jeſus haue mercy vpon me whom thou ſo dæerely haſt bought wich thy bloudſhed, pardon my ſinnes, and receiue mee into thy kingdome, as for my carcaſe be it as thou haſte appointed me, for death cannot betide me in a better time. After this hee ſtayed not as diſmayed, but paſſinge farther to ſee in what manner thys treaſon was compaſſed, he ſawe the gates of the one Caſtle ſet wyde open and thence iſſuinge a huge gyant vpon a myghty courſer with more then twentie knyghtes well armed at hys taple. At their firſt comminge they made a greate ſhowt as if they had got ſome great victory, & the gyant amongeſt the reſt ſayd vnto hym. Thou miſerable and

wretch-

wretched knight well shalte thou abye the shame which
thou diddeſt to my father Candramarte when thou diddeſt
cutte off hys armies at London . Roſicleer as deſperate
made aunſwere. I doubt not but fo2 all your th2eats you
will giue me leaue to dye, but ere that happen, it may be
you ſhall be diſappoynted of your purpoſe and with that
he d2ewe out Queene Iulias ſwo2de, with the which hee
encountred the tall Gyant which came agaynſt him with
a great ſpeare . The ſpeare hitte Roſicleer on the b2eſt,
and in dæde were it not fo2 the fineſſe of the armoure, it
had pearced him,but the mettall being ſuch as it was,the
Greeke made no mo2e fo2 the blowe then if he had bene
hitte with ſome delycate young knight,and befo2e that the
Gyant coulde recouer his ho2ſe raine to fetch the ſeconde
courſe, Roſicleer gaue him ſuch a blowe with his ſwo2de
that he clefte him to the bowelles , the greate Gyant fell
deade to the grounde, the blœde iſſuyng in greate aboun-
dance.Hære the great b2ag was quayled,when he which
came to aduenge an other mans quarrell coulde not warrant his owne ſafetie.

But truthe it is, that thoſe which vnmeaſurably doe
ſæke reuenge, doe oftentimes heape on themſelues the
greater miſchiefe . And what did this ty2annous Candramarte els which placing himſelfe at his windowe to beholde the battayle and to make mo2e ſolace at Roſicleers
harme as if the onely repo2t had not bene ſufficient, now
in ſtæde of his fo2mer w2ong he founde a greater by the
death of his ſonnes,but yet thys is the beginning only of
his miſery, fo2 the valyant knight not fearing deathe at
all , in greate choller ruſhed amonge the other knightes
which lykewiſe aſſayled him ceuragiouſly and had within a while with theire battayle axes hewen his ho2ſe in
pæces.

When he was on fœte he layde about him manfullye
that in ſho2t ſpace the ſcantlyng of grounde in which they
fought was couered with b2eſtplates and taigettes , and

es

as their number leſſened and that he had moꝛe roome, ſo
his courage encreaſed and he did them moꝛe ſcath : but
well fare his enchaunted armour , which hadde ſerued to
moꝛe purpoſe in defending, then his ſwoꝛde in offending,
oꝛ els his courage had tyꝛed befoꝛe the ende of ſo daungerous a fray . Now are there felwe alyue, and thoſe eyther ſtraining foꝛ lyfe vpon the graſſe, oꝛ in weake caſe v-
pon foote, readyer to flye then to fight : but pꝛeſently ther
came freſh ſuccours from the other Caſtle . Foꝛ the other
ſonne of Candramarte with moꝛe then thirtie knightes in
great haſt came agaynſt this good knight not being welly
ly occupyed among the other knightes . The Gyant foꝛ
other good moꝛow gaue the good knight ſo ſtrong a blow
with his battayle are vppon the headepæce , that had it
not bene rather in the headepæce to withſtand the blow,
then in himſelfe to reſiſt the Gyant, Roſicleer had layne
bꝛaynéleſſe on the grounde, but all this grieued him not,
ſauing that the wayghte of the blowe made him kiſſe the
earth, whence yet he ſtarte vp lyghtly,and minding to requite courteſie foꝛ courteſie, as hee was purpoſed at the
Gyant there ſtept in a knight betwéene them, whome Roſicleer deuided to the bꝛeſt bone, whereat the Gyant and
thoſe which beheldé him were much abaſhed , notwith-
ſtanding this they beyng many and he weryed he myghte
not defende himſelfe long from them, eſpecially from the
Gyant which only watched oppoꝛtunityé of aduauntagés
yet lengthened he the fight by his noble courage a longe
time, vntill foꝛ very fayntneſſe he was fayne to giue back
and to gette his ſhoulders agaynſt a wall,from which afterwarde he was dꝛiuen by mayne foꝛce, and being purſued, he withdꝛewe himſelfe to the Sea euer as he warded one blowe beſtowing an other . After hee had gotte
the Sea at his backe he waxed bolder and aboue all watched Candramartes ſonne , which had hurte him moſte e-
ſpecially him he hitte ſo ſure that the bloude guſhed oute
in thꝛée oꝛ foure places.

Jb

In the mean while Candramarte viewing the battayle to no great lyking blafphemed heauen and earth, and leuing the windowe ranne to the Sea fide, where the battayle was continued, and with a loude voyce hee called on his knights reuilyng them as cowardes and daſtardes if one knight might reſiſt them ſo longe, and aboue all to his ſonne he ſpake thus. Thou vile and daſtarde ſhape how lyke thou art to thy miſerable mother, I ſweare by heauen and earth, if thou eſcapeſt out of this battayle alyue, my cauſe and thy brothers death vnreuenged, that I will ſtarue thee in the ſame place where I ſtarued thy mother.

The Gyant and his knights thus rayled on for ſhame and feare gaue a freſh aſſault vppon the good knighte, ſo that as he diſpatched ſome, there ſtepped in newe in their roomes: and euer the battayle was as it were newe to beginne to poore Roſicleer, which draue him to ſeeke farther ſuccour in the water, and to ſtande vp to the nauell, thincking his death to be very nighe, he prayed to God with all his heart for his ſoules health as one that altogether deteſted his lyfe, and determined no longer to defende himſelfe then the water woulde giue him leaue. Then taketh he his ſworde with both his hands and layeth on ſo thicke that there are ſlayne more then tenne knightes ere hee leaueth, as the Sea gaue witnes which made the bancke ſeeme as all bedewed with bloude. Nowe beholde and ſee how God neuer forſaketh his, and eſpecially thoſe which abide his pleaſure: as hee did vnto this knight, which now ſtanding equally betwixt lyfe and death, though neither fearing the one nor hoping the other, and ſure of neyther yet hath he remedy beſides his hope and is comforted, of his owne brother, vnknowen to both.

So maye Fortune ſometyme vere and annoye vs: yet at the lengthe ſhe retourneth backe and relenteth agayne. But for this matter which wee entreate off, wee are to

re-

remember our selues of that valyaunt Grecian sonne to the Emperour Trebatio lefte in the lyttle boate saylinge through the Occean Seas with the which he had passed the bonnds of Africa and coasting by the Mediterraneum Seas was driuen along the Spanish shoare, and from thence at length sayled by the Ilande of Candramarte at suche time as Rosicleer nowe enforced himselfe to abide the vttermost of ŷ skirmish, with resolute mynd presently to receiue the death or to be conquerour. But this boat guyded by a wiseman as you hearde before toke landing almost agaynst Donzel del Febos will about a birdebolte shotte from Rosicleer where he espyed a cruell fight, but that which most amazed him was ŷ one knight (thoughe strong timbred and valyant) yet had sette himselfe against so many, & with their bodyes had made so great a slaughter. So with a great admiration rather amorous then ielous he sayd vnto himselfe. Who woulde beleue that in our dayes there might be founde a knighte furnished with suche excellencie of manhode. Assuredlye his fame is as worthy to be spoken off, as that Greekes which had killed the famous Troyan Hector. Thanckes be to the Gods which haue broughte mee hether, for althoughe I shoulde lose my lyfe, I wyll not leaue hym vnsuccoured.

Thus saying hee waded in the water to come nære him, and seing the Gyant to oppresse him so much and without a shielde, for hee had lost it in battayle with the first Gyant he toke his sworde with both his handes, and lette driue with all his force at the Gyants heade that he cleaued it vnto the brayne and afterward rushed among the rest killyng many of them. When Rosicleer sawe with one blowe the Gyant stroken downe and suche vnhoped for succours the greate wonder that hee receiued may not be tolde. And as if the enterprise had bene achieued or his lyfe saued, with a fresh courage hee wente out of the water, and valyauntly thruste himselfe among

hys

his enemies, where he well gaue them to vnderstand that he was desirous the battayle shoulde ende. Here two bretheren albeit vnknowen each to others, gaue brotherly helpe in time of neede. And there was neuer a one lefte, which eyther cryed not pardon, or fledde his wayr, the supplyants were pardoned. But lette vs thincke of Candramarte which now sawe his other and onely sonne slayne at one blowe, in what plyght dee you iudge him to be: but the worst is good inough, whereas if he had helde in his hungry desire of reuenge with a long delay, or had dissimuled his choller he might haue lyued quyetly wyth his sonnes by him, able sufficiently to defend soreyne inuasion, and mayntayne his. But now childlesse, knightlesse, and armelesse, besides at the mercye of his enemye, he was farre out of charity with all the worlde, that cursing heauen and earth and what was in them, he runne headlong into the sea there drowning himselfe among the waues, and bequeathing his soule to the Diuill who long ere that expected to be his executor.

Tell me I pray you gentill readers, howe often you haue seene the vnmeasurable desire of reuenge haue a lucky ende, or not rather to procure a farther harme, when as that which might be pardoned or dissimuled with honoure afterwarde is bewayled with sorrowe and griefe. It is writtenne that hee that seeketh reuendge, vengeance will lyght on him. For why the same God saythe. To me vengeance belongeth, and I will rewarde it. O ye malicious and wicked men which with infinit trauaile beate your heades to ordayne mischiefe for the least displeasure. Take this lesson for your amendment, and make Candramarte your example.

But lette vs continue our historie of the two brethren the Knight of the Sunne and Rosicleer which now the battayle being ended and the misdoers pardoned had little leysure to learne of eache other who he was. Rosicleer pulled off his visoure, and spake to the Knighte of the

Sunne

Sunne saying. Knight the most valyant that euer I met
withall, I knowe not how to reward you for the greate
friendthip you haue shewed to me,but tell me your name
I praye you and I shall account my selfe the happiest man
this day lyuing, and while I lyue will I remember your
valour. The knighte of the Sunne noting the greate
slaughter of knights with y manglyng of armour in that
place wher y first batattayle had bene sought, besides the
monstrous blow wherewith the firste Gyaunt had bane
slayne, and after viewing his personage, his bearde but
now burgening he pulled of his helmet and after the ma-
nifesting of his beautifull lookes suche as passed all the
knightes of his time he aunswered gently. Right valyant
knighte , I am to thancke my Gods for that they haue
brought me hether in so good a time as to know so valyant a knight, and to see with mine eyes the knighthoode
which I would scarse haue credited with mine eares:but
whereas you demaunde of me who I am, knew you that
I am called the knight of the Sunne for the deuise which
I beare in my armour, and for my birth I can shew you
no farther neither know I more of my estate:but the aduenture which brought me hether hath bene by occasion
of a storme which draue me on this shoare,and this is the
firste lande whereon I sette foote since this tempest tooke
my ship, and courtesie commaunded me to lend mine aide
when I saw you ouermatched with number . And thus
much for aunswere to your demaunde : but new agayne
that I haue tolde you that which you required,so I pray
you tell me your name,and for what cause this cruell battayle hath bene foughte betwéene these Gyants and you.
While the knight of the Sunne spake thus,Rosicleer beheld him very sadly,and hearing him say that he was the
knight of the Sunne and that he knew no more of hys
estate , he thought that peraduenture this same might be
his brother of whome Artemidoro had tolde him suche
aneru...ples, but leauing this suspicion til he might questi-

on

on of it moze at large, he satisfied the Knight of the Sun as to his question in shozte speache after this manner. Pour friendeshippe was great, and so I make reckning of it, otherwise I should not haue happened on so good a time to tell you my name in which bicause you woulde learne of mæ, you shall vnderstande that my name is Rosicleer, and that I was of good repozt in the court of kyng Oliuerio the king of great Britaine although my mishap causing it I doubte mee so much that my name is once mentioned amongest them, but that matter I will leaue off as not pertinent, this which you require aboute our fight spzong vppon thys occasion, and so hee shewed the whole ozder both of the receiuing of his Auant Cheualier at the kyngs hands: the first dayes iusting: the second dayes combatte with Candramarte: the honoure of the iustes: the enuye of Candramarte: and poynt by poynte the whole stozy as you hearde befoze.

Which tale Rosicleer had scarsely finished, when the gentlewoman which all this whyle remayned in the ship cryed out, wherat they tourning their heads, saw in what manner she outraged saying. O spightfull Foztune doe what thou canst, foz the succour which I haue wanted on lande, I hope to finde in the bottome of the Seas, and the God Neptune which hath power ouer the swelling waues shall kæpe mee from farther vengeaunce, wherewith she leaped into the Sea, but being clad in large garments she coulde not ozowne pzesently. The Knight of the Sunne and Rosicleer seeing hir in that estate, pitied hir greatly, but she was too far off foz them to wade nære, so the Knight of the Sunne tooke his boat hastely to helpe ȳ gentlewoman, wher otherwise then he looked foz, ȳ boat was carryed by vyolence another waye, and albeit hee stroue to bzinge it towardes hir, yet pzeuayled hee nothing, foz it sailed in ȳ Sea as swiftely as sometimes the cloudes racke in the ayze being oziuen by the windes, pzesently Rosicleer with greate griefe loste the sighte of the

boate

boate, wherfore fetching a dœpe sighe, as for that his former hope was cleane dashed to haue founde his brother, he sayd as followeth. Fortune, the thing which I moste detest, therein thou showest thy selfe most fauourable vnto me. This is my lyfe which now twise thou hast restored me without my will, but that which my heart most desired and with which my lyfe shoulde finde most ease, therein thou shewest thy selfe an aduersary to me: so that whatsoeuer good happeneth vnto me, thou makest mee thincke that it happeneth for the worste, for the longer I lyue, the more are my paynes encreased.

Now by that time that he had lamented a while for this sodayne losse of the straunge knight, he saw the gentlewoman cast vppon the sandes not as yet deade, whom he caused those knightes which were escaped in the battayle to carrye vnto the Castell, and there to finde some remedy for hir. Thus the knights did, with whome hee wente to one of the Castelles, where for this time wee wyll leaue him, to followe the Knighte of the Sunne on his iourney by Sea.

¶The Knight of the Sunne was carryed to the Ilande of Lyndaraza, where hee achieued manye straunge and fearefull aduentures. Cap. 44.

With great swiftenesse and incredible haste the boate whereas the knyght sayled, was carryed, passing in shorte time the dœpe Atlantike and West Occean, nare the vttermost Cape of the Ponent, till from thence it boue vppon the Pillours of Hercules, where his mightie arme and skaled forke made place for the Occean to enter and water the earthe. This Sea is called Mediterraneum Sea, and into this Sea the Knighte of the Sunne steard his boate, where he found well peepled townes and greater delyght then appeared in the wide and West Occean, and he beganne to receiue some ioy of his hether arryuall as if not without cause he were carryed in such hast, and that some great thing was therby hoped for: but as sory for his sodayne acquayntaunce with Rosicleer he besee-ched his gods with all his hearte, that they myghte once mæte agayne, and at more leysure recount each to other of their aduentures.

Well on all griefes whether for his friendes Brandy-zel and Clauergudo, or this vnacquaynted Rosicleer, or the vnskilfulnesse of his way were extinguished, by that his lerned gouernour guided their Barke whether it was conuenient. So still hoping for the Porte and Hauen, wherein his little boate shoulde ryde, he sayled as I sayd in the middell earthe Sea, where on the lefte hande hee sawe Spayne, Portugall and those countryes where hee coulde gladly haue bestowed himselfe, but that he was not to commaunde the stœreseman, but in god time came hee thether as shalbe recyted in the history hærafter. Although by shoare on the right hande he lefte Africke, Carthage, and Tures, and forewarde as he sayled he discouered the Ilandes Belears and Sardinia, with the warlyke Italy, and the fertill Sicily where the flames of Aetna hill a while stayed him. There might hee sæ the ruynous re-liques of olde Syracuse, and many perillous Mermaydes. haunting these shoares much feared by all the Maryners Then sawe he the fresh water of the ryuer Nylus, which entreth the Sea by seauen mouthes. From thence one the other hande might hæ sæ Greece. Wherewith hee woulde more willingly haue fedde his eyes, if he had then knowne the ryghte which he had thereto. But from thence hee lawnched into the broade Euxino where the wide Sea conuayed all thinges out of sighte, that nought appeared but cloudes aboue and waues beneath. Longe thus he sayled meruaylinge when his nauigation shoulde take ende.

After this as it were a faire calme following a stormy

T. tempest

tempest ther appeared aboue the water a faire Jlande vnto the which his boat draue, whereat he was merry and
pleasaunt thinking that there abode him some aduenture
wherein he might try his manly prowesse, and full fayne
hee was to leaue the Sea: here J say at this Jlande his
Barke stayed, whereby he knewe that his iourney was
thetherwarde.

Then the knighte leaped to lande, vppon the entrye
whereoff there was a banke cast of hard stone, and somewhat farther he sawe a freshe and pleasaunt soyle full of
the sweetest hearbes that euer he had seene. There was
a fence or closure made of tall high trees, some of them
with so loftye toppes that it weryed him for to looke vpwardes. Beneath this there was a meddowe platte
whereon grewe many flowers and hearbes of all sortes,
and it was compassed with a stil water gently rolling vppon the pumuise stones, the water was as cleere as a-
ny Christall.

Among the thicke trees he might haue seene the swifte
Harte and the faire Unicorne with the lyttle Beuerelte
and the small Connye bancking the greene boughs, besids
the lyght Squirel climbing the tall Oke, with the sweete
chirping layes, which the Birdes made, recording so plea-
sauntlye amonge the tender sprayes that it would haue
made a man vtterly forelorne to receiue comfort, and hee
that was surprised with loue or loues dartes might haue
founde a more present remedy then the Hartes of Creete
doe when they are wounded by the Hunter. This pleasure
to haue enioyed, you woulde haue thoughte your selfe to
haue bene transported into an other worlde or into a celestiall Paradise.

When the Knight of the Sunne had both beheld and
hearde all those thinges, he immagined presently that
the Iland was well stored with people thether resorting
for the delyght there to be founde, but yet he meruayled
why their pathes were no more trodden, and gazing one
euery

euery part which waye to take beſt, he tooke the waye
which was moſt beaten, therein he walked heauily laden
with his armour: but his deſire to know the end of thys
aduenture, and the ſwæte melody of the Birdes continually accompanying him, made him thincke his iourneye
ſho͛ter.

About a myle o͛ mo͛e out of this medowe he entred
into a playne paſture ſo beſette with flowers as the medowes were. In the middell of this paſture as it were
a bowe ſhotte from him he ſawe the faireſt Caſtell which
euer eye had ſæne aſwell fo͛ the height and largenes as
fo͛ coſt and wo͛kemanſhip.

The matter was all of Jaſper which when the Sunne
beganne to caſt his beames thereon ſhyned ſo b͛ight that
it dazeled the eyes of the beholder. The fo͛me was qua-
d͛angle after an euen p͛opo͛tion as b͛oad as long. In e-
uery of the co͛ners ther were ten faire Turrets which
reached by mans ſæming to the cloudes. The outward
wall of the Caſtle was harde Marble hewed out of the I-
lande Paros, rounde aboute the Caſtell there was a dæpe
ditche with a deuyce, that albeit there was no ſp͛inge
in it to nouriſh it, yet was it mayntayned with a freſhe
flowe partly by the fall of waters from the mountaynes,
partly by the ryuers we named amongeſt the medowes,
which at euery ſp͛ing clæred the channell. Uppon this
water there ſtode a b͛idge with th͛æ ſtrong Turrets one
in the beginning, the other in the middeſt, the other in
the ende towards the Caſtle. Th͛ough them a man cannot enter but by playne fo͛ce, fo͛ the kæpers open not but
conſtrayned and they næde to be right valyant fo͛ the po͛-
ters are fell.

The Knight of the Sunne gazed uppon this verye at-
tentiuelye, ſo amaſed at the ſtraungeneſſe of the wo͛ke
that hée coulde not thincke it to haue bene buylded by
mans hande. And hauing as then no other ſkill of God,
but the Gentiles lawe, he thought that peraduenture this

T.ij.   might

might be the house of his Gods, when they descended frō heauen to soiourne amongest vs . So very desirous to know the ende thereoff, he came vnto the bridge where he stayed a while ere he proceeded farther, for he iudged that according to the great strength of the archers, the depth of the water and the height of the wall, that no man might enter without leaue asked. And as he there wanted not matter of meruayle for the wonder of the castle, so meruayled hee that neere so rare & magnificent buildings he met no person of whom he might demaunde to whom the fayre Castle did belong. Amid these thoughts it seemed best in his fancie to call to them within, if perhaps any would aunswere him, and therefore comming to the gates of the first turret which was then neerest to him he found a porch opened, and right before a faire stately court enclosed with walles of Iasper, and in the midst before him a payer of stayers of a r. or rij. degrees which ledde vp to a fayre piller, wherevnto was fastened with a chaine of golde, a fayre horne and a rich brawdricke to it . The horne was tipped all with golde, and in the ende were set many precious stones . The riches thereoff might haue contented a right couetous eye : vnderneth the horne vppon the same piller there were engrauen letters which the knight of the Sunne perceiuing and hoping there to learne some more newes he mounted vp the stayres and read as hereafter followeth.

¶ This Castle belongeth to the beautifull Lindaraza, the gates may not be opened to any saue to him which windeth the horne. But let him take heede withall, for when they are open there shall not faile him cruell & · fierce porters to giue him the death if it bee possible.

When

When he had reade the letters and gathered by them
that there were Porters to aunswere him, hee feared not a whit for all the threates of ye writing, but wyth
an heroycall heart he vntyed his horne and winded it so
shrill that all the Castel eccowed wyth the noyfe, at the
founde heereoff the inner gates of steele flewe open as
if they had bene shaken with a tempest, and presently
there appeared a fierce Gyant bearinge in the one hande
a barre of yron, and in the other a chayne wherein hee
ledde tyed a Dragon the most hydious that euer man
loked on. This beast was from the breast downeward
as high as any man on horsebacke, and the tayle theroff
was tenne paces in length, wherewyth he sweeped the
grounde. Nowe the stronge Gyant comminge out of
the gates let lose the Dragon and toke the barre of yron
in his handes paceing towardes the knight whiche was
nowe in descending from the piller. Ere the knyght
could eafely come to the grounde the Gyant mette hym
with a counterbuffe on the sheelde that he miffed two or
three steppes in comminge downe. The monsterous
Dragon beneath was ready to receiue him. But the
nephewe of Alicante lightly esteamed all thys, and rather toke courage in thys that there was some thinge
worthy his paynes behinde when the Castell was kept
by fuche ougly porters, and drawinge out his swoorde
hee stroke at the Serpent a blowe on the toppe of the
head, but it dyd hym no more harme then if it had lyghted vppon a smythes anfelde, but it a little benummed
his fences and beguyled him of his forehoped grype.
Thys little harme which he had done to the Serpent
dyd much amaze hym, and the better to faue hymfelfe
from the Serpente he got vnder the piller, and then hee
bestowed an other blowe vppon the Serpents head with
all his force. The Serpent fo fore stricken waxed woode
and brayed out fo loude that all the courte range of the
noyfe, and faine would it haue got betwene the knight

T.ij.   of

of the Sunne, ⁊ the place vnder the piller where he ſtode
to haue raught him in his pawes, but the good knight defended himſelfe lightly from him and laide at the Dragon
ſtill with the ſword. The Gyant abode ſtill at the ſtayers foote to waite for the knightes tombling on the ſtayers, at length he came downe headlong where the ſtrong
Gyant let driue at him ſo great a blowe with his barre
that the barre burſt and the good knight thought his head
had bene bruſed, with this as well as he might, he roſe
vp, and driuing at the gyant he cut his legges cleane from
his body. The Gyant falling to grounde, the Serpent
rayſing his tayle graſped at the knight of the Sunne, but
I can not tell howe the knight eſcaped it, and withal he
toke vp the greateſt peece of the barre of yron which the
Gyant had, and haſting towarde the Serpent he gaue
him ſuch a blowe therewith vpon the head that hee fell
downe, and before he could riſe, the knight gaue him ſuch
an other that his ſcull as hard as flinte burſt into two
peeces, yet for al this y̌ great Serpent was not throughly
dead but bounded vp into the ayre, and ſwept the ground
with his tayle ſeeming to be more fierce then at the beginning. The knight of the Sunne purpoſed to ſtrike
no more but quickly gate vp higher on the ſtayers to be
out of daunger, in the ende the Dragon ſturred no more
whereby he iudged that he was dead, and meruaylinge
what beſides this there might be found in the Caſtle, he
hong the fayre horne about his necke, and with the bar
in his handes he entered the firſt Tower, and from thence
through the firſt arche of the bridge till he came to the
ſecond Tower which was in the midſt of the bridge, the
gates whereoff were of ſteele ⁊ ſhut as faſt as y̌ gates of
y̌ firſt arch were. Cheualiero del Febo winded his horne
and preſently the gates were opened and there came iſſu-
ng out a Gyant no leſſe ſtrong then the firſt, hauing in
the one hand a clubbe, and in the other a chayne wherein he ledde a Lyon, the wightyeſt of lymme and byggeſt

i   of

of bone that euer man sawe . The bodye as bigge as a
Bull, and euery of his clawes was a handfull longe, his
eyes shined lyke lampes.

This Lyon the Gyant vntyed strayght and sette vppon the knight, which with no litte courage as he had
a greater quest in hande awayted him, and at the firste
blowe hee strake him so fell vppon the heade , that the
braynes starte out, and the monsterous Lyon fell starke
deade without more sturring . When he had this done
he encountred the Gyant, and the Gyant latte dryue at
him : But the knight not minded at that time to assaye
or put his trust to the fine mettall of his enchaunted helmette starte aside, that the clubbe fell vppon the brydge :
but before the Gyant coulde reare his clubbe , the sonne
of Trebatio hitte him so stronglye beneathe the knees
that hys shinne bones were burst withall , and the Gyant wyth greate clamoures fell downe , the Knighte of
the Sunne leauing him sure inough for making resistance
toke vp his heauye clubbe to go farther and to see what
was within.

This passed he through the seconde tower , till hee
came to the thirde and last tower of the brydge, whereoff
finding the gates shut as the other he wynded his horne,
and with the shrylnesse thereoff the gates burst open making as great a noyse as if the brydge had rente in two
presently stepped forth a huge Gyant, nine fote in height
all his bodye couered with a toughe hide so harde and
strong that no sworde coulde enter at his wast he hadde
a sword, and in his hand a chayne of yron whereto were
fastened two Tygers of wonderfull greatnesse , by the
fiercenesse of theire lokes able for to haue affrayed anye
man.

For all this the hardy Grecian was nothing appalled,
for he lyfte vp the heauy club so stronge, as if the greate
Hercules shoulde haue come to ufighte with him onelye
with the showe it mighte haue made hym to tremble.

Those fierce beastes so soone as the Gyant had vnlosed them, opening their horrible mouthes, ranne with suche swiftnesse vpon him that it seemed their feete touched not the ground, at such time as they came both vppon him, he gaue one of them such a blowe vpon the shoulder that he burst all hys bones in peeces wherewith the Tyger fell to the grounde. Then came the other and caught holde of him in the shoulder so griping him that he coulde not stirre his arme, neither one way nor other, and grasping almost all the headpeece within his sharpe feeth he thougt to haue crushed it in peeces, but the hel-met defended the head and the Magicke armour kepte of the tearinge of his nayles. Nowe the good knyght seeing neither purpose of hys clubbe nor vse of his swoord while he was thus entertayned by the Tyger throwinge away his clubbe, he strugled and wrastled so longe with the Tyger, that in the ende he cast the beast vppon the harde flinte stones with such a fall that the braynes flew out of the head. The wylde Gyant when he sawe the Tyger thus slayne, with an hellishe furye he went to-ward the knight of the Sunne, and takinge his longe swoorde he gaue him such a blowe vppon the toppe of the helmet that there sparckeled out great flakes of fire, and the knight fell vppon handes and knees. But as soone as he coulde, the knight recouering his swoorde requited him so couragiously, the Gyaunt beeinge vnarmed, that had not the stronge hide stoode him in steede of complete armour the swoorde had entered the fleshe, whereoff at this time it missed. Veereat the wilde Gyant taking vp agayne the heauie swoord stroke the knight of the Sunne vpon the toppe of hys headpeece, but he auoided the blow lightly. In such sort ỹ the heauy swoord fel vpon ỹ ground & brake in peeces, the hilts onely remaining in his hands. Now before ỹ gyant could raise vp his swoord ỹ knight of the Sunne ranne him through. When the knight of the Sun had accompliſhed thus much of his purpose, he thought

there

there had bene no more to be done saue now to know the secrets which abode behinde, and wherefore this strayght warding was ordayned . Therefore he went throughe all the bridge vntill he came to a pathway which leede betweene the outwarde wall and the great Castle . When he had walked this path, about a bowe shotte off he saw a lyttle dore all engrauen with sundry kynde of portrayture, the straungenesse whereoff, with the varietie of the story therein portrayed, might haue helde a good caruer a long time: the Imagery was so drawn that it would haue troubled the witte of Praxites to haue matched it . The gates were not great, but the chiefe part was of stele as surely closed as the first.

The Knight of the Sunne thinking that percase they woulde open at the first push rushed against them with all his force but his laboure was lost and hee preuayled no more then if hee woulde haue broken downe the walles with his fete . Therefore he winded his horne whereat the gates burst open but no man appeared without , saue that when he was about to enter he sawe two Gyantes the one of the one side and the other armed from top toe, with headepeeces of fine stele, and their armoure a finger depe in thicken. se they helde in their hands two battayle arces raysed vp aloft ready to discharge their blows vppon the commer in. The fiercenesse of their semblance was so straunge that it is harde to belieue that any man had the courage to enter a gaynst his will, but if it hadde bene the dogge Cerberus he could not haue defended him the passage.

This valyant knyght seing them in such sort prepared for the fight albeit he wanted not courage to assaye that fearefull entry, yet he stayed in doubte howe he mighte enter without daunger and warde the two first blowes. For to receiue both their blowes at once was not possible without great hazarde, and otherwise enter he could not, but after long pawsing he came nerer and as if he would

T.b.   haue

haue passed through he shewed himselfe, whereat the
Gyants as if he had entred indæd let driue their blowes,
the wackest the knight stepte in betwæne them, and taking the nexte to hand he hit the one Gyant ouerthwart
the pawnch, but his sworde entred not. The Gyantes
which at their first blowes had broken their heauy clubs
drewe out their broade arminge swordes, and layde at
the knight of the Sunne. The one hee receiued on the
sworde, the other hee auoyded lightely by stepping aside.
And willyng to sæ the ende of the aduenture he stroke on
of them full vppon the visour wherewith he had thought
to haue hewed his face, but he was deceiued, for it dyd
the Gyant no more harme then if he hadde bene smitten
with an hasill wande.

The Gyants nowe layde on loade, but he disappoyn-
ted them by ye delyuernes of his body, And now consider
what thought this good knight was in to fæle himselfe assayled by two fierce enemyes & not able to hurt againe.
Neither was it possible to maister one of them by wrast-
lyng, for both the weaker of the two was to strong for
him, and perhappes while he shoulde deale with the one,
the other might displease him. So that neither of these
wayes were conuenient, without some present helpe the
daunger certeyne, yet in the ende he beganne to rebuke
himselfe, euer sayng, Sticke to it. thou cowarde, and albeit as yet it sæmes impossible for to escape this perillous
skirmish, yet stirre not thy foote, either shalte thou sone
ouercome or sone lose the victory, but neuer shalte thou
lose thy infamy if thou dye flying, many times such hard
aduentures haue bene occasion of greater glorye, and if
any body but my selfe achieue it, I shall not lyke my self
as long as I lyue,

So gazing about to sæke aduauntages he marked the
wickette standing open somewhat beneath the Porche
where through he mighte well passe by lyttle boweynge
himselfe, but neyther of the Gyantes mighte except they

fell

fell on all foure, fo2 they were higher then he by the b2eſt
downewarde, when he ſawe this do2e he bethought him
ſelfe how to be out from the daunger of blowes which fell
into his b2ayne at a time of nœde . Thus it was as the
Gyants were deſirous to hitte him he euer ſtouped vnder
and watchinge one of them , as hee was lyſting vp his
armes , befo2e the blowe could deſcende he ran and cloſed with him, and taking him by the gy2dell carryed him
by ſtrong hande and with all his fo2ce ranne agaynſt the
wickette that the Gyant not being able to paſſe th2ough
burſt both heade and ſhoulders agaynſt the wall, the Gyant there dyed in hys armour,

This done the ſtrong knight paſſed farther , and letting the body fall with ſo muche ſpœde as hee might hee
ranne to mœte with the other Gyant, which then app2o-
ched with his ſwo2de in both his handes to haue ſmitten
him . But theſe Gyants lyttle acquaynted with feates
of armes, and the knight of the Sunne by the derteryfe
of his body defended himſelfe lyghtly from them and obtayned victo2y.

Fo2 when the Gyant had lefte his ſwo2de fall out of
his handes he emb2aced the Gyant with both his hands
and tourning himſelfe twice about at the thirde time hœ
lette him fall that th2ough the wayghte of his body hys
gall burſt in his bodye,and he dyed p2eſently. This meruaylous combat bœing ended, the good knight was now
wery:and therefo2e tœke his eaſe vppon a ſeate of ſtone
which was in the po2ch there to occupy himſelfe he behelde the ſtrong buyldings of the Caſtle . After rœminge
about to finde ſome other way to departe thence he found
at one ende an other gate all of y2on and the gates ſhutte
as all the fir ſt, whereby he ſawe that he had yet farther
tryall to abide.

And therefo2e he reſted him ſelfe where he ſafe, after
which done he aroſe and paſſing th2ough the fir ſt wall to
the ſeconde hee founde the gates ſhutte , and therefo2e
he

he winded his horne, presently the Castle gates opened, and there came out thereoff a flame of fire accompanyed with great smoke, as if it had bene some place of hell, vntill the smoke vanished awaye he could see nothing. After hee saw before y gate a beast in forme lyke a Crocodile but somewhat more hydeous, as it wer a mishapen monster purposed by nature to shew the lothsomnesse of deformity. Out of his mouth he sent great flakes of fire, in the fangs ther sate a tusse without the mouth about halfe a yearde very sharpe and cutting.

The good knighte abashed nowe to see so many fierce keepers in that Castle as if it had ben nothing but a lodge of warders, (as he supposed) to keepe in durance the sons of Titan which once rebelled against Iupiter. The which tale he had often heard in his Gentiles lawe, and yet the trauayle of conquering grieued him not alyke to the long looking for of the end. but not minding to debate y matter at this time, he tooke his swoorde in hys hande, assayinge the entry, but the ougiy beast cast out suche a flash of fire that the Knighte of the Sunne lyttle lyked of it. And not being able to endure it, he gaue backe tyll the heat should slake.

This may a man say that it troubled the knight more then all that had passed, one cause was for the extremitye of heate, an other for that he sawe no waye to come nere the beast, for before he might approch it the beast woulde be all on a lyghte fire, but remembring himselfe of the club which he had lefte in the first entrye and thinking that it shoulde be the best weapon he might haue he ran to fetch it, and retourning speedelye he founde the monster as you hearde before spitting his fire. The Knight of the Sunne with his long reach in his hand gaue the beast vppon the foreheade such a blowe, that the heade rent into two, and the terrible beast fell to grounde, beating his feet against the grounde so harde that it seemed the Castle shooke with all, and the smoke which it sent foorth, as at the quenching

of

of a great fire so blinded the Knighte of the Sunne till it
was starke dead that hee might not enter : from thence
after he came to a faire courte the sumptuous buylbinge
whereoff amazed him much , that in comparison the golden statues which Nero the Emperour of Rome ereded
might not moze delyght him : no, noz yet the wonders of
the wozlde the stately Pyramides of Aegypt, wherein only their kings are buryed, and wherein they wasted the
most part of their substance might lyke delyght them. In
beholding the straungenesse of these buyldings I can not
tell pzecisely his thought foz euery circumstance , but if
his thought were as my thought, oz if the repozt be true
which first came from him, surely ther was matter inough
to gaze bppon, but what thinke you he noted especiallly ?
Nothing but a marble stone, but as it fell out to some
good purpose.

In the marble stone were engranen the valyant ades
of all knights alyue oz dead in such ozder of time as they
lyued . First the auncienter, then the later, till he came
to the neerest very sewe oz none omitted . A rare péce of
wozke, and must nædes haue bene done by other cunning
then stozy oz caruing, foz the one the paynes were insi-
nite, foz the other no mans reading stretcheth so farre as
to knowe euery stozy . But hærein he tooke great pleasure, and from the first to the last he ranne them ouer, he
stayed at his owne picture wherebnto ioyned nexte a-
boue was Trebatio, and the nexte beneath was Rosicleer
These thrée pictures were fresher to his fancie then the
others, as if they had bene newe made . Remembzing
by the picture of Rosicleer the countenance of that knight
whome he had founde in the Ilande of Candramarte, hee
yælded fozth a great sigh and blessing the picture from the
bottome of his heart, he spake these wozds vnto like purpose.

Thou art a ryghte good knyght and wozthely place
among the most famous knights of the wozld, foz I beleue,

ene not that among so many as are here painted ther is
ne so valyant as thou art. For albeit commonlye wee
make much of our Elders vertues, it is but as commonly many things shew fairer a far off whereas when they
come to tryall they are but as ordinary.

After this hee mused in himselfe who that Trebatio
might be for he neuer hearde of such a man: but by the
draught of the picture he tooke him to be a comlye personage, of a milde and sadde countenaunce and it did him
good to beholde him: so looking farther he saw the whole
story of the Emperour Trebatio drawen vnderneathe,
from his first landing in Hungary till that houre of hys
enchauntment in that Castle. Howe he was in the company of Lyndaraza without knowledge of himselfe, or
witting to his friendes. Now did he at length learne the
purpose of the strong wardes which was to holde in the
Emperour Trebatio there beitched for the companye of
Lyndaraza, whome before he could restore to the knowre-
ledge of himselfe, he must bringe from that pece of the
Castell which was enchaunted to that onely effect. This
when he vnderstoode it pitied him much that so good an
Emperour shoulde there be in holde by false meanes to
the great sorowe of his subiects and principally of his wife
tre Princesse Briana whome he sawe lykewise all cladde
in blacke lyke a widdow, and to worke some meanes of
his deliuery, he looked about him which way was best to
take, and lyking best one of the gallories the which was
nærest to the paued courte, that he followed mounting
vp a paire of stayrs all made of Iasper in the midst wheroff he mette comming downe a bigge knight armed with
rich and glistering armoure, his face bare and of a fresh
colour, which approching to him drewe out his sworde,
and without saying oughte, layde at the Knighte of the
Sunne as fiercely as he coulo.

The knight of the Sunne woulde rather haue talked
with him to haue learned some newes but it coulde not
be,

be, so it behoued him to drawe his sworde and to defend himselfe . There beganne a whotte skirmishe that the clattering of their armoure and the flashinge of theire swordes range throughout the pallayce , This fury notwithstanding lasted not longe for the knight of the Sun in a cholericke rage hitte his aduersary so sure vppon the toppe of his helmette that the bigge knighte fell downe, and laye for dead.

The knighte of the Sunne stayed not to make dispatch of hym but rather hauing compassien on him (for he seemed a noble knight) he vnlaced the knights helmet to giue him ayre, but not being able then to recouer him, he passed farther and comming to the gallorye hee then went vp an other payre of stayres so wide and bread that if two were goyng vp neere the two endes, scarcelye the the one might knowe the other . Nowe in this his way albeit many things were which might haue stayed either an idell gazer or a curious eye, and manye thinges beside to haue inuited a weryed man to take his rest,yet the desire of finding the Emperour carryed his feete , and ouercomming the paynes of the waye he came to a portall curiously wrought, to the entrye wheroff, there led three steps of beaten siluer . By them he entred into the great chamber where first Emperour Trebatio had a sighte of the faire and beautifull Lyndaraza and was bereaued of his wittes.

In this chamber he was greatly abashed at the coste and workemanshippe of riche Tapestrye and other ornaments, and euer though the stuffe were of the costlyest, yet the workemanship bettered the matter . Hence must he as I tolde you conuaye the Emperour if hee meane to make himselfe known . Now for your farther instruction knowe that among other things which the wise Lyrgandeo gaue vnto the knighte of the Sunne,at hys departure from Babilon, hee gaue him a lyttle stone sette in a ryng of excellent fine golde the same being of so straunge
ver

vertue that no enchauntment might preuayle agaynst it,
by this he was bolde to enter the chamber, & being within was free from the charme . Out of this chamber he
came to the Orcharde whereunto this chamber looked , so
fresh and delectable that if euer pleasure might rauish the
sences of man, a man might affirme it of that place . In
the arbour nære the entry he sawe a number of faire gentlewomen clothed with silke, their breasts bare and white
as snowe, some played on instrumentes and other sange
sweetly to them.

Such kinde of Mermaydes woulde haue beguyled a
well stayed Vlysses, or such Musicions, aswell for theire
cunning song as their company., woulde haue broughte
a watchfull Argus to a sleepy heade . A good way off he
sawe the Emperour Trebatio and the faire Lyndaraza
alone , sette in seuerall chaires all vnmindefull of other
thinges but of their loue and wish to other . The Emperour Trebatio leaned his heade vppon the white and delycate breasses of Lyndaraza with suche shewe of pleasure
therein that the young Greke feelyng thereby in himselfe
that which all men haue, coulde haue bene content wyth
the others roome, and for very loue he made an inuectiue
agaynst nature which hadde ordayned that kinde to haue
such souereintye ouer valyant knights, with many wordes
to the same matter, but this was yet the wantonnesse of
his immagination, his necke had not felte the yoke, hereafter perhappes he will speake more earnestly when you
shall beleeue him.

Nowe , when the gentlewomen espyed him as all a-
bashed they layde aside their Musicke, with the soddayne
staye whereoff Trebatio and Lyndaraza lyfted vp theire
heades and seeing a knight so strongly made to come towardes them,they were ouertaken with feare especially
Lyndaraza, which gessing at the trouth of the matter that
hir long loue shoulde now take ende for very sorrowe fel
to grounde, Trebatio comforted hir inasmuch as yet no

byolence was offered,but she replyed wyth terres, saying. Alas my Lord I shall dye vnlesse you do iustice on
this knight which hath here entered without my leaue,&
which hath interrupted our ioyes by the destroying of my
kæpers . Heerewith the Emperour very angry spake   to
the knight,saying. Sir knight why haue you come within this place without the lisence of this lady,it being hirs
& kept by strong kæpers for hir vse. The knight of the
Sunne gently aunswered. Noble Emperour I confesse I
demaunded no leaue,& till now I met with none which
would aske wherefore I came,but my arrant is for your
selfe which heere liue vnknowen,& haue forgotten your
wyfe and Empire. The Emperour angerly replyed:ney-
ther thou nor the whole world may bring me hence,& for
thy good zeale to put me from my ioy,stay awhile and I
will acquite thee thy fee. So hastely he flang to a chamber where he armed himselfe, the while that Lindaraza
whom it touched as in especiall reuiled the knight of the
Sunne for his thether comming. O saith she,thou sauctie
and vnmannerly knight howe hast thou had the face to
enter my castle in despight of my porters,either departe
hence quickly or tarry to abide the Emperours puissance.
And if my minde deceiue me not I shall soone be satisfied
for this disgrace. The knight of the Sun knowing how
grieuous it would be vnto hir that the Emperour should
leaue hir layd contrarywise w faire words to perswade
hir to giue consent to his departure,saying: Worthy lady may you not content your selfe with so many years in
which you haue detained this noble & famous Emperour:
both from wife & kindred,from land & subiect,but wil you
also for your pleasure,neither lasting nor honest vndoe a
whole countrey,& take a man from his wife which hath
mourned for him xx.years. I beseech you madame contet
your selfe with y which is past and let him not wade farther in this errour which if it may plese you to remoue
to your great honour at my entreatie. Hereat Lindaraza

all firie could not abide the end of his sute, but with great
outcries to insence ý poore emperour, ſhe put him off. The
Emperour being armed, in great choller ranne vpon the
knight of the Sunne, ¶ without ſaying any thing laide at
him with all his force. The knight of the Sun knowing
that what ý Emperour did, was but as done in a dreame,
would not ſtrike him to do him harme, but onely to ſaue
himſelfe ¶ to finde the meanes whereby to bring Trebatio
from that enchauntment. Thereupon by little ¶ little he
gaue backe, that the Emperour following him, he might in
the end bring him frō the inchāuted chamber. This came
to paſſe accordingly, for as he made ſhow of lacke of reſi-
ſtance, ſo ý emperour thinking to follow the aduauntage
purſued him to the great chamber wher the enchauntmēt
firſt tooke effect. In ſhort by this foreſaid meanes ther alſo
this emperour was brought to the point of auoiding the
chamber, whereat Lindaraza fearing leaſt he might be led
cryed w̄ a loude voice. Stay, ſtay, my lord, for this knight
is full of fallſhood, and if you go out of this chamber both
you ¶ I ſhall dye. Hereat the Emperour who was not
deſirous of any thing but to pleaſe hir retourned backe.
The knight of ý Sun would not follow him, but ſtil kept
at the pitch of the entry, ¶ the Emperour would not come
to him for feare of Lindaraza.

    Well, this deuiſe not ſuccæding the knight of ý Sun
thought now to try if he might carry him by maine force.
This he knew woulde be a daungerous matter for the
courage which he knewe in the Emperour, but all was
well employed if he might ſet him at libertie. So towardes the Emperour he goeth, whome not prepared to
fight, he ſodenly catcheth in his armes and with a luſty
courage raiſeth him from ground to haue carryed him a-
way, but before the knight might get to the dore ý Emperour catching holde likewiſe held the knight ſo ſhorte
that for a while they tumbled in the hall, neyther parte
gayning any great ſcantling of grounde, but the ods was

                                   ✠ the

the knightes,& in the ende he quickly lifting vp the Emperour would he or not,he brought him without y̆ chamber. The Emperour strugled to recouer the dore,but in
their strugling they both tumbled downe the stayers.
Nowe hath the knight of the Sunne played the man,for
ere they came fully to the ground the dores of the inchaunted chamber clapt together, wherewith and wyth
the noyse thereoff a great part of the edifices sanke withall. The Emperour retourned to his former wittes presently sawe that he thought he had not stayed there past
a day,and that which passed betwœne him and Lindaraza had bene but a short and pleasaunt dreame. After calling to minde his wife the faire Princesse Briana & the
great hoast which he had left before Belgrado he became
so sorrowfull that the teares trickled downe his chœkes
in great measure. But of this manner and condition are
we mortall men, that for our pleasures we sometimes
forget our spoufes the one halfe of our selues: sometimes
neglect our children the more halfe to our selues (as in
whom the hope of posteritie resteth)and lastly sometimes
we ouertourne our countrey which ought to be dœrer to
vs then our selues, neyther mindefull to what vse wœ
are created ,namely to the benefite of others , neyther
carefull what losse ensueth,as in especiall our owne dis-
commoditie,but that which is more then carelesse, is the
little thought of chaunge , and the lothinge to depart
from it.

That when we are at our wayes ende wœ sœme
but as it were nowe to begin a freshe : It is like a
swœte slœpe,but let vs shake off thys drousie humoure,
and let vs open our slœpy eyes . Let vs vse our selues so
that sometimes we haue recourse to matters of more
importaunce, and to thincke of heauen, to despise the
vayne temporall thinges of this world, to seperate our
selues from the man of fleshe,and willingly to leaue him
least he leaueth vs against our willes.

V.ij.   Lit-

Little shall remaine thereoff after scores of yeares, & that which remaineth shalbe shame & griefe for the life passed, beades desperate repentaunce which is a double torment. And much after this same manner was this valyant Emperour for his long delights with Lindaraza, now xx.yers was but a Summers day, & yet there left him not shame of his fact to fret his conscience, albeit he aduised himselfe the best remedy which I haue read off which is amendement of life, the safest hauen for a weatherbeaten penitent. First therefore knowing that this knight was hee which had as it were awaked him from this dreame, he pulled off his helmet & embraced him, giuing harty thanks for his deliueraunce. Withall, professing that he thought himselfe vnable to requite that great courtesy, yea, euen with the bestowing of his Empire, so assuredly hee ment not to forget it, if peraduenture God would shewe hym the occasion of doing him seruice. For (saith he) you haue not saued my life, here might I haue liued without daunger of swoord, but you haue saued my soule. &c. Extolling the greatnesse of the benefit, & in the ende, he prayed him of courtesie to tell him his name and countrey with the cause of his comming to that Iland. The knight of the Sun answered him gently. Valiaunt emperour y thing which I haue done in your seruice is not like to y which I wish for, as your valour forceth my will, so my wil sueth a desert on your part, more vnto you then to all the knights of the world. But wit you I am called y knight of the Sunne, my countrey I know not, but my bringing vp hath ben in Babilon, where I was tolde y I was found vpō y sea, being a very child, my cōming to this castle was by chaunce, my boat being driuen by tempest vpon y shore wher seeing it so fresh & faire I had desire to know y owners, & fortune being fauourable, I passed through al killing y keepers till I came within this court where I saw engrauen your whole history frō y time y you wer maried with y princes Briana til time you were brought hether.

Ther

There knewe I the manner of your bewitching, & albeit your selfe were vnknown to me, yet I thought I would set you free if that I might, from whence thys hath proceeded which you haue seene. When he had ended the Emperour embraced him many times with greate pleasure as well wondring at his great prowesse, for he could not be ignoraunt of Lindarazas power, as also at hys boldnesse for a matter not touching hym in any respecte by all appearaunce. For he neither knewe countrey nor parents. But as the remembraunce of his wyfe & Empyre caused in the Emperour much griefe, so he besought the knight of the Sunne that they might departe from thence to goe into Greece where he might better thancke him then he had earst done. The knight of y Sun with a good affection to beare him company condescended easily rather yet vpon desire to know the countrey wherin he had heard to be right valiant knightes, then of any hope of reward. So when they came neere the outward court they found that knight (whome the knight of the Sunne had left in a traunce) nowe retourned to himselfe and vpon his feet safe and sound. The knight when he sawe the Emperour and the knight of the Sunne cōming downe, giuing great sighes and weeping bitterly began to say. Oh what a dismall day is this for me, now my sister Lindaraza is dead and I haue lost a sweete companion, I would rather that I had bene killed by this straunger which hath destroyed all our good, then that I shoulde liue and susteyne such anguish. Little haue the monsterous keepers preuayled whome we put in our Castle to defende hir lyfe, and to defende the death which so sodeynly hath taken hir away. The Emperour hearinge him and knowing him ran to embrace him, saying. My deere friend Flamides howe chaunceth this heauinesse in your countenaunce? Why doe you fetch such deepe sighs and spill so many teares with so great sobbes. If it be for my departure and for the libertie which you haue

T.iij. re-

recciued by this knight, you know how long time I haue héere remained out of my remembraunce, and forgetfull of my Empire and kingdome, and shall I not go to comfort hir which long time by my absence hath bene comfortlesse. My Lorde sayde Flamides, I can not denye but your reason is good, and that the iniurie hath bene great in detayning you so long from thence, but as your excellencie knoweth there is no loue more naturall then betwéene brother and sister. O the death of my sister Lindaraza pearceth me to the heart, and I had rather then my life haue accompanied hir in death, then thus to bewayle hir lacke after death. For so soone as you came out of the inchaunted roome, my sister dyed presently, so was it appointed by ye destinies, that no longer then she should enioye your presence she should liue. Blessed man, sayde the Emperour, is Lindaraza dead, yea assuredly quoth he. Now on my honour (sayd the Emperour) hir death grieueth me, and during my life shall I be sad as oft as I shall call hir to remémbraunce, & although my case is such as in more néede of comfort then likely to comfort others, yet me thinckes I may tel you that you ought not to bewaile hir death so much, for belike a long time haue you knowé ye hir life should not last after my departure. Now wherefore do you lament hir so sore as if it were but now thought on & not before foreséene. Againe your ouermuch carefulnes in fortifying your castle was but néedlesse, for it is giuen to man to haue ye mastery ouer beasts which either by Art or Nature become tractable. And be it your castle had bene inexpugnable for all men in ye world, yet what fence had you to shut out death. A man in no place can warrant himselfe such safetie as that at euery step he draweth himselfe néerer vnto death. Whether we be frée or bond, on foot or horseback, sléeping or waking, whole or sick, we dayly draw nere vnto our end: or if you wil speak more truely to our perfection, for then man beginneth to liue in déede when he goeth out of this miserable world.

Lin-

Lindaraza is dead and wéeping may not recall hir, if you
beare vnto hir any loue you may shew it nowe after hir
death in recciuing to hir place hir daughter Lindaraza:for
hir prouide ý she may depart from hence,& J wil carry hir
to my kingdome wher she shalbe in ý estate as is due to
ý daughter of such parents:when the emperour had thus
sayd,Flamides forced himselfe so much as he might for to
speake,& thus aunswered him. Your reason satisfieth my
vnderstanding,& J confesse it true that we ought not to
wéepe when death assaileth vs,neither ought we to make
straunge of it,for in the end we must leaue this world,&
then is there nothing more certeine,but my conceit builded vpon outward sence béeing contrary to reason trou-
bleth againe that part where affections are & maketh it
rebellious,and howsoeuer men be prouided for death by
continuall thought that they muste dye : ordinarily notwithstanding we thincke our selues immortall till death
attacheth vs. And what olde man onely for age is so fée-
ble that he hopeth not for a day to liue:But as to Lindaraza my sister,J beléue that although you had stayed
here many dayes,the secret of this aduenture had neuer
bene disclosed vnto you,neither do you knowe the cause
why you were brought & put héere. ButJ will tell you
plainly. My sister Lindaraza & J had both one father named Palisteo being the second son to ý king of Phrygia,
my father not being borne to the kingdome fell rather to
seke his owne delight without enuy,then to trouble him
selfe with the care of gouerning . Aboue all he studied
the Arte Magicke, where by his paines at length came
to the most absolute perfection of all in Asia,he was
matched wyth a Lady of high parentage , by whome
he had two children,my sister Lindaraza and me, wee
were of young yeares when our mother dyed in labour
of ý third child,so ther remained none else but our father aliue,& louing to be solitarie came & dwelled in this
Iland,bringing w him my sister & those waiting women

U.iiij.   which

which you haue sæne, by his greate skill he buylded thys Castle, bære he lyued vntill my sister and I were of some discretion to guyde our selues. Hære he drewe many histories of thinges passed in the worlde, and among other the pictures of many valiant knightes which were thē on liue, with the rest you were so liuely drawen that it happening my sister to enter one day where ẙ Imagery was, by the sight of your picture she was surprised with your loue. Our father Palisteo knowing hirdisease deuised you should be brought by following your owne wife carried from you . For this cause was this enchauntment made in that quarter of the castle wherein you abode without making your selfe priuie to your owne estate, that if your knights came to sæke you they might not perswade you hence, neither could euer perswasion haue serued, onely force which this man hath vsed. When the wise man our father had done all this, he declared vnto vs the secretes of these thinges, and farther tolde vs by his Arte that the time should come when you should be deliuered from the enchauntment, although he knewe not when nor in what manner. He tolde vs that at such time as you should bé at large , my sister Lindaraza should dye, either for the griefe that she should conceiue, or for that the fates had so appointed. Moreouer that you shoulde haue a daughter by hir which might not hence depart till ther should come a knight which should winne the entries once againe, ẙ after marry hir. Of this knight he said that there should spring the race, whence issueth ẙ two noble families much spoken off throughout the world, the one house to be called Mongrana, ẙ other Claramonte, me he charged not to leaue the Castle till my næce Lindaraza should be acquited. After this, our father Palisteo bæing sore sicke dyed, since his death hitherto euery thing hath fallen out accordingly. And thus you haue heard the whole processe of my tale, and the cause why your daughter Lindaraza can not goe from hence at this time.

The

The Emperour and the the knight of the Sunne had very attentiuely lyſtened to all that which Flamides had ſpoken : and albeit the Emperour was deſirous to carry his daughter Lyndaraza with him, he could not yet refuſe to leaue hir when he coulde not otherwiſe chuſe, and he beſought Flamides that at ſuch time as they came both out that they ſhould take the way to Greece there to reioyce with him . After they had thus argued a little Flamides brought them through that part of the Caſtle which was not enchaunted ſhowing them manye thinges aſwell of halls of cloyſters, as of pictures and payntry whereat the Emperour and the Knight of the Sunne were greatly amaſed . And for that that day the Knight of the Sunne hadde not eaten , Flamides made them ſit in a faire parlour where they had plenty of daynty vyands:when they had eaten,the Emperour being deſirous to depart, deſired Flamides to conuey him through the gates . So (by the way) this péece of the ſtory as I haue hearde was afterward penned and portrayed in the court hall of the Emerours pallayce at Conſtantinople . But they wente through all the gates of the Caſtle and of the bridge tyll they came where the pillours ſtode. Ther Flamides toke his leaue of the Emperoure and of the Knighte of the Sunne .

When Flamides had departed from them , and they had paſſed through the bridges preſently the gates of the Towers clapt together with great noyſe, being as ſurely ſhutte as euer they were . The emperour and the knight of the Sunne were amaſed at the ſtraunge things which had happened in that Caſtle and toke the waye towards the Sea by the ſame path,in which they had come reioycing at the ſwéte harmonye which the birdes made in thoſe pleaſaunt trées,ſo that although they went a fóte, yet it ſéemed no payne vnto them. And the loue that they bare to each other was ſo great that it could not haue had bene more if they had knowen each other eſpeciallye the

U.b.   Em.

Emperour, who so often as he saw his face thought vppon the Princesse Briana whome he much resembled. In
this manner the father and the sonne trauayled running
ouer in their discourse straunge thinges of the enchaunted Castle, till that they approched the mayne sea wheras yet the lyttle boate stoode in which the Knighte of the
Sunne had come thether . Now for that along the shore
there were no more boats, the Emperour was somewhat
sorrowfull seeming to him that hee was ill furnished to
go whether he purposed, and telling it to the Knighte of
the Sunne . The knight of the Sunne aunswered. My
Lorde I pray you be not agrieued with this, for the boat
is guyded by a wise man a friende of mine, one as I belæue so carefull to carry me hence, as he hath friendelye
sent me to worke your delyueraunce. Besides, this boate
will holde vs both, and if it be so you will vouchsafe my
shippe you shall neuer sayle more safe neither better prouided for victualls . The Emperour was greatly amazed
at it that all things were so plentifull with the Knight of
the Sunne . But both very merry they entred into the
boat which being driuē from shore so soone as it tooke the
shore sayled amayne , neyther missed they oughte which
was the thought necessary. Quickly they hasted ouer the
Sea Euxinus where wee wyll leaue them vntill an o-
ther time, to write of other things which chaunced before
this time.

¶ The three Princes which went in the quest of Rosicleer, were transported into the Empire of Trabisond
where chaunced to them a faire aduenture. Cap. 45.

S the valyaunt dædes of Rosicleer while he was
there caused great ioy in the court of king Oliuerio : so no lesse was the grief ther for his sodeine
departure amongst his friendes, yet all these sor-
rowes ioyned in one might not be equall to that which
the

the faire Oliuia felt, foʒ ſhe ſeing ſhe had ben ẙ cauſe therⲟ
off , tⲱke thereat ſuch inwarde griefe thatſhe became
both weake and pale and hir father with the whole court
greatly lamented foʒ hir . In this generall ſoʒroⲱe foʒ
the loſſe of Roſicleer, you muſt thinke that the Pʒinceſ⸗
ſes Rodaſylua and Syluerina were not frœ, foʒ the loſſe
of Roſicleer pʒocured the abſence of their loues . So as
the hiſtoʒy recounteth that they tⲱo together with the va
lyant Pʒince Zoylo tⲱke vppon them the ſearch of him
and therefoʒe lette vs leaue the courte of kinge Oliue⸗
rio to tell you of them.

Thus it is, that after they were all embarked in the
hauen which was nœreſt to London they ſayled foʒ⸗
wards a months ſaylyng, not deſiring to bend either this
way oʒ that way . At the ende of the month rather vpon
chaunce then their purpoſe they were dʒyuen vppon the
coaſt of Trabiſond where yet glad they were when the
countrey was deſcryed to ſœ it and to abide there . Com⸗
ming to lande armed with their rich armour and theire
ẽquires accompanying them they tⲱke their hoʒſe and
riding thʒoughe a beaten pathe at the ſide of a pleaſaunt
wⲱde they heard a noyſe, wherat being moued they tour⸗
ned backe to ſœ what it might be.

Out of the thickeſt of the wⲱde they ſaⲱe a wylde
Boare dʒiuing ſo faſt as poſſibly it might,and in the pur⸗
ſuite thereoff , a young gentlewoman vppon a mightye
courſer and a Boare ſpeare in hir right hande , hir hun⸗
ters wœde was all of grœne veluet, hir treſſes hanging
doⲱne in colour lyke the golde of Araby,in hir left hand
a wande of golde and two rich Pearles hanging at hyʒ
eares . She came ſpurring hir hoʒſe in ſuch wiſe and
with ſuch courage to ouertake the Boare that ſhe much
delyghted them , and at ſuche time as the Boare croſſed
the way betwœne them and hir ſhe ſtrake the Boare on
the ſtancke, that hyʒ ſpeare appeared at the other ſide of
the Boare.

The

The game was gotte, and the Lady not taking héede of the other knights perhappes shadowed by the trées retourned with softe paces to hir company, but the knights ouertoke hir and as I may say abashed at that whiche they had séene, at hir graces and beautie, they only gased ene vppon the other not once making offer to salute hir, wherat the Lady more bolde then the men as it were to awake them out of their dreames toke and winded a faire horne which honge at hir necke so loude and shryll that all the forrest and valleyes rang thereoff, and when she had thus done she came to the thrée Princes in hir séeming the propresst knights that euer she set eye on, whom she friendly welcomed on this wise. God saue you gentle knights and sende you the comforte of your loues for by your sadde and demure lokes, it séemes you are either straungers or others thrall.

The knights tourning towardes hir made their courteous obeysaunce, and for them the valyaunt Tartarian spake in this manner. Madame we haue sode estonished neither for straungenesse, nor for ill successe in loue, with some of vs haue not yet tryed, but onely for the thought of your beautye being a Ladye huntresse as if you were Diana which in lyke attire was was wont to hunte the forrests : but as you say we are straungers indéede, and bicause wee woulde carrye somewhat worthe the tellyng wee craue youre name, and the fashions of the countrey.

The Lady delighted in the good behauiour of the thrée knights and tickeled with the wordes of the Tartarian, in great maiestye aunswered him. Assuredly sir knight I knowe no cause you haue to meruayle at me, but rather I at you. For if I séeme to you lyke to Diana the goddesse of the Gentiles, you lykewise séeme to me the thrée sonnes of Priamus : Hector, Paris and Troylus, not farre inferiour in renowne to the Gods themselues, whereas you desire me to make you knowe who I am, I will doe

it

it gladly but yet conditionally, that afterwardes you tell
me your name and countrey . This shall be one for
one, and by iust exchaunge wee shall hereafter finde
peace.

Wit you now that I am called Claridiana the daughter
to Theodoro Lord of this Empyre and to the Emprefse
Diana Quæne of the Amazones which two hauing bene
mortall enemyes as by long warres appeareth , continued hotly on either parte, they were after greate friendes
mæting in a pitched field either being then young and vn-
marryed . I am their onely childe which since my young
yeares haue bene brought vp in hunting and I am pro-
mifed to be made knight, for my mother being but young
achieued such enterpryfes that in hir time there was no
knight more famous, and I am defirous to be somewhat
lyke vnto hir especiallye in that poynte . And nowe fir
knights tel me who you are for I would wel accompany
fuch lufty knights.

The Tartarian who had first taken in hande to speak
aunfwered . Noble Princeffe we were fure inough that
there wanted not in you the diuinitye we fpake off: but
yet we fayled in the name, for fo many graces which accompany you could not be in a Lady of leffe eftate, as my
Relygion being Paganfiue woulde rather haue induced
mee to take you for the daughter of Iupiter , then of the
Emperour Theodoro. And now fith your excellency hath
fhewed vs fuch vndeferued fauour as to tell vs who you
are , it is reafon that we obaye in tellinge who wee are,
and where we were borne . This knight poynting to
Bargandel fayth he is the Prince Bargandel the kynges
fonne of Bohemia, this, by Liriamandro fayth he is the
Prince of Hungary called Liriamandro, and I am called
Zoylo fonne to the king of Tartary , we haue ioyned for
aduenture beginning in the great Britaine to finde a new
knighte a friende of ours taken from vs wee wotte not
howe . Him we are determined to looke in the worlde

and

and we haue already fayled a moneth since we left England, so this morning we landed heere very glad to haue founde your highnesse. God be praysed sayd the Princesse for the names of so high Princes oughte not to be concealed, especially heere where the Emperour my Father woulde be glad of such knights for the honour which his court shoulde receiue thereby, and I for my part would thinke it a great courtesie in you, if you would stay heere till I were knighted. for by such noble Princes might I be honoured. In the meane while, the courtesie which our court can afforde shalbe accomplished to the full, and after that you may tourne you to your purposed iourney. The Princesse had thus sayd, and strayght wayes there came from the forest thirtie gentlewomen on rych palfrayes, and in long weedes of greene taffeta, amonge them also a troupe of more then thirtie knights all surely armed with their speares in their handes comming to seeke the Princesse, which beinge better horsed then they had killed the Boare long before their approche. The Princes when she saw them said to the three Princes. My good Lords if you thought it not amisse, I would see what my knights woulde doe in my defence, Bargandel aunswered. Noble Lady the thing cannot displease vs which contēteth you, we will endanger our persons to serue you. The Princesse then called hir knightes, and sayde vnto them.

In good time my friends are you come. These three knightes whome you see heere would haue carryed me away against my wil, But I prayed them not to offer such wrong to a gentlewoman, and if they woulde therewith satisfie themselues, I offered them that of my knights so many, as they shoulde hurle downe or vnhorse, they shoulde haue so many of my gentlewomen for rewarde & themselues or any of them were ouerthrowen that then the party faulting shoulde forfette horse and harnesse. Heereto they haue agreed, now doe the best you can to defend the

gen-

gentlewomen which are in your company. Yeere the
Prince Zoylo which knew the Princesse meaning sayde
vnto hir. Nay madame let vs first know whether the gen
tlewomen will yeeld to our couenaunt or no, and let their
knights speak for them. Mary aunswered the knights we
are content. Yea but so are not we sayd the gentlewomē
shall we say they venture imprisonment vpon our knights
and they lose nothing, they may betray vs if they wyll,
but we feare rather that it will not be in theire power.
Ye mary aunswered the knights you are now wise: but
if you be so fearefull, we pray you alter the iustes to the
tryall of the sword, & you shall see presently these knights
both ashamed and vnhorsed.

Nay but yet quoth the gentlewomen we had néede of
better warrants then your wordes, but if you will deale
with our knights as we would haue you, you must wa-
ger your horse and armour to be giué them with vs if you
fayle, and hereto we request these knights straungers o-
therwise to discharge the Princesse of hir promise. The
thrée Princes sayned to mislyke the gentlewomans deuice, and the knightes of the countrey wer angrye to see
howe lyttle hope theire gentlewomen hadde in them.
So comminge vnto the thrée Princes, they sayde vnto
them.

Syr knights you may beholde héere that our gentlewomen are not content with the first match therefore we
will vnbind it and lose as much as you should therefore
take to your selues so much of the field as you shal thinke
good, and lette vs to the iust for we will decciue the women of the little hope they haue in our vertue. Thrée
of the knights at this Alarme prepared themselues to iust
and the thrée Princes did as much gladde to shew there
their manhood.

The thrée first knights were borne downe horse and
man to the great discomfitte of the Ladyes, whercoff one
mockt hir knight for his courage crying. Marry it seemes

sir knighte that I mighte haue beene safe betwéene your armes, when you knowe not how to sit sure within your saddle . Which wordes caused as great laughter in the Princesse, as shame and confusion to the knights which were on grounde.

Then came thrée other which doing as much as the other were in lyke manner welcomed. So that to make short tale from thrée to thrée the Princes vnhorsed whole thirtie, and no man offered a seconde course : but yet the shame of their falles so egged them on, that they demaunded the combat with the swordes . Heereat the knights which knew well inough the Princesse purpose made a great stay as it were to consult with their power being straungers and but thrée, in the ende saye they. You know that the price which was ordained at these iusts were your horse and armour the which you haue lost, if you will therefore needes vrge vs to the combatte with the swordes, lay away your horse and armour which are ours and come your wayes. Otherwise you must begge the vse of them at these gentlewomen to whome we surrender our whole title.

Mary sayde one of the gentlewomen . My Lordes we accepte of your courtesie, and heere we els staye the combat, for we will not giue them leaue the seconde tyme to lose both t' . . . ies and vs. The knights were so ashamed asw'. . . the Princes wordes as for the gentlewomans rebuke, that altogether with their swordes drawen they would haue rushed vpon the straungers, if the Princesse comminge betweene hadde not stayed them, speaking to the straungers . That this was sufficient, and it greatly lyked hir that they had thus shewed theire valour.

Where to Prince Zoylo aunswered . Madame wee haue besides to demaunde our prices which we will not otherwise remitte but to your selfe, wherat smiling they all vnbuckeled their helmets Bargandel and Liriamandro

dro bæing then of the age of rr.yeares,seeming so beautifull that as well the gentlewomen as the knights were
amazed at them. After them the Tartarian shewed himselfe,who although he was a Morian borne,& somewhat
of colour tawnie, yet had he a manly countenaunce,and
therwithall pleasant,that he pleased them as well as his
companions. With this there are no moe foes to be feared as it appeareth said the Princesse,if you challengers
vnarme your selues,but if it be no griefe to you let vs
go together to the citie of Trabisond not bæing farre off,
for at your instance I may p sooner receiue p order.The
Princes thancking the Lady for that fauour , prepared
themselues to obey hir commaund, so rid they on wyth
the Princesse towardes Trabisond where they stayed
about rv.dayes much encrealinge their honour at the
feastes proclaimed for the knighting of the enheritresse,
they bæing made known to none but to p princesse:hate
likewyse the great prowesse which the Princesse Claris-
diana shewed were suche that euery man was amazed at them.

Albeit the thrée Princes neuer iusted against hir,but
hæreafter you shall heare sufficiently of hir and them,
now to the two Princes Brandizel and Clauergudo
whome we left in the kingdome of Persia very sadde
for the losse of their dære friende the worthy knyght of
the Sunne.

¶The two Princes Brandizel and Clauergudo stale secretly out of the kingedome of Persia,to finde the knight of the
Sunne.　　　　　Cap.46.

NOwe you are to remember your selues of the two
valiant Princes Brandizel & Clauergudo which remained in p kingdome of Persia very pensiue for p losse
of their friend,touching whom the history saith that after

　　　　　　　　X.　　　　　　　these

these two princes wer in Persia some daies hauing great
desire to finde out the knight of ỹ Sun ⁊ to seeke straunge
aduentures:one day as they were with Armineo vnckle
to Clauergudo,they determined betwene themselues for
to depart closely frō them,⁊ to go by sea whethersoeuer
fortune would transport them,wherto although Clauergudo ⁊ Armineo would haue made the king Florion priuie,yet the Prince Brandizel would in no case consēt,be-
leuing ỹ if his parents knewe of it they would not giue
him leaue to go from them,so to pleasure him they kept
that counsell as priuie as they could.And when al things
wer in readines,one night secretly they coūaied thēselues
out of ỹ citie ⁊ so straight to ỹ sea side where they entered
into a ship prouided for that purpose,⁊ hoising vp sailes
they were carried,they neither knew nor cared whether,
for the courages of these two princes resolued to ỹ search
of worthy aduentures would not let them be quiet,so ỹ
any thing might better content their ease at home. But
as soone as they were gone the wise Lyrgandeo knew of
it,and waying the great commoditie which might ensue
thereoff to themselues ⁊ others, he would not hinder it,
nor it make as if he knew it,yet had he gret care to guide
their ship wherein they sailed,⁊ they reached thether in.xv
dayes which to other is an ordinary monethes sayling.
That the marriners were abashed to see the swiftnesse of
the shyp being more then vsuall, which when they had
discouered to their Lordes,the Princes knewe presently
by whose meanes it so happened , wherefore yet they
were the better apayed for nowe they were sure thether
to be carried which fitted best for their auayle . Well,
shortly after these princes departur,⁊ before it was either
so noised or suspected,Lyrgandeo declared ỹ truth to the
king Florion ⁊ the Queene Balisea willing them withall
not to afflict thē for ỹ they thereby should gaine much honour ⁊ should retourne safely with the knight of ỹ Sun in
their company. With this ỹ king ⁊ Queene were indifferently

rently appeafed. Now all matters quieted in Perfia fo2 ẏ
p2inces abfence, we may the fraelier beare ẏ knights company which are yet failing on the fea, fo ẏ the rv. day after
they were departed from Perfia, they landed in a haue of
Polonia where their ſhip ſtœd ſtil, ẝ taking land to learne
fome newes ẝ know the country ere they had long trauailed they faw befo2e them a little towne to their iudgemẽt
pleafant, ẝ round about great flocks of men ẝ women ſcat-
tered, ẝ making great cries as if fome great mifchance had
happened to them. Armineo demaunded of them the caufe
of their fo2row, whereto an auncient man amonge them
anfwered, ẏ a fierce gyant wt mo2e thẽ fiftie knights had
come in this mo2ning bpon thẽ to ſteale away ẏ p2inceſſe
Clarinea daughter to the king of Polonia their liege lo2d,
ẏ he had killed the greater number, ẝ fpoiled the refidue.
And as he thought was ere this time on his way with ẏ
p2inceſſe in his carriage, from whom if it fo be not all the
wo2ld may recouer hir: why fo faid Armineo ẝ where is ẏ
king, o2 where are his knights ẏ they do not defend their
lady. The olde man anfwered, they are in a town iiij. mile
off, not mindeful of any fuch matter ẝ it hath not ben paſt
biij. daies fince ẏ p2inceſſe came to this towne, ẝ now this
which you haue heard hath happened to hir: when ẏ th2ee
knights heard this of ẏ olde mans relation, wout ſtaying
longer they galloped to their ho2ſes fo faſt as they might,
ẝ comming neere to ẏ towne they faw iſſuing out of the
gates a great troup of knights, ẏ one part d2iuing ẏ other
befo2e it. Fo2 fo it was ẏ the gyant hauing the p2inceſſe
in his power was carying hir away ẝ ẏ townfmen fought
with him, but their power little p2euailed, the gyant was
ſtrong, his knights many, ẝ fo they murdered al ẏ came,
in fuch fo2t ẏ the town dwellers fled: then came ẏ other
knightes which flew many of them. Twenty of the gyants knights at once fell bpon them laying at them w al
their fo2ces, ẏ meane while ẏ the gyant held in his arma
ẏ p2inceſſe Clarinea, ẝ thinking ẏ his knights wold make

X.ij.   rue

riddaunce of thefe thꝛꝏ,he tꝏke no moꝛe kꝟpe but rodꝺ
away foftly with the pꝛinceffe. The pꝛinceffe cried out fo
loud ꝙ it was great pitie to heare hir,ꝸ thofe which heard
hir of hir own knights,came pitifully crying to ꝑ knights
ftraungers ꝙ foꝛ the honour of god they ſhould go help hir.
When this was fpoke,Brandizel befought his compani-
ens to ſtay ther in ꝑ battail,ꝸ to giue him leue to follow ꝑ
gyant.which whꝫ they graunted him,he putting the fpurs
to his hoꝛfe followed the ſrace, the whiles the knights of
Fraunce thꝛoughly galded their enimies. Foꝛ ꝑ one of thꝫ
matchable J dare anouch with ꝑ auncient Franconio the
Troyans fonne,of whom he defcended:foꝛ he putting himfelfe in pꝛeafe among them,to fome claue their heads,to
other fome their ſhꝏlds murdering many ꝸ felling many,
ꝑ at length there was none fo hardy which durſt ſtand
him a blow,but euery of thꝫ did his beſt to faue one.His
vnckle Armineo in ꝑ bꝛoile helped not a little,foꝛ he was
a valiant knight ꝸ much eſtꝫmed off in Fraunce'. But let
vs leaue them ꝸ fpeake of the pꝛince Brandizel who pur-
fued the Gyant. He rode fo faſt that ere the gyant came
within a flight ſhot of ꝑ fea,he ouertoke in a large plaine ꝸ
crying aloud bad him redeliuer ꝑ pꝛinces falfe faytour as
he was.The gyant loked back to fe what he was,ꝸ fꝏing
but one though riding in haſt he cared not foꝛ him,faue ꝑ
not to be foꝺ vnpꝛouided,he lofꝺ ꝑ pꝛinces fro betwꝏne
his arms ꝸ fet hir on grouꝺ:ꝑ pꝛince comuing to him fpake
neuer a woꝛd,but dꝛawing his fwoꝛd hit him fo great a
blow vpon ꝑ helmet ꝑ he made him bꝏwe his head to his
bꝛeſt,wherwith ꝑ gyant encreafed in choller ꝸ gaue him ꝑ
like:this begā ꝑ fkirmiſb betwꝏn thꝫ.wherin ꝑ noife was
fo great ꝑ ꝑ pꝛinceſſe Clarinea befoꝛe in a found returned
to hir felfe,ꝸ fꝏing ꝑ battaile with fo little hope as ꝑ one
onely knight ſhould aduenture hir deliuerance.fell into a
found again,wherin ſhe had dyed foꝛ foꝛrow had not god
pꝛouided hir ꝑ means ſhe loked not foꝛ,ꝸ the ccmfoꝛt ſhe
hoped not:ꝸ ſhe was ꝑ reſt of ꝑ battaile a ioyful beholder.

When

When they had thus fought an houre, it was a wōder to see
their bruised armour wt their hacked shieldes, but euer ȳ
steele coate defended the biting of their swoordes, especially Brandizels, which made by Art Magicke had this vertue that no mettalle might pearce it . The Gyant was
hurt in many places, whereat as at the force of his aduersary he was greatly estonished & blasphemed his gods
in desperate manner which had made him stay that good
knightes comming. The Princesse Clarinea seeinge the
Gyantes bloud thus couer the ground, was very glad &
hir colour became fresh which much encreased hir beautie
whereto also (Fortune willinge to be fauourable) it was
so that the Prince Brandizel beholding hir was enamored of hir beautie and entierly loued hir . For his heart
nowe set on fire augmented his courage, and he buffeted
ȳ Gyant, so that in short time he vnarmed hym in many
places. In the ende the Prince desirous to gyue end to ȳ
battaile, raysed in his styroppes, stroke a full blowe at
the Gyant vpon the shoulder that his swoorde entered a
handfull and the gyant fell dead. The Prince seeinge
him fall, presently leaped from his horse and pulling off
his helmet went to the Princesse to recōfort hir, sayinge.
Madame I besœch you accept in good part this little seruice at his handes which desireth to do you much more.
The Princesse very ioyfull to sée hir enemy on ground, &
more glad to sée hir friend so goodly a man, courteously answered. Noble knight you haue done so much for me that
wt al ȳ which my father hath, I shal not be able to requite
it you, but if you wil ȳ this good which you haue done me
do like me in déd, shew me so much fauour as to cary me
to ȳ king my father, for hither wil come ȳ residue of ȳ gyants knights, & thē my liberty is to begin again: ȳ prince
gently taking both hir handes in his, kissed them & said vnto hir. Madame if it please you we may retourne to the
towne frō whence we came, for I beléue ȳ these knights
of whō you speak, are but few aliue to put vs in danger,

I left my companions fighting with thē, who I am sure haue done their parts, and yet they shall do vs no wrong though they be many. But in far greater ieopardy am I of my life by you, if you vouchsafe me not your seruice, wherwith ý princesse was nothing offended to: she liked very wel his comely personage, but she answered nothing. The prince seing ý princesse without a palfray toke hir vp behinde him I with easy paces rid towards ý towne. In which way ý prince with many amorcus woords feasted the princesse I manifested to hir his loue, I after disclosing himselfe also he besæched hir to kæpe it secret, which she did, resoluing notwithstanding if hir father were so content, not to match otherwise. Well, nære ý towne they came where they sawe a great troupe of knights hasting so fast as they might, I in dæd they were the king I his knights, more then 500.in number, who by the report excited to succour their princesse came to the towne, I finding almost all the gyants knights taken or slaine by ý prince Clauergudo and Armineo with such ayde as the towne afforded they altogether follow on in the pursute of ý gyant which had led hir away. Now there were of ý comcompany which a farre off ascried the Princesse behinde Brandizel, I learning that it was the knight which rode to follow the gyant, they tolde it to the king, whereat he was very glad, and making much of the thræ straungers, especially of Brandizel, he spake on this wise. Sir knight how shall I be able to requite this friendship which you and your companions haue shewed to me. Assuredly I knowe not though I should giue you my kingdeme, for were it not for you I shoulde haue lost this day my daughter Clarinea, and with hir my ioye and pleasure which being lost what ioy should I haue found in ruling, but tell me I pray you how you dealt with ý Gyaunt for he was stronge and great. Sir sayth Brandizel offering to kisse his handes which the kinge gently refused.

Sir

Sir saith he, mightie Prince my companions & I thinke
our Fortune to be very good in that we are thether ar-
ued where we may doe seruice to so courteous a Prince,
and it is reward sufficient your acceptation. As touching the Gyant his ill purpose was his owne decay, for
he is already dead, not farre from hence. The king wen-
dered to heare tell that the Gyant was dead, for by the report of his bignesse he thought it impossible that one onely knight should coape with him, and then much more
making of the Princes, he imbraced them often times, &
desired them to tell him their names which at length they
did. And the king vnderstanding of their byrthes carried
them with himselfe towardes the towne where in the
way he tolde them who that gyant was, and what the
cause was why he had come thether in such sort, saying.
My lords this gyant was called Lamberdo, Lorde of the
Iland of Perda, not farre hence he hath since the time he
was first knighted neuer employed his time to other aduauntage but to robbing & spoyling and for this he hath
an Iland excæding strong, but very little and scarce well
peopled. In this he may defend him from any enimy, &
bestowing his espies in euery corner to watch for some
such cheuisance, he knewe that my daughter Clarinea
was in this towne with a fewe knightes, so hither hæ
made a voyage and had stolen hir away, but that God be
blessed, such valyaunt knightes as you came in suche
a time for hir succour, while the king tolde this tale they
were within the towne wals, & as they entered through
the streets, the whole towne gathered together to sæ the
Prince which had slayne Lambardo. And then through
the towne they came to the kings pallaice where they a-
bode a great while.

¶ Rosicleer departeth from the Iland of Cadramarte
and meeteth with certeine aduenturers on the Sea.
Cap. 47.

X.iiij.   The

He historie left þ valiant Roſicleer very ſad in þ Iland of Candramarte as well foꝛ hys ladies letter, as foꝛ that the knight of the Sunne departed from him ſo ſooꝺynly that he coulꝺ not knowe hym. Foꝛ remembꝛing himſelfe of the woꝛꝺes which the wiſe Artemidoro haꝺ tolꝺe him as concerninge his bꝛother, his minꝺe gaue him that it might be h̄, wherefoꝛe as without hope euer to ſee him, anꝺ not hauing to comfoꝛt his afflicteꝺ ſpirites, he burſt out into teares, ſayinge. O Foꝛtune howe haſt thou bene froward to me aboue all men. Firſt befoꝛe I was boꝛne I loſt my Father, anꝺ when I was boꝛne my Mother was in ſoꝛrowe anꝺ care foꝛ me, anꝺ ſcarcely began I to know the woꝛlꝺ when I was banniſheꝺ from hir whom I loueꝺ ꝺærer then my ſelfe. Anꝺ nowe by chaunce haue I bene bꝛought to the company of a noble knight with whome I might haue bene moꝛe frienꝺly acquainteꝺ, but the waues roſe vp a-gainſt mǽ, anꝺ haue carrieꝺ him awaye from me as if I were vnwoꝛthy of any goꝺ. When he haꝺ wept his fill he went to one of the Caſtles, there to ſet ſuch things in oꝛꝺer as were ꝺiſquieteꝺ by the ꝺeath of their Loꝛꝺ, anꝺ to comfoꝛt the wofull Gyanteſſe, whom he after matcheꝺ with one of þ beſt knights of all thoſe whom the gyant haꝺ left, giuing them liuerie & ſeaſon in that lanꝺ, & making others to ſweare obeꝺience. Shoꝛt time after hée woulꝺ nǽdes ꝺepart with full purpoſe to kǽpe in the ſea anꝺ not to ꝺepart till that he ſhoulꝺ haue ſayleꝺ ſo farre that no woꝛꝺes might be hearꝺ of him in thoſe quarters. Wherefoꝛe he tooke hys armour, wherein was ꝺꝛawen the God of loue, in ſuch ſoꝛt as our aunceſtoꝛs were wont to paynt him, with his eyes out, his bowe anꝺ arrowes in his hanꝺ: The picture bǽing ſo liuely ꝺꝛawen þ Roſi-cleer knewe it was ꝺone by the wiſe Artemidoro, anꝺ therevpon he tooke his name of that ꝺeuiſe, from whiche time he neuer calleꝺ himſelfe other then the knight of Cupid, vnꝺer which name he achiueꝺ many enterpꝛiſes,

and

and Roficleers name came neuer moze to the eares of Oliuia.

Hauing put on his armour he tooke his leaue of Candriana foz fo was called the daughter of Candramarte and foz remembzaunce onely the fhippe wherein he firfte fayled when he left great Britayne, with two marriners to conduct it, whom he charged not to call by other name then the knight of Cupide, and to guyde the fhippe Eaftwarde. When he had fo fayled fiftæne dayes without chauncing to him any thing wozthy of recytall. It was fo that one mozning by Sunne rifing he faw a little boat paffe by him, out of which he hearde many cryes as if it had bene the laboure of fome woman, and thincking that there might be næde of helpe, he was defirous to knowe what was in the fhippe, and therevpon he commaunted to ioyne with them.

Pzefently there ftept vppon the hatches a fadde auncient man with a white bearde all armed faue the heade which demaunded what he would. Roficleer fayde I woulde knowe who is in your fhippe foz mee thinckes I haue hearde fome woman complayne, and if it bee fo I will venture my perfon to doe hir good. The auncient knight beheld Roficleer, and taking him to be fome knight of great bountie, efpecially in that he had offered himfelfe fo fræly. When he had thzoughly beheloe, he opened the matter on this fozt. Affuredly good knighte I thancke you foz your great good wil and it is not mifbefæming youre outwarde beautye to haue fome inwarde vertue lyke thereto.

But knowe you that in this fhippe there abydeth a gentlewoman making towardes the great Britayne ther to complayne hir to the king Oliuerio & his knightes, of þ outrage which is done vnto hir. Now bicaufe our ftay is daungerous, I may not tel you farther of this matter, our enemyes followe vs, and fo refte you with G & D. When the olde man had fayde this, Roficeer hauinge

X.b.   defire

desire to knowe more stayed him and besought him to discourse more at large, for himselfe was a knighte of that court and could tell him what remedye was to be hoped for there. The olde man was loth to stay longer, yet hearing him say that he was of the same court he tolde hym in fewe wordes that this gentlewoman was the Princesse Arguirosa one of the sayrest Ladyes in the worlde, and a Princesse of Thessaly, only heire to that kingdome. That hir mother being dead, the king Arguidoro hir father fell in loue with a gentlewoman of Thessaly, not so honest nor of so high estate, as wanton and of base birth: and louing hir affectionately, after marryed hir, to the dispossessing of his owne childe. Then in the time of hir fathers lyfe ther was in the court a knight called Rolando, besides his great liuing one of y strongest knights in all those parties, but proude, and little respecting the whole worlde. That this knight during the lyfe of the king was lyked of Ipesea, and so sone as the kinge Arguidoro dyed of a soddayne disease, was promoted to the kings bedde by matching with the Quéene, and being of greate reuenues that he nowe enioyed the kingedome by fayes, and excluding the right heire, none of the kingdome daring to gaynesay him, for the most able are his nigh kinsmen, the other learne patience perforce. But that which worst of all was, that to vndoe hir rightfull claime hee mindeth to marrye hir with a kinsman of his and to giue onely some lyttle towne to dwell in in, reseruinge the title of the kingdome after his owne dayes to a sonne the which hee hath begotten on his Quéene Ipesea.

I am kinsmã saith he to the Princes being hir mothers brother, and therefore I haue aduentured to relieue my néece, but not knowing any remedy at home bicause my power is not equall with Rolandos, I haue broughte hir out from thence, and I determine to goe to the great Britaine, where as I haue heard arethere many valyaunt

knights

knights especially a new knight,of whom I haue hearde e-
specially since the great feasts therholden. If this knight
helpe me not,I knowe not who may withstand Rolando.
Three nights and dayes haue we bene vppon the Sea:
onely I,the Lady,two gentlewomen,and our marriners,
and I beleue that ther come after vs Rolandos knights.
Nowe haue I tolde you the whole of your desire, and I
besæch you tell vs, what newes you knowe of that good
knight.

Rosicleer nowe hauing hearde the whole state of the
Princes Arguirosas matter was much troubled,and desirous to helpe hir he aunswered the auncient man , that
for his stape he thancked him , and as touching your demaunde sayth he of the newe knight . Truth it is that
in Britayne none can tell you newes of him , wherefore
your labour shoulde be lost if you sought him there. But
the Princesses affliction so much moueth me, that albeit
I was purposed otherwhere, yet woulde I gladly fighte
with Rolando in the Princesse behalfe.

The auncient knight was very sad to heare that the
newe knighte was not in Britayne , but well eying this
knight which had so tolde him and made proffer of helpe,
he stoode in doubt whether to take or refuse, by and by he
discouered two shippes vnder sayle, and by theire toppes
to be of Thessaly, whereat striking himselfe on the brest
he cryed out, O most vnhappy that we are, here commeth Rolandos knights which will take vs, and being
brought agayne to Thessaly we shall there receiue most
cruel death,& he wept cursing the houre of his departure,
the Princesse Arguirosa hearing the complaynts which
hir vncle made, his great sorrowe which hee sustayned,
the extreame daunger they were in, and the cause why
he did it, tooke it as heauily, and wofully bewaylel their
miserp.

When Rosicleer sawe them in this plyghte, he much
pitied them, especially Arguirosa , which the Prince sse

Oluia

Oliuia not remembred mighte haue well contented him. Therefore he willed them to gette vnder the hatches agayne, and to lette him shifte for their safetie, the olde man thinking that Rosicleer would defende them by saying that they were his people, did so, not ceasing yet to feare the worst and to pray earn.stly for their escape. Rosicleer lept into the Princesse shippe, and sate vppon the bannue thereof to see what would happen, till that the other ship came nere, and that he which was the Captayn comm.unded to grappell, and espyinge Rosicleer with a proude voyce badde him say both who himselfe was, and what people he had in his shippe, and not to faile in anye poynt. Whe;to Rosicleer by and by aunswered. I am a straunger in these parts, and farther it is no reason that you know who they are that are with mee, for we keepe our way without molesting thee or thine. The Captaine angry for his short speach sayd to him. I will strike thy heade into the water vnlesse thou aunswer me directly to my question, and so sayng he halde and pulde Rosicleer to haue forced him. Rosicleer thus rudely entreated rose vp, and with his gauntlette gaue the Captayne such a blow vppon the helmette, that his braynes flewe aboute his heade, and presentlye hee fell into the water, where the weight of his armour kepte him downe. Strayghtwaies more then twentie knightes well armed and well angred for y death of their Captain altogether with their swords in their hads smote at him. Rosicleer drawing out Queene Iulias blade, stroke agayne with such courage that at three blowes three knights were slayne, and those which presently knewe his great prowesse drew backe, making no great hast to come nere hun. Rosicleer knowing his enemyes feare leaped into their ship and there layd so about hun that in short space he killed halfe of them. The Princesse Arguirosa and the auncient knight now began to shew themselues aboue boorde and they greatly wendred at his manhood.

So shortly after Roſicleer was alone in his enemyes
ſhippe without reſiſtaunce, eyther all being ſlayne, or all
ſlayne or wounded, or ſlayne, wounded, or by flyght eſ
ſcaped: for Roſicleers owne ſhippe was loſt in this gar
boyle. Now retourned he to Arguiroſas ſhippe wher
in ſhe with the olde man receyued him, Roſicleers ſaluta
cion to the Princeſſe after this exployt was in this wiſe.
Madame what hath bene done your ſelfe hath ſæne, but
for a recompence hereoff, I ſhall thinke my ſelfe through
ly ſatiſfied if you will venture that into my hands, which
you dare hazarde into the hands of the newe knight. For
I promiſe you, I will as willingly ieopard my perſon as
he ſhall. Now when Roſicleer had ſo ſayd the Princes
and ý olde man ſtaied a good while without ſpeking word
for the conſideration of their owne daunger, paſt recoue
ry if this man ſayled, made them the more wary, and ſo
betwæne the examination of Rolandos valour and Roſi
cleers hardineſſe. In the ende Arguiroſa hir ſelfe rather
uppon loue towardes him, then of aſſured confidence
woulde put hir matter to no other tryall then Roſicleers,
ſo ſhe commended hir quarrell to him on this ſort. The
courteſie valyaunt knighte, which you haue offered mee
thoughe unworthy, hath bene ſo greate that I wante the
boldeneſſe to accepte more, yet bicauſe you carſt defended
me from death by the vanquiſhing of Rolandos knights,
and now againe you will nædes take uppon you a further
matter, rather not to refuſe you, then willyng to trouble
you agayne, I will retourne with you to my countrey,
and committe wholy to your handes the whole ordering
both of my ſelfe and my cauſe: hir vnckle gaue his con
ſent thereto, and Roſicleer thanked them much. So they
ſayled to Theſſalya, where by the way Roſicleer caſting
in his thought how to redres ý Princ· wrong, to ý leaſt
diſpleaſure of hir and hir vnckle which were lothe to bee
knowen, determined as a ſtraunger to enter the land and
to demaunde iuſtice as it were agaynſt a perſon not kno
wen

wen. To which deuice after he had made them priuie, and promised that they should not be disclosed till it so serued for their auayle, they were better comforted, and sailed with so good winde that they tooke landing in a hauen neare the place where the king was, taking lande he made the Princesse to put on a muffler, & the olde knight to couer his heade, besides bidding both to counterfayte for the tyme some straunge behauiour either in holdyng downe theire heades or in disguysing their attyre. To either of them he gaue their horse, and himselfe mounted vppon a courser the best of all Candramartes stable. In the coole of the euening they tooke their waye to the neerest Citie, where then were many knightes and Ladyes comming out of the Citie to disporte them in the shadowe. Rosicleer being of a comly personage and so lustely mounted praunced forth to be seene, and was well lyked off and praysed amongst them all. As they followed on their iourney toward the gates of the Citie, the king at ý time came out accōpanyed with his nobilitye to solace himselfe in the fielde as at other times before hee was accustomed. The king rode vpon a mightie horse, with trappings and harnesse most of beaten golde, hys horse being so braue and himselfe so fierce and sterne to looke to that it would haue daunted a right good knighte to haue but spoke to him. So soone as the Princesse, and hir vnckle saw him, they counterfayted the best that they could, and for feare their blood sonke down into their bellies. The valyant Greeke knowing that this was Rolando whome he sought for, as nothing afrayd of his terrible lookes, but rather glad to haue met with him so conueniently, & in the company of so many knights, willed the Princesse & the knight to follow him. So come they al in before the king, Rosicleer speaking to him & saying. Mightie king in iustice stay thy horse to heare a poore Ladyes complaynt, & to right the greatest wrong that euer was offered to a gentlewomā. Why she complaineth to thee, is

for

for that thou art the king and shouldst aboue all men re-
pute the wrong doer, (so further discouering of the kings
ducty.) Now the while Roficleer spake thus, Rolando
beheide him very well, lyking both his courage and personage, and albeit of his owne nature he neither feared
God nor kept iuſtice in things which perteyned to hymselfe, yet hearing in Roficleers discourſe, himſelfe to bee
made on now and then as of a ryghte Iudge, and that he
woulde not conſent that other then iuſtice ſhoulo be executed in his kingdome, he was tickeled therwith, and
badde Roficleer tell on, for hee woulde heare his matter
willyngly . Roficleer ſtrayning his voyce, that what
hee ſayde might be hearde and noyſed abroade , ſpake as
followeth.

Knowe you mightie king that the father of thys gentlewoman was Lorde of great poſſeſſions, which marrying with an honourable woman begatte on hir this Lady. Few yeare after his wife deceaſing, this Lord marryed alſo an other woman, by whom, he had no childe, after
th..t the Lorde himſelfe dyed alſo , the ſtepdame remayning on lyue, and ſhortely marrying with an other man
whome in hir huſbands dayes ſhe had a lyking to. This
man ſir king matching with the mother in lawe hath diſ-
poſſeſſed the true heire of hir lawfull enheritaunce, inſo-
much to, as being ſo diſſeyſed ſhee hath in no wiſe bene
conſidered off as ſuch a mans daughter. Nowe ſeaking
hir redreſſe abroade , it was my chaunce to mæete wyth
hir, to whome after ſhee had declared hir caſe , I made
offer for to fighte for hir with anye which impugned
hir right . Theſe are therefore to require thee O kinge
ſo to tender hir ſuite in the honour of iuſtice, either that
ſhe may lawfully enioye hir owne , or that you autho-
riſe the lyſtes, that the conquerour may enter by a lawfull meane.

So Roficleer ended, expectinge the kynges aunſwere,
who neither warily nor aduiſedly waying and vnderſtanding

ding the drifte and purpose of this parable aunswered.
Sir knight thy demaunde is iust, and the knighte which
hath done this wronge cannot chuse but take the one of
the two, therefore tell me who thou art and I will send
for him to aunswere thy challenge. Be it as the kinge
hath spoken it sayde Rosicleer. And know for truth that
the knight which hath done this iniurye is thy selfe : the
gentlewoman which receiued it is the Princesse Arguiro=
la which here standeth by me the lawfull enheriteur as
thy selfe knoweth of this kingedome : thou without iuste
title hast intruded vppon it : therefore doe that which thy
mouth hath witnessed to be iust . When Rosicleer had
sayd, Rolando much amased at his greate presumption,
and not beinge able to bridle his choller aunswered de=
spitefully.

Thou foolish & vnhappy knight, how hath so great mad=
nes entred into thee, as to appeare before me with such a
demaunde, that were it not for the sentence which I haue
giuen, I would ere this haue abated thy pryde : but I
will not keepe long from thee the rod of due correction, I
am content to take the battayle, and with the condicions
which thou hast named harde enough I warrant thee for
thy selfe and that woman whome I will so cage vp that
she shall no more seeke such knights as thou art. When
the kinge had thus sayde hee wente on his waye, and all
those which hearde the demaund of Rosicleer were much
abashed at his boldnesse, for though he was bigge yet see=
med he nothing so stronge as to resist Rolando, presently
it was publyshed throughout the whole citie , and the
battayle was appoynted to be on the morrow, where you
shoulde haue seene most parte of the towne praye to God
for the ryght of their naturall Queene , many scaffoldes
were erected to see the lysts.

The auncient knight vnckle to the Princes was cal=
led Alberto , and he had a nepheive a strong and lustye
knighte , dwellyng a mile from the Cittie in a Castell of
his

his owne , whence he seldome departed for feare of the
king . Whether dyd the vnckle of the Princesse for
that night carry them,where they were receiued gladly &
toke their rest.

¶ The battaile which Roficleer had with Rolando.
	Cap.48.

ROlando made no account that night of the battayle
which he was to fight the next day , for he thought
no harme could happen him though there had bene ten
more such knightes as his aduerfary was . The days
bœing come he arose and armed himfelfe,where enqui-
ring whether the knight his aduerfary were in fielde or
no,it was tolde him,yea, wherefore he made the more
haft,and comming to the liftes with a troupe of armed
knightes, for his more honour he defied the knight of
Cupid,for fo was Roficleer then called of y̆ deuice which
he bare : the kinges woordes were to this effect. Tell me
now foolish knight,doeft thou not repent thy yesterdayes
challenge,wouldeft thou not giue much not to bœ hœre
nowe : whereto Roficleer. No,affuredly I repent mœ
not,for if thou vanquifh me I looke for naught but death,
which I fet fo light by as in fo right a quarrell,I would
not venture my life xx.times,but thou oughteft rather to
repent thy felfe,and to haue remorfe of thy ill dealinge.
Rolando heard him fay fo & began to laugh aloude . Art
thou (fayth he)become a Philofopher : who wantinge
ftrength of armes to purchafe honour , when they lye
ftriking themfelues on theyr couches can talke gallantly,which they account for as great a glory. Thou trufts
more I percevue in thy tongue philofophy then in chiual-
ry or manhœode,and yet to be fpoken off after thy iuft
punifhment,thou wilt dye forfooth in defence of iuftice.
But if death in fuch a quarel be fo acceptable,prepare thy
felfe for it,for thou fhalt ftay no longer then y̆ proofe of my

	P.	fpeare.

speare. So saying Rolando, tourned the raines of his horse to take the carryer. The meane whyle that the Iudges were placed on their bench, and that the Quæne wyth hir Ladyes had taken the windowes to beholde the battaile. The Prnncesse Arguirosa sat vpon hir palfray all heauy, and onely accompanyed with Alberto, for none els turst make any coūtenaunce of wel meaning towardes hir for feare of ý king: but to our matter, these two knights putting their spurs to their horses wt their speares in their restes, ran together, & with their force the earth shooke & their spears burst in sunder. The king in ý most of ý carryer being borne vpō his croupper, & Rosicleer not moued at all, saue that his horse peautrels burst with the rushing, and both knightes lighted downe, where began a fierce battaile on foote, eyther laying at other so thick that their shoeldes were burst in pæces, and themselues so weryed that either followed the other staggering and not certeyne of his gate. The beholders of the battayle were much amazed at Rosicleer, and at the daunger wherein he put the king, but if any meruayled, much more did Rolando which both felt it & could iudge what terrible shakes he had borne both on horse and foote, & he thought in himselfe neuer to haue met with like knight one or other, man or Gyant: Euer Rosicleers nimblenesse helped him much, for he could steppe easily aside and escape the blowe. but Rolando found a want of his horse for he was so heauy that he could not auoide one blowe. At length starke tyred, his bones akeing for very paine of trauaile, he would haue taken breath, but fearing to make hys aduersary priuie thereto, he forced himselfe quickly to kill or be killed, and heaping his blowes vppon Rosicleer, he so galde him that the lookers on mistrusted Rosicleers partie. But would he or not (Rosicleer enduring the vttermost,) Rolando was faine to gyue ouer, whereat Rosicleer though not hauing so much næde, yet not to take so foule on did the like.

They

They two leaning their breastes vpon the pommelles of
their swordes behelde each other a longe whyle, where
Rolando thincking it not best so to ende the matter, but
to take it vp some other way, spake to Rosicleer, saying.
I had not thought knight that so muche courage had
bene in thee, and yet ere the ende it will little further
thee agaynst mee, but for that I am gyuen to loue and
like of such knights as thou art I will vse clemency towardes thee, which I neuer determined to doe towardes
one which hath so much offended mee. This it is, I
will that thou leaue of the battaile which thou hast in
hande, for the Princesse Arguirola, and from thenceforth
that thou abide in my court where I will dee thee that
honour which thy person meriteth, & I will bestowe a liuing vpon thee wherewith thou shalt lyue contentedly.
Rosicleer heere well perceyuing what he went about,
sayd vnto him. I would willingly Rolando that as thou
hast in shewe offered me great honour, for the which I
thancke thee, so that thou wouldest in deede performe an
other thing which should be lesse empayre to my present
honour then the leauing of the battaile: the battaile as thou
sayest would I gladly end, not onely for mine owne danger which I am like to be in, but for thy sake whome I
rather wish to amend his fault by liuing and restoring the
Lady to hir owne, then by dying in a wrong cause to hazard the vtter perdition of thy soule. And for truth take
this that I will chose to die rather then to suffer hir cause
to be lost by my collusion. Take therefore some other
meanes to leaue this battaile, for this will not succede, or
let vs fight it out for I hope in God that he wyll defend
the innocent. When Rosicleer had sayde this, Rolando
thincking that his owne gentle speach had made his enimy more bold, became mad outright, and forgetting hys
wearinesse tooke his sworde with both his handes, and
therewith he strake Rosicleer so hard on the headpeece, y
he made bowe both handes and knees vnto the ground.

The

The blow being so heauy as if a tower had fallen vpon him. Rosicleer rising vp acquited it him, that he made him stagger fiue or sire paces backward. And betwæne them the combat was renued. Now this especially refreshed the poore Princesse Arguirosa, that hir knight troubled hir enimy moze now then at the beginning. And not long after it was apparaunt that Rosicleer had the better, for Rolando began to be wery, and coulde not moue out of his place. Rosicleer knowing the auadntage, and willing to ende the battaile the sooner both for the contentment of the Princesse and the safetie of Rolandos life, whome he iudged to be a valiaunt knight, offered agayne the conditions before mentioned. But it was not Rolandos good hap, and true it is that those which liue so wickedly, dye commonly as desperatly least they should repente their faultes and finde mercy: But Rolando moze then madde at the courtesie which was offered hym, woulde beare naught but stroke at Rosicleer with all hys force, Rosicleer stept aside and the swozd fell vpon the ground stickynge vp to the hyltes. The whiles that Rolando haled at his swozd Rosicleer discharged his blowe with great strength and cut the necke in sunder from the body. Wherewithall the whole multitude showted, but in diuers tunes some for sozrowe of the Tyzants death, but most crying. Liue thou Arguirosa our Quæne and Lady. Then albeit some of the kinges friendes woulde haue auenged hys death, the y durst not signifie it the people bæing so bent after the newe Quæne. The knight of Cupid when the battayle was ended thancked God and demaunded of the Iudges whether ought else were to be perfozmed for the restozing of the Princesse Arguirosa to hir kingdome. To which all sayde no, and the trumpettes sounded. Yet sat the Princesse vpon hir palfray tyll there came to hir of the most principall knightes, and other Citizens, which now all feare set aside durst discouer their good affection.

The

The Princesse therewith,and the knight of Cupid,with hir vnckle Alberto rode in great honour to the pallace, where that present day ý princesse was crowned Quæne, the chiefe lordes kissing hir hand in the name of ý gentlemen & commons. After this there was no talke but of ý marriage of the Quæne,euery man as he wished,naming the knight of Cupid,which hir selfe more desiret then they all,but knowing that the knight of Cupid had else where bestowed his liking (which she gathered by likelihood of speaches which she had heard in the shyp,by the deep sighs which he hourely fetched,and especially by his deuice which did not argue in a new beginner)she ruled hir passion the best she might,and for this time meued hym not therein,afterwardes she sent for Rolandos wife hir mother in lawe to kæpe hir company,but the roporte was that for anguish of minde she had slayne hir selfe. Well,yet she commaunded them both to be enfered as belonged to the kings and Quænes of that land. Rosicleer remained in that kingdome fire dayes at the greate entreaty of Quæne to helpe all thinges to good order. After fæling the wound which sat more dæply imprinted in his heart, then the Image thereof in his armour,he departed thece.And so let vs leue him to recout of the Emperour Trebatio and the knight of the Sunne who were lost sayling vpon the Sea.

¶The Emperour Trebatio and the kinght
    of the Sunne are in their waye to the
    kingdome of Hungary.   Cap.49.

THE Emperour Trebatio and the Knight of the Sunne departing from the Ilande of Lyndaraza, were left saylynge in the Sea Euxino. Nowe the shyppe wherin he was hauing so good and skilfull a gouernour as wæ haue tolde you, was carryed so swiftly that within two daies they entred ý mouth of Danubia, and being vpon the ryuer thrée dayes and thrée nightes, the fourth day in the morninge they were set on lande ere that they wist. The Emperour lokinge about him knewe the countrey very well since he had followed the charriot to the selfe same place. And béeing glad to haue arriued to Hungary so safe and so shortly, he embraced the knight of the Sunne for ioye, telling hym that this was Hungary where the Princesse Briana liued. So he deuised with him in what manner he might best make himselfe known to ye princesse, & conuay hir into Gréece. The knight of the Sunne béeing so friendly asked his aduice, aunswered as faythfully. My Lord it is requisite for vs first of all to knowe where the kinge Tiberio is, and in what order the princesse nowe abideth, which béeing done you may the better compasse that whiche you purpose. You say right well, aunswered the Emperour, let vs kéepe along the shoare, that if perhaps we méete with any one, we may enquire what newes there are. So on fote they walked through a forrest leading vp pon the ryuer, wherein they trauayled halfe a day without méeting any one, after somewhat wearied they sate them downe to rest themselues, where they fed on such viandes as they had brought with them from the boate, an halfe, houre after when they had rested indifferently, they sawe néere at hand a gentlewoman vpon a palfraye making as much hast as she could, and after hir a knight on fote with a naked swoyde threateninge hir if shée stayed not, when he ouertoke hir to runne hir throughe. The gentlewoman séeing the Emperour and the knyght of the Sunne lept from hir palfray, crying out: succour mée good knights for thys trayterous knight wyll rauish mée. The Emperour rose vp, & comforting the gentlewoman, stayed a while till the knight came to laye hands on hir, then he sayd, sir knight either let this gentlewoman alone or tell vs why thou wilt carry hir against hir wyll. The knight which was both proude and peuish, aunswered

red

red him, I will carrie hir away maugre your teeth, and I haue no charge to make you other answere, but as to the cause, witte you that it is for my selfe and for the other, wherof you shal be no let I warrant you. But you carrie hir not away, sayde the Emperour, for sooner shall you die then touch hir honour. The knight was ouerawed in wordes thought to make amendes in deedes, and soerinly he hit the Emperour vnder the ribbes. The Emperour to yelde it him agayne, strake at his head which hee receiued in his shielde, and not daring to abide an other, hee fled through the forrest as fast as he might, neither the Emperour nor the knight of the Sunne would followe him, but demaunded of the gentlewoman why that knight pursued hir.

Alas my Lordes sayd she, my fellowe and I came ryding through the forrest where we were met with foure knightes which would haue carryed vs awaye by force, my selfe fledde this way, my companion an other, and but if you doe helpe hir, these wicked knyghtes will doe hir villany. The Emperour hauing alone begun the battayle, desired the knight of the Sunne to abyde there. The while he tooke the gentlewomans palfray to succour the other Lady. The knyght of the Sunne woulde rather haue taken that trauayle vpon him, then to expede the report but not to importunate the Emperour, he promised to stay his comming or to followe hym. The Emperour tooke vp the gentlewoman behinde him to conduct on the way, & being brought by hir to the middt of y forrest about a flight shot, they heard y scriching of some gentlewoman, & following y soud they finde iiii knights laying hands vpon a gentlewoman, whereat she cryed out. The Emperour presentlyas he saw dismounted fro his horse, & cryed to y knights saying, knights let this gentlewoman alone for it is great villany to force a woman. One of them hearing the Emperour, cryed agayne. Who made you a Justice or doe you looke for an attournyes fee,

P.iiij.   and

and they all three layde at the Emperour, but it had ben better for them not to haue bene so hasty, for ere long they receiued iust reward for their insolencie. For the Emperour cleaued one of them to the scull, and one other from the shoulders downeward, the thirde as hee made hast to escape was taken shorter by the legges. For the Emperour albeit very inclinable to any reasonable pitie, yet was in this poynt very rigorous, not to spare the dishonourers of virginitie, his saying was, that it quenched the naturall loue betwœne father and mother, sister and brother, betwœne kisse and kinne: that the bastard broke seldome came to good purpose: that it was partly the sinne of Sodomy, &c. And for his owne fault it was in deed mœre ignorance or rather constraint, & therby the more pardonable, or perhaps ye detesting of it himselfe made him more seuerely exact the kœping of chastitie in others: But forward with our matter: The emperour beholding this gentlewoman whome he had succoured, knew hir presently to be Clandestria a gentlewoman belonging to ye Princesse Briana, wherewith he was the gladdest man in the world, as hopyng to heare some good newes at hir hands. Yet to couer himselfe he made the gentlewomen sit downe, hymselfe sitting by them, & to tell hym whether they went, & wherefore they were in those partes. The gentlewomen glad and fayne that they might without daunger tell of what countrey they were, and what their erraunt was thetherward, aunswered.

Syr knight we are belonging to the Princesse Briana daughter to the king of thys land: the cause of our comming is that long time agone our Lady lost hir husband the prince Edward prince of Britaine, & hath neuer since heard of him. For his sake shœ hath remayned a widow in the monastery of the ryuer, demeaning a very sorry lyfe, as pent vp in a religious cloyster. Hir beliefe was alwayes that he was dead tell within these fiftene

dayes

dayes she dreamed that she sawe him alyue, and that hee
came by Sea to this lande, very merry, of the same age
which he was off when he first lefte hir, which dreame
she hath dreamed three nights together, the last night of
the three there appeared to hir an auncient man much re-
buking hir for hir distrust, whereat the Princesse though
hardlye perswaded, yet being so admonished, the better
hath credited that night vision, and hath sent vs to a re-
lygious house, dedicated to our Lady the blessed Virgin,
with rich offerings and many good deuotions for his safe
retourne Whence after we were retourning by this forrest these knights besette vs, and had rauished vs but that
we cryed so loude that you hearde vs, and you haue
thancks be to God, well eased vs of them, and for your
so great courtesie, if it so please you to ride with vs, I
doubt not but our mistresse will well consider you. The
Emperour much reioycing at the great constancie of hys
wife Briana, and desiring to discouer himselfe, asked the
gentlewomen if any of them had seene the Prince Edward or no. Whereto Clandestria aunswered. Yea sir
knight very wel, and I woulde that God woulde once
shew him me, I should know him by his louely face, ex-
cellyng al other knights which I haue euer seene I wyll
see that presently sayd the Emperour. and so saying hee
put off his helmet: and how now sayth hee, whome take
you me for. O say they both, your selfe are Prince Edward
& kneelyng down before him would haue kissed his hands
& they earnestly entreated him to go with the to the mena-
sterie of the riuer. The Emperour consented glacly. for I
haue sayth he as great desire to see hir, but heere not farre
hence there is a knighte which stayeth for me, him must
we seeke and carry in our company, for he is the manne
next vnto God, to whome I am most beholding, for by
him haue I bene deliuered from prison and from enchauntment. The whole storye I wyll tell you by the
waye.

So the Emperour made the gentlewomen to mount
vppon their palfrayes, and himselfe tooke one of the horses pertayning to the dead knight for him elfe, and an o-
ther for the knight of the Sun and by the way he discoursed as he promised of his owne estate with Lindaraza till
that they mette with the Knighte of the Sunne; with
whome the Emperour communicated of his good aduenture to lyght vppon Brianas maydes, and what newes he
had hearde of them. Whereat the Knight of the Sunne
became as ioyous, and they made a merry iourney towardes Belgrado, which helde them foure dayes trauaile
from that place.

¶ The Emperour and the Knight of the Sunne riding towards the monasterie of the riuer are by
an aduenture seperated.   Cap.50.

The Emperour in the waye declared to the gentlewomen and to the knight of the Sunne who
he was, not Prince Edward as they thoughte,
but in his name Brianas bridegrome, and so forth
of that matter, which you may conceiue by that you heard
before . Whereat the gentlewomen were not a lyttle
amazed , but nothing sorye . And with the knighte of
the Sunne the Emperour entred into farther counsayle
in what order he might make the king Tiberio priuie to
his facte , and carrye the Princesse Briana into Greece.
Whereto the Knight of the Sunne counsayled thus. My
Lorde, you knowe the fayth of a Prince, a bonde verye
strayght for kings and great Lordes, as touching the pre-
seruation of theire honour in promise , for which many
times many haue preferred the trust layde vpon them before the safetie of their nere kinred . Thys I saye for
that peraduenture Tiberio wilbe right glad to haue matched his daughter with you, yet for the Prince Edwards
facte comming vnder his safe conduct he maye not take it

in

In god part, or if hee did, hadde not king Oliuerio iust cause to be angry being so abused as vnder his worde to to haue lost his sonne, and subiects withall, my counsaile is therefore for the better dispatch of your businesse, and auoyding of being shent if you venture rashly vppon an enemy not reconciled. That you go secretly to the monasterie and carry away the Princesse from thence, scarce letting hir selfe know whether you shall go, saue that behinde you you may leaue a letter which shall signifie the whole effect of that which is passed. By this meanes if the king of England bewayle the death of his sonne, the king Tiberio may complayne of the losse of his daughter and in time when these sores are skinned, there maye friendshippe be made on either part. The Emperour liked weil this counsayle, and giuing him many thanckes tolde him that he would put it in effect. So two dayes they kept company nothing in the meane time happening worth the telling.

The thirde day comming to a crosse waye well frode they sawe a pauilyon pitched and not farre off twelue gentlewomen clothed in blacke, and hauing verye sadde countenaunces, at the tente dore they sawe three knights which were their kepers. When the Emperour and the knighte of the Sunne approched, the gentlewomen cryed out, whereat the knight of the Sunne sayde, and spake vnto them. Gentlewomen, aswell by your countenaunces as by your outcryes wee perceiue you are distressed. Show vs now the cause thereof, and if the thing be such as that we may remedye it we will doe our best to doe it.

One of the chiefest of them answered. Sir your courteous wordes makes vs y bolder to vtter our griefe. Therfore know you that I haue a sister called Silandra Duchesse of Pannonia, and marryed to a knight the most wicked man that was euer borne, for he hath farmensed hir with such a mistrepart as the lyke hath not bene heard off.

S.

So it is that my sister and hee haue bene marryed eyghte yeares and haue had no children, wherefore he fearinge ý after hir deceafe the Dukedome fhould retourne to hys kinne, as by right it would being hir onely enheritaunce, and minding to eftablifh the ftate in his owne name, hath fuborned a defperate perfon to challenge hir of adultery. By which meanes fhe being executed as falfe to hir hufbande all hir lands and goods are forfayted to the hufband as it were to make him amendes of his wiues wronge. Now this fclaunder is apparant to all men, but bicaufe the Duke offereth that the combatte fhalbe graunted to him which fhall gaynfay the flaunder, the matter is made the lykelyer, and is borne out though not by ftrong hands yet by pollycy, and yet no man dare oppofe himfelfe to the challenger. For there is a knight in the lande called Arydon Lord of ý blacke who by reporte ý ftrongeft knight which euer was in thefe parts, albeit very lyke vnto the Duke in his ill lyuing, him hath the Duke made hys friende and accufer of the Princeffe. For a plot of ground adiacent to his fegniories, his accufation lyeth thus that with himfelfe fhe committed adultery, whereas though he was a long foiourner in hir court, yet he neither perfwaded hir to it, nor woulde euer moue hir in it, for hée knewe his aunfwere. But the matter was thus canuafed, the while the Duke kepte at the courte of the kynge Tiberio, thether word is brought of the falfe packing of the Duchefe and Arydon. The Duke prefently complaineth to the king, & both partyes are fent for in all haft. Arydon being firft afked confeffeth it, and is acquitted by his confeffion. As (by the way) our lawe in this cafe acquiteth the man once confeffing it though otherwife neuer fo great an offender, and onely ftretcheth to the woman in refpect of hir faythe giuen at marriage. Nowe what coulde the Princeffe doe ftanding before the kinge, and accufed not of hearefay, but by himfelfe with whom fhe is fayde to haue lyen? yet denyeth fhe it. Well, the

Duke

Duke charging hir with it and she purging hir selfe, she
was fayne to require respite for prouiding a sufficient
knight to maintayne hir innocency. Yet was she commaunded to prison vnder sure kæpinge, and there is a
day set for the tryall, Arydon being the accuser, agaynst
whome I doe not thincke that anye man in hir defence,
though the cause be righteous dare shewe himselfe, for
we haue tarryed hære these rr.dayes and haue not found
any. Now bicause hære are crossewayes, in which it is
lykely that many knights should passe, we determyne to
abide the rest of the præfired time. And this is the cause
sir knight why we mourne, and so she ended weping bitterly.

The Emperour and the Knight of the Sunne pitied
them much, meruaylyng so vngodly dealyng could haue
any place to rust in Hungary, but God is wise say they
yea, and sæth his time. So the Knighte of the Sunne
talking apart with the Emperour sayd to him. My Lord
you sæ good cause binding me to pittie the Duchesse in
hir extreame næde, if you be pleased therewith, I wyll
go aunswere for hir in the court of kyng Tiberio. In
the meane time it will be best for you to go to the monasterie of the riuer the most secretly that you may, and I
will not fayle to certefie you from the courte if I heare
ought which might auaile you being known. This being
done, I will with Gods helpe come to Greece, where I
loke to finde you very merry. The Emperour was loth,
but sæing the vrgent necessitye he was content and aunswered, ý he would not be agaynst his pleasure althoughe
it woulde grieue him to be long without his companye,
but at Constantinople shall we mæte.

Thereuppon the knighte of the Sunne tourned to
the gentlewomen, saying. Gentlewomen, your mourning
hath so much grieued this knight and me, that although
his affaires lye otherwhere and that he cannot be present,
yet for his sake will I go with you to the courte, ther to
aun-

aunſwere for the Ducheſſe if ſhe be ſo content . The gentlewomen willyngly accepted of the knight, and not ſtaying longer but to thancke him they pulled downe theire
tent and to herſebacke they go. By the way he had much
talke with Eliſea for ſo was the Ducheſſe ſiſter named, he
comforting hir and ſhee requeſting him to make ſpæde
for wee lacke not many dayes of our appoynted time,
when if wee fayle we ſhall loſe a good cauſe for lacke of
pitye in knightes aduenturous . But letteus leaue this
and tourne we to the Emperour in the companye of Brianas gentlewomen.

¶ The Emperour Trebatio came to the monaſterie of the
riuer & there was made known to his wife the Princeſſe.   Cap.51.

The Emperour hauing good hope to mæte with the
Princeſſe whom he loued no leſſe then before he had,
when he hazarded his perſon for hir ſake vppon Prince
Edward, made greate haſt, and hee trauayled with the
gentlewomen thræ dayes an thræ nights. Now we haue
tolde you often that that the Princes lodging was in one
quarter of the monaſterie ſeperate from ỹ other, wherto
ſhe had a poſterne gate towards the wood, by which Clandeſtria had carryed Donzel del Febo & Roſicleer to nur-
ſing, & by this gate no man either entred or went out, but
by Clandeſtrias leaue, ſhee was growne porter and kepte
the key hir ſelfe . And for to couer this matter which the
Emperour would in wiſe haue known it was very fit ỹ
Clandeſtria was ther in company. For when they approched ỹ monaſterie ſaith Clandeſtria. My Lord if you will
not be known by ỹ gentlewomen here belonging to our
Lade, beſt it were that I ſhould firſt enter & ſæ what they
do, & that I ſhould cauſe the Princeſſe to take hir moſt ſecret chamber, where as I ſhall finde hir ſo I will declare
                                                              of

of your comming, otherwise it maye be that your so sodayne approch might worke some alteration in hir bodye to the daunger of hir health she being so sore weakened by continual mourning, but this night shal passe & the morow you shal come vnto hir. The Emperour lyked well of Clandestrias speach, and so he stayed in a place which she prouided for him, the whilest that the gentlewomen went to the Princesse. Some will thinke that the Emperour shoulde be much chaunged this being the xx.yeare of his absence, but it was not so, for when he first entred the Castle of Lyndaraza he was but xxxb.yeares in age, and no more was he when he came from the enchauntment, neither his age encreasing, nor his beautie decreasing. When the Emperour lefte the Princesse Briana, she was but xiiii. yeares olde, and counting the time that she had liued afterward she was iust one yere vnder him wherein hir beautie best appeared, and the great sorrowe which she before had taken did not so abate hir coleure, but that the ioy of his retourne fetched it agayne more fresh and lyuely then it was before.

But the story saith that the gentlewomen found their mistresse alone prayinge deuoutlye vppon hir knees, and more merry then she was before, whether by inspiration or by immagination, conceiuing hope in the dreame I tolde you off: but hir gentlewomen were very gladde to be witnesses of hir mirth. The Princesse louingly welcommed the gentlewomen especially Clandestria which was hir sure friende, demaunding of them how they had sped in their iourney.

Clandestria aunswered .. Madame, wee were once in daunger to loose bothe our honoures and oure lyues after that wee hadde done as you commaunded vs . Ah blessed Virgin sayde the Princesse, and is it possible that you shoulde euer be in so greate daunger for my cause. Yea it is most certine madame aunsw▵

answered Clandestria, but as after a fowle euening coms a faire morning, so after this trouble we had some quyetnesse by the meanes of our flight, for we mette with a good knight, which not onely saued vs from great shame by killyng these wicked knightes which woulde haue spoyled vs, but after tolde vs suche newes as you haue cause to be the gladdest woman in the worlde. He sayd that not manye dayes before hee departed from youre husband, which was in good health, and of the same age as he was when you first knewe him, for since hee was with you, he hath bene enchaunted, and being now set at comming to you.

O good Lorde, and is it possible sayde the Princesse that thou art so fauourable vnto me, as to sende mee my husbande alyue: or is this some dreame the farther to encrease my dolour. Tell me Clandestria in good faythe, is it trewe which thou sayst, for I can hardly beleue thee. Yea assuredly sayde Clandestria for the knight which reported it, is so credible as that he will not tell other then troth. Ah Clandestria sayde the Princesse thou hast bene alwayes dilygent, discreete, and lyberall in those thinges which haue touched my seruice hetherto, but in this now concerning my lyfe especially thou hast bene neglygent or hast wanted discretion. For why didst thou not bringe him before me that my selfe might haue hearde it of his owne mouth, would it not then haue bene pleasaunt vnto me to haue sene that knighte, which so lately sawe my louing husband: and to haue knowen of him in what manner he mette with him, and for what cause he commeth not so sone as the other.

Madame be not agrieued with this sayde Clandestria for the knight which tolde it me is not so farre hence but that within a quarter of an houre you may se him if you haue desire thereto. Desire sayde the Princesse, I desire nothing so much in the worlo, therefore go and fetch him before me, that I may knowe whether that be trewe

which

which my heart thincketh so incredible, I wyll goe my
wayes sayde Clandeſtria, and ſo ſhe went out of the
Princeſſe lodginge and ſtraight to the Emperour to
whom ſhe tolde all that talke which ſhee had had wyth
hir Lady, whereat the Emperour was ſo gladde that vp
the ſtayers full faine hæ goeth, and by ſuch priuie waies
as none but Clandeſtria knewe, hæ is brought before
Briana . Clandeſtria firſt entering, then the Emperour
clothed in rich armour and hys viſour pulled downe.
The Princeſſe was ſomewhat afrayde to ſæ ſo bygge
a man all armed , but the Emperour pullinge off hys
helmette quickly ſhewed hys louely face, the whiche ſhee
had imprinted in hir remembraunce . And wyth ha-
ſty paces hæ made towardes the Princeſſe, whome
hæ kyſſed on the mouth ſo ſwætly that their tongues
this while were ſlent, not to interrupt the ioye of their
firſt mæting . Anone after the Princeſſe whiche in
dæde had the chiefeſt wrong ſpake to the Emperour
thus:

My Lorde and onely lyfe what cruell Fortune
hath detayned you from this lande , and banniſhed you
ſo long from my preſence . In what ſtraunge and hyd-
den countryes haue you bene that we coulde neuer
heare worde of you . Madame, aunſwered the Emperour, you may call that Fortune cruell, ſo it hath offered you a great wronge by forceing you to endure a
farre greater penaunce then Penelope dyd by Vlyſſes
abſence : but one thinge you maye aſſure your ſelfe
of that the fault was not in mæ thoughe I am not to
bæ excuſed , ſo if I had had lyfe and lybertie and
iudgement, all the worlde ſhould not haue ſtayed me from
you.

Since my frædome if I haue not had as loyall a
regarde of your conſtancye and my duetie, then blame
all mankinde for my ſake of vnſtedfaſtneſſe and wronge,
and for this tyme let theſe things ſlippe wyth leſſe

Z.   griefe

griefe to entertayne our p:efent ioye . So he kyffed
the P:inceſſe agayne,and they both ſatte downe toge=
ther kiſſing and collinge eache other lyke two younge
louers,when they were th:oughly entered thys delyght,
and that the Empereur was ſure of hir good lykinge
towardes himſelfe ,whoſomeuer hæ were he bew:ayed
to hir the whole matter,firſt that he was not the P:ince
Edward as ſhæ thought , but the Empereur Trebatio,
and ſo in fewe wo:des he tolde hir the whole ſto:ye of
hys firſt heate by the p:iſoners confeſſion , and from
thence in o:der to thys delyuerannce w:ought by the
knight of the Sunne.

    The P:inceſſe fo: a greate while ſtode hæreat a=
maʒed and began to gather mo:e of the wo:des whiche
Roſicleer had w:itten to hir,and not bæinge diſpleaſed
with hir fo:mer errour,in the ende ſhæ tolde him that
whoſomeuer he was in dæde, yet was hee the ſame to
whome ſhe was marryed , and that vowe which ſhæ
then made,ſhe ſayd ſhe woulde perfo:me to hym alóne.
The Empereur courteouſly thanckinge hir, badde hy:
ſaye on what had happened , whereat ſhe graciouſlye
bluſſinge,tolde him that ſhe had bene deliuered of two
child:en at one burthen bæing two godly boyes with
ſtraunge markes in their bodies . Of them ſhæ tolde
hym farther,pow:ing downe many a teare the manner
of their loſſe, the one called Donʒel del Febo at th:ee
years of his age,the other named Roſicleer at ſeuentene,
and fo: Roſicleer (ſayth ſhee) hæ hathe p:oued a ryght
manly knight , and therewith ſhe gaue him the letter
which Arinda had b:ought.

    The Empereur read the letter and was very gladde
to heare of that hope which Artemidoro had put hym
in as touchinge the recouery of hys b:other . And in
god time while we haue occaſion to entreat off Treba-
tios child:en, let us holde on w:th the knyght of the
Sunne

Sunne, whom we left in the way trauailing to the court of king Tiberio, which shall be declared in the chapter following.

¶ The Knight of the Sunne ridinge to the court of king Tiberio, iusteth with a knight for passage. Cap. 52.

THE Knight of the Sunne and the gentlwomen with their knightes ryode towardes the Citie of Ratisbona where the kinge Tiberio and his court for that tyme laye. Three dayes almost they trauayled hearynge of naught that myght be tolde you tyll towardes noone vppon the thirde daye they mette wyth a fayre gentlewoman vppon a palfraye whiche saluted them courteously in thys manner. God saue you Sir knyghtes, I praye you tell mee whether you are going, to the court of the kinge Tiberio or no, for if you goe thether I haue certeine newes to tell you.

Mary sayd one of the knyghtes that we doe, what do you commaunde vs thether fayre gentlewoman, I wyll tell you that willingly sayth shee if the knight whiche hath the deuice of the Sunne will graunt me my asking. I graunt it you gentlewoman aunswered the knight of the Sunne, if it bee neither let to my iourney nor preiudiciall to my person. I am content wyth these conditions sayth shee, and so I accept of your promise.

Nowe Sir knight trueth it is that riding thys waye I must of force passe ouer a bridge stretchinge ouer Danubia not passinge two myles from the greate citie of Ratisbona, ouer which you must also passe if you woulde goe to the citie. Thys bridge sayth she is kept

Z.ij.   by

by a knyght called Florinaldes for the loue of a Lady named Albamyra equally beloued of two knyghtes, The one is this Florinaldes, the other is an Earle named Orfeo, and they two haue bene at longe strife for hir loue. She to bee rydde of the one, shœ careth not whether hath commaunded that in hir presence they should seuerally kéepe thys passage fiftéene dayes space, promising that he which doth best shall bée hir knyght, Florinaldes hathe bene the first and hath kepte thys bridge twelue dayes in Albamyras presence, where are many knightes and gentlewomen . Nowe it béeing so nœre the courte there coms daylye many good knightes to proue themselues, but hee hathe the masterye of them all, and hys prayse is spredde farre abrode.

This morninge my selfe rydinge towardes Ratisbona for certeyne businesse I haue there woulde haue passed the bridge, but I coulde not bée suffered excepte I woulde haue confessed Albamyra to bee the fayrest Lady in all Hungary. Thys if I woulde not doe, they badde mée bringe some knight that shoulde wynne the passage for mée, when I heard thys I called to sée the beautie of Albamyra, that I myght iudge whether it were so or no. Then was I ledde into a riche tent wherein Albamyra satte accompanyed wyth many gentlewomen, and I behelde hir at the full, but truely if my glasse at home lye not, wherein I was wont to sée myne owne beautye, hyrs is nothinge equall to myne. So I tolde them that for ought I had séene I muste bee fayne to retourne backe and to finde a knight whiche woulde breake the passage.

Nowe the gyfte whiche I demaunde of you Syr knyght is, that hœreuppon you iuste wyth Florinaldes, and in the maintenaunce of my beautie agaynst hirs, be you assured of the victory.

When the gentlewoman had said thus, those that were

pre

present laughed a good, and the knight of the Sonne fo
shift hir off, aunswered. Gentlewoman if your busi-
niße had bene so great to the court as you woulde haue
vs thincke, you would not haue stayed fo so small a
matter. The gentlewoman very angry replyed shortly,
Call you it so small a matter, marke what I saye, you
are not so courteous as I toeke you fo, if you so little
esteeme womens sutes, you being a knight, nowe know
you that a woman esteemeth hir beautie aboue al, and that
there is no iniury so great fo a woman, as to say that an
other is fayrer then shee: I tell you that I had rather be
called any other name of reproch, then not a well fauourd
woman, and being as I am I account my selfe much
fairer then Albamyra, o rather would I all my greate
businesse vndone, then to confesse that which the knyght
of the bridge doth will me to. Nowe sith you haue gyuen me this graunt, perfoyme it o otherwise during my
lyfe I will complayne me of you. The knight of the
Sonne and those which were with him laughed to see
the gentlewoman so hot fo the light regardinge of hir
beautie, and they sayd, sith we must passe the bridge wee
will see the beautie of Albamyra, and if it be lesse then
yours then will we doe our best that you shall passe vn-
controlled.

Of the one part be you sure quoth y gentlewoman that
my beautie is moe, and if I had the maintenaunce
which Albamira hath, Florinaldes o the Earle Orfeo
would rather quarrell fo my beautie then fo hys. At
thys and other lyke thinges they laughed tyll they came
to the bridge where they sawe a bigge knyght armed,
and a fayre rich tente pytched, with certeine knightes
and gentlewomen walkinge by the ryuer side, who so
soone as they sawe these knightes come, gathered vnto
the tent.

The knight of the Sonne and hys company offred
to ryde ouer the bridge, but there came a gentlewoman

out agaynst him, saying. Sir knight this bridge is defended you by Florinaldes, ouer may you not passe vnlesse you iuste wyth him or confesse that Albamyra is the fayrest gentlewoman in thys kyngdome, and that Florinaldes is the knight which best deserueth hir, the which also must these gentlewomen saye which are in your company or bring knightes to aunswere for them. Wee could be content. aunswered the knyght of the Sunne to agree to these conditions which you speake off, but the gentlewomen in our company make such account of their beauties that they wyll rather retourne backe, then confesse that which you woulde. Nowe that they are in our company wee muste aunswere for them. Determine what to dee, and for your choice, it must bee one of those two, sayd the gentlewoman, and so she departed.

Florinaldes and Albamyra hearde all this, and presently they caused the tent dore to bee set open, where these straungers sawe Albamyra amongest the gentlewomen much excelling them all, whiche made them take vp a freshe laughter at their merry gentlewomen. Florinaldes issued forth of the tent taking a speare in hys hande and comming towards the knight, he spake saying. You haue knowne already knightes that this bridge is kept by mee, if you saye not that which I demaund of you, or otherwyse presently iust with mee. The knights aunswered, we will doe what we lyke best, and therewyth they required the knight of the Sunne that they might iust first, which he graunted them, and so the one taking a speare in his hande ranne to encounter Florinaldes, but he was vnhorsed, and so the seconde and the thirde all of them as easily and wyth no more a doe then I haue had in telling you.

The knyghte of the Sunne seeinge these three knyghtes thus cast downe, spake vnto the gentlewoman which had brought them thether. Gentlewoman

this

thys knyght is no babe youlee, were it not better for vs to sare as he sayth, then myght wee goe free. And the rather for that I haue seene Albamyra which in my eyes is much fairer then you.

Blessed Mary sayth the gentlewoman, if Albamyra bee fayrer then I, it is for hir apparell onely, but sithe you haue promised this, you muste performe it, and al thoughe I gaine nothing herein, yet shall it doe mee good to see you flye from your saddle, for the little skyll you haue in deserning beauties. Albamira hearde this and the other gentlewomen, and knowinge that this was the gentlewoman whiche had bene there be fore they laughed muche at hir, whereat she waxed angry. The knight of the Sunne then tooke a speare from the ratler and called for Florinaldes. Then ranne they together with such force that they made the bridge to shake. Florinaldes onely burst hys speare vppon the knyght of the Sunne, but the knyght of the Sunne bare Florinaldes ouer and ouer so strongly that hee had a sore bruse and myght not ryse, hys knyghtes tooke him in their armes into hys tent where he was beatup, and it is vncertaine whether more grieued wyth the sore of his bruse then wyth the shame of hys fall, so to be foyled before his mistrelle, but if I maye meddle in schole poyntes, I thincke he had rather burst an arme then so to haue cracked his credite wyth both Ladye and friendes, such as manye resorte thether from Tiberios court to see him iust.

And the knight of the Sunne seeing Florinaldes so vnhorsed before his Lady, was as sorry for hym and presentlye departed. The gentlewomen and theyr knights in whose company he trauailed were glad for the hope gyuen them of a farther triall, but aboue al, y gentle woman which had required hym to these iustes, try umphed nowe as if rather in hir quarrell, then by the knightes strength, Florinaldes had bene ouerthrowne,

Z.iiij.   and

and she bad them aloude to remember the comparison of Albamiras beautie & hirs, from this time she liked much better of hir selfe, but age comming vpon hir, hir beautie decayed, as there is nothing moze vncertayne, either empayzed by sicknesse, oz withered by age, oz by sundzy accidents in mannes lyfe cozrupted and depzaued, and what should I talke of the harme that thence issueth. It is at home a bzœder of vnrest, a robber of rase abzoade, a continuall care, a cause of many daungers, a sea of trauayles, and an euerlasting griefe whether comminge oz goinge: but what nœdeth this so long a digression, the rest let vs leaue to those that are ydle, to discourse at leysure, nowe moze at large of our necessary matter. The knyght of the Sunne with his company rydeth to Ratisbona, whether they cameere full sunne set, and lodged foz that night at a friendes house of Elisea. The stozye sayth also that Florinaldes and his company dislodged their tent and came that night to Rotisbona also, all greatly amazed at the knyght of the Sunne to whome Florinaldes bare such an euil wil that it had almost cost him hys lyfe, as the next booke shall tell you hereafter.

¶The knight of the Sunne aunswered before the king Tiberio for the Dutchesse Elisandra, and the battaile was appointed betweene him and Aridon of the black wood. Cap. 53.

The next day bœing come the knight of the Sunne armed himselfe, and bœing ready, onely with Elisea went towardes the pallaice, whether when he came he found the kinge amongest hys nobles, and wyth them the Duke of Pannonia, and Arydon of the blacke woode, either of them not a little pussed vp wyth vaine glozy, that the time pzefired was now spent almost,

and

and no man daring to aunſwer for the Ducheſſe . Now
at the comming in of this knighte with the deuice of the
Sunne there was ſodainly a great ſilence belyke by occaſion of ſome in the company which had ſæne his valour
proued vppon Florinaldes. And the knight of the Sunne
glad of ſuch cōuenient time of hearing,after he had hum
bly bowed to the king,ſpake as followeth . Mightie king
I am a knighte and a ſtraunger neither of your courte,
countrey , nor relygion : but Fortune caſting me vppon
this coaſt , it was my chaunce to mæte with this gentlewoman,ſiſter to the Ducheſſe of Pannonia,whom you
holde priſoner . This gentlewoman trauayled to ſæke a
knight which woulde aunſwere the accuſation that the
Duke hir huſband layeth agaynſt hir, and lyghting vpon
me ſhe hath opened to me the whole trechery and packing
of the Duke hir huſvande with the periured Arydon of
the blacke wode . In the iuſtifyng of which wordes
ſpoken by the gentlewoman, and the improuing of Arydons falſe and ſhameleſſe ſlaunder , I am hether come to
proue that he belyeth the Ducheſſe vppon his body. The
king now and all which were preſent beheld the knight
of the Sunne very earneſtly,and were abaſhed to ſæ him
being ſo young to ſpeake ſo couragiouſly . Arydon verye
angry roſe vp, and to the knight of the Sunne ſpake on
this wiſe . Sir knight it appeares that thou art bothe
young and a ſtraunger in this countrey, for if thou werſt
of yeares or kneweſt Arydon which nowe talketh wyth
thæ, thou wouloſt not be ſo hardy as to deſſe him in preſence, and were it not for the King my Lorde I woulde
in ſome wiſe tell thæ of thy rudeneſſe, but there nædeth
no ſuch haſt, I hope I ſhall haue time inoughe ſith thou
canſt not detract the battayle whereto thy ſelfe hath firſt
made offer, but lette vs go to it preſently and ende it in
this place . Arydons highe diſdayne ſore diſpleaſed the
knight of the Sunne as appeared by his loke, but he re-
frayned for honour to the king, and for the reſt he deſired

the king to authorize the lysts. The king aunswered him gently that daye it mighte not be, both for that it was needefull the Duchesse of Pannonia should appeare openly to put hir quarrell into his handes; and for that also Judges must be ordayned of the fieide, and the lysts erected: which coulde not be promised in so shorte warning. The knight of the Sunne yelded to the kinges pleasure; and after that he had witnessed his forwardenesse to defende the Duchesse, hee toke his leaue of the king and to his host he goeth. The king as soone as he was gone, by occasion of this young knight, calling to minde his sonne Liriamandro whome he had not hearde off in long tyme, wept bitterly and sayd a loude that diuers hearde it. If my sonne Liriamandro be lyke to this lusty knighte, and haue a care to be notable, no doubt he will excell all his auncestors. Whereat those which were there by declared to the king what themselues had seene of this knight and howe strongly hee had ouerthrowen Florinaldes: which report did in a manner discomfit Arydon, that he would haue wished his stake out at y dealing with all his heart, but in deede a very desperate contempt both of God and the worlde brought him to his ende.

¶The battaile betweene the Knight of the Sunne and the strong Arydon.   Cap.54.

The next day the king rose erlier then he was wont to doe, bicause of the battayle which was to be made betweene Arydon and the knight straunger. And Arydon lykewise made more hast, nor the Knight of the Sun fayled for his parte. When all were in the fielde, the king caused the Duchesse to be brought, which came thether in a mourning weede and with so sorrowfull a countenaunce that no heart so stony but woulde haue pityed hir, for shee had bene very fayre alwayes accounted as wise and honest. The king demaunded of hir whether she
                                        woulde

would referre the tryall of hir cause to the successe of hir knight whether good or bad, whereto she aunswered yea, and that she had no other helpe but in God and the innocencie of hir cause. So was she ledde to a scaffold prouided for hir and other gentlewomen . The Judges nexte were called for, which were named by the king, the Duke of Austrich & the Duke of Saxony two auncient knights and then resiant in ẏ court. The Judges thus placed Arydon and the Knight of the Sunne toke their spears in their hands forcing themselues agaynst each other. Now sounded a trumpette and a herauld cryed. Go to knights and God defende the righte . With this they ranne together with all the force they coulde : theire encountrey was such that Arydon burste his speare and diseased not his enemy, but the knight of the Sunne both burste his speare and vnhorsed Arydon and with the fall hee gaue him, almost burste his backe, while he payned himselfe to keepe the saddle..

Arydon thus bruised lyfte vp his eyes to heauen and in despaire of conscience murmured to himselfe some like thing . Thou O God as I beleue hast sent this young man from heauen to reuenge my misreport , otherwyse who is his hee in this worlde which mighte haue sate so quiet in his saddel after so violent a push as I haue giuen him, or who might haue annoyed Arydon so, and with a desperate rage he drew his swoorde to haue sheathed it in the knights horse bellye , but ẏ knighte descended & with hys swoorde before him went toward Arydon ẏ betwene them the battayle begunneth. The king and the Princes ther present were very glad to see so good a beginning of the Duchesse delyuerance. And Arydon fayled not to do his best, that the knight of ẏ Sun could not but take him for a strong knight, the battaile endured a great while no man being able to iudge who had ẏ better, til ẏ the knight of ẏ Suns courage grew as his honour encreased for he was not angred at the first . The ende of this battayle

(for

(for it was not long neither very equall) was in this manner, Arydon hitte the knight of the Sunne on the headpeece that he bowed his knees to the grounde. Then the
knight of the Sunne gaue him an other that he staggered
with it, the seconde time Arydon hitte the knight of the
Sunne a blowe vppon the headpeece, whereat the last
time the knight of the Sunne stretching himselfe and following his blow, withal his mighte hit Arydon so sure,
that Arydon fell vppon the grount mouing neither hand
nor foote . The knight of the Sunne thinking it to bee
but an amase stoode still while Arydon might recouer a-
gayne.

   The whilest all the beholders much praysed the knight
of the Sunne for the best knight lyuing, as well commending his courage as his actiuitye . The Duchesse Elisandra likewise now hauing some hope by hir knight gate
hir colour agayne, and hir ioye was as much as hir hus-
bands sorrowe . But you haue not yet hearde the worst
of the wicked Duke, for Arydon reuiued : whom when
the knight of the Sunne saw raysing himselfe vp he came
hastely and holding the poynt of his sword agaynst Arydons throate he spake saying . Thou shalt dye false Arydon vnlesse thou confesse the treason that thou hast deuised agaynst the Duchesse, and if thou deest dye in thys
obstinate minde of concealyng so great outrage thou ha-
zardest thy soules health. Arydon as it trer halfe awake,
and yet not so loth to die as strcken with a terrcur of his
owne conscience aunswered . Thy wortes haue abashed
me more then the death which thou threatnest, the faulte
which I haue committed hath bredde a greater sorroure
in my fleshe: but make the Iudges come nere and I will
declare the whole.

   The knightes of the Sunne called the Iudges, they
comming nere hearde these wordes of his owne mouth,
the substaunce of the Dukes shifting to wring his wiues
enheritaunce to himselfe, in such manner as you haue
                                                    hearde

heard in Eliseas report . The Judges straughtwayes
declared it to the king, who detesting theire fact , caused
the Duke to be apprehended and both to be executed in
that place.

For albeit many of his nobles entreated for their pardon, yet the king so abhorred ȳ villany that nought auailed : and at this time was the lawe first enacted in Hungary that the law of punnishment for whoredome should
stretche aswell to the man as to the woman, and that e-
quall penaltie should be assigned to lyke offendours, wheras before the men escaped the women onely were in danger . Nowe after this execution, the Duchesse Elisandra was sette at large, and the Quæne. Augusta receyued hir with great honour into hir company. The knight
of the Sunne was very desirous to leaue the Citie : but
the king desired much to knowe him , and to haue hym
abide for some time in his court. In the time of his abode
the knight of the Sunne grew in more familyar aquain-
taunce with the king , and was much lyked of him bycause he sæmed to resemble the Princesse Briana, but one
day the king importuning the younge knight to knowe
his kinred vsed such lyke wordes.

Sir knight wee thancke you heartely for the paynes
that you haue taken in the Duchesse of Pannonias behalfe
and for the maintayning of hir honour , whereby if shæ
haue recciued commoditie of lyuing and auoyding shame:
so haue I receiued some quietnesse in my realme by the
open detecting of such malefactours, & their punnishment
wilbe occasion of feare in others : for this cause I haue
willed you to stay hære, as thereto I pray you heartelye,
but I pray you lette me knowe your name and wher you
were borne, for I know not how to call you. The knight
of the Sunne well nurtered in ths Souldans court after
his humble thanckes for his Maiesties most gratious
proffer and the promise of acceptaunce being a thing in
dæde very conuenient for the certefiyng of the Emperour
began

began as followeth . Fo2 your maiesties fauour I shall most willyngly doe your highnesse seruice and fo2 the Duchesse I am glad that the equity of hir cause furdered my attempt, and fo2 my name o2 countrey, I can better tell you the sto2y of my lyfe since I came to yeares then declare that . Yet am I called the knight of the Sunne by my deuice,and my education hath bene in the Souldans courte at Babilon, thether I being b2ought by the kings sonne in lawe, the king of Persia when I was but a child and as it hath bene tolde me, found in a lyttle boate vp= the Sea , fo2 my lyfe hetherto it hath bene in armes, and that doe I meane to pursue . The king and those which were with him were greatly amased that hee had come from so farre a countrey, and had bene founde vp= pon the Sea,and that he knewe no mo2e of his estate,but they thought that yet he was of some noble birth . The king thancked him and in this o2der the knighte of the Sunne stayed with the king Tiberio fo2 certeine dayes where he gayned many friends and one onely enemy, by name Florinaldes which could not fo2gette the shame re= ceiued befo2e his mistresse, although it had done him no scathe:fo2 in the ende Albamira p2eferred him befo2e the Earle Orfeo . So as I say yet Florinaldes seing the ho= nour of the knight of the Sunne dayly to encrease to the discredite of the bo2ne Hungarian, his stomacke rose a= gaynst him, and one day he sette vppon the knight of the Sunne at vnawares , but to his owne losse,had not the knight of the Sunne bene mo2e merciful,after they were made friends. But let vs b2eake off this sto2y to dispatch the P2ince of Lusitania out of England.

¶Don Siluerio demaunded the Princesse Oliuia for wife of the kyng Oliuerio.   Cap.55.

THe great so2row which the losse of Rosicleer caused in ý court of ý king Oliuerio hath bene ere this decla=
red

red to you for all the good knights his friendes wente to
seeke him, leauing the court bare and naked for noble men
and about all the Princesse Oliuia was worse wrynged,
albeit hir griefe was not so manifest. Nowe yet there
stayed in the court the Prince Don Siluerio straungelie
surprised with the loue of Oliuia and vsing the helpe of
his sister Rodasylua to the perswading of Oliuia. One
day the last I take it he vnfolded his griefe vnto hir, tellyng hir that vnlesse she founde the meanes, hee shoulde
bare leaue his lyfe in a farre countrey. The matter is
mine olde sute ÿ you wot off, my desire is that at least I
may be assured of hir good will. Sure I am if I moue the
king in it that I shall obtayne. The Princesse Rodasylua
moued in deede wᵗ hir brothers afflictiō promised ÿ vttermost of hir paynes, and wit̲hin a while after she had some
talke with the Princesse about that matter, hir wordes
tending to lyke effect.

Madame you knowe right well the great loue which
since I came to this courte I haue borne vnto you, and
how I haue done you seruice in al that I was able, that
which more is, in what manner I haue absented my selfe
from my parents onely to be in your company, which if
you know and confesse to be true, you must lykewise belæue that that which I shall say now, rather proceedeth
of good zeale towards your honoure, then of any purpose
to worke mine owne contentment, though I cannot deny
but that if I obtaine it will content me highly. But I
doe not desire the thing which standeth not with your honour, and for my paynes reward seeke I none, but that
I may be heard.

If I erre in ought wherin I shall counsaile you, then
may you blame me, and yet I doubte not but when you
shall haue throughly examined the whole, you shall rather impute the faulte to lacke of skill, then to any lacke
of good meaning, and as I am certeyne that you haue
this same opinion of mee without any farther suspecte,

so

so will I tell you my minde flatly. You knowe that you
are the onely enheritrix of this kingedome. that your father the king my Lord muſt nædes marry you with ſuch
a one as may equall your eſtate,both for the naturall care
which he hath ouer you in reſpect that you are his daughter,and for the proſit which ſhall thereby redounde to his
ſubiects, which cannot be well gouerned, the ſtate wanting a rightfull heire : you are withall at this time mar-
riageable,my ſute therefore is that hærein you will haue
a more regard of the Prince Don Siluerio my brother a
worthy knight of perſonage and valour, of an high birth,
a kings ſonne and heir, beſides louing you ſo entirely as
he can nothing more, long hath he endured this torment
and neuer would bewray it to any but to me,and I haue
hetherto ſuppreſſed it not to moleſt you now for compaſſion towardes him whome I muſt loue and henounre
myne owne brother I require this that at leaſt you ſhew
him ſome good countenaunce whereby he may be encou-
raged to demaunde you of the kynge your father , which
ſuite ſhall not be impoſſible if onely your lyking maye be
wonne.

   The Princeſſe angry at the heart with this ſpeach for
it was the thing moſt contrary to hir wiſh replyed ſhort-
ly . Madame Rodaſylua,if I had thought that the zeale
and loue which you haue profeſſed and I doe confeſſe had
tended to this iſſue, I ſhoulde leſſe haue lyked your company,and I cannot thinke wel of it,that either you ſhould
breake with me of ſuch matters or ſhoulde haue commu-
nication thereabouts with your brother, who as you ſay
lacketh boldeneſſe to diſcouer his affection, which cannot
be, doth he loue ſo earneſtly, when he vouchſafeth not to
ſpeke vnto me but by a meſſenger. I ſuſpect your words
perhappes if I had hearde the man ſpeake I might haue
iudged in his countenaunce whether hee had lyed yea,or
no .

   But for truth you knowe I am of young yeares at
this

this instant, neither haue I will to marrie: I pray you therefore name it no moze vnto mee, and yet when I am of yeares I may not choose my husband, and I am at the kinges coummaundement whom I must obey. The princesse Rodasylua so sharply rebuked by the Princesse Celiuia, and thereby gathering the little good wyll shee bare vnto hir brother, demaunded pardon of hir speache, and retourned to hir lodging whether shee sent for the Prince Don Siluerio, and to him she tolde the whole taike, with the Princesse aunswere, willing him notwithstandinge not to gyue ouer but to make a better shewe as if hir aunswere mislyked hym not, and couertly to laboure the king for his consent.

This can hee not denye you, and after you maye winne the Princesse, for as yet hir excuse is but of yeares. The Prince liking hir counsayle departed from the Princesse his sister, and the next daye findinge the king at leysure he requyred his maiestie of a secret matter. The king commaunded those in presence to auoyd, & toke him to a windowe, where the Prince after his duetie done, began on this sort. Wyth your graces fauour I trust, I haue this longe time bene a welwiller to your daughter the Princesse Oliuia and to haue hir to wyfe, whereto if it might please your highnesse to condiscend, I know my parents would wel agrée therto, for ye great loue which they beare to your maiestie & to me their sonne, & thereby should I take my selfe to be the best rewarded for my long tarrying that euer prince was: I humbly beséech your highnesse to let me know your minde héerein. This demaund of the prince was nothing straunge to the king Oliuerio for he supeded this matter long befoze, & therfore his aunswere was shozt, that he was content to accept him for sonne in lawe, aswell for his owne worthinesse as for his birth, and for the friendship betwixt their people, yet sayth he, you shall giue me leaue to thinck thereon, & you shall haue a moze resolute answere: the prince hoping ye his

Aa. de

desire would take effect. Nowe the king to knowe the
princesse minde therin went himselfe to the princesse lodging, where finding hir alone, hee counsailed hir in this
sorte. It hath pleased God that the Prince Edwarde
thy brother should be lost in the realme of Hungary, I hauing none other child but thee thinck it conuenient both
for mine owne liking, and the common profit of my subiectes to haue thee marryed with some Prince of lyke e-
state. This haue I thought on a long time, and now vppon mature deliberation had wyth some speciall of my
counsaile, I haue founde one: a prince which both for his
power may, & for his courage will, & for his nobilitie is
worthy to beare sway in so great an estate as this is,
him am I content to take for sonne in lawe, and to commend my title vnto you. This Prince is Don Siluerio
Prince of Lusitania, whom you knowe right well, a comly knight of personage, valiant in armes, of a couragious
spirite aboue all vertuous, and in his dealinges circum-
spect, courteous of speach and of highe estate, as I knew
fewe like. Ther are besides to commend this match the
entercourse of trafficke betwæne our subiectes, and the
friendshippe betwæne his parents & mée. Hæerein therefore say your owne fancy, for so farre as reason wyll, I
am content to heare you: Thus sayd the kinge. But the
Princesse whom these wordes more galled then swoord
or speare, not knownig how to shift off the king hir father
and not to aunswere his demaund, stode in amaze for
feare. The king sæing hir so silent, asked the cause why?
she aunswered nothing yet a while. In the ende forced
to say somewhat, she rather excused hir silence then re-
resolued the doubt. My Lorde and father sayth shée, I
haue not aunswered you hetherto bicause I knowe not
how to doe, neither may you now lôke for a full answere.
The matter is so straunge vnto mée, as that I neuer
thought of it before, and your highnesse knoweth that I
am of young yeares, & as yet I haue no desire to marry,

the

the time groweth on when I shall be of moze age, and
then perhaps shall I haue moze desire, which whensoe=
uer it falles out shall be of your choise moze then of mine
owne. The kinge thinckinge that she had spoke as shee
ment, and that hir young age had bene hir onely staye,
toke in good part this excuse, willing hir notwithstanding
to remember what he had sayd. So the kinge departed
and the Pzincesse remayned somewhat better apayed by
the kinges liking of hir aunswere, but hir hope was that
Rosicleer would come, and that he beinge present the
kinges minde might be altered as touching Don Silue=
rio, and foz this cause she made many a secret bowe foz
his speedy retourne, but aboue all she looked foz Fidelia.
The king at his retourne caused Don Siluerio to be cal=
led, to whome hee declared his talke with his daughter,
and hir aunswere, adding mozeouer that hereafter hee
thought the matter possible inough, foz hir good likinge,
beside his, whercoff he might be assured. Don Siluerio
was the gladdest man aliue, and thancking the king, foz
so high fauour, foz that time he departed from the king,
but the Pzincesse grewe to be moze melancholyke then
befoze, foz she espyed what courage he had taken by the
comfozt which the king had gyuen him. After Don Sil=
uerio thincking the matter sure enough, departed the
Realme with his sister Rodasilua, where let vs leaue him
and tourne to the Emperour Trebatio.

¶The Emperour Trebatio carried away the prin=
cesse Briana from the monastery of the ryuer.
Cap. 56.

A great pleasure and contentation dyd the Empe=
rour Trebatio remayne with the Pzincesse Briana,
at the monastery of the ryuer, where by their continu=
aunce together, their loues encreased so towardes each
other, that either of them delighted in the other, and ey=

therof them thought themselues happy when they wer
in the others company. This loue betwæne them was
in other manner then that which aryseth by a blasse of
beautie : and it endured so longe betwæne them, that
neither yeares, noz sicknesse, noz death scarcely could once
empayze it, and foz thys loues sake could the Emperour
Trebatio willingly haue fozbozne both kisse and kinred,
and acquaintaunce in his owne countrey, and foz hys
loue durst the Princesse aduenture to flye hir Fathers
Realme, and to abanden hir selfe to vnknowne passages,
and to trauayle with Trebatio into Greece. As the Emperour Trebatio finding opoztunitie tolde hir that he had
counsayled with the knight of the Sunne as touchinge
their departure, by whom he vnderstod ý both foz themselues and foz the king Tiberio it was mætest to depart,
otherwise saith he, may ý king your father be blamed foz
the death of the Prince Edward, and our ioye might finde
ende if I were discouered, but foz the dispatche of thys
whole matter, he sayd that he would leaue a letter in hir
chamber wherein should be shewed both what and in
what manner all thinges had bene done which you haue
heard off. The Princesse yelded thereto gladly, and betwæne themselues they pzouided thinges necessary foz
their departure, none being pziuie thereto but Clandestria
and the other gentlewomen. The day befoze the Princesse should depart, she tolde hir gentlewomen that shé
had bowed ir. dayes fast in hir lodging, charging that foz
that time none should trouble hir, saue that she woulde
haue Clandestria as she was wont, and this gentlewoman foz necessary occasion. The Princesse was thus
wont to doe very often which made it pzobable. The
next day when all were ready and had voyded the princesse lodginge, the Emperour thzewe in his letter and
Clandestria shut the dooze. So by the secrete posterne
they all departed: This was a god while befoze daye,
and they toke such hozse as had bene pzouided by the

Prin

Princesse . By the opening of the morning they hadde ridden a prety way, and the Princesse being wery tourned out of the way to rest hir selfe in a shade , as euery thing made hir afrayde and wery, till that Clandestria hastened hir on, by saying that she thought their businesse would be suspected, in that she fetched not the broths as she was wont . So vp to horse they goe , and héere breaketh of the first booke, what happened by the way the seconde booke declareth. Now lette vs remember by the way where we lefte our worthy Princes, that when we haue néede of them we may there finde them. The Emperour is in way to Greece : the knight of the Sunne abideth in Tiberios court : Don Siluerio is vppon the Sea towards Lusitania : Rosicleer now departeth from Thessaly after the establishing of the kingdome to the Quéene Arguirosa : Brandizel and Clauergudo stay in the kinge of Polonias courte , where the Prince Brandizel maketh loue to the Princesse Clarinea : Zoylo Prince of Tartary, Bargandel Prince of Bohemia,& Liriamandro prince of Hungary, all thrée together soiourne at the Emperours court at Trabisond , with the princesse Claridiana a womã knight, of whom this whole story specially entreateth, but more at large héereafter. And thus endeth the first booke.

FINIS.

¶A TABLE CONTEINING ALL THE
Chapters which are in this booke.

CAPVT. I. The description of the kinred and chusing of the Emperour Trebatio. Fol.1.

Cap.2. The king of Hungary pretending a title to the Empire setteth himselt against the Emperour Trebatio. Fol.3.

Ca.3. The emperour Trebatio by the hearsay of hir beuty was surprised with the loue of the Princesse Briana. Fol.5.

Cap.4. Prince Edward entreth into Belgrado: the Emperour bethinketh himself of his remedy. Fo.7

Cap.5. Prince Edward riding towards the monasterie of the riuer, was by the emperour Trebatio encountred and slayne. Fol.8

Cap.6. The Emperour Trebatio was receiued at the monasterie by the Archbishop of Belgrado, and there betrothed by the name of Prince Edward. Fol.9

Cap.7. The Emperour Trebatio driueth in his cōceit the order how to cōsummate the marriage, which in the ende he bringeth to passe accordingly. Fol.11

Cap.8. The Emperour Trebatio pursuing those which had stolne his Lady, lefte all his knights and tooke an other way. Fol.12

Cap.9. The aduentures of the Emperour in following the inchanted chariot. fol.14

Cap.10. The Emperours knights finde not their Lord & the Hungarians misse the prince of England. fol.18

Cap.11. The Princesse Briana taketh great sorrow at the losse of Prince Edward. fol.19

Cap.12. The Princesse Briana was deliuered of two sonnes, Clandestria christeneth them & causeth thē to be noursed. fol.2c

Cap.13. The king of Boheme raysed the siege, and the king of Hungary returned the princes knights into England. Fol.22

Cap.14. Clandestria deuiseth with the Princesse Briana how chir sons might be brought vp in hri company. Fol 23.

Cap.15. Donzel del Febo was lost by misaduenture. Fol.25.

Cap.16. The pedegree of the valiant Prince Florion & other matters as touching him. Fol.29.

Cap.17. prince Florion in his way homewardes findeth by aduenture the young gentleman Clauergudo sonne to the king Oristeo king of Fraunce, & bringeth him with the gentleman of the Sunne to Babilon. Fol 31.

Cap.18. Prince Florion with the two young gētlemen entreth Babilō, & were ther honourably receiued by the Souldan. Fol.35.
C p.19

Cap.19. The deliuery of the Souldan by the gentleman of the Sun. Fol.36.

Cap.20. An aduēture in the court of the Souldan, which befell to the young gentleman of the Sunne. Fol.41

Cap.21. Donzel del Febo is dubbed knight & ouercommeth Raiartes. Fol.46.

Ca.22 Africano king of Media & Persia, inferred war vpō the Souldan of Babilon. Fol.50

Cap.23. The knight of the Sunne maketh aunfwer to Africano as to his letter: Fol.52

Cap.24. A cruel battaile between the knight of the Sunne and Africano: with the difcomfiture of Africanos hoaft. Fol.56.

Cap.25. The knight of the Sunne, the two Princes Florion and Clauergudo, with a great hoaft entred into Perfia and there put Florion in poffefsion of the crowne. Fol.61

Cap.26. The knight of the Sūnne and the Prince Clauergudo being in their way towards Babilon, wer deuided by a fodayne aduenture. Fol.63.

Cap.27. The Princeffe Briana difcouered to Roficleer fecretly that he was hir fonne Fol.66

Cap.28. Roficleer departed from he monaftery of the riuer withut the knowledge of the Princes is mother. Fol.68

Ca.29. Roficleer in Liuerbas name flayeth Argyon and remoueth the lawes. Fol.71

Cap.30. Roficleer departed from the valley of the mountaines, meteth with two Princes chriftened, and by aduenture is carryed from them agayne. Fol.74

Cap.31. Certeine accidents which befell Roficleer after his departure from the two Princes. Fol.79

Cap.32. The great feafts beganne in Oluerios court. Fol.82

Cap.33. An aduēture which chanced in king Oluerios court. Fol.90

Cap.34. A daungerous battayle betweene Candramarte and Roficleer, Fol.93.

Cap.35. A gentlewoman came to the court from the Princeffe Briana which made him follow Brandagedeon. Fol.97.

Cap.36. A cruell battaile between Roficleer and Brandagedeon wyth his knights. Fol.100.

Cap.37. Roficleer & the two princes feek aduentures in the lande of Britayne, and the two gentlewomen carrye the Gyants body to Oliuerios court. Fol.104

Cap38. The gentlewomē brought the bodye of Brandagedeon to the court, and the Princeffes receyue the letters of their knights. Fol.107

Cap.39. Arinda the gentlewomā belonging vnto the Princeffe Briana, todle the bringing vp of Roficleer ſicleer vnto the Princeſſe Oliuia. Fol.113.

Cap.40. Fidelia being on hir way to carry the letter to Roſicleer was taken by ſixe knights,& frō them deliuered by Roſicleer. Fol.118

Ca.41. The Princes Bargandel & Liriamandro retourning from the forreſt, miſſe Roſicleer. Fol.125

Ca.42 Roſicleers departure is publiſhed in the court of king Oliuerio, Oliuia after knowledge whoſe ſonne he was,reuerſeth iudgement paſſed by a countermaund in an other letter, whereoff Fidelia lykewiſe is the bearer. Fol 127

Ca.43. Roſicleer was betrayed into the Ilande of Candramarte that Gyant whoſe handes had bene cut off before by Roſicleer. Fol.131

Cap.44.The knight of the Sunne was carryed to the Ilande of Lindaraza, where he achieued many ſtraunge and fearefull aduentures. Fol.135.

Cap.45. The three Princes which wēt in the queſt of Roſicleer,wer tranſported into the Empire of Trabiſond where chaunced to thē a faire aduenture. Fol.149

Cap.46. The two Princes Brandizel and Clauergudo ſtale ſecretly out of the kingedome of Perſia to finde the knight of the Sun.Fo.153

Cap.47.Roſicleer departeth from the Iland of Cādramarte & meteth

with certeine aduentures on the Sea. Fol.156

Cap.48.The battaile which Roſicleer had with Rolando. Fol.161

Cap.49. The Emperour Trebatio & the knight of the Sunne are in their way to the kingdome of Hūgary. Fol.163.

Cap.50. The emperour and the knight of the Sun riding towardes the monaſterie of the riuer are by an aduenture ſeperated. Fol.165.

Cap. 51. The Emperour came to the monaſtery of the riuer and ther was made known to his wife the Princeſſe. Fol.169

Cap.52.The Knight of the Sunne ridinge to the court of king Tiberio,iuſteth with a knight for paſſage. fol.179.

Cap.53.The knight of the Sunne aunſwered before the king Tiberio for the Dutcheſſe Eliſandra, & the batttile was appoynted betweene him and Arydon of the blacke woode. fol.172

Cap.54. The battaile betweene the Knight of the Sunne and the ſtrong Arydon. Fol.173.

Cap.55. Don Siluerio demaunded the princeſſe Oliuia for wife of the kyng Oliuerio. fol.174.

Cap.56. The emperour Trebatio carryed away the Princes Briana from the monaſterie of the riuer. Fol.178.

FINIS TABVLAE.